The
Little, Brown
Compact
Handbook

Third Edition
Custom Version for University of Phoenix

❖

Jane E. Aaron
New York University

🔲 **LONGMAN**

An Imprint of Addison Wesley Longman, Inc

New York • Reading, Massachusetts • Menlo Park, California • Harlow, England
Don Mills, Ontario • Sydney • Mexico City • Madrid • Amsterdam

Addison Wesley Longman Custom Books consist of products that are produced from camera-ready copy. Peer review, class testing, and accuracy are primarily the responsibility of the author(s).

Manager of Addison Wesley Longman Custom Books: Elizabeth Owens
Production Administrator: Rohnda Barnes

The Little, Brown Compact Handbook, Third Edition, Custom Version for University of Phoenix

ISBN: 0-201-67649-4

99 00 3 2 1

FREQUENTLY ASKED QUESTIONS

The chapter titles on the left list the book's main topics. Across from the titles are questions commonly asked about the topics. Follow either a chapter title or a question to the appropriate page in the book. Or follow a blue-green bar to the appropriate tabbed divider, which contains a more detailed outline of that part of the book. For a complete detailed contents, see inside the back cover.

Preface
for Instructors

❖

The *Little, Brown Compact Handbook* is an accessible reference for writers of varying experience. With the authority of its parent, *The Little, Brown Handbook,* but briefer and more convenient, *The Little, Brown Compact Handbook* answers questions about the writing process, paragraphs, clarity and style, grammar, research writing, and more.

This third edition appears amid a sea change in writing instruction: electronic media are transforming classrooms, research methods, forms of presentation, even the writing process itself. The challenge of the revision was to revamp the handbook so that it serves computer-using students and teachers and yet retains its strengths as a concise, clear reference.

Computers in writing and research

Computers are woven into the cloth of the handbook:

- ❖ TIPS FOR COMPUTER USE appear throughout the book, always signaled by the computer image shown here.
- ❖ ELECTRONIC RESEARCH receives substantial attention, including guidance on developing keywords and searching electronically, using Internet resources such as the World Wide Web, and evaluating electronic sources.
- ❖ DOCUMENTING ELECTRONIC SOURCES receives special attention with each documentation style covered: MLA, APA, Chicago, and CBE.

❖ New material on DOCUMENT DESIGN includes advice about typefaces, illustrations, color, and other elements. Examples include a report and a newsletter.

❖ FOR COMPUTERS IN BUSINESS WRITING, the handbook shows a contemporary résumé and offers advice for writing faxes and electronic mail.

❖ A new chapter provides basic tips for WORD PROCESSING, guidelines for WRITING COLLABORATIVELY WITH COMPUTERS, and suggestions for CREATING HYPERTEXT DOCUMENTS.

Research writing

Along with the changes addressing electronic research, the following additions have greatly strengthened the chapters on research writing:

❖ Viewing research writing as a process.

❖ Keeping a research journal.

❖ Developing a research question.

❖ Setting goals for research.

❖ Conducting an interview.

❖ Evaluating and synthesizing sources.

❖ Avoiding plagiarism.

❖ Focusing, organizing, and drafting a research paper.

❖ Integrating sources in the paper.

❖ Revising, editing, and formatting a research paper.

The handbook is also stronger on documentation, with these changes:

❖ New separate tabbed dividers for MLA and APA styles.

❖ Expanded discussion of placing in-text citations.

❖ New MLA models for sources such as the Bible, reference works, and abstracts.

❖ New coverage of the Chicago and CBE styles, with their own tabbed divider.

English as a second language

As before, the material for nonnative speakers is thoroughly integrated into the main text, so that students do not have to distinguish between ESL problems and those they share with native speakers. A small color block (ESL) highlights the material.

Much ESL material is new to this edition:

❖ An ESL GUIDE just before the back endpapers provides a ready reference to all the ESL material so that it can be taught or consulted as a unit.

❖ THIRTY-FOUR NEW ESL NOTES (for a total of forty-seven) deal with issues of process and rhetoric as well as grammar.

❖ TWO NEW ESL SECTIONS (for a total of thirteen) treat ESL grammar issues in detail.

Other additions

Myriad other improvements, small and large, increase the handbook's usefulness for students and teachers. Following are some highlights:

❖ Chapters on the writing process benefit from new material on JOURNAL WRITING, the THESIS SENTENCE, and creating a WRITING PORTFOLIO.

❖ The chapter on READING AND WRITING ABOUT LITERATURE, contributed by Sylvan Barnet, includes a discussion of critical approaches to literature.

❖ An expanded section on BIASED LANGUAGE emphasizes stereotypes of sex, race, religion, age, and other characteristics.

❖ The material on using and punctuating TRANSITIONAL EXPRESSIONS is more detailed.

❖ Several PUNCTUATION TOPICS are new or expanded, such as comma splices, misuse of a comma after a conjunction, and the ellipsis mark.

Accessibility

Above all, *The Little, Brown Compact Handbook* aims to be an accessible reference, with features that help students find what they need:

❖ The COMB BINDING allows the book to lie flat. The notebook-style DIVIDERS make it easy to flip to any part of the book. Detailed PART OUTLINES and DOCUMENTATION INDEXES on the tabbed dividers provide direct routes into the handbook.

❖ "FREQUENTLY ASKED QUESTIONS," on the front endpapers, pairs a brief contents with questions like those students ask, using everyday language and examples in place of terms.

❖ A new "PREFACE FOR STUDENTS," following this preface, briefly introduces the uses and features of the handbook and includes a visual guide to the many reference aids.

❖ Headings use MINIMAL TERMINOLOGY whenever possible, replacing or substituting terms (such as *coordinating conjunction*) with examples (such as *and* or *but*). Thus the book's various tables of contents are inviting and comprehensible to students.

❖ The handbook provides DEFINITIONS WHEN NEEDED and so avoids confusing cross-references. Principal terms are defined in the text itself, and secondary terms are defined in out-of-the-way white boxes at the bottoms of pages.

❖ The ORGANIZATION arranges topics in ways that students can easily grasp without prior experience of handbooks. For instance, students who want to know when to use *good* or *well* or how to repair a dangling modifier do not have to distinguish between sentence effectiveness and sentence grammar but can turn to the one comprehensive section on modifiers.

❖ On the back endpapers, a COMPLETE CONTENTS provides an at-a-glance overview of the handbook, a list of EDITING SYMBOLS translates readers' marks, and a new "ESL GUIDE" provides a convenient index to the ESL material integrated throughout the book.

❖ FIFTY TINTED BOXES, twenty-three of them new, highlight key reference information, such as questions about audience, revision of comma splices, and indexes to documentation models.

Supplements

Accompanying *The Little, Brown Compact Handbook* is an array of supplements for students and instructors:

❖ *Exercises to Accompany The Little, Brown Compact Handbook* offers activities on everything from paragraph coherence to comma splices to paraphrasing. The exercises cover a range of academic disciplines, and all are in connected discourse. A separate answer key is also available.

❖ *Developmental Exercises to Accompany The Little, Brown Compact Handbook,* a new workbook, provides very practical activities for developmental writers. These exercises also range across disciplines and are written in connected discourse. A separate answer key is available.

❖ *The Writer's Workshop,* keyed to the handbook, is an electronic heuristics program that helps students explore, form, and express their ideas while writing arguments, research papers, and literary analyses. A new feature, peer review prompts, guides writers as they work together on drafting and revising. Also included is a tool for formatting source citations in MLA or APA style and an online version of the handbook. (IBM and Macintosh.)

❖ *Teaching Online: Internet Research, Conversation, and Composition* is an accessible introduction to Internet resources for teaching writing. Written by Daniel Anderson, Bret Benjamin, Chris Busiel, and Bill Paredes-Holt of the University of Texas at Austin, the book offers basic definitions and information on Internet access and shows how to integrate a variety of Internet tools into writing courses.

❖ A new guide for students, *Researching Online*, adapts *Teaching Online* to help students reach and use the Internet for their research projects.

❖ *Documenting Sources Across the Curriculum*, also for students, is a handy compilation of the handbook's material on preparing a working bibliography and documenting sources in MLA, APA, Chicago, and CBE styles.

Acknowledgments

The Little, Brown Compact Handbook benefits from the generous and insightful advice of many writing teachers. I especially thank Joseph A. Alvarez, Central Piedmont Community College; Mary M. Bendel-Simso, Western Maryland College; Lois Birky, Illinois Central College; Kay Bosgraaf, Montgomery College; Steve Brahlek, Palm Beach Community College; Deborah Burns, Merrimack College; Susan E. Carlisle, Boston University; H. Julie Chen, Southeast Missouri State University; Robert Dial, University of Akron; Suzanne Dixon, Carroll Community College; Peter Dorman, Central Virginia Community College; Scott Douglas, Chattanooga State Technical Community College; Dennis Gabriel, Cuyahoga Community College; Clinton R. Gardner, Salt Lake Community College; Michelle Guthrie Maynard, University of Texas, Austin; Carol Harrell, Ball State University; Will Hochman, University of Southern Colorado; Karen Jones, St. Charles County Community College; Scott Alan Kemp, University of Northern Colorado; Antoinette M. Mastin, University of Cincinnati; Shirley Nelson, Chattanooga State Technical Community College; Judy Pearce, Montgomery College, Rockville; Ruth Silon, Cuyahoga Community College; Bill Stiffler, Hartford Community College; Kip Strasma, Illinois Central College; Darlene Strawser, Lakeland Community College; Kimberly A. Sullivan, Clark College; Lulu C. H. Sun, University of Massachusetts, Dartmouth; Kristin Woolever, Northeastern University.

In addition, I am grateful to Susan Lang, Southern Illinois University, for her help with the new material on electronic research and writing and to Sylvan Barnet, Tufts University, for his chapter "Reading and Writing About Literature," adapted from his *Short Guide to Writing About Literature* and *Introduction to Literature* (with Morton Berman, William Burto, and William E. Cain).

The folks at and around Longman supported me with patience, intelligence, hard work, and good cheer. Patricia Rossi, Thomas Maeglin, Ann Stypuloski, Marina Vaynshteyn, Robert Ginsberg, Dorothy Bungert, Lynne Cattafi, and Reka Simonsen have my happy thanks.

Preface
for Students

❖

The Little, Brown Compact Handbook contains the basic information you'll need for writing in and out of school. Here you can find out how to get ideas, use commas, search the Internet, cite sources, craft an argument, and write a résumé—all in a convenient, accessible package.

This book is mainly a reference for you to dip into as needs arise. You probably won't read the book all the way through, nor will you use everything it contains: you already know much of the content anyway, whether consciously or not. The trick is to figure out what you *don't* know—taking cues from your own writing experiences and the comments of others—and then to find the answers to your questions in these pages.

The following page details the many ways you can find information in the handbook. In addition to the features illustrated, a computer image appears in the margin (as it does here) whenever the book offers a tip for using computers productively.

Before you begin using this book, you may need to banish a very common misconception: that writing is only, or even mainly, a matter of correctness. True, any written message will find a more receptive audience if it is correct in grammar, punctuation, and similar matters. But these concerns should come late in the writing process, after you've allowed yourself to discover what you have to say, freeing yourself to make mistakes along the way. As one writer put it, you need to get the clay on the potter's wheel before you can shape it into a bowl, and you need to shape it into a bowl before you can perfect it. So get your clay on the wheel and work with it until it looks like a bowl. Then worry about correctness.

FINDING WHAT YOU NEED

Use a directory.

* ❖ "Frequently Asked Questions" (inside the front cover) provides questions in everyday language that are commonly asked about the book's main topics.
* ❖ The "Contents" (inside the back cover) provides an overview of the entire book.
* ❖ Detailed outlines on the tabbed dividers direct you to the material covered in each part of the book.

Use the index.

An alphabetical list of all topics, terms, and problem words and expressions begins on p. 387.

Use the elements of the page.

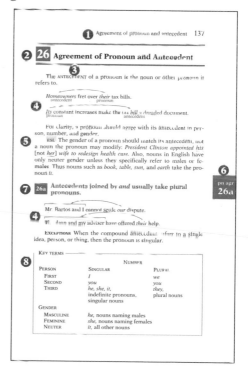

❶ Running head (header) showing the topic being discussed on this page.

❷ Chapter number and title.

❸ Key term for this discussion, defined in the text.

❹ Examples, always indented, often showing revision.

❺ ESL designation, highlighting material especially for those using English as a second language.

❻ Page tab, containing the code of the nearest section heading (**26a**) and the symbol or abbreviation for the topic being discussed (**pn agr**).

❼ Section heading, containing a main convention or topic. It is labeled with the section code, **26a**: the chapter number (**26**) and the section letter (**a**).

❽ Box defining secondary terms used on the page (always at the bottom of the page). Refer to these white boxes whenever a term is unclear. Otherwise, ignore them.

The Writing Process and Paragraphs

❖

I

The Writing Process and Paragraphs

❖

1 The Writing Situation

Like most writers (even very experienced ones), you may find writing sometimes easy but more often difficult, sometimes smooth but more often halting. Writing involves creation, and creation requires freedom, experimentation, and, yes, missteps. Instead of proceeding in a straight line over a clear path, you might start writing without knowing what you have to say, circle back to explore a new idea, or keep going even though you're sure you'll have to rewrite later.

As uncertain as the writing process may be, you can bring some control to it by understanding your WRITING SITUATION—the intersection of your subject (what you're writing about), your purpose (why you're writing), and your audience (whom you're writing to). These three elements together limit and clarify your choices each time you write.

1a Finding your subject

A subject for writing has several basic requirements:

❖ It should be suitable for the assignment.
❖ It should be neither too general nor too limited for the length of paper and deadline assigned.
❖ It should be something you care about.

When you receive a writing assignment, ask yourself these questions about it:

❖ *What's wanted from you?* Many writing assignments contain words such as *report, summarize, compare, define, analyze, interpret, evaluate,* or *argue.* These words specify the way you are to approach your subject and what your purpose is. (See p. 4.)
❖ *For whom are you writing?* Some assignments will specify your readers, but usually you will have to figure out for yourself whether your audience is your boss, the college community, your instructor, or some other group or individual. (See p. 5.)
❖ *What kind of research is required?* Sometimes an assignment specifies the kinds of sources you are expected to consult, and you can use such information to choose your subject. (If you are unsure whether research is expected, check with your instructor.)
❖ *What is the length of the paper and the deadline?* Having a week to write three pages or three weeks to write six pages can make a big difference in the subject you select.

3

1b

NOTE If you write on a computer, you can store question sets like the one on the previous page and the one on page 6 in a file or as a macro (a repeatable sequence of actions). Then, for each assignment, you can call up the file or macro and insert appropriate answers between the questions. Save the answers, and print a copy to use for reference while you draft your paper.

Answering questions about your assignment will help set some boundaries for your choice of subject. Then you can explore your own interests and experiences to narrow the subject so that you can cover it adequately within the space and time assigned. Federal aid to college students could be the subject of a book; the kinds of aid available or why the government should increase aid would be a more appropriate subject for a four-page paper due in a week. Here are some guidelines for narrowing broad subjects:

❖ Break your broad subject into as many specific topics as you can think of. Make a list.

❖ For each topic that interests you and fits the assignment, roughly sketch out the main ideas and consider how many paragraphs or pages of specific facts, examples, and other details you would need to pin those ideas down. This thinking should give you at least a vague idea of how much work you'd have to do and how long the resulting paper might be.

❖ If an interesting and appropriate topic is still too broad, break it down further and repeat the previous step.

1b Defining your purpose

Your PURPOSE in writing is your chief reason for communicating something about your subject to a particular audience of readers. Most writing you do will have one of four main purposes. Occasionally, you will *entertain* readers or *express yourself*—your feelings or ideas—to readers. More often you will *explain* something to readers or *persuade* readers to respect and accept, and sometimes even act on, your well-supported opinion. These purposes often overlap in a single essay, but usually one predominates. And the dominant purpose will influence your particular slant on your subject, the details you choose, and even the words you use.

Many writing assignments narrow the purpose by using a signal word, such as the following:

❖ *Report:* Survey, organize, and objectively present the available evidence on the subject.

❖ *Summarize:* Concisely state the main points in a text, argument, theory, or other work.

❖ *Discuss:* Examine the main points, competing views, or implications of the subject.

❖ *Compare and contrast:* Explain the similarities and differences between two subjects. (See also p. 49.)

❖ *Define:* Specify the meaning of a term or a concept—distinctive characteristics, boundaries, and so on. (See also p. 48.)

❖ *Analyze:* Identify the elements of the subject, and discuss how they work together. (See also p. 48.)

❖ *Interpret:* Infer the subject's meaning or implications.

❖ *Evaluate:* Judge the quality or significance of the subject, considering pros and cons. (See also pp. 252–53.)

❖ *Argue:* Take a position on the subject, and support your position with evidence. (See also pp. 341–50.)

1c Considering your audience

The readers likely to see your work—your audience—may influence your choice of subject and your definition of purpose. Your audience certainly will influence what you say about your subject and how you say it—for instance, how much background information you give and whether you adopt a serious or a friendly tone. Consider, for instance, these two memos written by a student who worked part-time at a small company and wanted to persuade the company to recycle paper:

ADDRESSED TO COWORKERS

Ever notice how much paper collects in your trash basket every day? Well, most of it can be recycled with little effort, I promise. Basically, all you need to do is set a bag or box near your desk and deposit wastepaper in it. I know, space is cramped in these little cubicles. But what's a little more crowding when the earth's at stake?. . .

Information: how employees could handle recycling; no mention of costs

Role: cheerful, equally harried colleague

Tone: informal, personal (*Ever notice; you; what's; Well; I know, space is cramped*)

ADDRESSED TO MANAGEMENT

In my four months here, I have observed that all of us throw out baskets of potentially recyclable paper every day. Considering the drain on our forest resources and the pressure on landfills that paper causes, we could make a valuable contribution to the environmental movement by helping to recycle the paper we use. At the company where I worked before, the employees separate clean wastepaper from other trash at their desks. The maintenance staff collects trash in two receptacles,

Information: specific reasons; view of company as a whole; reference to another company; problem of cost

Role: serious, thoughtful, responsible employee

Tone: formal, serious (*Considering the drain; forest resources; valuable contribution;* no *you* or contractions)

1c

Questions about audience

❖ Who *are* my readers?
❖ Why are readers going to read my writing? What will they expect?
❖ What do I want readers to know or do after reading my work, and how should I make that clear to them?
❖ How will readers' characteristics, such as those below, influence their attitudes toward my topic?

Age or sex
Occupation: students, professional colleagues, etc.
Social or economic role: adult children, car buyers, potential employers, etc.
Economic or educational background
Ethnic background
Political, religious, or moral beliefs and values
Hobbies or activities

❖ What do readers already know and *not* know about my topic? How much do I have to tell them?
❖ If my topic involves specialized language, how much should I use and define?
❖ What ideas, arguments, or information might surprise readers? excite them? offend them? How should I handle these points?
❖ What misconceptions might readers have of my topic and/or my approach to the topic? How can I dispel these misconceptions?
❖ What is my relationship to my readers? What role and tone should I assume? What role do I want readers to play?
❖ What will readers do with my writing? Should I expect them to read every word from the top, to scan for information, or to look for conclusions? Can I help them with a summary, headings, illustrations, or other special features? (See pp. 203–15 on document format.)

---

and the trash hauler (the same one we use here) makes separate pickups. I do not know what the hauler charges for handling recyclable material. . . .

The box above contains questions that can help you analyze and address your audience. Depending on your writing situation, some questions will be more helpful than others. For instance, your readers' knowledge of your topic will be important to consider if you are trying to explain how a particular computer program works, whereas readers' beliefs and values may be important if you are trying to gather support for a change in welfare policy.

ESL If English is not your native language, you may not be accustomed to appealing to your readers when you write. In some cultures, for instance, readers may accept a writer's statements with little or no questioning. In English, however, readers expect the writer to reach out to them by being accurate, fair, interesting, and clear.

2a

---

2   Invention

Writers use a host of techniques to help invent or discover ideas and information about their subjects. *Whichever of the following techniques you use, do your work in writing, not just in your head.* Your ideas will be retrievable, and the very act of writing will lead you to fresh insights.

ESL The discovery process encouraged here rewards rapid writing; you won't need to do a lot of thinking beforehand about what you will write or how. If you are not comfortable or fluent in English, you may find it helpful initially to do this exploratory writing in your native language first and then to translate the worthwhile material for use in your drafts.

2a   Keeping a journal

A JOURNAL is a diary of ideas kept on paper or on a computer. It gives you a place to record your thoughts and can provide ideas for writing. Because you write for yourself, you can work out your ideas without the pressure of an audience "out there" who will evaluate logic or organization or correctness. If you write every day, even just for a few minutes, the routine will loosen your writing muscles and improve your confidence.

You can use a journal for varied purposes: perhaps to confide your feelings, explore your responses to movies and other media, practice certain kinds of writing (such as poems or news stories), think critically about what you read (see p. 12), or pursue ideas from your courses. In both examples following, the students planted the seeds for essays they later wrote. Megan Polanyis pondered something she learned from her biology textbook:

> *Ecology* and *economics* have the same root—Greek word for house. Economy = management of the house. Ecology = study of the house. In ecology the house is all of nature, ourselves, the other animals, the plants, the earth, the air, the whole environment. Ecology has a lot to do with economy: study the house in order to manage it.

2c

Terry Perez responded to the day's news:

> The paper today was full of bad news. Does it only seem this way, or do newspapers and TV really play up conflicts between racial and ethnic groups? Here at school there are some conflicts, sure. But it's more interesting how many different types of people from different backgrounds manage to live together and learn from each other. Isn't that true elsewhere?

(Further examples of Perez's writing appear opposite and in the next three chapters.)

ESL A journal can be especially helpful if you're writing in English as a second language. You can practice writing to improve your fluency, try out sentence patterns, and experiment with vocabulary words. Equally important, you can experiment with applying what you know from experience to what you read and observe.

2b Observing your surroundings

Sometimes you can find a good subject or good ideas by looking around you, not in the half-conscious way most of us move from place to place in our daily lives but deliberately, all senses alert. On a bus, for instance, are there certain types of passengers? What seems to be on the driver's mind? To get the most from observation, you should have a tablet and pen or pencil handy for notes and sketches. Back at your desk, study your notes and sketches for oddities or patterns that you'd like to explore further.

2c Freewriting

A good way to find or explore a subject is to write without stopping for a certain amount of time (say, ten minutes) or to a certain length (say, one page). The goal of this FREEWRITING is to generate ideas and information from *within* yourself by going around the part of your mind that doesn't want to write or can't think of anything to write. You let words themselves suggest other words. *What* you write is not important; that you *keep* writing is. Don't stop, even if that means repeating the same words until new words come. Don't go back to reread, don't censor ideas, and don't stop to edit: grammar, punctuation, and spelling are irrelevant at this stage.

If you write on a computer, you can ensure that your freewriting keeps moving forward by turning off your computer's monitor or turning its brightness control all the way down so that the screen is dark. The computer will record what you type but keep it from you and thus prevent you from tinkering with your prose. This

INVISIBLE WRITING may feel uncomfortable at first, but it can free the mind for very creative results. When you've finished freewriting, simply turn the monitor on or turn up the brightness control to read your writing, and then save or revise it as appropriate.

2d

ESL Invisible writing can be especially helpful if English is a second language for you and you tend to worry about errors while writing. The blank computer screen leaves you no choice but to explore ideas without regard for their expression. ■

The physical act of freewriting may give you access to ideas you were unaware of. For example, the following freewriting by a student, Robert Benday, gave him the subject of writing as a disguise.

> Write to write. Seems pretty obvious, also weird. What to gain by writing? never anything before. Writing seems always—always Getting corrected for trying too hard to please the teacher, getting corrected for not trying hard enuf. Frustration, nail biting, sometimes getting carried away making sentences to tell stories, not even true stories, *esp.* not true stories, *that* feels like creating something. Writing just pulls the story out of me. The story lets me be someone else, gives me a disguise.

(A later phase of Benday's writing process appears on p. 11.)

Freewriting is also useful to discover ideas about a specific subject, as the following example shows. Terry Perez, the writer, had an assignment to explore some aspect of cultural diversity in the United States. She had written about the subject in her journal (see opposite) and then read a statement by the writer Ishmael Reed that conflict among cultural groups "is played up and often encouraged by the media."

> Cultural diversity in the media? The media has a one track mind, cultural diversity is bad. Like Reed says the media makes a big deal of conflict between racial and ethnic groups, it's almost constant in the papers, on TV. TV especially—the news vs. all the white bread programs, the sitcoms and ads. That's a whole other view—*no* conflict, *no* tension. No diversity. So we have all people the same except when they're not, then they're at war. Two unreal pictures.

(An outline and drafts of Perez's paper appear on pp. 18, 21–22, 25–26, and 29–31.)

2d Brainstorming

A method similar to freewriting is BRAINSTORMING—focusing intently on a subject for a fixed period (say, fifteen minutes), pushing yourself to list every idea and detail that comes to mind. Like freewriting, brainstorming requires turning off your internal editor so that

2e

you keep moving ahead. (The technique of invisible writing on a computer, described on pp. 8–9, can help you move forward.)

Here is an example of brainstorming by a student, Johanna Abrams, on what a summer job can teach:

> summer work teaches—
>> how to look busy while doing nothing
>> how to avoid the sun in summer
>> seriously: discipline, budgeting money, value of money
> which job? Burger King cashier? baby sitter? mail-room clerk?
> mail room: how to sort mail into boxes: this is learning??
> how to survive getting fired—humiliation, outrage
> Mrs. King! the mail-room queen as learning experience
> the shock of getting fired: what to tell parents, friends?
> Mrs. K was so rigid—dumb procedures
> initials instead of names on the mail boxes—confusion!
> Mrs. K's anger, resentment: the disadvantages of being smarter than your boss
> The odd thing about working in an office: a world with its own rules for how to act
> what Mr. D said about the pecking order—big chick (Mrs. K) pecks on little chick (me)
> a job can beat you down—make you be mean to other people

(A later phase of Abrams's writing process appears on p. 17.)

Working on a computer makes it fairly easy to edit and shape a brainstorming list into a preliminary outline of your paper (see p. 16). With a few keystrokes, you can delete weak ideas, expand strong ones, and rearrange items. You can also freewrite from the list if you think some ideas are especially promising and deserve more thought.

2e   Clustering

Like freewriting and brainstorming, CLUSTERING also draws on free association and rapid, unedited work. But it emphasizes the relations between ideas by combining writing and nonlinear drawing. When clustering, you radiate outward from a center point—your topic. When an idea occurs, you pursue related ideas in a branching structure until they seem exhausted. Then you do the same with other ideas, staying open to connections, continuously branching out or drawing arrows.

The example of clustering on the facing page shows how Robert Benday used the technique for ten minutes to expand on the topic of writing as a means of disguise, an idea he arrived at through freewriting (see the preceding page).

CLUSTERING

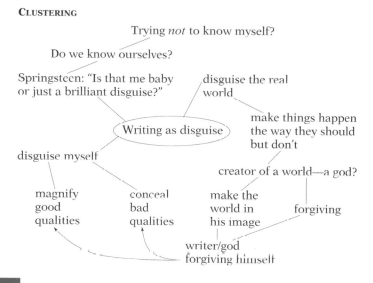

Trying *not* to know myself?

Do we know ourselves?

Springsteen: "Is that me baby
or just a brilliant disguise?"

disguise the real
world

make things happen
the way they should
but don't

Writing as disguise

disguise myself

creator of a world—a god?

magnify
good
qualities

conceal
bad
qualities

make the
world in
his image

forgiving

writer/god
forgiving himself

2f   Asking questions

Asking yourself a set of questions about your subject—and
writing out the answers—can help you look at the topic objectively
and see fresh possibilities in it.

If you write on a computer, you can create a file for each set of
questions below and duplicate the set for appropriate writing projects. Simply insert answers between the questions. Then print the
answers so they're handy while you draft, or split your computer
screen horizontally so that it shows the answers above while you
draft below. You may even be able to import passages from the answers into your draft.

1. Journalist's questions

A journalist with a story to report poses a set of questions:

Who was involved?
What happened, and what were the results?
When did it happen?
Where did it happen?
Why did it happen?
How did it happen?

These questions can also be useful in probing an essay subject,
especially when you are telling a story or examining causes and effects.

2. Questions about patterns

2g

We think about and understand a vast range of subjects through patterns such as narration, classification, and comparison and contrast. Asking questions based on the patterns can help you view your topic from many angles. Sometimes you may want to develop an entire essay using just one pattern.

> How did it happen? (Narration)
> How does it look, sound, feel, smell, taste? (Description)
> What are examples of it or reasons for it? (Illustration or support)
> What is it? What does it encompass, and what does it exclude? (Definition)
> What are its parts or characteristics? (Division or analysis)
> What groups or categories can it be sorted into? (Classification)
> How is it like, or different from, other things? (Comparison and contrast)
> Why did it happen? What results did or could it have? (Cause-and-effect analysis)
> How do you do it, or how does it work? (Process analysis)

For more on these patterns, including paragraph-length examples, see pages 46–51.

2g Reading and thinking critically

Even when reading is not required by an assignment, it can help you locate or develop your topic by introducing you to ideas you didn't know or expanding on what you do know.

People often read passively, absorbing content like blotters, not interacting with it. To read for ideas, you need to be more active, probing text and illustrations with your mind. In other words, you need to *think critically* while you read, questioning the material, testing it against what you know, building on what it says and what you yourself think. In this context *critical* does not mean "negative" but "skeptical," "exacting," "creative."

To read actively and critically, read with a pen or pencil in your hand or a keyboard nearby. Mark up the material if it's yours, or make separate notes if it's borrowed. (A journal can be useful for recording your responses to reading. See p. 7.) Question what you don't understand or find doubtful. Agree or disagree with the writer's ideas. Highlight or quote passages you find especially interesting or important. With such notes you create a record of what the material makes *you* think, and you begin to organize the material for your own purposes. (For more on critical reading, see pp. 251–54.)

ESL The idea of reading critically may require some adjustment if readers in your native culture tend to seek understanding or agreement more than engagement from what they read. Readers of English read for all kinds of reasons, including pleasure, reinforcement, enlightenment, information, and many others. But they also read skeptically, critically, to see the author's motives, test their own ideas, and arrive at new knowledge.

NOTE Whenever you use the information or ideas of others in your writing, you must acknowledge your sources in order to avoid the serious offense of plagiarism. (See pp. 258–61.)

3   Thesis and Organization

Shaping your raw material helps you clear away unneeded ideas, spot possible gaps, and energize your topic. The two main operations in shaping material are focusing on a thesis (below) and organizing ideas (p. 15).

3a   Conceiving a thesis sentence

Your readers will expect your essay to be focused on and controlled by a main idea, or THESIS. In your final draft you may express this idea in a THESIS SENTENCE (or sentences), often at the end of your introduction.

Functions of the thesis sentence

❖ It narrows your topic to a single, central idea that you want readers to gain from your essay. All the paragraphs in the essay will develop and support this idea.
❖ It asserts something specific and significant about the topic, conveying your opinion.
❖ It *may* concisely preview how you will arrange your ideas in the essay.

ESL In some cultures it is considered unnecessary or impolite for a writer to have an opinion or to state his or her main idea outright. But readers of English usually expect a clear and early idea of what a writer thinks.

All the thesis sentences on the next page fulfill the first two functions listed in the box (the nature of the assertion is highlighted in brackets). The last two examples also fulfill the third function, previewing organization.

Topic	Thesis sentence
1. The pecking order in an office	Two months working in a large agency taught me that an office's pecking order should be respected. [*Topic:* office's pecking order. *Assertion:* should be respected.]
2. The dynamics of single-parent families	In families consisting of a single parent and a single child, the boundaries between parent and child may disappear so that the two interact like siblings or like a married couple. [*Topic:* boundaries between parent and child. *Assertion:* may disappear.]
3. Federal aid to college students	To compete well in the global economy, the United States must make higher education affordable for any student who qualifies academically. [*Topic:* a competitive United States. *Assertion:* must make higher education affordable.]
4. Preventing juvenile crime	Juveniles can be diverted from crime by active learning programs, full-time sports, and intervention by mentors and role models. [*Topic:* juveniles. *Assertion:* can be diverted from crime in three ways.]
5. The effects of strip-mining	Strip-mining should be tightly controlled in this region to reduce its pollution of water resources, its destruction of the land, and its devastating effects on people's lives. [*Topic:* strip-mining. *Assertion:* should be tightly controlled for three reasons.]

A thesis will not usually leap fully formed into your head: you will have to develop and shape the idea as you develop and shape your essay. Still, try to draft a thesis sentence when you have a fairly good stock of ideas. Then it can help you start drafting and can serve as a point of reference when changes inevitably occur.

While you are developing your thesis sentence, ask questions about each attempt:

❖ Does the sentence make an *assertion* about your topic?
❖ Is the assertion *limited* to only one idea?
❖ Is the assertion *specific* and *significant?*
❖ Does the sentence convey your *purpose* and your *opinion?*

Here are examples of thesis sentences revised to meet these requirements:

FAULTY ORIGINAL	REVISED
This new product brought in over $300,000 last year. [A statement of fact, not an assertion: what is significant about the product's success?]	This new product succeeded because of its innovative marketing campaign, including widespread press coverage, in-store entertainment, and a consumer newsletter.
People should not go on fad diets. [A vague statement that needs limiting with one or more reasons: what's wrong with fad diets?]	Fad diets can be dangerous when they deprive the body of essential nutrients or rely on excessive quantities of potentially harmful foods.
Televised sports are different from live sports. [A general statement that needs to be made more specific: how are they different, and why is the difference significant?]	Although television cannot transmit all the excitement of being in a crowd during a game, its close-ups and slow-motion replays more than compensate.
Seat belts can save lives, but now carmakers are installing air bags. [Not unified: how do the two parts of the sentence relate to each other?]	If drivers had used lifesaving seat belts more often, carmakers might not have needed to install air bags.

3b

3b Organizing your ideas

Most essays share a basic pattern of introduction (states the subject), body (develops the subject), and conclusion (pulls the essay's ideas together). Introductions and conclusions are discussed on pages 51–54

Within the body, every paragraph develops some aspect of the essay's main idea, or thesis. See pages 29–31 for Terry Perez's essay, with annotations highlighting the body's pattern of support for the thesis sentence.

1. The general and the specific

To organize material for an essay, you need to distinguish general and specific ideas and see the relations between ideas. GENERAL and SPECIFIC refer to the number of instances or objects included in a group signified by a word. *Plant*, for example, is general because it encompasses all kinds of plants; *rose* is specific because it refers to a certain kind of plant; and *Uncle Dan's prize-winning American Beauty rose* is even more specific.

As you arrange your material, pick out the general ideas and then the specific points that support them. Set aside points that seem irrelevant to your key ideas. On a computer, you can easily experiment with various arrangements of general ideas and supporting information: save the master list, duplicate it, and then use the computer's copy and paste functions to move material around.

2. Schemes for organizing essays

An essay's body paragraphs may be arranged in many ways that are familiar to readers. The choice depends on your subject, purpose, and audience.

- ❖ *Spatial:* In describing a person, place, or thing, move through space systematically from a starting point to other features—for instance, top to bottom, near to far, left to right.
- ❖ *Chronological:* In recounting a sequence of events, arrange the events as they actually occurred in time, first to last.
- ❖ *General to specific:* Begin with an overall discussion of the subject; then fill in details, facts, examples, and other support.
- ❖ *Specific to general:* First provide the support; then draw a conclusion from it.
- ❖ *Climactic:* Arrange ideas in order of increasing importance to your thesis or increasing interest to the reader.

3. Outlines

It's not essential to craft a detailed outline before you begin drafting an essay; in fact, too detailed a plan could prevent you from discovering ideas while you draft. Still, even a rough scheme can show you patterns of general and specific, suggest proportions, and highlight gaps or overlaps in coverage.

There are several different kinds of outlines, some more flexible than others.

Scratch or informal outline

A scratch or informal outline includes key general points in the order they will be covered. It may also suggest the specific evidence for them.

Here is Terry Perez's scratch outline for her essay on diversity in the media:

THESIS SENTENCE
The media project unrealistic images of the United States as a nation of either constant ethnic conflict or untroubled homogeneity.

SCRATCH OUTLINE

Media images—
    Ethnic conflict
        —news stories—examples
        —the real story—examples
    Sameness—homogeneity
        —TV sitcoms and ads: the happy (white) family
        —the real story—examples

A scratch or informal outline may be all you need to begin drafting. Sometimes, though, it may prove too skimpy a guide, and you may want to use it as a preliminary to a more detailed outline. Indeed, Terry Perez used her scratch outline as a base for a detailed formal outline that gave her an even more definite sense of direction (see p. 18).

Tree diagram

In a tree diagram, ideas and details branch out in increasing specificity. Unlike more linear outlines, this diagram can be supplemented and extended indefinitely, so it is easy to alter. The following example was developed from Johanna Abrams's brainstorming about a summer job (p. 10).

THESIS SENTENCE

Two months working in a large agency taught me that an office's pecking order should be respected.

TREE DIAGRAM

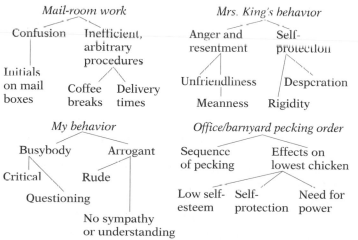

3b

Formal outline

A formal outline not only lays out main ideas and their support but also shows the relative importance of all the essay's elements. Following is Terry Perez's outline, developed from her scratch outline (p. 17).

THESIS SENTENCE

The media project unrealistic images of the United States as a nation of either constant ethnic conflict or untroubled homogeneity.

FORMAL OUTLINE

  I. Images of ethnic conflict, not coexistence
    A. News stories
      1. Ethnic gang wars
      2. Defaced Jewish synagogues and cemeteries
      3. Korean and non-Korean disputes
      4. Burned African American churches
    B. The real story
      1. No war among groups
      2. Coexistence among groups
 II. Images of untroubled homogeneity, not diversity
    A. People pictured in TV shows and ads
      1. Mainly white people
      2. Mainly middle-class people
      3. Mainly attractive people
    B. People missing from TV shows and ads
      1. Ethnic groups
      2. Poor people
      3. Other groups

This example illustrates several principles of outlining that can ensure completeness, balance, and clear relationships.

  ❖ All parts are systematically indented and labeled: Roman numerals (I, II) for primary divisions; indented capital letters (A, B) for secondary divisions; further indented Arabic numerals (1, 2) for supporting examples. (The next level down would be indented further still and labeled with small letters: a, b.)
  ❖ The outline divides the material into several groups. A long list of points at the same level should be broken up into groups.
  ❖ Topics of equal generality appear in parallel headings (with the same indentation and numbering or lettering).
  ❖ All subdivided headings break into at least two parts because a topic cannot logically be divided into only one part.
  ❖ All headings are expressed in parallel grammatical form—in the example, as phrases using a noun plus modifiers. This is a topic outline; in a sentence outline all headings are expressed as full sentences (see pp. 297–98).

NOTE Because of its structure, a formal outline can be an excellent tool for analyzing a draft before revising it. See page 23.

See page 23.

4. Unity and coherence

Two qualities of effective writing relate to organization: unity and coherence. When you perceive that someone's writing "flows well," you are probably appreciating these qualities.

To check an outline or draft for UNITY, ask these questions:

* Is each section relevant to the main idea (thesis) of the essay?
* Within main sections, does each example or detail support the principal idea of that section?

To check your outline or draft for COHERENCE, ask these questions:

* Do the ideas follow a clear sequence?
* Are the parts of the essay logically connected?
* Are the connections clear and smooth?

See also pages 40–46 on unity and coherence in paragraphs.

See also pages 40–46 on unity and coherence in paragraphs.

4 Drafting

Drafting is an occasion for exploration. Don't expect to transcribe solid thoughts into polished prose: solidity and polish will come with revision and editing. Instead, while drafting let the very act of writing help you find and form your meaning.

4a Starting to draft

Beginning a draft sometimes takes courage, even for seasoned professionals. Procrastination may actually help if you let ideas for writing simmer at the same time. At some point, though, you'll have to face the blank paper or computer screen. The following techniques can help you begin:

* Read over what you've already written—notes, outlines, and so on—and immediately start your draft with whatever comes to mind.
* Freewrite (see p. 8).
* Write scribbles or type nonsense until usable words start coming.
* Pretend you're writing to a friend about your topic.

4b

- ❖ Conjure up an image that represents your topic—a physical object, a facial expression, two people arguing over something, a giant machine gouging the earth for a mine, whatever. Describe that image.
- ❖ Skip the opening and start in the middle. Or write the conclusion.
- ❖ Write a paragraph on what you think your essay will be about when you finish it.
- ❖ Using your outline, divide your essay into chunks—say, one for the introduction, another for the first point, and so on. Start writing the chunk that seems most eager to be written, the one you understand best or feel most strongly about.

4b Keeping momentum

Drafting requires momentum: the forward movement opens you to fresh ideas and connections. To keep moving while drafting, try one or more of these techniques:

- ❖ Set aside enough time for yourself. (For a brief essay, a first draft is likely to take at least an hour or two.)
- ❖ Work in a place where you won't be interrupted, and make yourself comfortable.
- ❖ If you must stop working, leave a note with the draft about what you expect to do next. Then you can pick up where you stopped with minimal disruption.
- ❖ Be as fluid as possible, and don't worry about mistakes. Spontaneity will allow your attitudes toward your subject to surface naturally in your sentences, and it will also make you receptive to ideas and relations you haven't seen before. Mistakes will be easier to find and correct later, when you're not also trying to create.
- ❖ Keep going. Skip over sticky spots; leave a blank if you can't find the right word; put alternative ideas or phrasings in brackets so that you can consider them later without bogging down. If an idea pops out of nowhere but doesn't seem to fit in, quickly jot it down on a separate sheet, or write it into the draft and bracket or boldface it for later attention. You can use an asterisk (*) or some other symbol to mark places where you feel blocked or uncertain. On a computer you can find these places later by using the search command to locate the symbol.
- ❖ Resist self-criticism. Don't worry about your style, grammar, spelling, punctuation, and the like. Don't worry about what your readers will think. These are very important matters, but save them for revision. If you can't seem to resist self-criticism and you're using a computer, try invisible writing as described on pages 8–9.

❖ Use your thesis sentence and outline to remind you of your planned purpose, organization, and content.

❖ But don't feel constrained by your thesis and outline. If your writing leads you in a more interesting direction, follow.

If you write on a computer, frequently save or file the text you're drafting—at least every fifteen minutes or every couple of pages and every time you leave the computer. In addition, back up your drafts on a separate disk, and perhaps even print paper copies (so-called hard copy) in case anything happens to your disks.

4c Examining a sample first draft

The following is Terry Perez's first draft on the subject of cultural diversity in the media. (Perez's journal writing appears on p. 8, her freewriting on p. 9, and her outline on p. 18.) Like most first drafts, this one is rough, with holes, digressions, and grammatical errors. But it gave Perez a good start.

Title?

In "America: The Multinational Society," Ishmael Reed mentions that the communications media sensationalizes the "conflict between people of different backgrounds." Either that, or it depicts Americans as homogeneous. The media projects unrealistic images of the US as a nation either of constant ethnic conflict or untroubled homogeneity.

It is easy to find examples of the emphasizing of conflict among ethnic groups. The news is full of stories of Hispanic gangs fighting African American gangs, Korean shopkeepers pitted against non-Korean customers, African American churches are burned by white teenagers. In fact, New York City, with its dense and ethnically diverse population, regularly supplies stories for other cities' news media when they run out of local stories of hate and mayhem. My brother who lives in San Francisco is always complaining about all the New York stories in the news. What he doesn't realize is that it's not New York's fault, it's the media's for always playing up the bad news. Bad news is what the media specializes in--as everyone is always complaining. When it comes to ethnic relations, this is certainly the case. All sorts of different people mingle together peacefully, but not in the media.

There the only peace belongs to a very narrow band of people. Especially in television fiction and advertising. They have usual characteristics: they are white, married or expecting to be someday, unethnic, white-collar, well-to-do, settled, materialistic, good-looking, and thin. A certain commercial is typical of TV with the happy prosperous nuclear family enjoying breakfast together. Many, many groups are excluded from this TV type, such as ethnic groups, poor people, and the disabled.

The problem with this media image, with its extremes of peace and conflict, is that it is untrue. It caters to the ones who feel that the US should be a "monoculture" and would be. If only we could battle down the ones who don't belong or won't. A different picture is possible, but we aren't getting it.

5   Revising and Editing

During revision—literally "re-seeing"—you shift your focus outward from yourself and your subject toward your readers, concentrating on what will help them respond as you want. It's wise to revise in at least two stages, one devoted to fundamental meaning and structure (here called REVISING) and one devoted to word choice, grammar, punctuation, and other features of the surface (here called EDITING). Knowing that you will edit later gives you the freedom at first to look beyond the confines of the page or screen to the whole paper.

5a   Revising

To revise your writing, you have to read it critically (see p. 12), and that means you have to create some distance between your draft and yourself. One of the following techniques may help you see your work objectively:

- ❖ Take a break after finishing the draft to pursue some other activity. A few hours may be enough; a whole night or day is preferable.
- ❖ Ask someone to read and react to your draft.
- ❖ If you compose your draft in handwriting, retype it on a typewriter or computer before revising it. The act of transcription can reveal gaps in content or problems in structure.
- ❖ If you compose on a computer, print your draft on paper. You'll be able to view all pages of the draft at once, and the different medium can reveal weaknesses you didn't see on screen.

(Save each draft in its own file so that you can retrieve it if you need to.)

❖ Outline your draft. While reading it, highlight the main points supporting the thesis. Write these sentences down separately in outline form. (If you're working on a computer, you can copy and paste these sentences.) Then examine the outline you've made for logical order, gaps, and digressions. A formal outline can be especially illuminating because of its careful structure (see p. 18).

❖ Listen to your draft: read it out loud, read it into a tape recorder and play the tape, or have someone read the draft to you.

Set aside at least as much time to revise your essay as you took to draft it. Plan on going through the draft several times to answer the questions in the checklist below and to resolve any problems you uncover.

Checklist for revision

❖ *Purpose:* What is the essay's purpose? Does that purpose conform to the assignment? Is it consistent throughout the paper? (See pp. 4–5.)

❖ *Thesis:* What is the thesis of the essay? Where does it become clear? How well do thesis and paper match: Does the paper stray from the thesis? Does it fulfill the commitment of the thesis? (See pp. 13–15.)

❖ *Structure:* What are the main points of the paper? (List them.) How well does each support the thesis? How effective is their arrangement for the paper's purpose? (See pp. 15–16.)

❖ *Development:* How well do details, examples, and other evidence support each main point? Where, if at all, might readers find support skimpy or have trouble understanding the content? (See pp. 5–7, 47–51.)

❖ *Tone:* What is the tone of the paper? How do particular words and sentence structures create the tone? How appropriate is it for the purpose, topic, and intended readers? Where is it most or least successful? (See pp. 5–6.)

❖ *Unity:* What does each sentence and paragraph contribute to the thesis? Where, if at all, do digressions occur? Should these be cut, or can they be rewritten to support the thesis? (See pp. 19, 40–41.)

❖ *Coherence:* How clearly and smoothly does the paper flow? Where does it seem rough or awkward? Can any transitions be improved? (See pp. 19, 41–46.)

❖ *Title, introduction, conclusion:* How accurately and interestingly does the title reflect the essay's content? (See p. 24.) How well does the introduction engage and focus readers' attention? (See pp. 51–53.) How effective is the conclusion in providing a sense of completion? (See pp. 53–54.)

A note on titling your essay

The revision stage is a good time to consider a title because attempting to sum up your essay in a phrase can focus your attention sharply on your topic, purpose, and audience.

Here are some suggestions for titling an essay:

❖ A DESCRIPTIVE TITLE is almost always appropriate and is often expected for academic writing. It announces the topic clearly, accurately, and as briefly as possible. The title Terry Perez finally chose, "America's Media Image,'" is an example. Other examples: "Images of Lost Identity in *North by Northwest*"; "An Experiment in Small-Group Dynamics"; "Why Lincoln Delayed Emancipating the Slaves."

❖ A SUGGESTIVE TITLE—the kind often found in popular magazines—may be appropriate for more informal writing. Examples include "Making Peace" (for an essay on the Peace Corps) and "Royal Pain" (for an essay on Prince Charles of England). For a more suggestive title, Perez might have chosen something like "Distorted Pictures." Such a title conveys the writer's attitudes and main concerns but not the precise topic, thereby pulling readers into the essay to learn more. A source for such a title may be a familiar phrase, a fresh image, or a significant expression from the essay itself.

❖ A title tells readers how big the topic is. For Perez's essay, the title "Watching the Media" or "Cultural Diversity" would have been too broad, whereas "The Media and Cultural Conflict" or "Exclusion in the Media" would have been too narrow.

❖ A title should not restate the assignment or the thesis sentence, as in "What Ishmael Reed Means by Cultural Diversity" or "How I Feel About Cultural Diversity."

For more information on essay titles, see pages 205 (the format of a title in the final paper) and 224 (capitalizing words in a title).

5b   Examining a sample revision

The material opposite is the first half of Terry Perez's revision (first draft pp. 21–22). Some changes are especially notable. (This list is keyed to the revision by number.)

1. Perez added a descriptive title to give readers a sense of her topic.
2. Perez rewrote and expanded the previous abrupt introduction to give more of a sense of Reed's essay and to make a clearer transition to her additional point about the media (the new sentence beginning *Another false media picture*).

3. Perez added examples and other details to support her general statements. This and the following category of changes occupied most of Perez's attention during revision.

4. In response to a reader's comments, Perez added several concessions and exceptions to balance her strong point of view.

5. Perez cut a digression that her reader had found distracting and irrelevant.

6. To clarify the connection between a portion of her text and her thesis sentence, Perez started a new paragraph and rewrote the paragraph's opening.

rev
5b

Title? *America's Media Image*   1

Is the United States a "monoculture," a unified, homogeneous society?   2
Many Americans would like it to be or they think that it is now. But the
writer Ishmael Reed says no. His essay is titled "America: The Multinational
Society." In it he speaks out for cultural diversity. He thinks it makes the
nation stronger. In passing he

In "America: The Multinational Society," Ishmael Reed mentions
that the communications media sensationalizes the "conflict between
Another false media picture can be added to Reed's point. The picture of
people of different backgrounds." Either that, or it depicts Americans
Americans as socially, economically, and ethnically similar.
as homogeneous. The media projects unrealistic images of the US as a

nation either of constant ethnic conflict or untroubled homogeneity.

It is easy to find examples of the emphasizing of conflict among

ethnic groups. The news is full of stories of Hispanic gangs fighting
swastikas are painted on Jewish synagogues and cemeteries,
African American gangs, Korean shopkeepers pitted against non-   3
Haitians battle Cubans,
Korean customers, African American churches are burned by white
These are real stories, and all-too-real ethnic conflict should not
teenagers. In fact, New York City, with its dense and ethnically diverse   4
be covered up. However, these stories are blown out of proportion.
population, regularly supplies stories for other cities' news media when

they run out of local stories of hate and mayhem. My brother who lives   5

in San Francisco is always complaining about all the New York stories

in the news. What he doesn't realize is that it's not New York's fault, it's

the media's for always playing up the bad news. Bad news is what the

media specializes in--as everyone is always complaining. When it comes
¶ While emphasizing conflict, the media show little of the good news about   6
to ethnic relations, this is certainly the case. All sorts of different people
ethnic relations. Pakistanis, Russians, Mexicans, Chinese, Mayflower
mingle together peacefully, but not in the media.   3
descendants, great-grandchildren of African slaves. All these and more

mingle on the nation's streets, attend school together, work together, even

intermarry. Integration is very far from complete, severe inequality persists. 4
Real conflict exists. But for the most part, cultural groups are not at war
and instead practice toleration and cooperation.

5c Editing and proofreading

Editing, like revision, is a two-step process. First edit the revised draft for style, sense, and correctness; then proofread the final draft for correctness.

1. Editing

After you've revised your essay so that all the content is in place, then turn to the important work of removing any surface problems that could interfere with a reader's understanding or enjoyment of your ideas.

Try these approaches to discover what needs editing:

- Take a break, even fifteen or twenty minutes, to clear your head.
- Read the draft *slowly,* and read what you *actually see.* Otherwise, you're likely to read what you intended to write but didn't.
- As you read the draft, imagine yourself encountering it for the first time, as a reader will.
- Have a friend or relative read your work. (If your native language is not English, you may find it especially helpful to have a native speaker read your revised drafts.) When you share your work in class, listen to the responses of your classmates or instructor. (See p. 31.)
- As when revising, read the draft aloud, preferably into a tape recorder, listening for awkward rhythms, repetitive sentence patterns, and missing or clumsy transitions.
- Learn from your own experience. Keep a record of the problems that others have pointed out in your writing. When editing, check your work against this record.

If you write on a computer, consider these additional approaches to editing:

- If possible, work on a double-spaced paper copy. Most people find it much harder to spot errors on a computer screen than on paper.
- Use the search command to find and correct mistakes or stylistic problems that tend to crop up in your writing—certain misspellings, overuse of *there is,* wordy phrases such as *the fact that,* and so on.

Checklist for editing

❖ *Clarity:* How well do words and sentences convey their intended meanings? Which if any words and sentences are confusing? Check the paper especially for these:

Exact words (pp. 72–79)
Parallelism (pp. 59–61)
Clear modifiers (pp. 152–57)
Clear reference of pronouns (pp. 140–43)
Complete sentences (pp. 159–61)
Sentences separated correctly (pp. 161–65)

❖ *Effectiveness:* How well do words and sentences engage and direct readers' attention? Where, if at all, does the writing seem wordy, choppy, or dull? Check the paper especially for these:

Smooth and informative transitions (pp. 44–46)
Variety in sentence length and structure (pp. 64–66)
Appropriate words (pp. 67–72)
Concise sentences (pp. 80–86)

❖ *Correctness:* How little or how much do surface errors interfere with clarity and effectiveness? Check the paper especially for these:

Spelling (pp. 216–20)
Verb forms, especially -*s* and -*ed* endings and correct forms of irregular verbs (pp. 104–12)
Verb tenses, especially consistency (pp. 113–19)
Agreement between subjects and verbs, especially when words come between them or the subject is *each, everyone,* or a similar word (pp. 123–27)
Pronoun forms (pp. 132–37)
Agreement between pronouns and antecedents, especially when the subject contains *or* or it is *each, everyone,* or a similar word (pp. 137–40)
Commas, especially with *and* or *but* (pp. 174, 183), with introductory elements (174–75), with nonrestrictive elements (175–78), and with series (179–80)
Apostrophes in possessives but not plural nouns (*Dave's/witches,* pp. 189–91) and in contractions but not possessive personal pronouns (*it's/its,* pp. 191–92)

❖ Computer programs such as spelling checkers and grammar and style checkers can be helpful, but they cannot substitute for your own care and attention. Spelling checkers can't distinguish a misuse of a correctly spelled word, such as *their* for *there* or *not* for *now.* Grammar and style checkers often misidentify errors and ignore errors they're not capable of spotting. Use such programs only as a starting point. (For more on optional word-processing programs, see pp. 34–35.)

❖ The ease of editing on a computer can lead to overediting and steal the life from your prose. Resist any temptation to rewrite sentences over and over.

❖ Inserting or deleting text on a computer requires special care not to omit needed words or leave in unneeded words.

In your editing, work first for clarity and a smooth movement among sentences and then for correctness. Use the questions in the checklist on the preceding page to guide your editing, referring to the page numbers in parentheses as needed.

2. Proofreading

After editing your essay, recopy, retype, or print it one last time. Follow the guidelines in Chapter 40 or the wishes of your instructor for an appropriate document format. Be sure to proofread the final essay several times to spot and correct errors. To increase the accuracy of your proofreading, you may need to experiment with ways to keep yourself from relaxing into the rhythm and the content of your prose. Here are a few tricks, including some used by professional proofreaders:

❖ Read printed copy, even if you will eventually submit the paper electronically. Most people proofread more accurately when reading type on paper than when reading it on a computer screen. (At the same time, don't view the printed copy as necessarily error-free just because it's clean. Clean-looking copy may still harbor errors.)

❖ Read the paper aloud, very slowly, and distinctly pronounce exactly what you see.

❖ Place a ruler under each line as you read it.

❖ Read "against copy," comparing your final draft one sentence at a time against the edited draft you copied it from.

❖ Take steps to keep the content of your writing from distracting you while you proofread. Read the essay backward, end to beginning, examining each sentence as a separate unit. Or, taking advantage of a computer, isolate each paragraph from its context by printing it on a separate page. (Of course, reassemble the paragraphs before submitting the paper.)

5d Examining a sample editing and a final draft

Excerpts from Terry Perez's edited draft and her complete final draft appear below (first draft pp. 21–22; revision pp. 25–26). With the final draft are annotations that point out the relations among the essay's parts.

EDITED FIRST PARAGRAPH

Is the United States a "monoculture," a unified, homogeneous so-
~~think that it is or should be.~~
ciety? Many Americans ~~would like it to be or they think that it is now.~~

But the writer Ishmael Reed says no. ~~His essay is titled~~ *In* "America: The
Reed
Multinational Society," ~~In it he~~ speaks out for cultural diversity. He

thinks it makes the nation stronger. In passing he mentions that the

communications media sensationalize the "conflict between people of
To Reed's point can be added the media's other
different backgrounds." ~~Another false media picture of America can be~~
false picture of
~~added to Reed's point.~~ The picture of Americans as socially, economi-

cally, and ethnically similar. The media project unrealistic images of
United States
the ~~US~~ as a nation either of constant ethnic conflict or untroubled

homogeneity.

FINAL DRAFT

America's Media Image

Is the United States a "monoculture," a unified,
homogeneous society? Many Americans think that it
is or should be. But the writer Ishmael Reed says no.
In "America: The Multinational Society," Reed speaks
out for cultural diversity. He thinks it makes the
nation stronger. In passing he mentions that the
communications media sensationalize the "conflict
between people of different backgrounds." To Reed's
point can be added the media's other false picture of
Americans as socially, economically, and ethnically
similar. The media project unrealistic images of the
United States as a nation of either constant ethnic conflict or untroubled homogeneity.

It is easy to find examples of the emphasizing of
conflict among ethnic groups. The news is full of
stories of Hispanic gangs fighting African American
gangs, swastikas painted on Jewish synagogues and

Introduction:
opening question
to draw readers in;
then transition to
thesis sentence.

Thesis sentence:
media's depiction
of conflict and ho-
mogeneity.

First main point:
emphasis on con-
flict among groups.

cemeteries, Korean shopkeepers pitted against non-Korean customers, Haitians battling Cubans, or African American churches burned by white teen-agers. It's not that these aren't real stories, or that all-too-real ethnic conflict should be covered up. It's just that these stories are blown out of proportion.

While emphasizing conflict, the media show little of the good news about ethnic relations. Pakistanis, Russians, Mexicans, Chinese, Mayflower descendants, great-grandchildren of African slaves--all these and more mingle peacefully on the nation's streets, attend school together, work together, even intermarry. Granted, integration is very far from complete. Severe inequality and real conflict do exist. For the most part, however, cultural groups are not at war but practice toleration and cooperation.

Continuation of first main point: de-emphasis on tolerance and cooperation.

In the media, especially in television fiction and advertising, the only peace belongs to a homogeneous band of people. They are usually white, married or ex-pecting to be someday, unethnic, white collar, well-to-do, settled, materialistic, good looking, and thin. The norm is easy to recognize in a cereal commercial with a mother who is overseeing her husband's and children's breakfasts. The kitchen is full of the latest appliances and decorations. Everyone is white. Everyone is fit and cute, beautiful, or handsome. Everyone is well dressed and cheerful.

Second main point: emphasis on homogeneity.

The few exceptions to this norm, such as the working-class and overweight Roseanne and more recent African American situation comedies, simply highlight the lack of diversity everywhere else. These are but a few of the groups excluded from the homogeneous TV type (some overlap): Polish Americans, home-less families, homosexuals, factory workers, Lebanese

Continuation of second main point: de-emphasis on diversity.

immigrants, teenage mothers, amputees, Japanese Americans, unmarried couples, loners, stay-at-home fathers, transients, people with disabilities, elderly pensioners, homely people, fat people, small people.

The media's two extremes of peace and conflict create a composite picture of a nation where a "monoculture" is desirable and all but achieved, if only we could battle down the ones who don't belong or won't belong. Imagine a different picture, though. In this one, people coexist who have diverse backgrounds, interests, incomes, living arrangements, and appearances. Sometimes they stay apart; sometimes they blend. Sometimes they clash or prey on each other; sometimes they laugh together. It all happens now, and we could be watching.

> Conclusion: two main points tied together and related to the title.

5c   Revising collaboratively

In many writing courses students work together on writing, most often commenting on each other's work to help with revision. This collaborative writing gives experience in reading written work critically and in reaching others through writing. Collaboration often occurs face to face in small groups or via drafts and comments on paper. Increasingly, it also occurs on computers, a situation discussed on pages 36–37.

Whether you collaborate in person, on paper, or on a computer, you will be more comfortable and helpful and will benefit more from others' comments if you follow a few guidelines.

When reading someone else's writing, focus on content:

* Be sure you know what the writer is saying. If necessary, summarize or outline the paper to understand its content. Ask the writer for more information when you need it.
* Read closely and critically. (See p. 12.)
* Unless you have other instructions, address only the most significant problems in the work. Use the revision checklist on page 23 as a guide to what is significant in a piece of writing.
* Be specific. Explain *why* you are confused or *why* you disagree with a conclusion.

❖ Remember that you are the reader, not the writer. Resist the temptation to edit sentences, add details, or otherwise assume responsibility for the paper.

❖ Word your comments supportively. Question the writer in a way that emphasizes the effect of the work on *you*, the reader ("I find this paragraph confusing"), and avoid measuring the work against a set of external standards (instead of "This essay is poorly organized," say "I have difficulty following your argument").

❖ Be positive as well as honest. Instead of saying "This paragraph bores me," say "You have an interesting detail here that seems buried." And tell the writer what you like about the paper.

When you *receive* the comments of others, whether your classmates or your instructor, try to be open:

❖ Think of your readers as counselors or coaches who will help you see the virtues and flaws in your work and sharpen your awareness of readers' needs.

❖ Read or listen to comments closely.

❖ Make sure you know what the critic is saying. If you need more information, ask for it, or consult the appropriate section of this handbook.

❖ Don't become defensive. Letting comments offend you will only erect a barrier to improvement in your writing. As one writing teacher advises, "Leave your ego at the door."

❖ When comments seem appropriate, revise your work in response to them. You will learn more from the act of revision than from just thinking about changes.

❖ Though you should be open to suggestions, you are the final authority on your paper. You are free to decline advice when you think it is inappropriate.

❖ Keep track of both the strengths and weaknesses others identify. Then in following assignments you can build on your successes and give special attention to problem areas.

ESL Collaboration may be uncomfortable if you come from a culture where writers do not expect criticism from readers or readers do not expect to think and speak critically about what they read. Writers in English often consider a draft or even a final paper to be more an exploration of ideas than the last word on a subject. They usually welcome questions and suggestions from readers. Readers of English, in turn, often approach a text in a skeptical frame of mind. Their tactful questions and suggestions are usually considered appropriate.

5f   Preparing a writing portfolio

Your writing teacher may ask you to assemble samples of your writing into a portfolio, or folder, once or more during the course. Such a portfolio gives you chance to consider all your writing over a period and showcase your best work.

Although the requirements for portfolios vary, most teachers are looking for a range of writing that demonstrates your progress and strengths as a writer. You, in turn, see how you have advanced from one assignment to the next, as you've had time for new knowledge to sink in and time for practice. Teachers often allow students to revise papers before placing them in the portfolio, even if the papers have already been submitted earlier. In that case, every paper in the portfolio can benefit from all your learning.

An assignment to assemble a writing portfolio will probably also provide guidelines for what to include, how the portfolio will be evaluated, and how (or whether) it will be weighted for a grade. Be sure you understand the purpose of the portfolio and who will read it. For instance, if your composition teacher will be the only reader and his or her guidelines encourage you to show evidence of progress, you might include a paper that took big risks but never entirely succeeded. In contrast, if a committee of teachers will read your work and the guidelines urge you to demonstrate your competence as a writer, you might include only papers that did succeed.

Unless the guidelines specify otherwise, provide error-free copies of your final drafts, label all your samples with your name, and assemble them all in a folder. Add a cover letter or memo that lists the samples and explains why you've included each one. The self-evaluation involved should be a learning experience for you and will help your readers assess your development as a writer.

6   Writing with a Computer

At the symbol printed here in the margin, this handbook suggests specific ways to use or accommodate computers in writing and research. This chapter offers general advice for word processing (next page), for writing collaboratively with computers (p. 36), and for creating hypertext documents (p. 37).

6a Using a word processor

6a

Although a word processor cannot think for you, it can save you time and make writing easier. Specific tips for using a word processor during writing and research appear throughout Chapters 1–5 and 47–49, and Chapter 40 offers advice on designing word-processed documents. This section recommends some precautions and options.

1. Word-processing basics

You'll work more efficiently and prevent loss of your work by following a few guidelines:

* Become familiar with the software's "Help" menus, usually accessible at the top of the screen.
* Make a list of the basic keystrokes you need to perform important commands, such as moving the cursor around and inserting, deleting, and saving text.
* Save your work every fifteen minutes or so, either by instructing the computer to do so automatically or by manually saving the text you're working on.
* Label each project with its own file name—perhaps the paper's title or the assignment number. To ensure against loss of material as your ideas develop, consider making a separate file for each draft of a project as well, labeled with the draft number. At least copy passages before you delete them from a draft so that you can retrieve them if necessary.
* Make a backup disk of your work at the end of each word-processing session as insurance against the loss or damage of your working disk.
* Keep your disks in dustproof containers, and store them safely away from heat, cold, or sources of magnetism such as the computer itself or a stereo or television.
* Regularly print paper copies of your work. They serve as second backup copies, and you may find revising and editing easier and more productive on paper than on screen (see pp. 22 and 26–28).

2. Optional programs

Many word processors either come with optional programs such as spelling checkers or are compatible with optional programs. The programs are often limited, for the reasons given below, but they can support and speed your efforts.

6a

❖ *Invention or discovery programs* help you develop a topic by prompting you with a structured set of questions or by providing creative analogies that help you think imaginatively. These programs can help you get started, develop new insights, and conceive a purpose for your writing. One example, *The Writer's Workshop,* is available with this handbook.

❖ *Outlining programs* help you organize your work by providing automatic indentions, easy resequencing, and other features.

❖ *Documentation programs* help you format your source citations in just about any style (see p. 267 for more on these programs). The *Writer's Workshop* software available with this handbook includes such a documentation program.

❖ *Style-checking programs* point out wordy and awkward phrases and incorrect grammar and punctuation. However, these programs can only call your attention to passages that *may* be faulty. They miss many errors because they are not yet capable of analyzing the language in all its complexity. And the programs often question passages that don't need editing, such as an emphatic use of repetition. When you use a style-checking program, you must determine each time it questions something whether a change is needed at all and what change will be most effective. And you must read your text carefully on your own to find any errors the program may have missed.

❖ *Thesaurus programs* help with word choices by responding to your word with a display of several synonyms (words with similar meanings). A single keystroke allows you to replace your word with a displayed word. Thesaurus programs are limited because they display only some synonyms, not all, and because even a narrow list may contain words that do not suit your meaning. Like a printed thesaurus (see p. 73), an electronic thesaurus is no help if it leads you to misuse words whose meanings you don't know. Before you use a word suggested by a thesaurus, always check its meaning in a dictionary.

❖ *Spell-checking programs* help you find typographical errors and misspelled words, and they display correct spellings on the screen. They can be valuable proofreading aids. However, they are limited because they cannot store every possible word and thus may identify a word you use as misspelled even though it is correct. More important, they are unreliable because they cannot identify errors such as a confusion between *now* and *not, its* and *it's, your* and *you're,* or *there, their,* and *they're.* Maintain a file of your frequent misspellings and use the search command to check them yourself.

6b

6b   Collaborating using computers

Collaborating by computer can extend the advantages of collaborating in person and on paper, discussed on pages 31–32. The guidelines there can help you work effectively in computer groups as well.

1. Etiquette

Computer communication demands a certain etiquette:

❖ You wouldn't shout at a fellow student face to face, so don't do so by computer either. Temper your comments, and avoid using all-capital letters. (See p. 369 for more about online courtesy.)
❖ You may not be present to clarify your comments for your readers when they receive them. If you mean a remark to be taken humorously, you may need to say so. Or use common *emoticons*, combinations of punctuation marks and other symbols that signal emotions: for instance, :-) read sideways shows a smile.

2. E-mail and discussion groups

When you are collaborating by personal electronic mail or a discussion group, keep these guidelines in mind:

❖ In case other members of the group do not have the original message that prompts your response, take advantage of the common e-mail feature that allows you to extract portions of the earlier text into your own text.
❖ If you are joining a discussion already in progress, take the time to read all earlier messages before contributing comments or asking questions. (If you don't know how to obtain past messages, ask your instructor or another group member.)
❖ If you are responding to another group member's request for information, send a personal reply unless you think the entire group will benefit from your response.

3. Synchronous communication

Your class may have a chance to discuss papers or topics in "real time" through environments for synchronous, or simultaneous, communication, such as IRC or a MOO. (See p. 248 for more on these environments.) A few tips can help you make the most of a conversation that sometimes lags and sometimes proceeds rapidly:

❖ Always save a transcript of your session for future reference. Check with your instructor or your computer center if you don't know how to create a transcript.

❖ Have a clear sense of what your group's goals are for a session before beginning. If you sense at first that everyone is waiting for someone else to start, then do so by raising questions about the goals and plans for the session.

❖ If your group is meeting to comment on a paper, e-mail a copy of the paper to individual participants before the meeting time.

❖ If you find it impossible to read everyone's comments, pick a thread of conversation that seems most interesting or relevant to you and focus on the comments from the people involved. You can always go back and read the transcripts of other threads.

❖ Remember that you are participating in a conversation, not making a speech. You don't need to have a thought perfectly formed and worded in your mind before trying it out. Sometimes the smallest fragment of a thought may be just what the conversation needs.

6c Creating hypertext documents

In some of your courses you may be asked to create electronic HYPERTEXT documents that provide varied paths through the information they present. You have seen hypertext if you have browsed the World Wide Web (p. 244): sites there offer highlighted links to other spots in the same site (including text, graphics, video, and so on) or links to other sites on the Web. The user chooses his or her own path of exploration. You might create a Web site yourself, or you might create a hypertext document intended only for an instructor and perhaps classmates, such as a history project that shows text and images and provides links to primary-source documents.

Whether you plan to post a hypertext document on the Web or just on your own computer, you'll need to code the document using special software. Beyond the technical requirements, however, the medium involves other considerations as well.

1. Planning

Because of its complexities, a hypertext document rewards careful planning. Consider the following questions:

* What is your purpose in creating this document? Your choice of links, images, and other features should be geared to this purpose.
* Who is your audience? Use the questions on page 6 to analyze the audience's interests, biases, expectations, and so on.
* What do you want your document to look like? Plan your document so that headings, text, and any photographs, video, or other elements don't crowd together on a small computer screen.
* What elements will best achieve your purpose? Add elements to your document to further your purpose, not simply for the sake of including them. A single image may help you illustrate a concept more efficiently than a page of text alone. However, no such element should be used as a distraction from an otherwise weak document.

2. Links

Aside from the technical requirements, probably the trickiest part of creating a hypertext document is making effective links within the document and to other documents. The following questions raise the key issues:

* How does each of your links further your purpose? Every link in your document should add some information that is vital to your central idea.
* Will readers understand the reason for each link? Think about what readers probably understand, and provide a variety of links geared to their understanding.
* Are the sources of your links clear? You have the same obligation to acknowledge sources in a hypertext document as you do in other academic writing. (See pp. 258–61 on what to acknowledge and pp. 265–67 on documenting sources.)
* Have you sought permission for links to copyrighted material? If your hypertext document will be distributed privately (for instance, to your instructor and classmates), then it is enough to acknowledge the use of copyrighted material (see pp. 258–61). But if you are publishing your document on the World Wide Web, then you may be obliged to seek permission for using copyrighted material—just as print publishers do.

3. Nontext media

Images, backgrounds, icons, animation, video, and sound can add interest as well as substance to your hypertext document. When using such material, consider these questions:

* What does each element add to your document? A certain amount of window dressing may be appropriate, especially in the use of graphics. But an overloaded text will distract and even annoy readers.
* Can you find the elements you need on the Web? A number of image libraries allow users (especially nonprofit users) to download visual and audio elements without formal permission and to reproduce the elements in the users' own documents. If you reproduce elements from such a source, always acknowledge the source (see pp. 258–61).
* Do you need to seek permission for use of nontext elements? You can download nontext materials from many Web sites, not just image libraries. But unless the site explicitly allows copying without permission, you should seek permission to publish the material in your own Web document. (Text and nontext material are alike in this respect.)

7   Paragraphs

A PARAGRAPH is a group of related sentences set off by a beginning indention or, sometimes, by extra space. Paragraphs give you and your readers a breather from long stretches of text, and they indicate key steps in the development of your thesis.

In the body of your essay, you may use paragraphs for any of these purposes:

* To introduce one of the main points supporting your essay's central idea (its thesis) and to develop the point with examples, facts, or other supporting evidence. (See pp. 13–15 for a discussion of an essay's thesis.)
* Within a group of paragraphs centering on one main point, to introduce and develop a key example or other important evidence.
* To shift approach—for instance, from pros to cons, from problem to solution, from questions to answers.
* To mark movement in a sequence, such as from one reason or step to another.

This chapter discusses the three qualities of an effective body paragraph: unity (next page), coherence (p. 41), and development (p. 46). In addition, the chapter discusses two special kinds of paragraphs: introductions and conclusions (pp. 51 and 53).

¶ un
7a

ESL The conventions of paragraphing described here are not common to all languages. If your native language is not English and you have difficulty with paragraphs, don't worry about paragraphing during drafting. Instead, during a separate step of revision, divide your text into parts that develop your main points. Mark those parts with indentions.

7a   Maintaining paragraph unity

An effective paragraph develops one central idea—in other words, it is UNIFIED. For example:

> Some people really like chili, apparently, but nobody can agree how the stuff should be made. C. V. Wood, twice winner at Terlingua, uses flank steak, pork chops, chicken, and green chilis. My friend Hughes Rudd of CBS News, who imported five hundred pounds of chili powder into Russia as a condition of accepting employment as Moscow correspondent, favors coarse-ground beef. Isadore Bleckman, the cameraman I must live with on the road, insists upon one-inch cubes of stew beef and puts garlic in his chili, an Illinois affectation. An Indian of my acquaintance, Mr. Fulton Batisse, who eats chili for breakfast when he can, uses buffalo meat and plays an Indian drum while it's cooking. I ask you.   —CHARLES KURALT, *Dateline America*

Kuralt's paragraph works because it follows through on its central idea, which is stated in the underlined first sentence, the TOPIC SENTENCE. After the topic sentence, each of the next four sentences offers an example of a chili concoction. (In the final sentence Kuralt comments on the examples.)

What if Kuralt had written his paragraph as follows instead? Here the topic of chili preparation is forgotten mid-paragraph, as the sentences digress to describe life in Moscow:

> Some people really like chili, apparently, but nobody can agree how the stuff should be made. C. V. Wood, twice winner at Terlingua, uses flank steak, pork chops, chicken, and green chilis. My friend Hughes Rudd, who imported five hundred pounds of chili powder into Russia as a condition of accepting employment as Moscow correspondent, favors coarse-ground beef. He had some trouble finding the beef in Moscow, though. He sometimes had to scour all the markets and wait in long lines. For any American used to overstocked supermarkets and department stores, Russia can be quite a shock.

Instead of following through on its topic sentence, the paragraph loses its way. It is not unified.

A topic sentence need not always come first in the paragraph, and in some paragraphs the central idea may not be stated at all. But always the idea should govern the paragraph's content as if it were standing guard at the opening.

¶ coh
7b

7b Achieving paragraph coherence

When a paragraph is COHERENT, readers can see how it holds together: the sentences seem to flow logically and smoothly into one another. Exactly the opposite happens with this paragraph:

> The ancient Egyptians were masters of preserving dead people's bodies by making mummies of them. Mummies several thousand years old have been discovered nearly intact. The skin, hair, teeth, finger- and toenails, and facial features of the mummies were evident. It is possible to diagnose the diseases they suffered in life, such as smallpox, arthritis, and nutritional deficiencies. The process was remarkably effective. Sometimes apparent were the fatal afflictions of the dead people. a middle-aged king died from a blow on the head, and polio killed a child king. Mummification consisted of removing the internal organs, applying natural preservatives inside and out, and then wrapping the body in layers of bandages.

The paragraph is hard to read. The sentences lurch instead of gliding from point to point.

The paragraph as it was actually written is much clearer. Not only did the writer arrange information differently; he also built links into his sentences so that they would flow smoothly. The highlighting on the actual paragraph below emphasizes the techniques:

- ❖ After stating the central idea in a topic sentence, the writer moves to two more specific explanations and illustrates the second with four sentences of examples.
- ❖ Circled words repeat or restate key terms or concepts.
- ❖ Boxed words link sentences and clarify relationships.
- ❖ Underlined phrases are in parallel grammatical form to reflect their parallel content.

Central idea
The ancient Egyptians were masters of preserving dead people's bodies by making mummies of them. Basically, mummification consisted of removing the internal organs, applying natural preservatives inside and out, and then wrapping the body in layers of bandages. And the process was remarkably effective. Indeed,

(mummies) several thousand years old have been discovered nearly
Specific examples
intact. (Their) skin, hair, teeth, finger- and toenails, and facial fea-

tures are still evident. (Their) diseases in life, such as smallpox,

arthritis, and nutritional deficiencies, are still diagnosable. Even

(their) fatal afflictions are still apparent: a middle-aged king died

from a blow on the head; a child king died from polio.

—MITCHELL ROSENBAUM (student), "Lost Arts of the Egyptians"

1. Paragraph organization

A coherent paragraph organizes information so that readers can
easily follow along. These are the most common paragraph schemes:

* *General to specific:* Sentences downshift from more general
statements to more specific ones. (See the paragraph above by
Rosenbaum.)
* *Climactic:* Sentences increase in drama or interest, ending in a
climax. (See the paragraph by Lawrence Mayer opposite.)
* *Spatial:* Sentences scan a person, place, or object from top to
bottom, from side to side, or in some other way that approxi-
mates the way people actually look at things. (See the paragraph by Virginia Woolf on p. 47.)
* *Chronological:* Sentences present events as they occurred in
time, earlier to later. (See the paragraph by Kathleen LaFrank
on p. 44.)

2. Parallelism

Parallelism helps tie sentences together. In the following paragraph the underlined parallel structures of *She* and a verb link all
sentences after the first one. Parallelism also appears *within* many
of the sentences. Aphra Behn (1640–89) was the first English-
woman to write professionally.

> In addition to her busy career as a writer, Aphra Behn also
> found time to briefly marry and spend a little while in debtor's
> prison. She found time to take up a career as a spy for the English
> in their war against the Dutch. She made the long and difficult

---
KEY TERM

PARALLELISM   The use of similar grammatical structures for similar
elements of meaning within or among sentences: *The book caused a
stir in the media* and *aroused debate in Congress.* (See also Chapter 9.)

voyage to Suriname [in South America] and became involved in a slave rebellion there. <u>She plunged</u> into political debate at Will's Coffee House and defended her position from the stage of the Drury Lane Theater. <u>She</u> actively <u>argued</u> for women's rights to be educated and to marry whom they pleased, or not at all. <u>She defied</u> the seventeenth-century dictum that ladies must be "modest" and wrote freely about sex.   —ANGELINE GOREAU, "Aphra Behn"

¶ coh
7b

3. Repetition and restatement

Repeating or restating key words helps make a paragraph coherent and also reminds readers what the topic is. In the following paragraph note the underlined repetition of *sleep* and restatement of *adults*.

> Perhaps the simplest fact about <u>sleep</u> is that individual needs for it vary widely. Most <u>adults sleep</u> between seven and nine hours, but occasionally <u>people</u> turn up who need twelve hours or so, while some <u>rare types</u> can get by on three or four. Rarest of all are those <u>legendary types</u> who require almost no <u>sleep</u> at all; respected researchers have recently studied three <u>such people</u>. One of them— a healthy, happy woman in her seventies—<u>sleeps</u> about an hour every two or three days. The other two are <u>men</u> in early middle age, who get by on a few minutes a night. One of them complains about the daily fifteen minutes or so he's forced to "waste" in <u>sleeping</u>.
>   —LAWRENCE A. MAYER, "The Confounding Enemy of Sleep"

4. Pronouns

Because pronouns refer to nouns, they can help relate sentences to each other. In the paragraph by Angeline Goreau beginning on the facing page, *she* works just this way by substituting for *Aphra Behn*.

5. Consistency

Consistency (or the lack of it) occurs primarily in the person and number of nouns and pronouns and in the tense of verbs. Any inconsistencies not required by meaning will interfere with a reader's ability to follow the development of ideas.

Note the underlined inconsistencies in the next paragraphs.

KEY TERMS

PRONOUN   A word that refers to and functions as a noun, such as *I, you, he, she, it, we, they: The patient could not raise her arm.* (See p. 91.)

TENSE   The form of a verb that indicates the time of its action, such as present (*I run*), past (*I ran*), or future (*I will run*). (See p. 113.)

SHIFTS IN TENSE

In the Hopi religion, water is the driving force. Since the Hopi lived in the Arizona desert, they needed water urgently for drinking, cooking, and irrigating crops. Their complex beliefs are focused in part on gaining the assistance of supernatural forces in obtaining water. Many of the Hopi kachinas, or spirit essences, were directly concerned with clouds, rain, and snow.

SHIFTS IN NUMBER

Kachinas represent spiritually the things and events of the real world, such as cumulus clouds, mischief, cornmeal, and even death. A kachina is not worshipped as a god but regarded as an interested friend. They visit the Hopi from December through July in the form of men who dress in kachina costumes and perform dances and other rituals.

SHIFTS IN PERSON

Unlike the man, the Hopi woman does not keep contact with kachinas through costumes and dancing. Instead, one receives a tihu, or small effigy, of a kachina from the man impersonating the kachina. You are more likely to receive a tihu as a girl approaching marriage, though a child or older woman may receive one, too.

6. Transitional expressions

Transitional expressions such as *therefore, in contrast,* or *meanwhile* can forge specific connections between sentences, as do the underlined expressions in this paragraph:

> Medical science has thus succeeded in identifying the hundreds of viruses that can cause the common cold. It has also discovered the most effective means of prevention. One person transmits the cold viruses to another most often by hand. For instance, an infected person covers his mouth to cough. Then he picks up the telephone. Half an hour later, his daughter picks up the same telephone. Immediately afterward, she rubs her eyes. Within a few days, she, *too,* has a cold. And thus it spreads. To avoid colds, therefore, people should wash their hands often and keep their hands away from their faces.
> —KATHLEEN LaFRANK (student), "Colds: Myth and Science"

KEY TERMS

NUMBER The form of a noun, pronoun, or verb that indicates whether it is singular (one) or plural (more than one): *boy, boys.*

PERSON The form of a pronoun that indicates whether the subject is speaking (first person: *I, we*), spoken to (second person: *you*), or spoken about (third person: *he, she, it, they*). All nouns are in the third person.

Note that you can use transitional expressions to link paragraphs as well as sentences. In the first sentence of LaFrank's paragraph, the word *thus* signals that the sentence refers to an effect discussed in the preceding paragraph.

The following box lists many transitional expressions by the functions they perform.

Transitional expressions

To ADD OR SHOW SEQUENCE

again, also, and, and then, besides, equally important, finally, first, further, furthermore, in addition, in the first place, last, moreover, next, second, still, too

To COMPARE

also, in the same way, likewise, similarly

To CONTRAST

although, and yet, but, but at the same time, despite, even so, even though, for all that, however, in contrast, in spite of, nevertheless, notwithstanding, on the contrary, on the other hand, regardless, still, though, yet

To GIVE EXAMPLES OR INTENSIFY

after all, an illustration of, even, for example, for instance, indeed, in fact, it is true, of course, specifically, that is, to illustrate, truly

To INDICATE PLACE

above, adjacent to, below, elsewhere, farther on, here, near, nearby, on the other side, opposite to, there, to the east, to the left

To INDICATE TIME

after a while, afterward, as long as, as soon as, at last, at length, at that time, before, earlier, formerly, immediately, in the meantime, in the past, lately, later, meanwhile, now, presently, shortly, simultaneously, since, so far, soon, subsequently, then, thereafter, until, until now, when

To REPEAT, SUMMARIZE, OR CONCLUDE

all in all, altogether, as has been said, in brief, in conclusion, in other words, in particular, in short, in simpler terms, in summary, on the whole, that is, therefore, to put it differently, to summarize

To SHOW CAUSE OR EFFECT

accordingly, as a result, because, consequently, for this purpose, hence, otherwise, since, then, therefore, thereupon, thus, to this end, with this object

NOTE Draw carefully on this list of transitional expressions because the ones in each group are not interchangeable. For instance, *besides, finally,* and *second* may all be used to add information, but each has its own distinct meaning.

ESL If you are writing in English as a second language, you may be tempted to add transitional expressions at the beginnings of most sentences. But such explicit transitions aren't needed everywhere, and in fact too many can be intrusive and awkward. When inserting transitional expressions, consider the reader's need for a signal: often the connection from sentence to sentence is already clear from the context or can be made clear by relating the content of sentences more closely (see pp. 42–43). When you do need transitional expressions, try varying their positions in your sentences, as illustrated in the sample paragraph on page 44.

7c   Developing paragraphs

An effective, well-developed paragraph always provides the specific information that readers need and expect in order to understand you and to stay interested in what you say. Paragraph length can be a rough gauge of development: anything much shorter than 100 to 150 words may leave readers with a sense of incompleteness.

To develop or shape an idea in a paragraph, one or more of the following patterns may help. (These patterns may also be used to develop entire essays. See p. 12.)

1. Narration

Narration retells a significant sequence of events, usually in the order of their occurrence (that is, chronologically). A narrator is concerned not just with the sequence of events but also with their consequence, their importance to the whole.

> Jill's story is typical for "recruits" to religious cults. She was very lonely in college and appreciated the attention of the nice young men and women who lived in a house near campus. They persuaded her to share their meals and then to move in with them. Between intense bombardments of "love," they deprived her of sleep and sometimes threatened to throw her out. Jill became increasingly confused and dependent, losing touch with any reality besides the one in the group. She dropped out of school and refused to see or communicate with her family. Before long she, too, was preying on lonely college students.
>
> —HILLARY BEGAS (student), "The Love Bombers"

2. Description

Description details the sensory qualities of a person, scene, thing, or feeling, using concrete and specific words to convey a dominant mood, to illustrate an idea, or to achieve some other purpose.

> The sun struck straight upon the house, making the white walls glare between the dark windows. Their panes, woven thickly with green branches, held circles of impenetrable darkness. Sharp-edged wedges of light lay upon the window-sill and showed inside the room plates with blue rings, cups with curved handles, the bulge of a great bowl, the criss-cross pattern in the rug, and the formidable corners and lines of cabinets and bookcases. Behind their conglomeration hung a zone of shadow in which might be a further shape to be disencumbered of shadow or still denser depths of darkness.   — VIRGINIA WOOLF, *The Waves*

3. Illustration or support

An idea may be developed with several specific examples, like those used by Charles Kuralt on page 40, or with a single extended example, as here:

> The language problem that I was attacking loomed larger and larger as I began to learn more. When I would describe in English certain concepts and objects enmeshed in Korean emotion and imagination, I became slowly aware of nuances, of differences between two languages even in simple expression. The remark "Kim entered the house" seems to be simple enough, yet, unless a reader has a clear visual image of a Korean house, his understanding of the sentence is not complete. When a Korean says he is "in the house," he may be in his courtyard, or on his porch, or in his small room! If I wanted to give a specific picture of entering the house in the Western sense, I had to say "room" instead of house sometimes. I say "sometimes" because many Koreans entertain their guests on their porches and still are considered to be hospitable, and in the Korean sense, going into the "room" may be a more intimate act than it would be in the English sense. Such problems!
> —KIM YONG IK, "A Book-Writing Venture"

Sometimes you can develop a paragraph by providing your reasons for stating a general idea. For instance:

> There are three reasons, quite apart from scientific considerations, that mankind needs to travel in space. The first reason is the need for garbage disposal: we need to transfer industrial processes into space, so that the earth may remain a green and pleasant place for our grandchildren to live in. The second reason is the need to escape material impoverishment: the resources of this

planet are finite, and we shall not forgo forever the abundant solar energy and minerals and living space that are spread out all around us. The third reason is our spiritual need for an open frontier: the ultimate purpose of space travel is to bring to humanity not only scientific discoveries and an occasional spectacular show on television but a real expansion of our spirit.

—FREEMAN DYSON, "Disturbing the Universe"

4. Definition

Defining a complicated, abstract, or controversial term often requires extended explanation. The following definition of the word *quality* comes from an essay asserting that "quality in product and effort has become a vanishing element of current civilization." Notice how the writer pins down her meaning by offering examples and by setting up contrasts with nonquality.

In the hope of possibly reducing the hail of censure which is certain to greet this essay (I am thinking of going to Alaska or possibly Patagonia in the week it is published), let me say that quality, as I understand it, means investment of the best skill and effort possible to produce the finest and most admirable result possible. Its presence or absence in some degree characterizes every man-made object, service, skilled or unskilled labor—laying bricks, painting a picture, ironing shirts, practicing medicine, shoemaking, scholarship, writing a book. You do it well or you do it half-well. Materials are sound and durable or they are sleazy; method is painstaking or whatever is easiest. Quality is achieving or reaching for the highest standard as against being satisfied with the sloppy or fraudulent. It is honesty of purpose as against catering to cheap or sensational sentiment. It does not allow compromise with the second-rate.   —BARBARA TUCHMAN, "The Decline of Quality"

5. Division or analysis

With division or analysis, you separate something into its elements to understand it better—for instance, you might divide a newspaper into its sections, such as national news, regional news, life-style, and so on. As in the paragraph below, you may also interpret the meaning and significance of the elements you identify.

The surface realism of the soap opera conjures up an illusion of "liveness." The domestic settings and easygoing rhythms encourage the viewer to believe that the drama, however ridiculous, is simply an extension of daily life. The conversation is so slow that some have called it "radio with pictures." (Advertisers have always assumed that busy housewives would listen, rather than watch.)

Conversation is casual and colloquial, as though one were eaves-dropping on neighbors. There is plenty of time to "read" the character's face; close-ups establish intimacy. The sets are comfortably familiar: well-lit interiors of living rooms, restaurants, offices, and hospitals. Daytime soaps have little of the glamour of their prime-time relations. The viewer easily imagines that the conversation is taking place in real time.   —RUTH ROSEN, "Search for Yesterday"

Analysis is a key skill in critical reading of research sources and literature. See pages 251–54 and 351–54.

6. Classification

When you sort many items into groups, you classify the items to see their relations more clearly. For instance:

In my experience, the parents who hire daytime sitters for their school-age children tend to fall into one of three groups. The first group includes parents who work and want someone to be at home when the children return from school. These parents are looking for an extension of themselves, someone who will give the care they would give if they were at home. The second group includes parents who may be home all day themselves but are too disorganized or too frazzled by their children's demands to handle child care alone. They are looking for an organizer and helpmate. The third and final group includes parents who do not want to be bothered by their children, whether they are home all day or not. Unlike the parents in the first two groups, who care for their children however they can, these parents seek a permanent substitute for themselves.   — NANCY WHITTLE (student), "Modern Parenting"

7. Comparison and contrast

Comparison and contrast may be used separately or together to develop an idea. The following paragraph illustrates one of two common ways of organizing a comparison and contrast: SUBJECT BY SUBJECT, first one subject and then the other.

Consider the differences also in the behavior of rock and classical music audiences. At a rock concert, the audience members yell, whistle, sing along, and stamp their feet. They may even stand during the entire performance. The better the music, the more active they'll be. At a classical concert, in contrast, the better the performance, the more *still* the audience is. Members of the classical audience are so highly disciplined that they refrain from even clearing their throats or coughing. No matter what effect the powerful music has on their intellects and feelings, they sit on their hands.
—TONY NAHM (student), "Rock and Roll Is Here to Stay"

The next paragraph illustrates the other common organization: POINT BY POINT, with the two subjects discussed side by side and matched feature for feature.

> The first electronic computer, ENIAC, went into operation not even fifty years ago, yet the differences between it and today's home computer are enormous. ENIAC was enormous itself, consisting of forty panels, each two feet wide and four feet deep. Today's PC or Macintosh, by contrast, can fit on one's lap. ENIAC had to be configured by hand, with its programmers taking up to two days to reset switches and cables. Today, the average home user can change programs in an instant. And for all its size and inconvenience, ENIAC was also slow. In its time, its operating speed of 100,000 pulses per second seemed amazingly fast. However, today's home machine can operate at 4 million pulses per second or faster.
>
> —SHIRLEY KAJIWARA (student), "The Computers We Deserve"

8. Cause-and-effect analysis

When you use analysis to explain why something happened or what did or may happen, then you are determining causes or effects. In the following paragraph the author looks at the cause of an effect—Japanese collectivism:

> The *shinkansen* or "bullet train" speeds across the rural areas of Japan giving a quick view of cluster after cluster of farmhouses surrounded by rice paddies. This particular pattern did not develop purely by chance, but as a consequence of the technology peculiar to the growing of rice, the staple of the Japanese diet. The growing of rice requires the construction and maintenance of an irrigation system, something that takes many hands to build. More importantly, the planting and the harvesting of rice can only be done efficiently with the cooperation of twenty or more people. The "bottom line" is that a single family working alone cannot produce enough rice to survive, but a dozen families working together can produce a surplus. Thus the Japanese have had to develop the capacity to work together in harmony, no matter what the forces of disagreement or social disintegration, in order to survive.
>
> —WILLIAM OUCHI, *Theory Z: How American Business Can Meet the Japanese Challenge*

9. Process analysis

When you analyze how to do something or how something works, you explain the steps in a process. For example:

> What used to be called "laying on of hands" is now practiced seriously by nurses and doctors. Studies have shown that therapeutic touch, as it is now known, can aid relaxation and ease pain,

¶
7d

two effects that may in turn cause physiological healing. A "healer" must first concentrate on helping the patient. Then, hands held a few inches from the patient's body, the healer moves from head to foot. The state of concentration allows the healer to detect energy disturbances in the patient that indicate localized tension, pain, or sickness. With further hand movements, the healer can redirect the energy. Patients report feeling heat from the healer's hands, perhaps indicating an energy transfer between healer and patient.

—LISA KUKLINSKI (student), "Old Ways to Noninvasive Medicine"

7d Writing introductory and concluding paragraphs

1. Introductions

An introduction draws readers from their world into your world.

* It focuses readers' attention on the topic and arouses their curiosity about what you have to say.
* It specifies your subject and implies your attitude.
* Often it states your thesis sentence (see p. 13).
* It is concise and sincere.

To focus readers' attention, you have a number of options:

Some strategies for introductions

* Ask a question.
* Relate an incident.
* Use a vivid quotation.
* Create a visual image that represents your subject.
* Offer a surprising statistic or other fact.
* State an opinion related to your thesis.
* Provide background.
* Outline the argument your thesis refutes.
* Make a historical comparison or contrast.
* Outline a problem or dilemma.
* Define a word central to your subject.
* In some business or technical writing, simply state your main idea.

ESL These options for an introduction may not coincide with what you are used to if your native language is not English. In other cultures readers may seek familiarity or reassurance from an author's introduction, or they may prefer an indirect approach to the subject. In English, however, writers and readers prefer originality and concise, direct expression.

A very common introduction opens with a statement of the essay's general subject, clarifies or limits the subject in one or more

¶
7d

sentences, and then asserts the point of the essay in the thesis sentence (underlined in the examples below).

> We Americans are a clean people. We bathe or shower regularly and spend billions of dollars each year on soaps and deodorants to wash away or disguise our dirt and odor. Yet cleanliness is a relatively recent habit with us. <u>From the time of the Puritans until the turn of the twentieth century, bathing in the United States was rare and sometimes even illegal.</u>
> —AMANDA HARRIS (student), "The Cleaning of America"

> Can your home or office computer make you sterile? Can it strike you blind or dumb? The answer is: probably not. Nevertheless, reports of side effects relating to computer use should be examined, especially in the area of birth defects, eye complaints, and postural difficulties. <u>Although little conclusive evidence exists to establish a causal link between computer use and problems of this sort, the circumstantial evidence can be disturbing.</u>
> —THOMAS HARTMANN, "How Dangerous Is Your Computer?"

In much business writing, it's more important to tell readers immediately what your point is than to try to engage them. This introduction to a brief memo quickly outlines a problem and (in the thesis sentence) suggests a way to solve it:

> Starting next month, the holiday rush and staff vacations will leave our department short-handed. We need to hire two or perhaps three temporary keyboarders to maintain our schedules for the month.

Additional examples of effective introductions appear in complete writing samples on pages 29, 299, 321, 348, 358, and 367.

When writing and revising your introduction, avoid some approaches that are likely to bore readers or make them question your sincerity or control.

❖ Don't reach back too far with vague generalities or truths, such as those beginning "Throughout human history . . ." or "In today's world. . . ." You may have needed a warm-up paragraph to start drafting, but your readers can do without it.

❖ Don't start with "The purpose of this essay is . . . ," "In this essay I will . . . ," or any similar flat announcement of your intention or topic.

❖ Don't refer to the title of the essay in the first sentence—for example, "This is my favorite activity" or "This is a big problem."

❖ Don't start with "According to Webster . . ." or a similar phrase leading to a dictionary definition. A definition can be an effective springboard to an essay, but this kind of lead-in has become dull with overuse.

❖ Don't apologize for your opinion or for inadequate knowledge with "I'm not sure if I'm right, but I think . . . ," "I don't know much about this, but . . . ," or similar lines.

2. Conclusions

Your conclusion finishes off your essay and tells readers where you think you have brought them. It answers the question "So what?"

Usually set off in its own paragraph, the conclusion may consist of a single sentence or a group of sentences. It may take one or more of the following approaches:

Some strategies for conclusions

❖ Strike a note of hope or despair.
❖ Give a symbolic or powerful fact or other detail.
❖ Give an especially compelling example.
❖ Create a visual image that represents your subject.

❖ Use a quotation.
❖ Recommend a course of action.
❖ Summarize the paper.
❖ Echo the approach of the introduction.
❖ Restate your thesis and reflect on its implications.

The following paragraph concludes the essay on bathing habits whose introduction is on the preceding page. The writer both summarizes her essay and echoes her introduction.

> Thus changed attitudes and advances in plumbing finally freed us to bathe whenever we want. Perhaps partly to make up for our ancestors' bad habits, we have transformed that freedom into a national obsession.
> —AMANDA HARRIS (student), "The Cleaning of America"

In the next paragraph the author concludes an essay on environmental protection with a call for action.

> Until we get the answers, I think we had better keep on building power plants and growing food with the help of fertilizers and such insect-controlling chemicals as we now have. The risks are well known, thanks to the environmentalists. If they had not created a widespread public awareness of the ecological crisis, we wouldn't stand a chance. But such awareness by itself is not enough. Flaming manifestos and prophecies of doom are no longer much help, and a search for scapegoats can only make matters worse. The time for sensations and manifestos is about over. Now we need rigorous analysis, united effort and very hard work.
> —PETER F. DRUCKER, "How Best to Protect the Environment"

Conclusions have several pitfalls you'll want to avoid:

❖ Don't simply restate your introduction—statement of subject, thesis sentence, and all. Presumably the paragraphs in the body of your essay have contributed something to the opening statements, and it's that something you want to capture in your conclusion.

❖ Don't start off in a new direction, with a subject different from or broader than the one your essay has been about.

❖ Don't conclude more than you reasonably can from the evidence you have presented. If your essay is about your frustrating experience trying to clear a parking ticket, you cannot reasonably conclude that *all* local police forces are too tied up in red tape to be of service to the people.

❖ Don't apologize for your essay or otherwise cast doubt on it. Don't say, "Even though I'm no expert," or "This may not be convincing, but I believe it's true," or anything similar. Rather, to win your readers' confidence, display confidence.

II

Clarity and Style

❖

II

Clarity and Style

❖

8 Coordination

Use COORDINATION to show that two or more elements in a sentence are equally important in meaning and thus to clarify the relation between them.

coord

8

Methods of coordinating equal information

❖ Link two main clauses with a comma and a coordinating conjunction, such as *and* or *but*.

equally
important

Independence Hall in Philadelphia is now restored, but *fifty years ago it was in bad shape.*

❖ Link two main clauses with a semicolon alone or with a semicolon and a conjunctive adverb, such as *however*.

equally important

The building was standing; however, *it suffered from decay.*

❖ Within clauses, link words and phrases with a coordinating conjunction, such as *and* or *or*.

equally
important

The *people* and *officials* of the nation *were indifferent to Indepen-*

equally important

dence Hall or *took it for granted.*

❖ Link main clauses, words, or phrases with a correlative conjunction such as *not only . . . but also.*

equally important

People not only *took the building for granted* but also *neglected it.*

KEY TERMS

MAIN CLAUSE A word group that contains a subject and a verb and does not begin with a subordinating word: *The books were expensive.* (See p. 101.)

COORDINATING CONJUNCTIONS *And, but, or, nor,* and sometimes *for, so, yet.* (See p. 95.)

CONJUNCTIVE ADVERBS Modifiers that describe the relation of the ideas in two clauses, such as *hence, however, indeed,* and *thus.* (See p. 164.)

CORRELATIVE CONJUNCTIONS Pairs of connecting words, such as *both . . . and, either . . . or, not only . . . but also.* (See pp. 96–97.)

8a Using coordination to relate equal ideas

Coordination shows the equality between elements, as illustrated on the preceding page. At the same time that it clarifies meaning, it can also help smooth choppy sentences.

> **CHOPPY SENTENCES**
>
> We should not rely so heavily on oil. Coal and uranium are also overused. We have a substantial energy resource in the moving waters of our rivers. Smaller streams add to the total volume of water. The resource renews itself. Coal and oil are irreplaceable. Uranium is also irreplaceable. The cost of water does not increase much over time. The costs of coal, oil, and uranium rise dramatically.

The revision groups coal, oil, and uranium and clearly opposes them to water. The connecting words are underlined.

> **IDEAS COORDINATED**
>
> We should not rely so heavily on coal, oil, and uranium, for we have a substantial energy resource in the moving waters of our rivers and streams. Coal, oil, and uranium are irreplaceable and thus subject to dramatic cost increases; water, however, is self-renewing and more stable in cost.

8b Using coordination effectively

Use coordination only to express the *equality* of ideas or details. A string of coordinated elements—especially main clauses—implies that all points are equally important.

> **EXCESSIVE COORDINATION**
>
> The weeks leading up to the resignation of President Nixon were eventful, and the Supreme Court and the Congress closed in on him, and the Senate Judiciary Committee voted to begin impeachment proceedings, and finally the President resigned on August 9, 1974.

Such a passage needs editing to stress the important points (in italics below) and to de-emphasize the less important information.

> **REVISED**
>
> *The weeks leading up the resignation of President Nixon were eventful,* as the Supreme Court and the Congress closed in on him and the Senate Judiciary Committee voted to begin impeachment proceedings. Finally, *the President resigned on August 9, 1974.*

Even within a single sentence, coordination should express a logical equality between ideas.

coord
8b

FAULTY   John Stuart Mill was a nineteenth-century utilitarian, and he believed that actions should be judged by their usefulness or by the happiness they cause. [The two clauses are not separate and equal: the second expands on the first by explaining what a utilitarian such as Mill believed.]

REVISED   John Stuart Mill, *a nineteenth-century utilitarian,* believed that actions should be judged by their usefulness or by the happiness they cause.

9 Parallelism

PARALLELISM is a similarity of grammatical form for similar elements of meaning within a sentence or among sentences.

The air is dirtied by *factories belching smoke*

and

cars spewing exhaust.

In this example the two italicized phrases have the same function and importance (both specify sources of air pollution), so they also have the same grammatical construction. Parallelism makes form follow meaning.

9a Using parallelism with *and, but, or, nor, yet*

The coordinating conjunctions *and, but, or, nor,* and *yet* always signal a need for parallelism.

The industrial base was *shifting* and *shrinking.* [Parallel words.]

Politicians rarely *acknowledged the problem* or *proposed alternatives.* [Parallel phrases.]

Industrial workers were understandably disturbed *that they were losing their jobs* and *that no one seemed to care.* [Parallel clauses.]

When sentence elements linked by coordinating conjunctions are not parallel in structure, the sentence is awkward and distracting.

KEY TERM

COORDINATING CONJUNCTIONS   Words that connect elements of the same kind and importance: *and, but, or, nor,* and sometimes *for, so, yet.*

//
9b

NONPARALLEL	Three reasons why steel companies kept losing money were that their plants were inefficient, high labor costs, <u>and</u> foreign competition was increasing.
REVISED	Three reasons why steel companies kept losing money were *inefficient plants,* high labor costs, <u>and</u> *increasing foreign competition.*
NONPARALLEL	Success was difficult even for efficient companies because of the shift away from all manufacturing in the United States <u>and</u> the fact that steel production was shifting toward emerging nations.
REVISED	Success was difficult even for efficient companies because of the shift away from all manufacturing in the United States <u>and</u> *toward steel production in emerging nations.*

All the words required by idiom or grammar must be stated in compound constructions (see also p. 79).

FAULTY	Given training, workers can acquire the skills <u>and</u> interest in other jobs. [Idiom dictates different prepositions with *skills* and *interest.*]
REVISED	Given training, workers can acquire the skills *for* <u>and</u> interest in other jobs.

9b Using parallelism with *both . . . and, not . . . but,* or another correlative conjunction

Correlative conjunctions stress equality and balance between elements. Parallelism confirms the equality.

It is <u>not</u> *a tax bill* <u>but</u> *a tax relief bill,* providing relief <u>not</u> *for the needy* <u>but</u> *for the greedy.* —FRANKLIN DELANO ROOSEVELT

With correlative conjunctions, the element after the second connector must match the element after the first connector.

NONPARALLEL	Huck Finn learns <u>not only</u> that human beings have an enormous capacity for folly <u>but also</u> enormous dignity. [The first element includes *that human beings have;* the second element does not.]

┌─ KEY TERM ───

CORRELATIVE CONJUNCTIONS Pairs of words that connect elements of the same kind and importance, such as *both . . . and, either . . . or, neither . . . nor, not . . . but, not only . . . but also.* (See pp. 96–97.)

REVISED   Huck Finn learns *that human beings have* <u>not only</u>
              an enormous capacity for folly <u>but also</u> enormous
              dignity. [Repositioning *not only* makes the two ele-
              ments parallel.]

9c Using parallelism in comparisons

Parallelism confirms the likeness or difference between two elements being compared using *than* or *as.*

NONPARALLEL   Huck Finn proves less a bad boy <u>than</u> to be an inde-
               pendent spirit. In the end he is <u>as</u> determined in re-
               jecting help <u>as</u> he is to leave for "the territory."
REVISED   Huck Finn proves less a bad boy <u>than</u> *an indepen-*
               dent spirit. In the end he is as determined *to reject*
               help <u>as</u> he is to leave for "the territory."

(See also pp. 146–47 on making comparisons logical.)

9d Using parallelism with lists, headings, and outlines

The items in a list or outline are coordinate and should be parallel. Parallelism is essential in the headings that divide a paper into
sections (see p. 209) and in a formal topic outline (p. 18).

NONPARALLEL	REVISED
Changes in Renaissance England	Changes in Renaissance England
1. Extension of trade routes	1. Extension of trade routes
2. Merchant class became more powerful	2. Increased power of the merchant class
3. The death of feudalism	3. Death of feudalism
4. Upsurging of the arts	4. Upsurge of the arts
5. Religious quarrels began	5. Rise of religious quarrels

10 Subordination

Use SUBORDINATION to indicate that some elements in a sentence
are less important than others for your meaning. Usually, the main
idea appears in the main clause, and supporting details appear in
subordinate structures.

sub
10

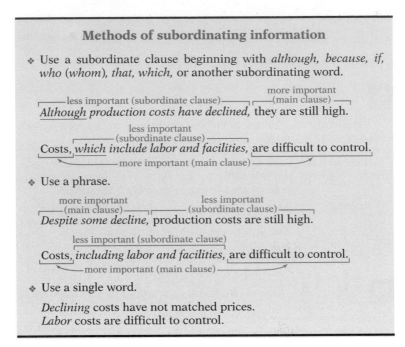

Methods of subordinating information

❖ Use a subordinate clause beginning with *although, because, if, who (whom), that, which,* or another subordinating word.

┌──────less important (subordinate clause)──────┐ ┌──(main clause)──┐
more important
Although production costs have declined, they are still high.

less important
┌──────(subordinate clause)──────┐
Costs, *which include labor and facilities,* are difficult to control.
└──────more important (main clause)──────┘

❖ Use a phrase.

more important   less important
┌──(main clause)──┐ ┌──(subordinate clause)──┐
Despite some decline, production costs are still high.

less important (subordinate clause)
┌──────────────────────────────┐
Costs, *including labor and facilities,* are difficult to control.
└──────more important (main clause)──────┘

❖ Use a single word.

Declining costs have not matched prices.
Labor costs are difficult to control.

10a Emphasizing main ideas

A string of main clauses can make everything in a passage seem equally important. Subordination with words, phrases, or subordinate clauses will highlight what's important.

STRING OF MAIN   In recent years computer prices have dropped,
CLAUSES   and production costs have dropped more slowly,
                  and computer manufacturers have had to strug-
                  gle, for their profits have been shrinking.

┌─ KEY TERMS ───

MAIN CLAUSE   A word group that contains a subject and a verb and does not begin with a subordinating word: *Words can do damage.* (See p. 101.)

SUBORDINATE CLAUSE   A word group that contains a subject and a verb, begins with a subordinating word such as *because* or *who,* and is not a question: *Words can do damage when they hurt feelings.* (See p. 101.)

PHRASE   A word group that lacks a subject or verb or both: *Words can do damage by hurting feelings.* (See p. 99.)

REVISED   *Because* production costs have dropped more
                   slowly *than prices* in recent years, computer man-
                   ufacturers have had to struggle *with shrinking
                   profits.*

10b Using subordination effectively

Use subordination only for the less important information in a
sentence.

FAULTY   Ms. Angelo was in her first year of teaching, al-
                   though she was a better instructor than others
                   with many years of experience. [The sentence sug-
                   gests that Angelo's inexperience is the main idea,
                   whereas the writer intended to stress her skill *de-
                   spite* her inexperience.]

REVISED   Although Ms. Angelo was in her first year of
                   teaching, *she was a better instructor than others
                   with many years of experience.*

Subordination loses its power to organize and emphasize information when too much loosely related detail crowds into one long
sentence.

OVERLOADED   The boats that were moored at the dock when the
                   hurricane, which was one of the worst in three
                   decades, struck were ripped from their moorings,
                   because the owners had not been adequately pre-
                   pared, since the weather service had predicted the
                   storm would blow out to sea, which they do at
                   this time of year.

REVISED   *Struck by one of the worst hurricanes in three
                   decades, the boats at the dock were ripped from
                   their moorings. The owners were unprepared* be-
                   cause the weather service had said that hurricanes
                   at this time of year blow out to sea. [The details
                   are sorted into two sentences, each with its own
                   main clause.]

11 Variety and Details

Writing that's interesting as well as clear has at least two features: the sentences vary in length and structure, and they are well
textured with details.

var
11

11a   Varying sentence length

In most contemporary writing, sentences tend to vary from about ten to about forty words, with an average of between fifteen and twenty-five words. If your sentences are mostly at one extreme or the other, your readers may have difficulty focusing on main ideas and seeing the relations among them.

❖ If most of your sentences contain thirty-five words or more, you probably need to break some up into shorter, simpler sentences.
❖ If most of your sentences contain fewer than ten or fifteen words, you probably need to add details to them (p. 66) or combine them through coordination (p. 57) and subordination (p. 61).

var
11b

11b   Varying sentence structure

A passage will be monotonous if all its sentences follow the same pattern, like soldiers marching in a parade. Try these techniques for varying structure.

1. Subordination

A string of main clauses in simple or compound sentences can be especially plodding.

MONOTONOUS   The moon is now drifting away from the earth. It moves away at the rate of about one inch a year. Our days on earth are getting longer, and they grow a thousandth of a second longer every century. A month will someday be forty-seven of our present days long, and we might eventually lose the moon altogether. Such great planetary movement rightly concerns astronomers, but it need not worry us. It will take 50 million years.

┌─ KEY TERMS ─────────────────────────────

MAIN CLAUSE   A word group that contains a subject and a verb and does not begin with a subordinating word: *Tourism is an industry. It brings in over $2 billion a year.* (See p. 101.)

SUBORDINATE CLAUSE   A word group that contains a subject and verb, begins with a subordinating word such as *because* or *who*, and is not a question: *Tourism is an industry that brings in over $2 billion a year.* (See p. 101.)

PHRASE   A word group that lacks a subject or verb or both: *Tourism is an industry valued at over $2 billion a year.* (See p. 99.)

Enliven such writing—and make the main ideas stand out—by expressing the less important information in subordinate clauses and phrases. In the revision below, italics indicate subordinate structures that used to be main clauses.

> **REVISED**   The moon is now drifting away from the earth *at the rate of about one inch a year. At a thousandth of a second every century,* our days on earth are getting longer. A month will someday be forty-seven of our present days long, *if we don't eventually lose the moon altogether.* Such great planetary movement rightly concerns astronomers, but it need not worry us. It will take 50 million years.

var
11b

2. Varied sentence beginnings

Another cause of monotony is an unbroken sequence of sentences beginning with their subjects.

> **MONOTONOUS**   The lawyer cross-examined the witness for two weeks. The witness had expected to be dismissed within an hour and was visibly irritated. He did not cooperate. He was reprimanded by the judge.

Simply beginning some of these sentences with a modifier or conjunction dramatically improves readability.

> **REVISED**   *For two weeks,* the lawyer cross-examined the witness. *Expecting to be dismissed within an hour,* the witness was visibly irritated. He did not cooperate. *Indeed,* he was reprimanded by the judge.

The italicized expressions represent the most common choices for varying sentence beginnings:

* Adverb modifiers, such as *For two weeks* (modifies the verb *cross-examined*).
* Adjective modifiers, such as *Expecting to be dismissed within an hour* (modifies *witness*).
* Transitional expressions, such as *Indeed*. (See p. 45 for a list.)

ESL Placing certain adverb modifiers at the beginning of a

KEY TERMS

ADVERB   A word or word group that describes a verb, an adjective, another adverb, or a whole sentence: *dressed _sharply_, _clearly_ unhappy, soaring _from the mountain_*. (See p. 93.)

ADJECTIVE   A word or word group that describes a noun or pronoun: *_sweet_ smile, _certain_ someone*. (See p. 93.)

sentence requires you to change the normal subject-verb order as well. The most common of these modifiers are negatives, including *seldom, rarely, in no case, not since,* and *not until.*

>   ┌──── adverb ────┐   subject verb phrase
> **FAULTY**   Not since 1992 a *witness has held* the stand so long.
>
>   helping   main
>   ┌──── adverb ────┐ verb   subject   verb
> **REVISED**   Not since 1992 *has* a *witness held* the stand so long.

3. Varied word order

Occasionally, you can vary a sentence and emphasize it at the same time by inverting the usual order of parts:

> A dozen witnesses testified for the prosecution, and the defense attorney barely questioned eleven of them. *The twelfth, however, he grilled.* [Normal word order: *He grilled the twelfth, however.*]

Inverted sentences used without need are artificial. Use them only when emphasis demands.

11c   Adding details

Relevant details such as facts and examples create the texture and life that keep readers awake and help them grasp your meaning. For instance:

> **FLAT**   Constructed after World War II, Levittown, New York, consisted of thousands of houses in two basic styles. Over the decades, residents have altered the houses so dramatically that the original styles are often unrecognizable.
>
> **DETAILED**   Constructed *on potato fields* after World War II, Levittown, New York, consisted of *more than 17,000* houses in *Cape Cod and ranch* styles. Over the decades, residents have *added expansive front porches, punched dormer windows through roofs, converted garages to sun porches, and otherwise* altered the houses so dramatically that the original styles are often unrecognizable.

12   Appropriate and Exact Words

The clarity and effectiveness of your writing will depend greatly on the use of words that are appropriate for your writing situation (opposite) and that express your meaning exactly (p. 72).

12a Choosing the appropriate word

Appropriate words suit your writing situation—your subject, purpose, and audience. In most college and career writing you should rely on what's called STANDARD ENGLISH, the written English normally expected and used in schools, businesses, government, and other places where people of diverse backgrounds must communicate with one another. Standard English is "standard" not because it is better than other forms of English but because it is accepted as the common language, much as dimes and quarters are accepted as the common currency.

The vocabulary of standard English is huge, allowing expression of an infinite range of ideas and feelings; but it does exclude words that only some groups of people use, understand, or find inoffensive. Some of these more limited vocabularies should be avoided altogether; others should be used cautiously and in relevant situations, as when aiming for a special effect with an audience you know will appreciate it. Whenever you doubt a word's status, consult a dictionary (see p. 73).

NOTE Many computerized style-checking programs will highlight and question nonstandard language, slang, colloquialisms, and other words whose appropriateness may be doubtful. When using such a program, you'll need to determine whether the flagged language is or is not appropriate for your writing situation, as explained below. (See p. 35 for more on style-checking programs.)

appr
12a

1. Dialect and nonstandard language

Like many countries, the United States includes scores of regional, social, or ethnic groups with their own distinct DIALECTS, or versions of English. Standard English is one of those dialects, and so are Black English, Appalachian English, Creole, and the English of coastal Maine. All the dialects of English share many features, but each also has its own vocabulary, pronunciation, and grammar.

If you speak a dialect of English besides standard English, you need to be careful about using your dialect in situations where standard English is the norm, such as in academic or business writing. Otherwise, your readers may not understand your meaning, or they may perceive your usage as incorrect. (Dialects are not wrong in themselves, but forms imported from one dialect into another may still be perceived as wrong.)

Your participation in the community of standard English does not require you to abandon your own dialect. Of course, you will want to use it with others who speak it. You may want to quote it in an academic paper (as when analyzing or reporting conversation in dialect). And you may want to use it in writing you do for yourself, such as journals, notes, and drafts, which should be composed as freely as possible. But edit your drafts carefully to eliminate dialect expressions, especially those which dictionaries label "nonstandard," such as *hisn, hern, hisself, theirselves, them books, them courses, this here school, that there building, knowed, throwed, hadn't ought, could of, didn't never,* and *haven't no.*

2. Slang

SLANG is the language used by a group, such as musicians or computer programmers, to reflect common experiences and to make technical references efficient. The following example is from an essay on the slang of "skaters" (skateboarders):

> Curtis slashed ultra-punk crunchers on his longboard, while the Rube-man flailed his usual Gumbyness on tweaked frontsides and lofty fakie ollies.   —MILES ORKIN, "Mucho Slingage by the Pool"

Among those who understand it, slang may be vivid and forceful. It often occurs in dialogue, and an occasional slang expression can enliven an informal essay. But most slang is too flippant and imprecise for effective communication, and it is generally inappropriate for college or business writing. Notice the gain in seriousness and precision achieved in the following revision.

SLANG   Many students start out *pretty together* but then *get weird.*
REVISED Many students start out *with clear goals* but then *lose their direction.*

3. Colloquial language

COLLOQUIAL LANGUAGE is the everyday spoken language, including expressions such as *get together, go crazy, do the dirty work,* and *get along.*

When you write informally, colloquial language may be appropriate to achieve the casual, relaxed effect of conversation. An occasional colloquial word dropped into otherwise more formal writing can also help you achieve a desired emphasis. But most colloquial language is not precise enough for college or career writing. In such writing you should generally avoid any words and expressions labeled "informal" or "colloquial" in your dictionary.

COLLOQUIAL   According to a Native American myth, the Great Creator *had a dog hanging around with him* when he created the earth.

REVISED   According to a Native American myth, the Great Creator *was accompanied by a dog* when he created the earth.

4. Technical words

All disciplines and professions rely on specialized language that allows the members to communicate precisely and efficiently with each other. Chemists, for instance, have their *phosphatides*, and literary critics have their *motifs* and *subtexts*. Without explanation technical words are meaningless to nonspecialists. When you are writing for nonspecialists, avoid unnecessary technical terms and carefully define terms you must use.

appr

12a

5. Indirect and pretentious writing

Small, plain, and direct words are almost always preferable to big, showy, or evasive words. Take special care to avoid euphemisms, double-talk, and pretentious writing.

A EUPHEMISM is a presumably inoffensive word that a writer or speaker substitutes for a word deemed potentially offensive or too blunt, such as *passed away* for *died* or *misspeak* for *lie*. Use euphemisms only when you know that blunt, truthful words would needlessly hurt or offend members of your audience.

A kind of euphemism that deliberately evades the truth is DOUBLE-TALK (also called DOUBLESPEAK or WEASEL WORDS): language intended to confuse or to be misunderstood. Today double-talk is unfortunately common in politics and advertising—the *revenue enhancement* that is really a tax, the *peace-keeping function* that is really war making, the *biodegradable* bags that last decades. Double-talk has no place in honest writing.

Euphemism and sometimes double-talk seem to keep company with PRETENTIOUS WRITING, fancy language that is more elaborate than its subject requires. Choose your words for their exactness and economy. The big, ornate word may be tempting, but pass it up. Your readers will be grateful.

PRETENTIOUS   To perpetuate our endeavor of providing funds for our elderly citizens as we do at the present moment, we will face the exigency of enhanced contributions from all our citizens.

REVISED   We cannot continue to fund Social Security and
Medicare for the elderly unless we raise taxes.

6. Sexist and other biased language

Even when we do not mean it to, our language can reflect and perpetuate hurtful prejudices toward groups of people. Such biased language can be obvious—words such as *nigger, honky, mick, kike, fag, dyke,* or *broad.* But it can also be subtle, generalizing about groups in ways that may be familiar but that are also inaccurate or unfair.

Biased language reflects poorly on the user, not on the person or persons whom it mischaracterizes or insults. Unbiased language does not submit to false generalizations. It treats people respectfully as individuals and labels groups as they wish to be labeled.

appr
12a

Stereotypes of race, ethnicity, religion, age, and other characteristics

A STEREOTYPE is a generalization based on poor evidence, a kind of formula for understanding and judging people simply because of their membership in a group.

Men are uncommunicative.
Women are emotional.
Liberals want to raise taxes.
Conservatives are affluent.

At best, stereotypes betray a noncritical writer, one who is not thinking beyond notions received from others. In your writing, be alert for statements that characterize whole groups of people.

STEREOTYPE   Elderly drivers should have their licenses limited to daytime driving only. [Asserts that all elderly people are poor night drivers.]

REVISED   Drivers with impaired night vision should have their licenses limited to daytime driving only.

Some stereotypes have become part of the language, but they are still potentially offensive.

STEREOTYPE   The administrators are too blind to see the need for a new gymnasium.

REVISED   The administrators do not understand the need for a new gymnasium.

Sexist language

Among the most subtle and persistent biased language is that expressing narrow ideas about men's and women's roles, position, and value in society. Like other stereotypes, this SEXIST LANGUAGE can wound or irritate readers, and it indicates the writer's thoughtlessness or unfairness. The following box suggests some ways of eliminating sexist language:

appr

12a

Eliminating sexist language

❖ Avoid demeaning and patronizing language.

SEXIST   Ladies are entering almost every occupation.

REVISED *Women* are entering almost every occupation.

SEXIST   President Reagan came to Nancy's defense.

REVISED President Reagan came to *Mrs. Reagan's* defense.

❖ Avoid occupational or social stereotypes.

SEXIST   The considerate doctor commends a nurse when she provides his patients with good care.

REVISED The considerate doctor commends a nurse *who provides good care for patients.*

SEXIST   The grocery shopper should save her coupons.

REVISED *Grocery shoppers* should save *their* coupons.

❖ Avoid referring needlessly to gender.

SEXIST   Marie Curie, a woman chemist, discovered radium.

REVISED Marie Curie, *a chemist,* discovered radium.

SEXIST   The patients were tended by a male nurse.

REVISED The patients were tended by *a nurse.*

❖ Avoid using *man* or words containing *man* to refer to all human beings. Here are a few alternatives:

businessman	businessperson
chairman	chair, chairperson
congressman	representative in Congress, legislator
craftsman	craftsperson, artisan
layman	layperson
mankind	humankind, humanity, human beings, humans
manmade	handmade, manufactured, synthetic, artificial
manpower	personnel, human resources
policeman	police officer
salesman	salesperson, sales representative

SEXIST   Man has not reached the limits of social justice.

REVISED *Humankind* [or *Humanity*] has not reached the limits of social justice.

SEXIST   The furniture consists of manmade materials.

REVISED The furniture consists of *synthetic* materials.

(continued)

> ## Eliminating sexist language
> *(continued)*
>
> ❖ Avoid using *he* to refer to both genders. (See also pp. 139–40.)
>
> **SEXIST**   The newborn child explores his world.
>
> **REVISED**   The newborn child explores *his or her* world. [Male and female pronouns.]
>
> **REVISED**   Newborn *children* explore *their* world. [Plural.]
>
> **REVISED**   The newborn child explores *the* world. [Pronoun avoided.]

exact
12b

Appropriate labels

We often need to label groups: *swimmers, politicians, mothers, Christians, Westerners, students.* But labels can be shorthand stereotypes, slighting the person labeled and ignoring the preferences of the group members themselves. Although sometimes dismissed as "political correctness," showing sensitivity when applying labels reveals you to be alert to readers' concerns.

Be careful to avoid labels that (intentionally or not) disparage the person or group you refer to. A person with emotional problems is not a *mental patient.* A person with cancer is not a *cancer victim.* A person using a wheelchair is not *wheelchair-bound.*

Take care also that the name you use for a group reflects the preferences of the group's members, or at least many of them. Group labels change often, so the list below is tentative. To learn current preferences, ask the group members themselves, attend to usage in reputable newspapers and magazines, or check a recent dictionary.

> African American, black
> Asian, Asian American, Japanese American, etc.
> Latino/Latina (Spanish speaking), Mexican American, Puerto Rican, Central American, etc.
> Native American, Indian
> Muslim
> deaf, hearing impaired
> blind, visually impaired
> disabled, physically challenged
> gay, lesbian, homosexual, bisexual

12b   Choosing the exact word

To write clearly and effectively, you will want to find the words that fit your meaning exactly and convey your attitude precisely.

1. Word meanings and synonyms

For writing exactly, a dictionary is essential and a thesaurus can be helpful.

Desk dictionaries

A desk dictionary defines about 150,000 to 200,000 words and provides pronunciation, grammatical functions, history, and other information. Here is a sample from *Merriam-Webster's Collegiate Dictionary:*

Spelling and
word division | Pronunciation

reck•on \'re-kən\ *vb* reck•oned; reck•on•ing \'re-kə-niŋ, 'rek-niŋ\
[ME *rekenen,* fr. OE *-recenian* (as in *gerecenian* to narrate); akin to OE ⌉ Etymology
reccan] *vt* (13c) **1 a :** COUNT ⟨~ the days till Christmas⟩ **b :** ESTI-
MATE, COMPUTE ⟨~ the height of a building⟩ **c :** to determine by reference to a fixed basis ⟨the existence of the U.S. is ~*ed* from the Decla- ⌉ Meanings
ration of Independence⟩ **2 :** to regard or think of as : CONSIDER **3**
chiefly dial ; THINK, SUPPOSE ⟨I ~ I've outlived my time —Ellen Glas ⌉ Quotation
gow⟩ ~ *vi* **1 :** to settle accounts **2 :** to make a calculation **3 a** and source
; JUDGE **b** *chiefly dial* : SUPPOSE, THINK **4 :** to accept something as
certain ⟨ place reliance ⟨I ~ on your promise to help⟩ — **reckon with :** ⌉ Idioms
to take into consideration — **reckon without :** to fail to consider
: IGNORE

Grammatical   Label (*dial=*   Synonym
functions   *dialect*)
and forms

Good desk dictionaries, in addition to *Merriam-Webster's,* include the *American Heritage College Dictionary,* the *Random House
Webster's College Dictionary,* and *Webster's New World Dictionary.*

ESL If English is not your first language, you probably should
have a dictionary prepared especially for ESL students, containing
special information on prepositions, count versus noncount nouns,
and many other matters. Reliable ESL dictionaries include the
Longman Dictionary of Contemporary English and the *Oxford Advanced Learner's Dictionary.*

NOTE Some of the dictionaries listed here are available in both
print and electronic form (on diskette and/or CD-ROM), and the
others will soon be available electronically as well. With an electronic dictionary, you can look up words from your word processor
to check spellings, meanings, synonyms, and other information.
You may even be able to customize the dictionary with words and
meanings it does not include. But you can use an electronic dictionary only with a computer, of course, and it is more expensive than
its print equivalent.

Thesauruses

To find a word with the exact shade of meaning you intend,
you may want to consult a thesaurus or book of SYNONYMS—words

with approximately the same meaning. A thesaurus such as *Roget's International Thesaurus* lists most imaginable synonyms for thousands of words. The word *news*, for instance, has half a page of synonyms in *Roget's International*, including *tidings, dispatch, gossip,* and *journalism.*

Since a thesaurus aims to open up possibilities, its lists of synonyms include approximate as well as precise matches. The thesaurus does not define synonyms or distinguish among them, however, so you need a dictionary to discover exact meanings. In general, don't use a word from a thesaurus—even one you like the sound of—until you are sure of its appropriateness for your meaning.

exact

12b

NOTE An electronic thesaurus—available independently or as part of an electronic dictionary—makes it easy to look up synonyms and insert the chosen word into your text. But still you should consult a dictionary unless you are certain of the word's meaning.

2. The right word for your meaning

All words have one or more basic meanings (called DENOTATIONS)—the meanings listed in the dictionary, without reference to emotional associations. If readers are to understand you, you must use words according to their established meanings.

- Consult a dictionary whenever you are unsure of a word's meaning.
- Distinguish between similar-sounding words that have widely different denotations.

INEXACT   Older people often suffer *infirmaries* [places for the sick].
EXACT   Older people often suffer *infirmities* [disabilities].

Some words, called HOMONYMS, sound exactly alike but differ in meaning: for example, *principal/principle* or *rain/reign/rein.* (See pp. 216–17 for a list of commonly confused homonyms.)

- Distinguish between words with related but distinct meanings.

INEXACT   Television commercials *continuously* [unceasingly] interrupt programming.
EXACT   Television commercials *continually* [regularly] interrupt programming.

In addition to their emotion-free meanings, many words also carry associations with specific feelings. These CONNOTATIONS can shape readers' responses and are thus a powerful tool for writers. The following word pairs have related denotations but very different connotations:

pride: sense of self-worth
vanity: excessive regard for oneself

firm: steady, unchanging, unyielding
stubborn: unreasonable, bullheaded

lasting: long-lived, enduring
endless: without limit, eternal

enthusiasm: excitement
mania: excessive interest or desire

A dictionary can help you track down words with the exact connotations you want. Besides providing meanings, your dictionary may also list and distinguish synonyms to guide your choices. A thesaurus can also help if you use it carefully, as discussed on pages 73–74.

exact
12b

3. Concrete and specific words

Clear, exact writing balances abstract and general words, which outline ideas and objects, with concrete and specific words, which sharpen and solidify.

* ABSTRACT WORDS name qualities and ideas: *beauty, inflation, management, culture, liberal.* CONCRETE WORDS name things we can know by our five senses of sight, hearing, touch, taste, and smell: *sleek, humming, brick, bitter, musty.*
* GENERAL WORDS name classes or groups of things, such as *buildings, weather,* or *birds,* and include all the varieties of the class. SPECIFIC WORDS limit a general class, such as *buildings,* by naming one of its varieties, such as *skyscraper, Victorian courthouse,* or *hut.*

Abstract and general words are useful in the broad statements that set the course for your writing.

The wild horse in America has a *romantic* history.

Relations between the sexes today are only a *little* more *relaxed* than they were in the past.

But such statements need development with concrete and specific detail. Look at how such detail turns a vague sentence into an exact one:

VAGUE   The size of his hands made his smallness real. [How big were his hands? How small was he?]

EXACT   Not until I saw his white, doll-like hands did I realize that he stood a full head shorter than most other men.

If you write on a computer, you can use its search function to help you find and revise abstract and general words that you tend to overuse. Examples of such words include *nice, interesting, things, very, good, a lot, a little,* and *some.*

4. Idioms

IDIOMS are expressions in any language that do not fit the rules for meaning or grammar—for instance, *put up with, plug away at, make off with.*

Idiomatic combinations of verbs or adjectives and prepositions can be confusing for both native and nonnative speakers of English. A number of these pairings are listed on the opposite page. (More appear on pp. 130–31.)

exact

12b

ESL   Those learning English as a second language are justified in stumbling over its prepositions because their meanings can shift depending on context and because they have so many idiomatic uses. In mastering English prepositions, you probably can't avoid memorization. But you can help yourself by memorizing related groups, such as those below:

 ❖ *At/in/on* in expressions of time: Use *at* before actual clock time: *at 8:30.* Use *in* before a month, year, century, or period: *in April, in 1985, in the twenty-first century, in the next month.* Use *on* before a day or date: *on Tuesday, on August 31.*
 ❖ *At/in/on* in expressions of place: Use *at* before a specific place or address: *at the school, at 511 Iris Street.* Use *in* before a place with limits or before a city, state, country, or continent: *in the house, in a box, in Oklahoma City, in China.* Use *on* to mean "supported by" or "touching the surface of": *on the table, on Iris Street, on page 150.*
 ❖ *For/since* in expressions of time: Use *for* before a period of time: *for an hour, for two years.* Use *since* before a specific point in time: *since 1995, since yesterday.*

A good ESL dictionary is the best source for the meanings of prepositions; see the recommendations on page 73. In addition, some references focus on prepositions. One is *Oxford Dictionary of Current Idiomatic English,* volume 1: *Verbs with Prepositions and Particles* (1985).

5. Figurative language

FIGURATIVE LANGUAGE (or a FIGURE OF SPEECH) departs from the literal meanings of words, usually by comparing very different ideas or objects.

Idioms with prepositions

abide *by* a rule
abide *in* a place or state

accords *with*
according *to*

accuse *of* a crime

accustomed *to*

adapt *from* a source
adapt *to* a situation

afraid *of*

agree *on* a plan
agree *to* a proposal
agree *with* a person

angry *with*

aware *of*

based *on*

capable *of*

certain *of*

charge *for* a purchase
charge *with* a crime

concur *in* an opinion
concur *with* a person

contend *for* a principle
contend *with* a person

dependent *on*

differ *about* or *over* a question
differ *from* in some quality
differ *with* a person

disappointed *by* or *in* a person
disappointed *in* or *with* a thing

familiar *with*

identical *with* or *to*

impatient *at* her conduct
impatient *of* restraint
impatient *for* a raise
impatient *with* a person

independent *of*

infer *from*

inferior *to*

involved *in* a task
involved *with* a person

oblivious *of* or *to* one's surroundings
oblivious *of* something forgotten

occupied *by* a person
occupied *in* study
occupied *with* a thing

opposed *to*

part *from* a person
part *with* a possession

prior *to*

proud *of*

related *to*

rewarded *by* the judge
rewarded *for* something done
rewarded *with* a gift

similar *to*

superior *to*

wait *at* a place
wait *for* a train, a person
wait *on* a customer

LITERAL   As I try to write, I can think of nothing to say.
FIGURATIVE   As I try to write, *my mind is a slab of black slate.*

Imaginatively and carefully used, figurative language can capture meaning more precisely and feelingly than literal language. Here is a figure of speech at work in technical writing (paraphrasing the physicist Edward Andrade):

The molecules in a liquid move continuously like couples on an overcrowded dance floor, jostling each other.

The two most common figures of speech are the simile and the metaphor. Both compare two things of different classes, often one abstract and the other concrete. A SIMILE makes the comparison explicit and usually begins with *like* or *as*.

Whenever we grow, we tend to feel it, *as* a young seed must feel the weight and inertia of the earth when it seeks to break out of its shell on its way to becoming a plant.   —ALICE WALKER

exact
12b

A METAPHOR claims that the two things are identical, omitting such words as *like* and *as*.

A school is a hopper into which children are heaved while they are young and tender; therein they are pressed into certain standard shapes and covered from head to heels with official rubber stamps.
—H. L. MENCKEN

To be successful, figurative language must be fresh and unstrained, calling attention not to itself but to the writer's meaning. Be especially wary of mixed metaphors, which combine two or more incompatible figures.

MIXED   Various thorny problems that we try to sweep under the rug continue to bob up all the same.

IMPROVED   Various thorny problems that we try to weed out continue to thrive all the same.

6. Trite expressions

TRITE EXPRESSIONS, or CLICHÉS, are phrases so old and so often repeated that they have become stale. They include the following:

add insult to injury	a needle in a haystack
better late than never	point with pride
cool, calm, and collected	pride and joy
crushing blow	ripe old age
easier said than done	rude awakening
face the music	sadder but wiser
few and far between	shoulder the burden
green with envy	shoulder to cry on
hard as a rock	sneaking suspicion
heavy as lead	stand in awe
hit the nail on the head	strong as an ox
hour of need	thin as a rail
ladder of success	tried and true
moving experience	wise as an owl

Clichés may slide into your drafts while you are trying to find the words for your meaning. To edit clichés, listen to your writing for any expressions that you have heard or used before. You can also supplement your efforts with a computerized style-checking program, which may include a cliché detector. No such program can flag all possible clichés, though, so you'll have to rely on your own editing as well. When you find a cliché, substitute fresh words of your own or restate the idea in plain language.

13 Completeness

The most serious kind of incomplete sentence is the grammatical fragment (see Chapter 30). But sentences are also incomplete when they omit one or more words needed for clarity.

13a Writing complete compounds

You may omit words from a compound construction when the omission will not confuse readers.

> Environmentalists have hopes for alternative fuels and [for] public transportation.
>
> Some cars will run on electricity; some [will run] on methane.

Such omissions are possible only when the words omitted are common to all the parts of a compound construction. When the parts differ in any way, all words must be included in all parts.

> One new car *gets* eighty miles per gallon; some old cars *get* as little as five miles per gallon. [One verb is singular, the other plural.]
>
> Environmentalists believe *in* and work *for* fuel conservation. [Idiom requires different prepositions with *believe* and *work*.]

┌─ KEY TERM ──────────────────────────────────

COMPOUND CONSTRUCTION   Two or more elements (words, phrases, clauses) that are equal in importance and that function as a unit: *Rain fell; streams overflowed* (clauses); *dogs and cats* (words).

13b   Adding needed words

In haste or carelessness, do not omit small words that are needed for clarity.

> INCOMPLETE   Regular payroll deductions are a type painless savings. You hardly notice missing amounts, and after period of years the contributions can add a large total.
>
> REVISED   Regular payroll deductions are a type *of* painless savings. You hardly notice *the* missing amounts, and after *a* period of years the contributions can add *up to* a large total.

con
14a

Attentive proofreading is the only insurance against this kind of omission. *Proofread all your papers carefully.* See page 28 for tips.

ESL   If your native language is not English, you may have difficulty knowing when to use the English articles *a, an,* and *the.* For guidelines on using articles, see pages 148–51.

14   Conciseness

Writing concisely means making every word count toward your meaning. Conciseness is not the same as mere brevity: detail and originality should not be cut with needless words. Rather, the length of an expression should be appropriate to the thought.

NOTE   Any computerized style-checking program will identify at least some of the wordy structures discussed on the following pages, such as repeated words, weak verbs, passive voice, and *there is* and *it is* constructions. No program can identify all these structures, however, nor can it tell you whether the structure is appropriate for your ideas. In short, such programs can't substitute for your own careful reading and editing. (See p. 35 for more on style checkers.)

14a   Focusing on the subject and verb

The heart of every sentence is its subject, which names who or what the sentence is about, and its verb, which specifies what the subject does or is. When the subject and verb do not identify the key actor and action, the sentence is bound to be wordy. In the examples following, the subjects and verbs are italicized.

Ways to achieve conciseness

WORDY (87 WORDS)

The highly pressured nature of critical-care nursing is due to the fact that the patients have life-threatening illnesses. Critical-care nurses must have possession of steady nerves to care for patients who are critically ill and very sick. The nurses must also have possession of interpersonal skills. They must also have medical skills. It is considered by most health-care professionals that these nurses are essential if there is to be improvement of patients who are now in critical care from that status to the status of intermediate care.

- Cut or shorten empty words and phrases (p. 81), and focus on subject and verb (p. 80).

- Use strong verbs (p. 83).

- Cut unneeded repetition (p. 82).

- Combine sentences (p. 85).

- Rewrite passive sentences as active (p. 84).

- Eliminate expletive constructions (p. 85)

- Cut unneeded repetition (p. 82), and reduce clauses and phrases (p. 83).

CONCISE (37 WORDS)

Critical-care nursing is highly pressured because the patients have life-threatening illnesses. Critical-care nurses must possess steady nerves and interpersonal and medical skills. Most health-care professionals consider these nurses essential if patients are to improve to intermediate care.

WORDY   The *occurrence* of the winter solstice, the shortest day of the year, *is* an event occurring about December 22.

REVISED   The winter *solstice*, the shortest day of the year, *occurs* about December 22.

Focusing on the subject and verb can help you with most of the editing techniques discussed below.

14b Cutting empty words

Empty words walk in place, gaining little or nothing in meaning. Many can be cut entirely. The following are just a few examples:

all things considered
as far as I'm concerned
for all intents and purposes
for the most part

in a manner of speaking
in my opinion
last but not least
more or less

con
14b

Other empty words can also be cut, usually along with some of the words around them:

area	element	kind	situation
aspect	factor	manner	thing
case	field	nature	type

Still others can be reduced from several words to a single word:

FOR	SUBSTITUTE
at all times	always
at the present time	now, yet
because of the fact that	because
by virtue of the fact that	because
due to the fact that	because
for the purpose of	for
in order to	to
in the event that	if
in the final analysis	finally

con
14c

Cutting or reducing such words and phrases will make your writing move faster and work harder.

WORDY   *As far as I am concerned,* because *of the fact that a situation of* discrimination continues *to exist* in *the field of* medicine, women have not *at the present time* achieved equality with men.

CONCISE   Because of continuing discrimination in medicine, women have not yet achieved equality with men.

14c Cutting unneeded repetition

Unnecessary repetition weakens sentences.

WORDY   Many unskilled workers *without training in a particular job* are unemployed *and do not have any work.*

CONCISE   Many unskilled workers are unemployed.

Be especially alert to phrases that say the same thing twice. In the examples below, the unneeded words are italicized.

circle *around*	*important* (*basic*) essentials
consensus *of opinion*	puzzling *in nature*
continue *on*	repeat *again*
cooperate *together*	return *again*
final completion	revert *back*
frank and honest exchange	square (round) *in shape*
the future *to come*	*surrounding* circumstances

ESL The preceding phrases are redundant because the main word already implies the italicized word or words. A dictionary will tell you what meanings a word implies. *Assassinate,* for instance, means "murder someone well known," so the following sentence is redundant: *Julius Caesar was assassinated and killed.*

14d Reducing clauses and phrases

Modifiers—subordinate clauses, phrases, and single words—can be expanded or contracted depending on the emphasis you want to achieve. (Generally, the longer a construction, the more emphasis it has.) When editing your sentences, consider whether any modifiers can be reduced without loss of emphasis or clarity.

> **WORDY**   The Channel Tunnel, *which links Britain and France,* bores through *a bed of solid chalk that is* twenty-three miles across.
>
> **REVISED**   The Channel Tunnel *linking Britain and France* bores through *twenty-three miles of solid chalk.*

14e Using strong verbs

Weak verbs such as forms of *be, have,* and *make* stall sentences. Strong verbs such as *slice, bicker,* and *stroll* energize sentences, moving them along. Weak verbs usually carry extra baggage, too, such as unneeded prepositional phrases and long, abstract nouns or adjectives.

> **WORDY**   The drillers *made slow advancement,* and costs *were over* $5 million a day. The slow progress *was worrisome for* backers, who *had had expectations of* high profits.

─ KEY TERMS ───────────────

MODIFIER   A word or word group that limits or qualifies another word: *slippery road.*

PHRASE   A word group that lacks a subject or a verb or both. Many phrases serve as modifiers: *road with a slippery surface.* (See p. 99.)

SUBORDINATE CLAUSE   A word group that contains a subject and a verb, begins with a subordinating word such as *because* or *who,* and is not a question. Most subordinate clauses serve as modifiers: *Two accidents occurred on the road, which was unusually slippery.* (See p. 101.)

con
14e

CONCISE   The drillers *advanced slowly,* and costs *topped* $5 million a day. The slow progress *worried* backers, who *had expected* high profits.

Don't try to eliminate every use of *be, have,* or *make: be* and *have* are essential as helping verbs (*is* going, *has* written); *be* links subjects and words describing them (*Planes are noisy*); and *have* and *make* have independent meanings (among them "possess" and "force," respectively).

In general, consider replacing forms of *be, have,* and *make* when one of the words following the verb could be made into a strong verb itself, as in these examples:

con
14f

WORDY	REVISED
was influential	influenced
is a glorification	glorifies
have a preference	prefer
had the appearance	appeared, seemed
made a claim	claimed
makes a good start	starts well

14f   Using the active voice

The active voice uses fewer words than the passive voice and is much more direct, because it names the performer of the verb's action up front. Change passive sentences to active by changing the verb and positioning the actor as the subject. (If you need help with this change, see p. 121.)

WORDY PASSIVE   As many as *fifteen feet* of chalk an hour *could be devoured* by the drill.

CONCISE ACTIVE   The *drill could devour* as many as fifteen feet of chalk an hour.

Retain the passive voice when the performer of the action is unknown or unimportant: *The candidate was elected.* (See p. 122.)

KEY TERMS

HELPING VERB   A verb used with another verb to convey time, obligation, and other meanings: *was* drilling, *would have been* drilling. (See p. 93.)

ACTIVE VOICE   The verb form when the subject names the *performer* of the verb's action: *The drillers used huge rotary blades.*

PASSIVE VOICE   The verb form when the subject names the *receiver* of the verb's action: *Huge rotary blades were used by the drillers.*

14g Cutting *there is* or *it is*

You can postpone the sentence subject with the words *there is* (*there are, there was, there were*) and *it is* (*it was*): *There is reason for voting. It is your vote that counts.* These EXPLETIVE CONSTRUCTIONS can be useful to emphasize the subject (as when introducing it for the first time) or to indicate a change in direction. But often they just add words and create limp substitutes for more vigorous sentences.

> **WORDY**   *There were more than half a million shareholders who* had invested in the tunnel. *It was they and the banks that* expected to profit.
>
> **CONCISE**   *More than half a million shareholders* had invested in the tunnel. *They and the banks* expected to profit.

con
14i

ESL When you do use an expletive construction, be careful to include *there* or *it*. Only commands and some questions can begin with verbs.

14h Combining sentences

Often the information in two or more sentences can be combined into one tight sentence.

> **WORDY**   Profits have not materialized. Even the banks have not profited. In 1996 the tunnel narrowly escaped bankruptcy. It restructured $1.56 billion of its debt.
>
> **CONCISE**   Profits have not materialized, even for the banks, and in 1996 the tunnel narrowly escaped bankruptcy by restructuring $1.56 billion of its debt.

14i Rewriting jargon

JARGON can refer to the special vocabulary of any discipline or profession (see p. 69). But it has also come to describe vague, inflated language that is overcomplicated, even incomprehensible. When it comes from government or business, we call it *bureaucratese*. It sounds almost as if the writer deliberately ignored every suggestion for clear, concise writing.

You may find yourself writing jargon when you are unsure of your subject or when your thoughts are tangled. It's fine, even necessary, to stumble and grope while drafting. But you should straighten out your ideas and eliminate jargon during revision and editing.

JARGON   The necessity for individuals to become separate entities in their own right may impel children to engage in open rebelliousness against parental authority or against sibling influence, with resultant confusion of those being rebelled against.

TRANSLATION   Children's natural desire to become themselves may make them rebel against bewildered parents or siblings.

con
14i

III

Sentence Parts and Patterns

III

Sentence Parts and Patterns

❖

III Sentence Parts and Patterns

89

BASIC GRAMMAR

Grammar describes how language works, and understanding it can help you create clear and accurate sentences. This section explains the kinds of words in sentences (Chapter 15) and how to build basic sentences (16), expand them (17), and classify them (18).

15 Parts of Speech

All English words fall into eight groups, called PARTS OF SPEECH: nouns, pronouns, verbs, adjectives, adverbs, prepositions, conjunctions, and interjections.

NOTE In different sentences a word may serve as different parts of speech. For example:

> The government sent *aid* to the city. [*Aid* is a noun.]
> Governments *aid* citizens. [*Aid* is a verb.]

The *function* of a word in a sentence always determines its part of speech in that sentence.

15a Recognizing nouns

Nouns name. They may name a person (*Rosie O'Donnell, Jesse Jackson, astronaut*), a thing (*chair, book, Mt. Rainier*), a quality (*pain, mystery, simplicity*), a place (*city, Washington, ocean, Red Sea*), or an idea (*reality, peace, success*).

The forms of nouns depend partly on where they fit in certain groups. As the examples indicate, the same noun may appear in more than one group.

❖ COMMON NOUNS name general classes of things and do not begin with capital letters: *earthquake, citizen, earth, fortitude, army.*

❖ PROPER NOUNS name specific people, places, and things and begin with capital letters: *Helen Hunt, Washington Monument, El Paso, US Congress.*

❖ COUNT NOUNS name things considered countable in English. Most add *-s* or *-es* to distinguish between singular (one) and plural (more than one): *citizen, citizens; city, cities.* Some count nouns form irregular plurals: *woman, women; child, children.*

❖ NONCOUNT NOUNS name things that aren't considered countable in English (*earth, sugar*), or they name qualities (*chaos, fortitude*). Noncount nouns do not form plurals.

❖ COLLECTIVE NOUNS are singular in form but name groups: *army, family, herd, US Congress.*

In addition, most nouns form the POSSESSIVE by adding *-'s* to show ownership (*Nadia's books, citizen's rights*), source (*Auden's poems*), and some other relationships.

15b Recognizing pronouns

Most PRONOUNS substitute for nouns and function in sentences as nouns do: *Susanne Ling enlisted in the Air Force when she graduated.*

Pronouns fall into several subclasses depending on their form or function:

❖ PERSONAL PRONOUNS refer to a specific individual or to individuals: *I, you, he, she, it, we,* and *they.*

❖ INDEFINITE PRONOUNS, such as *everybody* and *some,* do not substitute for any specific nouns, though they function as nouns (*Everybody speaks*).

❖ RELATIVE PRONOUNS—*who, whoever, which, that*—relate groups of words to nouns or other pronouns (*The book that won is a novel*).

❖ INTERROGATIVE PRONOUNS, such as *who, which,* and *what,* introduce questions (*Who will contribute?*).

❖ DEMONSTRATIVE PRONOUNS, including *this, that,* and *such,* identify or point to nouns (*This is the problem*).

❖ INTENSIVE PRONOUNS—a personal pronoun plus *-self* or *-selves* (*himself, ourselves*)—emphasize a noun or other pronoun (*He himself asked that question*).

❖ REFLEXIVE PRONOUNS have the same form as intensive pronouns but indicate that the sentence subject also receives the action of the verb (*They injured themselves*).

The personal pronouns *I, he, she, we,* and *they* and the relative pronouns *who* and *whoever* change form depending on their function in the sentence. (See Chapter 25.)

gr
15c

15c Recognizing verbs

Verbs express an action (*bring, change, grow, consider*), an occurrence (*become, happen, occur*), or a state of being (*be, seem, remain*).

1. Forms of verbs

Verbs have five distinctive forms. If the form can change as described here, the word is a verb:

❖ The PLAIN FORM is the dictionary form of the verb. When the subject is a plural noun or the pronoun *I, we, you,* or *they,* the plain form indicates action that occurs in the present, occurs habitually, or is generally true.

A few artists *live* in town today.
They *hold* classes downtown.

❖ The -S FORM ends in *-s* or *-es.* When the subject is a singular noun, a pronoun such as *everyone,* or the personal pronoun *he, she,* or *it,* the *-s* form indicates action that occurs in the present, occurs habitually, or is generally true.

The artist *lives* in town today.
She *holds* classes downtown.

❖ The PAST-TENSE FORM indicates that the action of the verb occurred before now. It usually adds *-d* or *-ed* to the plain form, although most irregular verbs create it in different ways (see pp. 104–07).

Many artists *lived* in town before this year.
They *held* classes downtown. [Irregular verb.]

❖ The PAST PARTICIPLE is usually the same as the past-tense form, except in most irregular verbs. It combines with forms of *have* or *be* (*has climbed, was created*), or by itself it modifies nouns and pronouns (*the sliced apples*).

Artists have *lived* in town for decades.
They have *held* classes downtown. [Irregular verb.]

❖ The PRESENT PARTICIPLE adds *-ing* to the verb's plain form. It combines with forms of *be* (*is buying*), modifies nouns and pronouns (*the boiling water*), or functions as a noun (*Running exhausts me*).

A few artists are *living* in town today.
They are *holding* classes downtown.

The verb *be* has eight forms rather than the five forms of most other verbs.

PLAIN FORM	be
PRESENT PARTICIPLE	being
PAST PARTICIPLE	been

	I	*he, she, it*	*we, you, they*
PRESENT TENSE	am	is	are
PAST TENSE	was	was	were

2. Helping verbs

Some verb forms combine with HELPING VERBS to indicate time, possibility, obligation, necessity, and other kinds of meaning: *can run*, *was sleeping*, *had been working*. In these VERB PHRASES *run*, *sleeping*, and *working* are MAIN VERBS—they carry the principal meaning.

VERB PHRASE

Helping   Main

Artists *can   train* others to draw.
The techniques *have   changed* little.

These are the most common helping verbs:

be able to	had better	must	used to
be supposed to	have to	ought to	will
can	may	shall	would
could	might	should	

Forms of *be:* be, am, is, are, was, were, been, being
Forms of *have:* have, has, had, having
Forms of *do:* do, does, did

See pages 108–12 for more on helping verbs.

15d Recognizing adjectives and adverbs

ADJECTIVES describe or modify nouns and pronouns. They specify which one, what quality, or how many.

old   city
adjective noun

generous   one
adjective   pronoun

two   pears
adjective noun

ADVERBS describe or modify verbs, adjectives, other adverbs, and whole groups of words. They specify when, where, how, and to what extent.

nearly destroyed
adverb   verb

too quickly
adverb adverb

very generous
adverb adjective

Unfortunately, taxes will rise.
adverb   word group

gr
15d

An *-ly* ending often signals an adverb, but not always: *friendly* is an adjective; *never, not,* and *always* are adverbs. The only way to tell whether a word is an adjective or an adverb is to determine what it modifies.

Adjectives and adverbs appear in three forms: POSITIVE (*green, angrily*), COMPARATIVE (*greener, more angrily*), and SUPERLATIVE (*greenest, most angrily*).

See Chapter 28 for more on adjectives and adverbs.

15e Recognizing connecting words: Prepositions and conjunctions

Connecting words are mostly small words that link parts of sentences. They never change form.

1. Prepositions

PREPOSITIONS form nouns or pronouns (plus any modifiers) into word groups called PREPOSITIONAL PHRASES: *about love, down the stairs.* These phrases usually serve as modifiers in sentences, as in *The plants trailed down the stairs.* (See p. 99 for more on prepositional phrases.)

gr
15e

Common prepositions				
about	before	except for	of	throughout
above	behind	excepting	off	till
according to	below	for	on	to
across	beneath	from	onto	toward
after	beside	in	on top of	under
against	between	in addition to	out	underneath
along	beyond	inside	out of	unlike
along with	by	inside of	outside	until
among	concerning	in spite of	over	up
around	despite	instead of	past	upon
as	down	into	regarding	up to
aside from	due to	like	round	with
at	during	near	since	within
because of	except	next to	through	without

ESL The meanings and uses of English prepositions can be difficult to master. See pages 76–77 for a discussion of prepositions in idioms. See pages 130–31 for uses of prepositions in two-word verbs such as *look after* or *look up.*

2. Subordinating conjunctions

SUBORDINATING CONJUNCTIONS form sentences into word groups called SUBORDINATE CLAUSES, such as *when the meeting ended.* These clauses serve as parts of sentences: *Everyone was relieved when the meeting ended.* (See p. 101 for more on subordinate clauses.)

Common subordinating conjunctions			
after	even if	rather than	until
although	even though	since	when
as	if	so that	whenever
as if	if only	than	where
as long as	in order that	that	whereas
as though	now that	though	wherever
because	once	till	whether
before	provided	unless	while

ESL Subordinating conjunctions convey meaning without help from other function words, such as the coordinating conjunctions *and, but, for,* or *so.*

FAULTY   *Even though* the parents are illiterate, *but* their children may read well. [*Even though* and *but* have the same meaning, so both are not needed.]

REVISED *Even though* the parents are illiterate, their children may read well.

gr
15e

3. Coordinating and correlative conjunctions

Coordinating and correlative conjunctions connect words or word groups of the same kind, such as nouns, adjectives, or sentences. COORDINATING CONJUNCTIONS consist of a single word.

Coordinating conjunctions			
and	nor	for	yet
but	or	so	

Biofeedback *or* simple relaxation can relieve headaches.
Relaxation works well, *and* it is inexpensive.

CORRELATIVE CONJUNCTIONS are combinations of coordinating conjunctions and other words.

Common correlative conjunctions	
both . . . and	neither . . . nor
not only . . . but also	whether . . . or
not . . . but	as . . . as
either . . . or	

Both biofeedback *and* relaxation can relieve headaches.

The headache sufferer learns *not only* to recognize the causes of headaches *but also* to control those causes.

15f Recognizing interjections

INTERJECTIONS express feeling or command attention. They are rarely used in academic or business writing.

Oh, the meeting went fine.
They won seven thousand dollars! *Wow!*

gr
16a

16 The Sentence

The SENTENCE is the basic unit of expression. It is grammatically complete and independent: it does not serve as an adjective, adverb, or other single part of speech.

16a Recognizing subjects and predicates

Most sentences make statements. First the SUBJECT names something; then the PREDICATE makes an assertion about the subject or describes an action by the subject.

SUBJECT   PREDICATE
    Art   thrives.

The SIMPLE SUBJECT consists of one or more nouns or pronouns, whereas the COMPLETE SUBJECT also includes any modifiers. The SIMPLE PREDICATE consists of one or more verbs, whereas the COMPLETE PREDICATE adds any words needed to complete the meaning of the verb plus any modifiers. Sometimes, as in the short example *Art thrives*, the simple and complete subject and predicate are the same. More often, they are different:

	SUBJECT	PREDICATE
	┌────complete────┐ simple	┌────complete────┐ simple
	Some contemporary *art*	*stirs* controversy.
	┌────complete────┐ simple	┌────complete────┐ simple
	Congress and the *media*	*discuss* and *dispute* its value.

In the last example, the simple subject and simple predicate are both COMPOUND: in each, two words joined by a coordinating conjunction (*and*) serve the same function.

ESL The subject of an English sentence may be a noun (*art*) or a pronoun that refers to the noun (*it*), but not both: *Some art* [not *art it*] *stirs controversy.* (See p. 167.)

16b Recognizing predicate patterns

All English sentences are based on five patterns, each differing in the complete predicate (the verb and any words following it).

ESL The word order in English sentences may not correspond to word order in the sentences of your native language. English, for instance, strongly prefers subject first, then verb, then any other words, whereas some other languages prefer the verb first.

Pattern 1: The earth trembled.

In the simplest pattern the predicate consists only of an INTRANSITIVE VERB, a verb that does not require a following word to complete its meaning.

	SUBJECT	PREDICATE
		Intransitive verb
	The earth	trembled.
	The hospital	may close.

Pattern 2: The earthquake destroyed the city.

In pattern 2 the verb is followed by a DIRECT OBJECT, a noun or pronoun that identifies who or what receives the action of the verb. A verb that requires a direct object to complete its meaning is called TRANSITIVE.

	SUBJECT	PREDICATE	
		Transitive *verb*	*Direct* *object*
	The earthquake	destroyed	the city.
	Education	opens	doors.

ESL Only transitive verbs can be used in the passive voice: *The city was destroyed* (see p. 121). Your dictionary will indicate whether a verb is transitive or intransitive. For some verbs (*begin, learn, read, write,* and others), it will indicate both uses.

Pattern 3: The result was chaos.

In pattern 3 the verb is followed by a SUBJECT COMPLEMENT, a word that renames or describes the subject. A verb in this pattern is called a LINKING VERB because it links its subject to the description following. The linking verbs include *be, seem, appear, become, grow, remain, stay, prove, feel, look, smell, sound,* and *taste.* Subject complements are usually nouns or adjectives.

SUBJECT	PREDICATE	
	Linking verb	*Subject complement*
The result	was	chaos.
The man	became	an accountant.

Pattern 4: The government sent the city aid.

In pattern 4 the verb is followed by a direct object and an IN-DIRECT OBJECT, a word identifying to or for whom the action of the verb is performed. The direct object and indirect object refer to different things, people, or places.

SUBJECT	PREDICATE		
	Transitive verb	*Indirect object*	*Direct object*
The government	sent	the city	aid.
One company	offered	its employees	bonuses.

A number of verbs can take indirect objects, including those above and *allow, bring, buy, deny, find, get, give, leave, make, pay, read, sell, show, teach,* and *write.*

ESL Some verbs expressing action done to or for someone must be followed by *to* or *for.* These verbs include *admit, announce, demonstrate, explain, introduce, mention, prove, recommend, say,* and *suggest: The manual explains the new procedure to workers.*

Pattern 5: The citizens considered the earthquake a disaster.

In pattern 5 the verb is followed by a direct object and an OB-JECT COMPLEMENT, a word that renames or describes the direct object. Object complements may be nouns or adjectives.

SUBJECT	PREDICATE		
	Transitive verb	*Direct object*	*Object complement*
The citizens	considered	the earthquake	a disaster.
Success	makes	some people	nervous.

gr
16b

17 Phrases and Subordinate Clauses

Most sentences contain word groups that serve as adjectives, adverbs, or nouns and thus cannot stand alone as sentences.

❖ A PHRASE lacks either a subject or a predicate or both: *fearing an accident; in a panic.*
❖ A SUBORDINATE CLAUSE contains a subject and a predicate (like a sentence) but begins with a subordinating word: *when prices rise; whoever laughs.*

17a Recognizing phrases

1. Prepositional phrases

A PREPOSITIONAL PHRASE consists of a preposition plus a noun, a pronoun, or a word group serving as a noun, called the OBJECT OF THE PREPOSITION. A list of prepositions appears on page 94.

PREPOSITION	OBJECT
of	spaghetti
on	the surface
with	great satisfaction
upon	entering the room
from	where you are standing

Prepositional phrases usually function as adjectives or adverbs.

Life *on a raft* was an opportunity *for adventure.*
adjective phrase   adjective phrase

Huck Finn rode the raft *by choice.*
adverb phrase

2. Verbal phrases

Certain forms of verbs, called VERBALS, can serve as modifiers or nouns. Often these verbals appear with their own modifiers and objects in VERBAL PHRASES.

NOTE Verbals cannot serve as verbs in sentences. *The sun rises over the dump* is a sentence; *The sun rising over the dump* is a sentence fragment. (See pp. 158–59.)

Participial phrases

Phrases made from present participles (ending in *-ing*) or past participles (usually ending in *-d* or *-ed*) serve as adjectives.

Strolling shoppers fill the malls.
adjective

They make selections *determined by personal taste.*
adjective phrase

NOTE With irregular verbs, the past participle may have a different ending—for instance, *hidden funds.* (See p. 104.)

ESL For verbs expressing feeling, the present and past participles have different meanings: *It was a boring lecture. The bored students slept.* (See p. 148.)

Gerund phrases

A GERUND is the *-ing* form of a verb when it serves as a noun. Gerunds and gerund phrases can do whatever nouns can do.

sentence
subject
Shopping satisfies personal needs.

noun
     object of preposition
Malls are good at *creating such needs.*
     noun phrase

Infinitive phrases

gr
17a

An INFINITIVE is the plain form of a verb plus *to: to hide.* Infinitives and infinitive phrases serve as adjectives, adverbs, or nouns.

sentence subject   subject complement
To design a mall is *to create an artificial environment.*
noun phrase   noun phrase

Malls are designed *to make shoppers feel safe.*
     adverb phrase

The environment supports the impulse *to shop.*
      adjective

ESL Infinitives and gerunds may follow some verbs and not others and may differ in meaning after a verb: *The singer stopped to sing. The singer stopped singing.* (See pp. 128–30.)

3. Absolute phrases

An ABSOLUTE PHRASE consists of a noun or pronoun and a participle, plus any modifiers. It modifies the entire rest of the sentence it appears in.

absolute phrase
Their own place established, many ethnic groups are making way
for new arrivals.

Unlike a participial phrase (pp. 99–100), an absolute phrase always contains a noun that serves as a subject.

┌ participial phrase ┐
Learning English, many immigrants discover American culture.

┌─────────── absolute phrase ───────────┐
The immigrants having learned English, their opportunities widen.

4. Appositive phrases

An APPOSITIVE is usually a noun that renames another noun. An appositive phrase includes modifiers as well.

╱──── appositive phrase
Bizen ware, *a dark stoneware*, is produced in Japan.

Appositives and appositive phrases sometimes begin with *that is, such as, for example,* or *in other words.*

╱──── ┌ appositive phrase
Bizen ware is used in the Japanese tea ceremony, *that is, the Zen*

Buddhist observance that links meditation and art.

17b Recognizing subordinate clauses

A CLAUSE is any group of words that contains both a subject and a predicate. There are two kinds of clauses, and the distinction between them is important.

❖ A MAIN CLAUSE makes a complete statement and can stand alone as a sentence: *The sky darkened.*
❖ A SUBORDINATE CLAUSE is just like a main clause except that it begins with a subordinating word: *when the sky darkened; whoever calls.* The subordinating word reduces the clause from a complete statement to a single part of speech: an adjective, adverb, or noun.

NOTE A subordinate clause punctuated as a sentence is a sentence fragment. (See pp. 158–61.)

Adjective clauses

An ADJECTIVE CLAUSE modifies a noun or pronoun. It usually begins with the relative pronoun *who, whom, whose, which,* or *that.* The relative pronoun is the subject or object of the clause it begins. The clause ordinarily falls immediately after the word it modifies.

╱──── adjective clause
Parents *who are illiterate* may have bad memories of school.

╱── ┌─── adjective clause ───┐
One school, *which is open year-round*, helps parents learn to read.

Adverb clauses

An ADVERB CLAUSE modifies a verb, an adjective, another adverb, or a whole word group. It always begins with a subordinating conjunction, such as *although, because, if,* or *when* (see p. 95 for a list).

The school began teaching parents *when adult illiteracy gained national attention.* — adverb clause —

Because it was directed at people who could not read, advertising had to be inventive. — adverb clause — main clause

Noun clauses

A NOUN CLAUSE replaces a noun in a sentence and serves as a subject, object, or complement. It begins with *that, what, whatever, who, whom, whoever, whomever, when, where, whether, why,* or *how.*

Whether the program would succeed depended on door-to-door advertising. — sentence subject — noun clause

Teachers explained in person *how the program would work.* — direct object — noun clause

18 Sentence Types

The four basic sentence structures vary in the number of main and coordinate clauses.

18a Recognizing simple sentences

A SIMPLE SENTENCE consists of a single main clause and no subordinate clause.

Last summer was unusually hot. — main clause —

The summer made many farmers leave the area for good or reduced them to bare existence. — main clause —

18b Recognizing compound sentences

A COMPOUND SENTENCE consists of two or more main clauses and no subordinate clause.

```
  ┌──main clause──┐      ┌────main clause────┐
```
Last July was hot, but August was even hotter.

```
  ┌────── main clause──────────┐    ┌──────main clause──────┐
```
The hot sun scorched the earth, and the lack of rain killed many
crops.

18c Recognizing complex sentences

A COMPLEX SENTENCE consists of one main clause and one or
more subordinate clauses.

```
  ┌──main clause──┐ ┌─────── subordinate clause──────┐
```
Rain finally came, although many had left the area by then.

```
  ┌──────────main clause───────────┐   ┌─subordinate clause──
```
Those who remained were able to start anew because the govern-
                 subordinate clause
ment came to their aid.

18d Recognizing compound-complex sentences

A COMPOUND-COMPLEX SENTENCE has the characteristics of both
the compound sentence (two or more main clauses) and the complex sentence (at least one subordinate clause).

```
  ┌────────── subordinate clause────┐  ┌──── main clause────
```
Even though government aid finally came, many people had al-
```
  ────────────────────────────┐   ┌──────main clause────────
```
ready been reduced to poverty, and others had been forced to
move.

gr
18d

VERBS

VERBS express actions, conditions, and states of being. The basic uses and forms of verbs are described on pages 91–93. This section explains and solves the most common problems with verbs' forms (Chapter 19), tenses (20), mood (21), and voice (22). It shows how to make verbs match their subjects (23). And it treats some special challenges of English verbs for nonnative speakers (24).

19 Verb Forms

Verb forms may give you trouble when the verb is irregular, when you omit certain endings, or when you stumble over helping verbs.

19a Use the correct forms of *sing/sang/sung* and other irregular verbs.

Most verbs are REGULAR: they form their past tense and past participle by adding *-d* or *-ed* to the plain form.

PLAIN FORM	PAST TENSE	PAST PARTICIPLE
live	lived	lived
act	acted	acted

About two hundred English verbs are IRREGULAR: they form their past tense and past participle in some irregular way. Check a dictionary under the verb's plain form if you have any doubt about its other forms. If the verb is irregular, the dictionary will list the plain form, the past tense, and the past participle in that order (*go,*

KEY TERMS

PLAIN FORM   The dictionary form of the verb: *I walk. You forget.* (See p. 92.)

PAST-TENSE FORM   The verb form indicating action that occurred in the past: *I walked. You forgot.* (See p. 92.)

PAST PARTICIPLE   The verb form used with *have, has,* or *had: I have walked.* It may also serve as a modifier: *This is a forgotten book.* (See p. 92.)

Common irregular verbs

PLAIN FORM	PAST TENSE	PAST PARTICIPLE
arise	arose	arisen
become	became	become
begin	began	begun
bid	bid	bid
bite	bit	bitten, bit
blow	blew	blown
break	broke	broken
bring	brought	brought
burst	burst	burst
buy	bought	bought
catch	caught	caught
choose	chose	chosen
come	came	come
cut	cut	cut
dive	dived, dove	dived
do	did	done
draw	drew	drawn
dream	dreamed, dreamt	dreamed, dreamt
drink	drank	drunk
drive	drove	driven
eat	ate	eaten
fall	fell	fallen
find	found	found
flee	fled	fled
fly	flew	flown
forget	forgot	forgotten, forgot
freeze	froze	frozen
get	got	got, gotten
give	gave	given
go	went	gone
grow	grew	grown
hang (suspend)	hung	hung
hang (execute)	hanged	hanged
hear	heard	heard
hide	hid	hidden
hold	held	held
keep	kept	kept
know	knew	known
lay	laid	laid
lead	led	led
leave	left	left

vb
19a

(continued)

Common irregular verbs
(continued)

PLAIN FORM	PAST TENSE	PAST PARTICIPLE
lend	lent	lent
let	let	let
lie	lay	lain
lose	lost	lost
pay	paid	paid
prove	proved	proved, proven
ride	rode	ridden
ring	rang	rung
rise	rose	risen
run	ran	run
say	said	said
see	saw	seen
set	set	set
shake	shook	shaken
shrink	shrank, shrunk	shrunk, shrunken
sing	sang, sung	sung
sink	sank, sunk	sunk
sit	sat	sat
slide	slid	slid
speak	spoke	spoken
spring	sprang, sprung	sprung
stand	stood	stood
steal	stole	stolen
swim	swam	swum
swing	swung	swung
take	took	taken
tear	tore	torn
throw	threw	thrown
wear	wore	worn
write	wrote	written

vb
19b

went, gone). If the dictionary gives only two forms (as in *think, thought*), then the past tense and the past participle are the same.

The list on the previous page and above includes the most common irregular verbs. (When two forms are possible, as in *dove* and *dived,* both are included.)

19b Distinguish between *sit* and *set, lie* and *lay,* and *rise* and *raise.*

The forms of *sit* and *set, lie* and *lay,* and *rise* and *raise* are easy to confuse.

PLAIN FORM	PAST TENSE	PAST PARTICIPLE
sit	sat	sat
set	set	set
lie	lay	lain
lay	laid	laid
rise	rose	risen
raise	raised	raised

In each of these confusing pairs, one verb is intransitive (it does not take an object) and one is transitive (it does take an object). (See p. 97 for more on this distinction.)

INTRANSITIVE

The patients *lie* in their beds. [*Lie* means "recline" and takes no object.]

Visitors *sit* with them. [*Sit* means "be seated" or "be located" and takes no object.]

Patients' temperatures *rise*. [*Rise* means "increase" or "get up" and takes no object.]

TRANSITIVE

Orderlies *lay* the dinner trays on tables. [*Lay* means "place" and takes an object, here *trays*.]

Orderlies *set* the trays down. [*Set* means "place" and takes an object, here *trays*.]

Nursing aides *raise* the shades. [*Raise* means "lift" or "bring up" and takes an object, here *shades*.]

19c Use the *-s* and *-ed* forms of the verb when they are required.

> vb
> **19c**

Speakers of some English dialects and nonnative speakers of English sometimes omit verb endings required by standard English. One is the *-s* form of a verb, which is required when *both* of these situations hold:

❖ The subject is a singular noun (*boy*), an indefinite pronoun (*everyone*), or *he, she,* or *it.*
❖ The verb's action occurs in the present.

> The letter *asks* [not *ask*] for a quick response.
> Delay *is* [not *be*] costly.

Watch especially for the *-s* forms *has, does,* and *doesn't* (for *does not*).

> The company *has* [not *have*] delayed responding.
> It *doesn't* [not *don't*] have the needed data.
> The contract *does* [not *do*] depend on the response.

Another ending sometimes omitted is *-d* or *-ed,* as in *we bagged* or *used cars.* The ending is particularly easy to omit if it isn't pronounced clearly in speech, as in *asked, discussed, fixed, mixed, supposed, walked,* and *used.* Use the ending for a regular verb in *any* of these situations:

❖ The verb's action occurred in the past:

The company *asked* [not *ask*] for more time.

❖ The verb form functions as a modifier:

The data *concerned* [not *concern*] should be retrievable.

❖ The verb form combines with a form of *be* or *have:*

The company is *supposed* [not *suppose*] to be the best.
It has *developed* [not *develop*] an excellent reputation.

ESL Some languages do not require endings equivalent to the *-s* or *-ed* in English. If English is not your native language and you find you omit one or both of these endings, you may need to edit your drafts just for them.

vb
19d

19d   Use helping verbs with main verbs appropriately.

Helping verbs combine with main verbs in verb phrases: *The line should have been cut. Who was calling?*

1. Required helping verbs

Some English dialects omit helping verbs required by standard English. In the sentences below, the underlined helping verbs are essential.

Archaeologists *are conducting* fieldwork all over the world. [Not *Archaeologists conducting. . . .*]
Many *have been* fortunate in their discoveries. [Not *Many been. . . .*]
Some *could be* real-life Indiana Joneses. [Not *Some be. . . .*]

KEY TERMS

HELPING VERB   A verb such as *can, may, be, have,* or *do* that forms a verb phrase with another verb to show time, permission, and other meanings. (See p. 93.)

MAIN VERB   The verb that carries the principal meaning in a verb phrase: *has walked, could be happening.* (See p. 93.)

VERB PHRASE   A helping verb plus a main verb: *will be singing, would speak.* (See p. 93.)

The omission of a helping verb may create an incomplete sentence, or SENTENCE FRAGMENT, because a present participle (*conducting*), an irregular past participle (*been*), or the infinitive *be* cannot stand alone as the only verb in a sentence (see pp. 158–59). To work as sentence verbs, these verb forms need helping verbs.

2. Combination of helping verb + main verb   ESL

Helping verbs and main verbs combine into verb phrases in specific ways.

NOTE The main verb in a verb phrase (the one carrying the main meaning) does not change to show a change in subject or time: *she has sung, you had sung.* Only the helping verb may change, as in these examples.

Form of *be* + present participle

The PROGRESSIVE TENSES indicate action in progress. Create them with *be, am, is, are, was, were,* or *been* followed by the main verb's present participle.

She *is working* on a new book.

Be and *been* require additional helping verbs to form progressive tenses.

can	might	should		have	
could	must	will	*be* working	has	*been* working
may	shall	would		had	

vh
19d

When forming the progressive tenses, be sure to use the *-ing* form of the main verb.

FAULTY   Her ideas are *grow* more complex. She is *developed* a new approach to ethics.

REVISED   Her ideas are *growing* more complex. She is *developing* a new approach to ethics.

KEY TERMS

PRESENT PARTICIPLE   The *-ing* form of the verb: *flying, writing.* (See p. 92.)

PAST PARTICIPLE   The *-d* or *-ed* form of a regular verb: *hedged, walked.* Most irregular verbs have distinctive past participles: *eaten, swum.* (See p. 92.)

PROGRESSIVE TENSES   Verb tenses expressing action in progress— for instance, *I am flying* (present progressive), *I was flying* (past progressive), *I will be flying* (future progressive). (See p. 115.)

Form of *be* + past participle

The PASSIVE VOICE of the verb indicates that the subject *receives* the action of the verb. Create the passive voice with *be, am, is, are, was, were, being,* or *been* followed by the main verb's past participle.

Her latest book *was completed* in four months.

Be, being, and *been* require additional helping verbs to form the passive voice.

$$\left.\begin{array}{l}\text{have}\\\text{has}\\\text{had}\end{array}\right\}\textit{been} \text{ completed}\qquad\left.\begin{array}{ll}\text{am}&\text{was}\\\text{is}&\text{were}\\\text{are}&\end{array}\right\}\textit{being} \text{ completed}$$

will *be* completed

Be sure to use the main verb's past participle for the passive voice.

FAULTY   Her next book will be *publish* soon.
REVISED   Her next book will be *published* soon.

NOTE Use only transitive verbs to form the passive voice:

FAULTY   A philosophy conference *will be occurred* in the same week. [*Occur* is not a transitive verb.]
REVISED   A philosophy conference *will occur* in the same week.

See page 122 for advice on when to use and when to avoid the passive voice.

Forms of *have*

Four forms of *have* serve as helping verbs: *have, has, had, having.* One of these forms plus the main verb's past participle creates one of the perfect tenses, those expressing action completed before another specific time or action.

Some students *have complained* about the laboratory.
Others *had complained* before.

vb 19d

┌─ KEY TERMS ────────────────────────────────

PASSIVE VOICE   The verb form when the subject names the receiver of the verb's action: *An essay was written by every student.* (See p. 121.)

TRANSITIVE VERB   A verb that requires an object to complete its meaning: *Every student completed an essay* (*essay* is the object of *completed*). (See p. 97.)

PERFECT TENSES   Verb tenses expressing an action completed before another specific time or action: *We have eaten* (present perfect), *We had eaten* (past perfect), *We will have eaten* (future perfect). (See pp. 113–14.)

Will and other helping verbs sometimes accompany forms of *have* in the perfect tenses.

Several more students *will have complained* by the end of the week.

Forms of *do*

Do, does, and *did* have three uses as helping verbs, always with the plain form of the main verb:

❖ To pose a question: *How did the trial end?*
❖ To emphasize the main verb: *It did end eventually.*
❖ To negate the main verb, along with *not* or *never: The judge did not withdraw.*

Be sure to use the main verb's plain form with any form of *do.*

FAULTY   The judge did *remained* in court.
REVISED   The judge did *remain* in court.

Modals

The modal helping verbs include *can, could, may,* and *might,* along with several two- and three-word combinations, such as *have to* and *be able to.* (See p. 93 for a list of modals.)

Modals convey various meanings, with these being most common:

❖ Ability: *can, could, be able to*

The equipment *can detect* small vibrations. [Present.]

The equipment *could detect* small vibrations. [Past.]

The equipment *is able to detect* small vibrations. [Present. For past: *was able to.* For future: *will be able to.*]

❖ Possibility: *could, may, might, could/may/might have* + past participle

The equipment *could fail.* [Present.]
The equipment *may fail.* [Present and future.]
The equipment *might fail.* [Present and future.]
The equipment *may have failed.* [Past.]

❖ Necessity or obligation: *must, have to, be supposed to*

The lab *must purchase* a backup. [Present or future.]
The lab *has to purchase* a backup. [Present or future. Past: *had to.*]
The lab *will have to purchase* a backup. [Future.]
The lab *is supposed to purchase* a backup. [Present. Past: *was supposed to.*]

vb
19d

- Permission: *may, can, could*

  The lab *may spend* the money. [Present or future.]
  The lab *can spend* the money. [Present or future.]
  The lab *could spend* the money. [Present or future, more tentative.]
  The school then announced that the lab *could spend* the money. [Past.]

- Intention: *will, shall, would*

  The lab *will spend* the money. [Future.]
  Shall we *offer* advice? [Future. Use *shall* for questions requesting opinion or consent.]
  We knew we *would offer* advice. [Past.]

- Request: *could, can, would*

  Could (or *can* or *would*) you please *obtain* a bid? [Present or future.]

- Advisability: *should, had better, ought to, should have* + past participle

  You *should obtain* three bids. [Present or future.]
  You *had better obtain* three bids. [Present or future.]
  You *ought to obtain* three bids. [Present or future.]
  You *should have obtained* three bids. [Past.]

- Past habit: *would, used to*

  In years past we *would obtain* five bids.
  We *used to obtain* five bids.

The following conventions govern the combination of modals and main verbs shown in the examples:

- One-word modals do not change form to show a change in subject: *I could run, she could run.* Most two- and three-word modals do change form, like other helping verbs: *I have to run, she has to run.*
- Modals can sometimes indicate past, present, or future time, occasionally with a word change (*can* to *could,* for instance), with a form change in a two- or three-word modal (such as *is/was able to*), or with *have* before the past participle of the main verb (*might have driven*).
- Don't use *to* between a one-word modal and the main verb: *can drive,* not *can to drive.* (Most of the two- and three-word modals do include *to: ought to drive.*)
- Don't use two one-word modals together: *I will be able to drive,* not I *will can drive.*

20 Verb Tenses

TENSE shows the time of a verb's action. The table on the next page illustrates the tense forms for a regular verb. (Irregular verbs have different past-tense and past-participle forms. See pp. 104–06.)

20a Observe the special uses of the present tense (*sing*).

Most academic and business writing uses the past tense (*the rebellion occurred*), but the present tense has several distinctive uses.

ACTION OCCURRING NOW
She *understands* the problem.
We *define* the problem differently.

HABITUAL OR RECURRING ACTION
Banks regularly *undergo* audits.
The audits *monitor* the banks' activities.

A GENERAL TRUTH
The mills of the gods *grind* slowly.
The earth *is* round.

DISCUSSION OF LITERATURE, FILM, AND SO ON
Huckleberry Finn *has* adventures we all envy.
In that article the author *examines* several causes of crime.

FUTURE TIME
Next week we *draft* a new budget.
Funding *ends* in less than a year.

(Time is really indicated here by *Next week* and *in less than a year*.)

20b Observe the uses of the perfect tenses (*have/had/will have sung*).

The perfect tenses consist of a form of *have* plus the verb's past participle (*closed, hidden*). They indicate an action completed before another specific time or action. The present perfect tense also indicates action begun in the past and continued into the present.

present perfect
The dancer *has performed* here only once. [The action is completed at the time of the statement.]

Tenses of a regular verb (active voice)

PRESENT Action that is occurring now, occurs habitually, or is generally true

SIMPLE PRESENT Plain form or *-s* form

I *walk.*
You/we/they *walk.*
He/she/it *walks.*

PRESENT PROGRESSIVE *Am, is,* or *are* plus *-ing* form

I *am walking.*
You/we/they *are walking.*
He/she/it *is walking.*

PAST Action that occurred before now

SIMPLE PAST Past-tense form (*-d* or *-ed*)

I/he/she/it *walked.*
You/we/they *walked.*

PAST PROGRESSIVE *Was* or *were* plus *-ing* form

I/he/she/it *was walking.*
You/we/they *were walking.*

FUTURE Action that will occur in the future

SIMPLE FUTURE Plain form plus *will*

I/you/he/she/it/we/they *will walk.*

FUTURE PROGRESSIVE *Will be* plus *-ing* form

I/you/he/she/it/we/they *will be walking.*

PRESENT PERFECT Action that began in the past and is linked to the present

PRESENT PERFECT *Have* or *has* plus past participle (*-d* or *-ed*)

I/you/we/they *have walked.*
He/she/it *has walked.*

PRESENT PERFECT PROGRESSIVE *Have been* or *has been* plus *-ing* form

I/you/we/they *have been walking.*
He/she/it *has been walking.*

PAST PERFECT Action that was completed before another past action

PAST PERFECT *Had* plus past participle (*-d* or *-ed*)

I/you/he/she/it/we/they *had walked.*

PAST PERFECT PROGRESSIVE *Had been* plus *-ing* form

I/you/he/she/it/we/they *had been walking.*

FUTURE PERFECT Action that will be completed before another future action

FUTURE PERFECT *Will have* plus past participle (*-d* or *-ed*)

I/you/he/she/it/we/they *will have walked.*

FUTURE PERFECT PROGRESSIVE *Will have been* plus *-ing* form

I/you/he/she/it/we/they *will have been walking.*

t
20b

present perfect
Critics *have written* about the performance ever since. [The action began in the past and continues now.]

past perfect
The dancer *had trained* in Asia before his performance. [The action was completed before another past action.]

future perfect
He *will have performed* here again by next month. [The action begins now or in the future and will be completed by a specified time in the future.]

ESL With the present perfect tense, the words *since* and *for* are followed by different information. After *since*, give a specific point in time: *The United States has been a member of the United Nations since 1945.* After *for*, give a span of time: *The United States has been a member of the United Nations for half a century.*

20c **Observe the uses of the progressive tenses (*is/was/will be singing*).** **ESL**

The progressive tenses indicate continuing (therefore progressive) action. They consist of a form of *be* plus the verb's *-ing* form (present participle). (The words *be* and *been* must be combined with other helping verbs. See p. 109.)

present progressive
The economy *is improving*.

past progressive
Last year the economy *was stagnating*.

future progressive
Economists *will be watching* for signs of growth.

present perfect progressive
The government *has been expecting* an upturn.

past perfect progressive
Various indicators *had been suggesting* improvement.

future perfect progressive
By the end of this year, investors *will have been watching* the markets nervously for nearly a decade.

NOTE Verbs that express unchanging states (especially mental states) rather than physical actions do not usually appear in the progressive tenses. These verbs include *adore, appear, believe, belong, care, hate, have, hear, know, like, love, mean, need, own, prefer, remember, see, sound, taste, think, understand,* and *want*.

FAULTY   She *is wanting* to study ethics.
REVISED   She *wants* to study ethics.

20d Keep tenses consistent.

Within a sentence, the tenses of verbs and verb forms need not be identical as long as they reflect actual changes in time: *Ramon will graduate from college twenty years after his father arrived in America.* But needless shifts in tense will confuse or distract readers.

INCONSISTENT   Immediately after Booth *shot* Lincoln, Major Rathbone *threw* himself upon the assassin. But Booth *pulls* a knife and *plunges* it into the major's arm.

REVISED   Immediately after Booth *shot* Lincoln, Major Rathbone *threw* himself upon the assassin. But Booth *pulled* a knife and *plunged* it into the major's arm.

INCONSISTENT   The main character in the novel *suffers* psychologically because he *has* a clubfoot, but he eventually *triumphed* over his disability.

REVISED   The main character in the novel *suffers* psychologically because he *has* a clubfoot, but he eventually *triumphs* over his disability. [Use the present tense when discussing the content of literature, film, and so on.]

20e Use the appropriate sequence of verb tenses.

The SEQUENCE OF TENSES is the relation between the verb tense in a main clause and the verb tense in a subordinate clause. The tenses are often different, as in *He will leave before I arrive.*

English tense sequence can be tricky for native speakers and especially challenging for nonnative speakers. The main difficulties are discussed below.

1. Past or past perfect tense in main clause

When the verb in the main clause is in the past or past perfect tense, the verb in the subordinate clause must also be past or past perfect:

┌ KEY TERMS ──────────────────────────────

MAIN CLAUSE   A word group that contains a subject and a verb and does not begin with a subordinating word: *Books are valuable.* (See p. 101.)

SUBORDINATE CLAUSE   A word group that contains a subject and a verb, begins with a subordinating word such as *because* or *who*, and is not a question: *Books are valuable when they enlighten.* (See p. 101.)

main clause: subordinate clause:
    past   past

The researchers *discovered* that people *varied* widely in their knowledge of public events.

main clause: subordinate clause:
   past   past perfect

The variation *occurred* because respondents *had been born* in different decades.

main clause: subordinate clause:
past perfect   past

None of them *had been born* when Warren G. Harding *was* President.

EXCEPTION Always use the present tense for a general truth, such as *The earth is round:*

main clause: subordinate clause:
  past   present

Most *understood* that popular Presidents *are* not necessarily good Presidents.

2. Conditional sentences FSL

A CONDITIONAL SENTENCE states a factual relation between cause and effect, makes a prediction, or speculates about what might happen. Such a sentence usually consists of a subordinate clause beginning with *if, when,* or *unless* and a main clause stating the result. The three kinds of conditional sentences use distinctive verbs.

seq
20e

Factual relation

For statements asserting that something always or usually happens whenever something else happens, use the present tense in both clauses:

subordinate clause: main clause:
  present   present

When a voter *casts* a ballot, he or she *has* complete privacy.

If the linked events occurred in the past, use the past tense in both clauses:

subordinate clause: main clause:
  past   past

When voters *registered* in some states, they *had* to pay a poll tax.

Prediction

For a prediction, generally use the present tense in the subordinate clause and the future tense in the main clause:

subordinate clause: main clause:
  present   future

Unless citizens *regain* faith in politics, they *will* not *vote.*

Sometimes the verb in the main clause consists of *may, can, should,* or *might* plus the verb's plain form: *If citizens regain faith, they may vote.*

Speculation

Speculations are mainly of two kinds, each with its own verb pattern. For events that are possible in the present but unlikely, use the past tense in the subordinate clause and *would, could,* or *might* plus the verb's plain form in the main clause:

> subordinate clause: main clause:
> past   *would* + verb
> If voters *had* more confidence, they *would vote* more often.

Use *were* instead of *was* when the subject is *I, he, she, it,* or a singular noun. (See p. 120 for more on this distinctive verb form.)

> subordinate clause: main clause:
> past   *would* + verb
> If the voter *were* more confident, he or she *would vote* more often.

For events that are impossible now, that are contrary to fact, use the same forms as above (including the distinctive *were* when applicable):

> subordinate clause: main clause:
> past   *might* + verb
> If Lincoln *were* alive, he *might inspire* confidence.

For events that were impossible in the past, use the past perfect tense in the subordinate clause and *would, could,* or *might* plus the present perfect tense in the main clause:

> subordinate clause: main clause:
> past perfect   *might* + present perfect
> If Lincoln *had lived* past the Civil War, he *might have helped* stabilize the country.

t seq

20e

3. Indirect quotations ESL

An INDIRECT QUOTATION reports what someone said or wrote but not in the exact words and not in quotation marks: *Lincoln said that events had controlled him* (quotation: "Events have controlled me"). An indirect quotation generally appears in a subordinate clause (underlined above), with certain conventions governing verb tense in most cases:

> ❖ When the verb in the main clause is in the present tense, the verb in the indirect quotation (subordinate clause) is in the same tense as the original quotation:

main clause: subordinate clause:
  present   present

Haworth *says* that Lincoln *is* our noblest national hero. [Quotation: "Lincoln *is* our noblest national hero."]

main clause: subordinate clause:
   present   past

He *says* that Lincoln *was* a complicated person. [Quotation: "Lincoln *was* a complicated person."]

❖ When the verb in the main clause is in the past tense, the verb in the indirect quotation usually changes tense from the original quotation. Present tense changes to past tense:

main clause: subordinate clause:
  past   past

An assistant to Lincoln *said* that the President *was* always generous. [Quotation: "The President *is* always generous."]

Past tense and present perfect tense change to past perfect tense. (Past perfect tense does not change.)

main clause;   subordinate clause:
  past   past perfect

Lincoln *said* that events *had controlled* him. [Quotation: "Events *have controlled* me."]

❖ When the direct quotation states a general truth or reports a situation that is still true, use the present tense in the indirect quotation regardless of the verb in the main clause:

main clause: subordinate clause:
  past   present

Lincoln *said* that right *makes* might. [Quotation: "Right *makes* might."]

NOTE As several of the examples show, an indirect quotation differs in at least two additional ways from the original quotation. (1) the indirect quotation is usually preceded by *that*, and (2) the indirect quotation changes pronouns, especially from forms of *I* or *we* to forms of *he, she,* or *they.*

vb
21

21 Verb Mood

MOOD in grammar is a verb form that indicates the writer's or speaker's attitude toward what he or she is saying. The INDICATIVE MOOD states a fact or opinion or asks a question: *The theater needs help.* The IMPERATIVE MOOD expresses a command or gives a direction. It omits the subject of the sentence, *you: Help the theater.*

The SUBJUNCTIVE MOOD is trickier and requires distinctive verb forms described below.

21a   Use the subjunctive verb forms appropriately, as in *I wish I were.*

The subjunctive mood expresses a suggestion, requirement, or desire, or it states a condition that is contrary to fact (that is, imaginary or hypothetical).

❖ Verbs such as *ask, insist, urge, require, recommend,* and *suggest* indicate request or requirement. They often precede a subordinate clause beginning with *that* and containing the substance of the request or requirement. For all subjects, the verb in the *that* clause is the plain form.

Rules require that every donation *be* mailed.
<small>plain form</small>

❖ Contrary-to-fact clauses state imaginary or hypothetical conditions and usually begin with *if* or *unless* or follow *wish.* For present contrary-to-fact clauses, use the verb's past-tense form (for *be,* use the past-tense form *were*).

If the theater *were* in better shape and *had* more money, its future would be assured.
<small>past   past</small>

I wish I *were* able to donate money.
<small>past</small>

For past contrary-to-fact clauses, use the verb's past perfect form (*had* + past participle).

The theater would be better funded if it *had been* better managed.
<small>past perfect</small>

NOTE Do not use the helping verb *would* or *could* in a contrary-to-fact clause beginning with *if.*

NOT   Many people would have helped if they *would have* known.
BUT   Many people would have helped if they *had* known.

See also page 118 for more on verb tenses in sentences like these.

21b   Keep mood consistent.

Shifts in mood within a sentence or among related sentences can be confusing. Such shifts occur most frequently in directions.

| INCONSISTENT | *Cook* the mixture slowly, and *you should stir* it until the sugar is dissolved. [Mood shifts from imperative to indicative.] |
| REVISED | *Cook* the mixture slowly, and *stir* it until the sugar is dissolved. [Consistently imperative.] |

22 Verb Voice

The VOICE of a verb tells whether the subject of the sentence performs the action (ACTIVE) or is acted upon (PASSIVE).

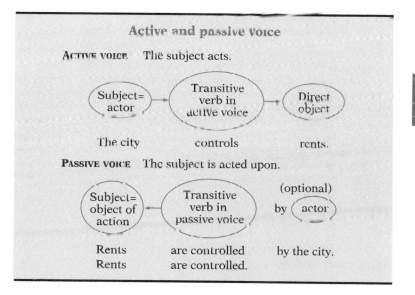

Active and passive voice

ACTIVE VOICE   The subject acts.

Subject= actor → Transitive verb in active voice → Direct object

The city   controls   rents.

PASSIVE VOICE   The subject is acted upon.

Subject= object of action ← Transitive verb in passive voice   (optional) by actor

Rents   are controlled   by the city.
Rents   are controlled.

The actor in a passive sentence may be named in a prepositional phrase (as in the first passive example above), or the actor may be omitted (as in the second passive example).

ESL A passive verb always consists of a form of *be* plus the past participle of the main verb: *rents are controlled, people were inspired.* Other helping verbs must also be used with the words *be, being,* and *been: rents have been controlled, people would have been inspired.* Only a transitive verb (one that takes an object) may be used in the passive voice. (See p. 110.)

22a Generally, prefer the active voice. Use the passive voice when the actor is unknown or unimportant.

The active voice is usually clearer, more concise, and more forthright than the passive voice.

WEAK PASSIVE	The *Internet is used* for research by many scholars, and its *expansion* to the general public *has been criticized* by some.
STRONG ACTIVE	Many *scholars use* the Internet for research, and *some have criticized* its expansion to the general public.

The passive voice is useful in two situations: when the actor is unknown and when the actor is unimportant or less important than the object of the action.

The Internet *was established* in 1969 by the US Department of Defense. The network *has* now *been extended* internationally to governments, universities, foundations, corporations, and private individuals. [In the first sentence the writer wishes to stress the Internet rather than the Department of Defense. In the second sentence the actor is unknown or too complicated to name.]

After the solution *had been cooled* to 10°C, the acid *was added.* [The person who cooled and added, perhaps the writer, is less important than the facts that the solution was cooled and acid was added. Passive sentences are common in scientific writing.]

pass 22b

22b Keep voice consistent.

Shifts in voice that involve shifts in subject are usually unnecessary and confusing.

INCONSISTENT	Internet *newsgroups cover* an enormous range of topics for discussion. *Forums* for meeting people with like interests *are provided* in these groups.
REVISED	Internet *newsgroups cover* an enormous range of topics for discussion *and provide* forums for meeting people with like interests.

A shift in voice is appropriate when it helps focus the reader's attention on a single subject, as in *The candidate campaigned vigorously and was nominated on the first ballot.*

23 Agreement of Subject and Verb

A subject and its verb should agree in number and person.

More *Japanese Americans live* in Hawaii and California than elsewhere.
subject   verb

Daniel Inouye was the first Japanese American in Congress.
subject   verb

Most problems of subject-verb agreement arise when endings are omitted from subjects or verbs or when the relation between sentence parts is uncertain.

23a The -s and -es endings work differently for nouns and verbs.

An -s or -es ending does opposite things to nouns and verbs: it usually makes a noun *plural*, but it always makes a present-tense verb *singular*. Thus if the subject noun is plural, it will end in -s or -es and the verb will not. If the subject is singular, it will not end in -s and the verb will.

SINGULAR	PLURAL
The boy plays.	The boys play.
The bird soars.	The birds soar.

The only exceptions to these rules involve the nouns that form irregular plurals, such as *child/children, woman/women*. The irregular plural still requires a plural verb: *The children play. The women read.*

ESL Most noncount nouns—those that do not form plurals—take singular verbs: *That information is helpful.* (See p. 125 on collective nouns.)

KEY TERMS

	NUMBER	
PERSON	SINGULAR	PLURAL
FIRST	I eat.	We eat.
SECOND	You eat.	You eat.
THIRD	He/she/it eats.	They eat.
	The bird eats.	Birds eat.

23b   Subject and verb should agree even when other words come between them.

The catalog of course requirements often *baffles* [not *baffle*] students.

The requirements stated in the catalog *are* [not *is*] unclear.

NOTE Phrases beginning with *as well as, together with, along with,* and *in addition to* do not change the number of the subject.

The president, as well as the deans, *has* [not *have*] agreed to revise the catalog.

23c   Subjects joined by *and* usually take plural verbs.

Frost and Roethke *were* contemporaries.

EXCEPTIONS When the parts of the subject form a single idea or refer to a single person or thing, they take a singular verb.

Avocado and bean sprouts *is* a California sandwich.

vb agr
23e

When a compound subject is preceded by the adjective *each* or *every,* the verb is usually singular.

Each man, woman, and child *has* a right to be heard.

23d   When parts of a subject are joined by *or* or *nor,* the verb agrees with the nearer part.

Either the painter or the carpenter *knows* the cost.

The cabinets or the bookcases *are* too costly.

When one part of the subject is singular and the other plural, avoid awkwardness by placing the plural part closer to the verb so that the verb is plural.

AWKWARD   Neither the owners nor the contractor *agrees.*

REVISED   Neither the contractor nor the owners *agree.*

23e   With *everyone* and other indefinite pronouns, use a singular or plural pronoun as appropriate.

Most indefinite pronouns are singular in meaning (they refer to a single unspecified person or thing), and they take singular verbs.

Something *smells.*   Neither *is* right.

The plural indefinite pronouns refer to more than one unspecified thing, and they take a plural verb:

Both *are* correct.   Several *were* invited.

The other indefinite pronouns take a singular or a plural verb depending on the meaning of the word they refer to:

All of the money *is* reserved for emergencies.

All of the funds *are* reserved for emergencies.

ESL See page 152 for the distinction between *few* ("not many") and *a few* ("some").

23f Collective nouns such as *team* take singular or plural verbs depending on meaning.

Use a singular verb with a collective noun when the group acts as a unit:

The group *agrees* that action is necessary.

But when the group's members act separately, use a plural verb:

The old group *have* gone their separate ways.

The collective noun *number* may be singular or plural. Preceded by *a*, it is plural; preceded by *the*, it is singular:

vb agr
23f

KEY TERMS

INDEFINITE PRONOUN A pronoun that does not refer to a specific person or thing:

			Singular or plural	Plural
Singular				
anybody	everyone	no one	all	both
anyone	everything	nothing	any	few
anything	much	one	more	many
each	neither	somebody	most	several
either	nobody	someone	some	
everybody	none	something		

COLLECTIVE NOUN A noun with singular form that names a group of individuals or things—for instance, *army, audience, committee, crowd, family, group, team.*

A number of people *are* in debt.

The number of people in debt *is* very large.

ESL Some noncount nouns (nouns that don't form plurals) are collective nouns because they name groups: for instance, *furniture, clothing, mail.* These noncount nouns usually take singular verbs: *Mail arrives daily.* But some of these nouns take plural verbs, including *clergy, military, people, police,* and any collective noun that comes from an adjective, such as *the poor, the rich, the young, the elderly.* If you mean one representative of the group, use a singular noun such as *police officer* or *poor person.*

23g Who, which, and that take verbs that agree with their antecedents.

When used as subjects, *who, which,* and *that* refer to another word in the sentence, called the ANTECEDENT. The verb agrees with the antecedent.

Mayor Garber ought to listen to the people who *work* for her.

Bardini is the only aide who *has* her ear.

Agreement problems often occur with relative pronouns when the sentence includes *one of the* or *the only one of the:*

Bardini is one of the aides who *work* unpaid. [Of the aides who work unpaid, Bardini is one.]

Bardini is the only one of the aides who *knows* the community. [Of the aides, only one, Bardini, knows the community.]

ESL In phrases like those above beginning with *one of the,* be sure the noun is plural: *Bardini is one of the aides* [not *aide*] *who work unpaid.*

23h News and other singular nouns ending in -s take singular verbs.

Singular nouns ending in *-s* include *athletics, economics, linguistics, mathematics, measles, mumps, news, physics, politics,* and *statistics,* as well as place names such as *Athens, Wales,* and *United States.*

vb agr
23h

After so long a wait, the news *has* to be good.

Statistics *is* required of psychology majors.

A few of these words also take plural verbs, but only when they describe individual items rather than whole bodies of activity or knowledge: *The statistics prove him wrong.*

Measurements and figures ending in -*s* may also be singular when the quantity they refer to is a unit.

Three years *is* a long time to wait.

Three-fourths of the library *consists* of reference books.

23i **The verb agrees with the subject even when the normal word order is inverted.**

Inverted subject-verb order occurs mainly in questions and in constructions beginning with *there* or *it* and a form of *be*.

Is voting a right or a privilege?

Are a right and a privilege the same thing?

There *are* differences between them.

23j *Is, are,* **and other linking verbs agree with their subjects, not subject complements.**

Make a linking verb agree with its subject, usually the first element in the sentence, not with the noun or pronoun serving as a subject complement.

The child's sole support *is* her court-appointed guardians.

Her court-appointed guardians *are* the child's sole support.

vb agr
23j

KEY TERMS

LINKING VERB   A verb that connects or equates the subject and subject complement: for example, *seem, become,* and forms of *be.* (See p. 98.)

SUBJECT COMPLEMENT   A word that describes or renames the subject: *They became chemists.* (See p. 98.)

23k Use singular verbs with titles and with words being described or defined.

Hakada Associates *is* a new firm.

Dream Days *remains* a favorite book.

Folks *is* a down-home word for people.

24 Other Complications with Verbs   ESL

If your native language is not English, you may have difficulty with combinations of verbs and other words: gerunds and infinitives (below) and prepositions and adverbs (p. 130).

vb
24a

24a Use a gerund or an infinitive after a verb as appropriate.   ESL

Gerunds and infinitives may follow certain verbs but not others. And sometimes the use of a gerund or infinitive with the same verb changes the meaning of the verb.

1. Either gerund or infinitive

A gerund or an infinitive may follow these verbs with no significant difference in meaning:

begin	continue	intend	prefer
can't bear	hate	like	pretend
can't stand	hesitate	love	start

The pump began *working*. The pump began *to work*.

KEY TERMS

GERUND   The *-ing* form of the verb used as a noun: *Smoking is unhealthful*. (See p. 100.)

INFINITIVE   The plain form of the verb usually preceded by *to: to smoke*. An infinitive may serve as an adjective, adverb, or noun. (See p. 100.)

2. Meaning change with gerund or infinitive

With four verbs, a gerund has quite a different meaning from an infinitive.

forget   remember   stop   try

The engineer stopped *eating*. [He no longer ate.]
The engineer stopped *to eat*. [He stopped in order to eat.]

3. Gerund, not infinitive

Do not use an infinitive after these verbs:

admit	discuss	mind	recollect
adore	dislike	miss	resent
appreciate	enjoy	postpone	resist
avoid	escape	practice	risk
consider	finish	put off	suggest
deny	imagine	quit	tolerate
detest	keep	recall	understand

FAULTY   He finished *to eat* lunch.
REVISED   He finished *eating* lunch.

4. Infinitive, not gerund

Do not use a gerund after these verbs:

agree	decide	mean	refuse
ask	expect	offer	say
assent	have	plan	wait
beg	hope	pretend	want
claim	manage	promise	wish

FAULTY   He decided *checking* the pump.
REVISED   He decided *to check* the pump.

vb
24a

5. Noun or pronoun + infinitive

Some verbs may be followed by an infinitive alone or by a noun or pronoun and an infinitive. The presence of a noun or pronoun changes the meaning.

ask	dare	need	wish
beg	expect	promise	would like
choose	help	want	

He expected *to watch*.
He expected *his workers to watch*.

Some verbs *must* be followed by a noun or pronoun before an infinitive:

admonish	encourage	oblige	require
advise	forbid	order	teach
allow	force	permit	tell
cause	hire	persuade	train
challenge	instruct	remind	urge
command	invite	request	warn
convince			

He instructed *his workers to watch.*

Do not use *to* before the infinitive when it follows one of these verbs and a noun or pronoun:

feel	make ("force")
have	see
hear	watch
let	

He let his workers *learn* by observation.

24b Use the appropriate particles with two-word verbs. ESL

vb
24b

Some verbs consist of two words: the verb itself and a PARTI-CLE, a preposition or adverb that affects the meaning of the verb. For example:

Look up the answer. [Research the answer.]
Look over the answer. [Examine the answer.]

The meanings of these two-word verbs are often quite different from the meanings of the individual words that make them up. (There are some three-word verbs, too, such as *put up with* and *run out of.*) A good ESL dictionary, such as one of those mentioned on page 73, will define two-word verbs for you. It will also tell you whether the verbs may be separated in a sentence, as explained opposite.

NOTE Many of these two-word verbs are more common in speech than in more formal academic or business writing. For formal writing, consider using *research* instead of *look up, examine* or *inspect* instead of *look over.*

KEY TERMS

PREPOSITION   A word such as *about, for,* or *to* that takes a noun or pronoun as its object: <u>at</u> *the house,* <u>in</u> *the woods.* (See p. 94 for a list of prepositions.)

ADVERB   A word that modifies a verb (*went <u>down</u>*), adjective (<u>*very*</u> *pretty*), another adverb (<u>*too*</u> *sweetly*), or a whole word group (<u>*Eventually*</u>, *the fire died*). (See p. 93.)

1. Inseparable two-word verbs

Verbs and particles that may not be separated by any other words include the following:

catch on	go over	play around	stay away
come across	grow up	run into	stay up
get along	keep on	run out of	take care of
give in	look into	speak up	turn up at

FAULTY   Children *grow* quickly *up.*
REVISED   Children *grow up* quickly.

2. Separable two-word verbs

Most two-word verbs that take direct objects may be separated by the object.

Parents *help out* their children.
Parents *help* their children *out.*

If the direct object is a pronoun, the pronoun *must* separate the verb from the particle.

FAULTY   Parents *help out* them.
REVISED   Parents *help* them *out.*

vb
24b

The separable two-word verbs include the following:

bring up	give back	make up	throw out
call off	hand in	point out	try on
call up	hand out	put away	try out
drop off	help out	put back	turn down
fill out	leave out	put off	turn on
fill up	look over	take out	turn up
give away	look up	take over	wrap up

PRONOUNS

PRONOUNS—words such as *she* and *who* that refer to nouns—merit special care because all their meaning comes from the other words they refer to. This section discusses pronoun forms (Chapter 25), matching pronouns and the words they refer to (26), and making sure pronouns refer to the right nouns (27).

25 Pronoun Case

CASE is the form of a noun or pronoun that shows the reader how it functions in a sentence.

- ❖ The SUBJECTIVE CASE indicates that the word is a subject or subject complement.
- ❖ The OBJECTIVE CASE indicates that the word is an object of a verb or preposition.
- ❖ The POSSESSIVE CASE indicates that the word owns or is the source of a noun in the sentence.

case
25a

Nouns change form only to show possession: *teacher's* (see pp. 189–91). The following pronouns change much more frequently.

SUBJECTIVE	OBJECTIVE	POSSESSIVE
I	me	my, mine
you	you	your, yours
he	him	his
she	her	her, hers
it	it	its
we	us	our, ours
you	you	your, yours
they	them	their, theirs
who	whom	whose
whoever	whomever	—

25a **Distinguish between compound subjects and compound objects: *she and I* vs. *her and me*.**

Compound subjects or objects—those consisting of two or more nouns or pronouns—have the same case forms as they would if one noun or pronoun stood alone.

compound
subject
She and Novick discussed the proposal.

compound
object
The proposal disappointed *her and him.*

If you are in doubt about the correct form, try the test below:

A test for case forms in compound constructions

❖ Identify a compound construction (one connected by *and, but, or, nor*).

(*He, Him*) and (*I, me*) won the prize.
The prize went to (*he, him*) and (*I, me*).

❖ Write a separate sentence for each part of the compound.

(*He, Him*) won the prize. (*I, Me*) won the prize.
The prize went to (*he, him*). The prize went to (*I, me*).

❖ Choose the pronouns that sound correct.

He won the prize. *I* won the prize. [Subjective.]
The prize went to *him.* The prize went to *me.* [Objective.]

❖ Put the separate sentences back together.

He and *I* won the prize.
The prize went to *him* and *me.*

case
25a

SUBJECT   Who or what a sentence is about: *Biologists often study animals. They often work in laboratories.* (See p. 96.)

SUBJECT COMPLEMENT   A word that renames or describes the sentence subject: *Biologists are scientists. The best biologists are she and Scoggins.* (See p. 98.)

OBJECT OF VERB   The receiver of the verb's action (DIRECT OBJECT): *Many biologists study animals. The animals teach them.* Or the person or thing the action is performed for (INDIRECT OBJECT): *Some biologists give animals homes. The animals give them pleasure.* (See pp. 97–98.)

OBJECT OF PREPOSITION   The word linked by *with, for,* or another preposition to the rest of the sentence: *Many biologists work in a laboratory. For them the lab often provides a second home.* (See p. 99.)

25b Use the subjective case for subject complements: *It was she.*

After a linking verb, a pronoun renaming the subject (a subject complement) should be in the subjective case.

subject
complement
The ones who care most are *she and Novick.*

subject
complement
It was *they* whom the mayor appointed.

If this construction sounds stilted to you, use the more natural order: <u>She and Novick</u> are the ones who care most. The mayor appointed <u>them</u>.

25c The use of *who* vs. *whom* depends on the pronoun's function in its clause.

1. Questions

At the beginning of a question use *who* for a subject and *whom* for an object.

subject ⟶   object ⟵⎯⎯⎯⎯
Who wrote the policy? *Whom* does it affect?

To find the correct case of *who* in a question, follow the steps below.

case
25c

❖ Pose the question.

(*Who, Whom*) makes that decision?
(*Who, Whom*) does one ask?

❖ Answer the question, using a personal pronoun. Choose the pronoun that sounds correct, and note its case.

(*She, Her*) makes that decision. *She* makes that decision. [Subjective.]

One asks (*she, her*). One asks *her.* [Objective.]

❖ Use the same case (*who* or *whom*) in the question.

Who makes that decision? [Subjective.]
Whom does one ask? [Objective.]

> ⎯ KEY TERM ⎯⎯⎯⎯⎯⎯⎯⎯⎯⎯⎯⎯⎯⎯⎯⎯⎯⎯⎯⎯⎯⎯⎯
>
> LINKING VERB   A verb, such as a form of *be,* that connects a subject and a word that renames or describes the subject (subject complement): *They <u>are</u> biologists.* (See p. 98.)

2. Subordinate clauses

In subordinate clauses use *who* and *whoever* for all subjects, *whom* and *whomever* for all objects.

subject ⟶
Give old clothes to *whoever* needs them.

object ⟵
I don't know *whom* the mayor appointed.

To determine which form to use, try the test below.

❖ Locate the subordinate clause.

Few people know (*who, whom*) they should ask.
They are unsure (*who, whom*) makes the decision.

❖ Rewrite the subordinate clause as a separate sentence, substituting a personal pronoun for *who, whom*. Choose the pronoun that sounds correct, and note its case.

They should ask (*she, her*). They should ask *her*. [Objective.]
(*She, her*) usually makes the decision. *She* usually makes the decision. [Subjective.]

❖ Use the same case (*who* or *whom*) in the subordinate clause.

Few people know *whom* they should ask. [Objective.]
They are unsure *who* makes the decision. [Subjective.]

NOTE Don't let expressions such as *I think* and *she says* mislead you into using *whom* rather than *who* for the subject of a clause.

subject ⟶
He is the one *who* I think is best qualified.

To choose between *who* and *whom* in such constructions, delete the interrupting phrase so that you can see the true relation between parts: *He is the one who is best qualified.*

25d Use the appropriate case in other constructions.

1. *We* or *us* with a noun

The choice of *we* or *us* before a noun depends on the use of the noun.

--- KEY TERM ---

SUBORDINATE CLAUSE   A word group that contains a subject and a verb and also begins with a subordinating word, such as *who, whom,* or *because.* (See p. 101.)

object of
preposition

Freezing weather is welcomed by *us* skaters.

subject

We skaters welcome freezing weather.

2. Pronoun in an appositive

In an appositive the case of a pronoun depends on the function of the word the appositive describes or identifies.

appositive
identifies object

The class elected two representatives, DeShawn and *me*.

appositive
identifies subject

Two representatives, DeShawn and *I*, were elected.

3. Pronoun after *than* or *as*

When a pronoun follows *than* or *as* in a comparison, the case of the pronoun indicates what words may have been omitted. A subjective pronoun must be the subject of the omitted verb:

subject

Some critics like Glass more than *he* [does].

An objective pronoun must be the object of the omitted verb:

object

Some critics like Glass more than [they like] *him*.

4. Subject and object of infinitive

Both the object *and* the subject of an infinitive are in the objective case.

subject of
infinitive

The school asked *him* to speak.

object of
infinitive

Students chose to invite *him*.

case
25d

┌─ KEY TERMS ───

APPOSITIVE   A noun or noun substitute that renames another noun immediately before it. (See p. 101.)

INFINITIVE   The plain form of the verb plus *to: to run*. (See p. 100.)

GERUND   The *-ing* form of a verb used as a noun: *Running is fun.* (See p. 100.)

5. Case before a gerund

Ordinarily, use the possessive form of a pronoun or noun immediately before a gerund.

The coach disapproved of *their* lifting weights.

The *coach's* disapproving was a surprise.

---

26 Agreement of Pronoun and Antecedent

The ANTECEDENT of a pronoun is the noun or other pronoun it refers to.

Homeowners fret over *their* tax bill.
  antecedent   pronoun

Its constant increases make the tax *bill* a dreaded document.
pronoun   antecedent

For clarity, a pronoun should agree with its antecedent in person, number, and gender.

ESL The gender of a pronoun should match its antecedent, not a noun the pronoun may modify: *President Clinton appointed his* [not *her*] *wife to redesign health care.* Also, nouns in English have only neuter gender unless they specifically refer to males or females. Thus nouns such as *book, table, sun,* and *earth* take the pronoun *it.*

pn agr
26

```
┌─ KEY TERMS ──────────────────────────────────────────┐
```

	NUMBER	
PERSON	SINGULAR	PLURAL
FIRST	*I*	*we*
SECOND	*you*	*you*
THIRD	*he, she, it,*	*they,*
	indefinite pronouns,	plural nouns
	singular nouns	
GENDER		
MASCULINE	*he,* nouns naming males	
FEMININE	*she,* nouns naming females	
NEUTER	*it,* all other nouns	

26a **Antecedents joined by *and* usually take plural pronouns.**

Mr. Bartos and I cannot settle *our* dispute.

The dean and my adviser have offered *their* help.

EXCEPTIONS When the compound antecedent refers to a single idea, person, or thing, then the pronoun is singular.

My friend and adviser offered *her* help.

When the compound antecedent follows *each* or *every*, the pronoun is singular.

Every girl and woman took *her* seat.

26b **When parts of an antecedent are joined by *or* or *nor*, the pronoun agrees with the nearer part.**

Tenants or owners must present *their* grievances.

Either the tenant or the owner will have *her* way.

When one subject is plural and the other singular, the sentence will be awkward unless you put the plural subject second.

AWKWARD   Neither the tenants nor the owner has yet made *her* case.

REVISED   Neither the owner nor the tenants have yet made *their* case.

26c **With *everyone* and other indefinite pronouns, use a singular or plural pronoun as appropriate.**

Most indefinite pronouns are singular in meaning. When they serve as antecedents to other pronouns, the other pronouns are singular:

Everyone on the women's teams now has *her* own locker.

Each of the men still has *his* own locker.

When an indefinite pronoun is plural in meaning, refer to it with a plural pronoun:

Few realize how *their* athletic facilities have changed.

When an indefinite pronoun may be singular or plural, figure out what it refers to and use a corresponding pronoun:

Few women athletes had changing spaces, so most had to change in *their* rooms.

Most of the changing space was dismal, *its* color a drab olive green.

In speech we commonly use a plural pronoun when the singular indefinite pronoun is intended to mean "many" or "all" rather than "one." In writing, however, you should revise sentences to avoid the misuse.

FAULTY   Everyone deserves *their* privacy.

REVISED   *All of the athletes* deserve *their* privacy.

The generic *he*

The meaning of an indefinite pronoun often includes both masculine and feminine genders, not one or the other. The same is true of other indefinite words such as *child, adult, individual,* and *person.* In such cases tradition has called for *he* (*him, his*) to refer to the antecedent. But this so-called GENERIC *HE* (or generalized *he*) appears to exclude females. To avoid it, try one of the techniques below:

pn agr
26c

GENERIC *HE*   None of the students had the credits *he* needed.

❖ Substitute *he or she.*

REVISED   None of the students had the credits *he or she* needed.

To avoid awkwardness, don't use *he or she* more than once in several sentences.

┌ **KEY TERM** ─────────────────────────────────

INDEFINITE PRONOUN   A pronoun that does not refer to a specific person or thing:

Singular			*Singular or plural*	*Plural*
anybody	everyone	no one	all	both
anyone	everything	nothing	any	few
anything	much	one	more	many
each	neither	somebody	most	several
either	nobody	someone	some	
everybody	none	something		

❖ Recast the sentence using a plural antecedent and pronoun.

REVISED   *All the students* in the class lacked the credits *they* needed.

❖ Rewrite the sentence to avoid the pronoun.

REVISED   None of the students had the *needed credits.*

For more on avoiding sexist and other biased language, see pages 70–72.

26d Collective nouns such as *team* take singular or plural pronouns depending on meaning.

Use a singular pronoun with a collective noun when referring to the group as a unit.

The committee voted to disband *itself.*

When referring to the individual members of the group, use a plural pronoun.

The old group have gone *their* separate ways.

ESL Collective nouns that are noncount nouns (they don't form plurals) usually take singular pronouns: *The mail sits in its own basket.* A few noncount nouns take plural pronouns, including *clergy, military, people, police, the rich,* and *the poor: The police support their unions.*

27 Reference of Pronoun to Antecedent

A pronoun should refer clearly to its ANTECEDENT, the noun it substitutes for. Otherwise, readers will have difficulty grasping the pronoun's meaning.

ESL A pronoun needs a clear antecedent nearby, but don't use both a pronoun and its antecedent as the subject of the same clause: *Jim* [not *Jim he*] *told Mark to go alone.* (See also p. 167.)

> ┌─ KEY TERM ───
> COLLECTIVE NOUN   A noun with singular form that names a group of individuals or things—for instance, *army, audience, committee, crowd, family, group, team.*

27a Make a pronoun refer clearly to one antecedent.

When either of two nouns can be a pronoun's antecedent, the reference will not be clear.

CONFUSING   Emily Dickinson is sometimes compared with Jane Austen, but *she* was quite different.

Revise such a sentence in one of two ways:

❖ Replace the pronoun with the appropriate noun.

CLEAR   Emily Dickinson is sometimes compared with Jane Austen, but *Dickinson* [or *Austen*] was quite different.

❖ Avoid repetition by rewriting the sentence. If you use the pronoun, make sure it has only one possible antecedent.

CLEAR   Despite occasional comparison, Emily Dickinson and Jane Austen were quite different.

CLEAR   Though sometimes compared with *her*, Emily Dickinson was quite different from Jane Austen.

27b Place a pronoun close enough to its antecedent to ensure clarity.

A clause beginning *who, which,* or *that* should generally fall immediately after the word it refers to.

CONFUSING   Jody found a dress in the attic *that* her aunt had worn.

CLEAR   In the attic Jody found a dress *that* her aunt had worn.

27c Make a pronoun refer to a specific antecedent, not an implied one.

A pronoun should refer to a specific noun or other pronoun. A reader can only guess at the meaning of a pronoun when its antecedent is implied by the context, not stated outright.

1. Vague *this, that, which,* or *it*

This, that, which, or *it* should refer to a specific noun, not to a whole word group expressing an idea or situation.

CONFUSING   The faculty agreed on changing the requirements, but *it* took time.

ref
27c

CLEAR   The faculty agreed on changing the requirements, but *the agreement* took time.

CLEAR   The faculty agreed on changing the requirements, but *the change* took time.

CONFUSING   The British knew little of the American countryside, and they had no experience with the colonists' guerrilla tactics. *This* gave the colonists an advantage.

CLEAR   The British knew little of the American countryside, and they had no experience with the colonists' guerrilla tactics. This *ignorance and inexperience* gave the colonists an advantage.

2. Implied nouns

A noun may be implied in some other word or phrase, such as an adjective (*happiness* implied in *happy*), a verb (*driver* implied in *drive*), or a possessive (*mother* implied in *mother's*). But a pronoun cannot refer clearly to an implied noun, only to a specific, stated one.

ref
27c

CONFUSING   Cohen's report brought *her* a lawsuit.

CLEAR   Cohen was sued over *her* report.

CONFUSING   Her reports on psychological development are generally unnoticed outside *it.*

CLEAR   Her reports on psychological development are generally unnoticed outside *the field.*

3. Indefinite *it, they,* or *you*

It, they, and *you* should have definite antecedents—nouns for *it* and *they,* an actual reader being addressed for *you.* Rewrite the sentence if the antecedent is missing.

CONFUSING   In Chapter 4 of this book *it* describes the early flights of the Wright brothers.

CLEAR   *Chapter 4* of this book describes the early flights of the Wright brothers.

CONFUSING   In the average television drama *they* present a false picture of life.

CLEAR   The average television *drama* presents a false picture of life.

In all but very formal writing, *you* is acceptable when the meaning is clearly "you, the reader." But the context must be appropriate for such a meaning.

INAPPROPRIATE   In the fourteenth century *you* had to struggle simply to survive.

REVISED   In the fourteenth century *one* [or *a person*] had to struggle simply to survive.

27d Keep pronouns consistent.

Within a sentence or a group of related sentences, pronouns should be consistent. Partly, consistency comes from making pronouns and their antecedents agree (see Chapter 26). In addition, the pronouns within a passage should match each other.

INCONSISTENT   *One* finds when reading that *your* concentration improves with practice, so that *I* now comprehend more in less time.

REVISED   *I* find when reading that *my* concentration improves with practice, so that I now comprehend more in less time.

ref
27d

MODIFIERS describe or limit other words in a sentence. They are adjectives, adverbs, or word groups serving as adjectives or adverbs. This section identifies and solves problems in the forms of modifiers (Chapter 28) and in their relation to the rest of the sentence (29).

28 Adjectives and Adverbs

ADJECTIVES modify nouns (*happy child*) and pronouns (*special someone*). ADVERBS modify verbs (*almost see*), adjectives (*very happy*), other adverbs (*not very*), and whole word groups (*Otherwise, the room was empty*). The only way to tell whether a modifier should be an adjective or an adverb is to determine its function in the sentence.

ESL In English an adjective does not change along with the noun it modifies to show plural number: *white* [not *whites*] shoes, *square* [not *squares*] spaces. Only nouns form plurals.

28a Use adjectives only to modify nouns and pronouns.

Using adjectives instead of adverbs to modify verbs, adverbs, or other adjectives is nonstandard.

NONSTANDARD Educating children *good* is everyone's focus.

STANDARD Educating children *well* is everyone's focus.

NONSTANDARD Some children suffer *bad*.

STANDARD Some children suffer *badly*.

ESL To negate a verb or an adjective, use the adverb *not*.

They are *not* learning. They are *not* stupid.

To negate a noun, use the adjective *no*.

No child should fail to read.

144

28b Use an adjective after a linking verb to modify the subject. Use an adverb to modify a verb.

Some verbs may or may not be linking verbs, depending on their meaning in the sentence. When the word after the verb modifies the subject, the verb is linking and the word should be an adjective: *He looked happy.* When the word modifies the verb, however, it should be an adverb: *He looked carefully.*

Two word pairs are especially tricky. One is *bad* and *badly:*

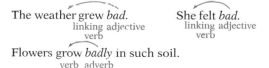

The weather grew *bad.*
    linking adjective
      verb

She felt *bad.*
    linking adjective
      verb

Flowers grow *badly* in such soil.
    verb adverb

The other is *good* and *well. Good* serves only as an adjective. *Well* may serve as an adverb with a host of meanings or as an adjective meaning only "fit" or "healthy,"

Decker trained *well.*
    verb   adverb

She felt *well.*
    linking adjective
      verb

Her health was *good.*
    linking adjective
      verb

28c Use the comparative and superlative forms of adjectives and adverbs appropriately.

ad
28c

Adjectives and adverbs can show degrees of quality or amount with the endings *-er* and *-est* or with the words *more* and *most* or *less* and *least.* Most modifiers have three forms:

	ADJECTIVES	ADVERBS
POSITIVE The basic form listed in the dictionary	red awful	soon quickly
COMPARATIVE A greater or lesser degree of the quality named	redder more/less awful	sooner more/less quickly
SUPERLATIVE The greatest or least degree of the quality named	reddest most/least awful	soonest most/least quickly

---

KEY TERM

LINKING VERB A verb that connects a subject and a word that describes the subject: *They are golfers.* Linking verbs are forms of *be,* the verbs of our five senses (*look, sound, smell, feel, taste*), and *appear, seem, become, grow, turn, prove, remain, stay.* (See p. 98.)

If sound alone does not tell you whether to use *-er/-est* or *more/most*, consult a dictionary. If the endings can be used, the dictionary will list them. Otherwise, use *more* or *most*.

1. Irregular adjectives and adverbs

The irregular modifiers change the spelling of their positive form to show comparative and superlative degrees.

POSITIVE	COMPARATIVE	SUPERLATIVE
Adjectives		
good	better	best
bad	worse	worst
little	littler, less	littlest, least
many		
some	more	most
much		
Adverbs		
well	better	best
badly	worse	worst

2. Double comparisons

A double comparative or double superlative combines the *-er* or *-est* ending with the word *more* or *most*. It is redundant.

Chang was the *wisest* [not *most wisest*] person in town.
He was *smarter* [not *more smarter*] than anyone else.

3. Logical comparisons

Absolute modifiers

Some adjectives and adverbs cannot logically be compared—for instance, *perfect, unique, dead, impossible, infinite*. These absolute words can be preceded by adverbs like *nearly* or *almost* that mean "approaching," but they cannot logically be modified by *more* or *most* (as in *most perfect*).

NOT   He was the *most unique* teacher we had.
BUT   He was a *unique* teacher.

Completeness

To be logical, a comparison must also be complete in the following ways:

❖ The comparison must state a relation fully enough for clarity.

UNCLEAR	Carmakers worry about their industry more than environmentalists.
CLEAR	Carmakers worry about their industry more than environmentalists *do*.
CLEAR	Carmakers worry about their industry more than *they worry about* environmentalists.

❖ The items being compared should in fact be comparable.

| ILLOGICAL | The cost of an electric car is greater than a gasoline-powered car. [Illogically compares a cost and a car.] |
| REVISED | The cost of an electric car is greater than *the cost of* [or *that of*] a gasoline-powered car. |

See also page 61 on parallelism with comparisons.

Any versus *any other*

Use *any other* when comparing something with others in the same group. Use *any* when comparing something with others in a different group.

| ILLOGICAL | Los Angeles is larger than *any* city in California. [Since Los Angeles is itself a city in California, the sentence seems to say that Los Angeles is larger than itself.] |
| REVISED | Los Angeles is larger than *any other* city in California. |

| ILLOGICAL | Los Angeles is larger than *any other* city in Canada. [The cities in Canada constitute a group to which Los Angeles does not belong.] |
| REVISED | Los Angeles is larger than *any* city in Canada. |

28d Avoid double negatives.

A DOUBLE NEGATIVE is a nonstandard construction in which two negative words such as *no, none, neither, barely, hardly,* or *scarcely* cancel each other out. For instance, *Jenny did not feel nothing* asserts that Jenny felt other than nothing, or something. For the opposite meaning, one of the negatives must be eliminated (*She felt nothing*) or one of them must be changed to a positive (*She did not feel anything*).

| FAULTY | The IRS *cannot hardly* audit all tax returns. *None* of its audits *never* touch many cheaters. |
| REVISED | The IRS *cannot* audit all tax returns. Its audits *never* touch many cheaters. |

28e Distinguish between present and past participles as adjectives. ESL

Both present participles and past participles may serve as adjectives: *a burning building, a burned building.* As in the examples, the two participles usually differ in the time they indicate.

But some present and past participles—those derived from verbs expressing feeling—can have altogether different meanings. The present participle refers to something that causes the feeling: *That was a frightening storm.* The past participle refers to something that experiences the feeling: *They quieted the frightened horses.*

The following participles are among those likely to be confused:

amazing/amazed
amusing/amused
annoying/annoyed
astonishing/astonished
boring/bored
confusing/confused
depressing/depressed
embarrassing/embarrassed
exciting/excited
exhausting/exhausted

fascinating/fascinated
frightening/frightened
frustrating/frustrated
interesting/interested
pleasing/pleased
satisfying/satisfied
shocking/shocked
surprising/surprised
tiring/tired
worrying/worried

det
28f

28f Use *a, an, the,* and other determiners appropriately. ESL

DETERMINERS are special kinds of adjectives that mark nouns because they always precede nouns. Some common determiners are *a, an,* and *the* (called ARTICLES) and *my, their, whose, this, these, those, one, some,* and *any.*

Native speakers of English can rely on their intuition when using determiners, but nonnative speakers often have difficulty with them because many other languages use them quite differently or not at all. In English the use of determiners depends on the context they appear in and the kind of nouns they precede:

KEY TERMS

PRESENT PARTICIPLE   The *-ing* form of a verb: *flying, writing.* (See p. 92.)

PAST PARTICIPLE   The *-d* or *-ed* form of a regular verb: *slipped, walked.* Most irregular verbs have distinctive past participles, such as *eaten* or *swum.* (See p. 92.)

❖ A PROPER NOUN names a particular person, place, or thing and begins with a capital letter: *February, Joe Allen, Red River.* Most proper nouns are not preceded by determiners.

❖ A COUNT NOUN names something that is countable in English and can form a plural: *girl/girls, apple/apples, child/children.* A singular count noun is always preceded by a determiner; a plural count noun sometimes is.

❖ A NONCOUNT NOUN names something not usually considered countable in English, and so it does not form a plural. A noncount noun is sometimes preceded by a determiner. Here is a sample of noncount nouns, sorted into groups by meaning:

Abstractions: confidence, democracy, education, equality, evidence, health, information, intelligence, knowledge, luxury, peace, pollution, research, success, supervision, truth, wealth, work

Food and drink: bread, candy, cereal, flour, meat, milk, salt, water, wine

Emotions: anger, courage, happiness, hate, joy, love, respect, satisfaction

Natural events and elements: air, blood, dirt, gasoline, gold, hair, heat, ice, oil, oxygen, rain, silver, smoke, weather, wood

Groups: clergy, clothing, equipment, furniture, garbage, jewelry, junk, legislation, machinery, mail, military, money, police, vocabulary

Fields of study: accounting, architecture, biology, business, chemistry, engineering, literature, psychology, science

det

28f

An ESL dictionary will tell you whether a noun is a count noun, a noncount noun, or both. (See p. 73 for recommended dictionaries.)

NOTE Many nouns are sometimes count nouns and sometimes noncount nouns.

The library has *a room* for readers. [*Room* is a count noun meaning "walled area."]

The library has *room* for reading. [*Room* is a noncount noun meaning "space."]

1. *A, an,* and *the*

With singular count nouns

A or *an* precedes a singular count noun when the reader does not already know its identity, usually because you have not mentioned it before.

A scientist in our chemistry department developed *a* process to strengthen metals. [*Scientist* and *process* are being introduced for the first time.]

The precedes a singular count noun that has a specific identity for the reader, usually because (1) you have mentioned it before, (2) you identify it immediately before or after you state it, (3) it is unique (the only one in existence), or (4) it refers to an institution or facility that is shared by a community.

A scientist in our chemistry department developed a process to strengthen metals. *The* scientist patented *the* process. [*Scientist* and *process* were identified in the preceding sentence.]

The most productive laboratory is *the* research center in the chemistry department. [*Most productive* identifies *laboratory,* and *in the chemistry department* identifies *research center.*]

The sun rises in *the* east. [*Sun* and *east* are unique.]

Many men and women aspire to *the* Presidency. [*Presidency* is a shared institution.]

The fax machine has changed business communication. [*Fax machine* is a shared facility.]

det
28f

The is not used before a singular noun that names a general category.

Wordsworth's poetry shows his love of *nature* [not *the nature*].

General Sherman said that *war* is hell. [*War* names a general category.]

The war in Croatia left many dead. [*War* names a specific war.]

With plural count nouns

A or *an* never precedes a plural noun. *The* does not precede a plural noun that names a general category. *The* does precede a plural noun that names specific representatives of a category.

Men and *women* are different. [*Men* and *women* name general categories.]

The women formed a team. [*Women* refers to specific people.]

With noncount nouns

A or *an* never precedes a noncount noun. *The* does precede a noncount noun that names specific representatives of a general category.

Vegetation suffers from drought. [*Vegetation* names a general category.]

The vegetation in the park withered or died. [*Vegetation* refers to specific plants.]

With proper nouns

A or *an* never precedes a proper noun. *The* generally does not precede proper nouns.

> *Garcia* lives in *Boulder.*

There are exceptions, however. For instance, we generally use *the* before plural proper nouns (*the Murphys, the Boston Celtics*) and before the names of groups and organizations (*the Department of Justice, the Sierra Club*), ships (*the Lusitania*), oceans (*the Pacific*), mountain ranges (*the Alps*), regions (*the Middle East*), rivers (*the Mississippi*), and some countries (*the United States, the Netherlands*).

2. Other determiners

The uses of English determiners besides articles also depend on context and kind of noun. The following determiners may be used as indicated with singular count nouns, plural count nouns, or noncount nouns.

With any kind of noun (singular count, plural count, noncount)

my, our, your, his, her, its, their, possessive nouns (*boy's, boys'*)
whose, which(ever), what(ever)
some, any, the other
no

> *Their* account is overdrawn. [Singular count.]
> *Their* funds are low. [Plural count.]
> *Their* money is running out. [Noncount.]

Only with singular nouns (count and noncount)

this, that

> *This* account has some money. [Count.]
> *This* information may help. [Noncount.]

Only with noncount nouns and plural count nouns

most, enough, other, such, all, all of the, a lot of

> *Most* funds are committed. [Plural count.]
> *Most* money is needed elsewhere. [Noncount.]

Only with singular count nouns

one, every, each, either, neither, another

> *One* car must be sold. [Singular count.]

**det
28f**

Only with plural count nouns

these, those
both, many, few, a few, fewer, fewest, several
two, three, and so forth

Two cars are unnecessary. [Plural count.]

NOTE *Few* means "not many" or "not enough." *A few* means "some" or "a small but sufficient quantity."

Few committee members came to the meeting.
A few members can keep the committee going.

Do not use *much* with a plural count noun.

Many [not *much*] members want to help.

Only with noncount nouns

much, more, little, a little, less, least, a large amount of

Less luxury is in order. [Noncount.]

NOTE *Little* means "not many" or "not enough." *A little* means "some" or "a small but sufficient quantity."

Little time remains before the conference.
The members need *a little* help from their colleagues.

Do not use *many* with a noncount noun.

Much [not *many*] work remains.

---

mm
29a

---

29 Misplaced and Dangling Modifiers

The arrangement of words in a sentence is an important clue to their relationships. Modifiers will be unclear if readers can't connect them to the words they modify.

29a Reposition misplaced modifiers.

A MISPLACED MODIFIER falls in the wrong place in a sentence. It may be awkward, confusing, or even unintentionally funny.

1. Clear placement

Readers tend to link a modifier to the nearest word it could modify. Any other placement can link the modifier to the wrong word.

| CONFUSING | He served steak to the men *on paper plates.* |
| CLEAR | He served the men steak *on paper plates.* |

| CONFUSING | According to the police, many dogs are killed by automobiles and trucks *roaming unleashed.* |
| CLEAR | According to the police, many dogs *roaming unleashed* are killed by automobiles and trucks. |

2. *Only* and other limiting modifiers

LIMITING MODIFIERS include *almost, even, exactly, hardly, just, merely, nearly, only, scarcely,* and *simply.* For clarity place such a modifier immediately before the word or word group you intend it to limit.

UNCLEAR	The archaeologist *only* found the skull on her last dig.
CLEAR	The archaeologist found *only* the skull on her last dig.
CLEAR	The archaeologist found the skull *only* on her last dig.

3. Adverbs with grammatical units

Adverbs can often move around in sentences, but some will be awkward if they interrupt certain grammatical units:

❖ A single-word adverb can interrupt subject and verb: *Bo gladly accepted.* But a longer adverb stops the flow of the sentence:

| | subject   adverb   verb |
| AWKWARD | *Kuwait,* after the Gulf War ended in 1991, *began* returning to normal. |

| | adverb   subject   verb |
| REVISED | After the Gulf War ended in 1991, *Kuwait began* returning to normal. |

❖ Any adverb is awkward between a verb and its direct object:

KEY TERMS

ADVERB   A word that describes a verb, adjective, other adverb, or whole word group, specifying how, when, where, or to what extent: *quickly see, solid like a boulder.*

DIRECT OBJECT   The receiver of the verb's action: *The car hit a tree.* (See p. 97.)

mm
29a

| verb | adverb | object |

AWKWARD   The war *had damaged* badly *many* of Kuwait's oilfields.

| verb | object |

REVISED   The war *had* badly *damaged many* of Kuwait's oilfields.
adverb

❖ A SPLIT INFINITIVE—an adverb placed between *to* and the verb—
annoys many readers:

infinitive

AWKWARD   The weather service expected temperatures *to* not *rise*.

infinitive

REVISED   The weather service expected temperatures not *to rise*.

A split infinitive may sometimes be natural and preferable,
though it may still bother some readers.

infinitive

Several US industries expect *to* more than *triple* their use of robots.

Here the split infinitive is more economical than the alternatives, such as *Several US industries expect to increase their use of
robots by more than three times.*

❖ A single-word adverb may interrupt a verb phrase after the first
helping verb: *Scientists have lately been using spacecraft to study
the sun.* But a longer adverb is usually awkward inside a verb
phrase:

helping
verb ———————— adverb ————————

AWKWARD   The spacecraft *Ulysses will* by traveling near the sun
main verb
report on the sun's energy fields.

verb
phrase
———— adverb ————

REVISED   By traveling near the sun, the spacecraft *Ulysses will report* on the sun's energy fields.

ESL In a question, place a one-word adverb after the first helping verb and subject:

helping   rest of
verb   subject   adverb   verb phrase
Will spacecraft ever *be able to leave* the solar system?

┌─ KEY TERMS ───

INFINITIVE A verb form consisting of *to* plus the verb's plain (or
dictionary) form: *to produce, to enjoy.* (See p. 100.)

VERB PHRASE A verb consisting of a helping verb and a main verb
that carries the principal meaning: *will have begun, can see.* (See p.
93.)
└──

mm
29a

4. Other adverb positions ESL

A few adverbs are subject to special conventions for placement:

❖ Adverbs of frequency include *always, never, often, rarely, seldom, sometimes,* and *usually*. They generally appear at the beginning of a sentence, before a one-word verb, or after the helping verb in a verb phrase:

helping   main
verb   adverb   verb

Robots *have* sometimes *put* humans out of work.

adverb   verb phrase

Sometimes robots *have put* humans out of work.

Adverbs of frequency always follow the verb *be*.

verb adverb

Robots *are* often helpful to workers.

❖ Adverbs of degree include *absolutely, almost, certainly, completely, definitely, especially, extremely, hardly,* and *only*. They fall just before the word modified (an adjective, another adverb, sometimes a verb):

adverb   adjective

Robots have been especially *useful* in making cars.

▪ Adverbs of manner include *badly, beautifully, openly, sweetly, tightly, well,* and others that describe how something is done. They usually fall after the verb:

verb   adverb

Robots *work* smoothly on assembly lines.

❖ The position of the adverb *not* depends on what it modifies. When it modifies a verb, place it after the helping verb (or the first helping verb if more than one):

helping   main
verb   verb

Robots *do* not *think*.

When *not* modifies another adverb or an adjective, place it before the other modifier:

adjective

Robots are not *sleek* machines.

mm
29a

5. Order of adjectives ESL

English follows distinctive rules for arranging two or three adjectives before a noun. (A string of more than three adjectives before a noun is rare.) The adjectives follow this order:

DETERMINER	OPINION	SIZE OR SHAPE	AGE	COLOR	ORIGIN	MATERIAL	NOUN USED AS ADJECTIVE	NOUN
many			new				state	laws
	lovely			green	Thai			birds
a		square				wooden		table
all			recent				business	reports
the				blue		litmus		paper

See page 180 on punctuating adjectives before a noun.

29b Connect dangling modifiers to their sentences.

A DANGLING MODIFIER does not sensibly modify anything in its sentence.

DANGLING *Passing the building,* the vandalism became visible. [The modifying phrase seems to describe *vandalism,* but vandalism does not pass buildings. Who was passing the building? Who saw the vandalism?]

Dangling modifiers usually introduce sentences, contain a verb form, and imply but do not name a subject: in the example above, the implied subject is the someone or something passing the building. Readers assume that this implied subject is the same as the subject of the sentence (*vandalism* in the example). When it is not, the modifier "dangles" unconnected to the rest of the sentence. Here is another example:

DANGLING Although intact, graffiti covered every inch of the walls and windows. [The walls and windows, not the graffiti, were intact.]

To revise a dangling modifier, you have to recast the sentence it appears in. (Revising just by moving the modifier will leave it dangling: *The vandalism became visible passing the building.*) Choose a revision method depending on what you want to emphasize in the sentence:

KEY TERM

ADJECTIVE A word that describes a noun or pronoun, specifying which one, what quality, or how many: <u>good</u> one, <u>three</u> cars. (See p. 144.)

---

dm
29b

Identifying and revising dangling modifiers

❖ If the modifier lacks a subject of its own (e.g., *when in diapers*), identify what it describes.
❖ Verify that what the modifier describes is in fact the subject of the main clause. If it is not, the modifier is probably dangling.

         ┌── modifier ──┐   subject
DANGLING   *When in diapers,* my mother remarried.

❖ Revise a dangling modifier (*a*) by recasting it with a subject of its own or (*b*) by changing the subject of the main clause.

REVISION A   When *I was* in diapers, my mother remarried.
REVISION B   When in diapers, *I attended my mother's second wedding.*

❖ Rewrite the dangling modifier as a complete clause with its own stated subject and verb. Readers can accept that the new subject and the sentence subject are different.

DANGLING   *Passing the building,* the vandalism became visible.

REVISED   *As we passed* the building, the vandalism became visible.

❖ Change the subject of the sentence to a word the modifier properly describes.

DANGLING   *Trying to understand the causes,* vandalism has been extensively studied.

REVISED   Trying to understand the causes, *researchers have* extensively *studied* vandalism.

dm
29b

A word group punctuated as a sentence will confuse or annoy readers if it lacks needed parts, has too many parts, or has parts that don't fit together.

30 Sentence Fragments

A SENTENCE FRAGMENT is part of a sentence that is set off as if it were a whole sentence by an initial capital letter and a final period or other end punctuation. Although writers occasionally use fragments deliberately and effectively (see 30c), readers perceive most fragments as serious errors.

Complete sentence versus sentence fragment

A COMPLETE SENTENCE OR MAIN CLAUSE
1. contains a subject and a verb (*The wind blows*)
2. and is not a subordinate clause (beginning with a word such as *because* or *who*).

A SENTENCE FRAGMENT
1. lacks a verb (*The wind blowing*),
2. or lacks a subject (*And blows*),
3. or is a subordinate clause not attached to a complete sentence (*Because the wind blows*).

ESL Some languages other than English allow the omission of the subject or verb from a sentence. Except in commands (*Close the door*), English always requires you to state the subject and verb.

frag
30a

30a Test your sentences for completeness.

A word group punctuated as a sentence should pass *all three* of the following tests. If it does not, it is a fragment and needs to be revised.

Test 1: Find the verb.

Look for a verb in the group of words.

FRAGMENT   Thousands of new sites on the World Wide Web.
[Compare a complete sentence: *Thousands of new
sites have appeared on the World Wide Web.*]

Any verb form you find must be a FINITE VERB, one that changes
form as indicated below. A verbal does not change; it cannot serve
as a sentence verb without the aid of a helping verb.

	FINITE VERBS IN COMPLETE SENTENCES	VERBALS IN SENTENCE FRAGMENTS
SINGULAR	The network *grows.*	The network *growing.*
PLURAL	Networks *grow.*	Networks *growing.*
PRESENT	The network *grows.*	
PAST	The network *grew.*	The network *growing.*
FUTURE	The network *will grow.*	

ESL   Some languages allow forms of *be* to be omitted as helping
verbs or linking verbs. But English requires stating forms of *be.*

FRAGMENTS   The network growing It already larger than its devel-
opers anticipated. [Compare complete sentences: *The
network is growing. It is already larger than its develop-
ers anticipated.*]

Test 2: Find the subject.

The subject of the sentence will usually come before the verb. If
there is no subject, the word group is probably a fragment.

FRAGMENT   And has enormous popular appeal. [Compare a complete sentence: *And the Web has enormous popular
appeal.*]

frag
30a

KEY TERMS

VERB   The part of a sentence that asserts something about the subject: *Ducks swim.* Also called PREDICATE. (See p. 96.)

VERBAL   A verb form that can serve as a noun, a modifier, or a part
of a sentence verb, but not alone as the only verb of a sentence:
drawing, to draw, drawn. (See p. 99.)

HELPING VERB   A verb such as *is, were, have, might,* and *could* that
combines with various verb forms to indicate time and other kinds
of meaning: for instance, *were drawing, might draw.* (See p. 93.)

SUBJECT   The part of a sentence that names who or what performs
the action or makes the assertion of the verb: *Ducks swim.* (See
p. 96.)

Test 3: Make sure the clause is not subordinate.

A subordinate clause usually begins with a subordinating word, such as one of the following:

SUBORDINATING CONJUNCTIONS			RELATIVE PRONOUNS	
after	once	until	that	who/whom
although	since	when	which	whoever/whomever
as	than	where		
because	that	whereas		
if	unless	while		

Subordinate clauses serve as parts of sentences (nouns or modifiers), not as whole sentences.

> FRAGMENT When the government devised the Internet. [Compare a complete sentence: *The government devised the Internet.* Or: *When the government devised the Internet, no expansive computer network existed.*]

> FRAGMENT The reason that the government devised the Internet. [This fragment is a noun (*reason*) plus its modifier (*that . . . Internet*). Compare a complete sentence: *The reason that the government devised the Internet <u>was to provide secure links among departments and defense contractors</u>.*)

frag

30b

NOTE Questions beginning with *how, what, when, where, which, who, whom, whose,* and *why* are not sentence fragments: *Who was responsible? When did it happen?*

30b **Revise sentence fragments.**

Correct sentence fragments in one of two ways depending on the importance of the information in the fragment and thus how much you want to stress it.

❖ Rewrite the fragment as a complete sentence. The information in the fragment will then have the same importance as that in other complete sentences.

> FRAGMENT A recent addition to the Internet is the World Wide Web. *Which allows users to move easily between sites.*

KEY TERM

SUBORDINATE CLAUSE A word group that contains a subject and a verb, begins with a subordinating word such as *because* or *who,* and is not a question: *Ducks can swim <u>when they are young</u>.* A subordinate clause may serve as a modifier or as a noun. (See p. 101.)

REVISED	A recent addition to the Internet is the World Wide Web. *It* allows users to move easily between sites.
FRAGMENT	The Internet and now the Web are a boon to researchers. *A vast and accessible library.*
REVISED	The Internet and now the Web are a boon to researchers. *They form* a vast and accessible library.

❖ Combine the fragment with the appropriate main clause. The information in the fragment will then be subordinated to that in the main clause.

FRAGMENT	The Web is easy to use. *Loaded with links and graphics.*
REVISED	The Web, loaded with links and graphics, is easy to use.
FRAGMENT	With the links, users can move to other Web sites. *That they want to consult.*
REVISED	With the links, users can move to other Web sites that they want to consult.

30c Be aware of the acceptable uses of incomplete sentences.

A few word groups lacking the usual subject-predicate combination are incomplete sentences, but they are not fragments because they conform to the expectations of most readers. They include exclamations (*Oh no!*); questions and answers (*Where next? To Kansas.*); and commands (*Move along. Shut the window.*).

Experienced writers sometimes use sentence fragments when they want to achieve a special effect. Such fragments appear more in informal than in formal writing. Unless you are experienced and thoroughly secure in your own writing, you should avoid all fragments and concentrate on writing clear, well-formed sentences.

cs / fs
31

---

31 Comma Splices and Fused Sentences

When a sentence contains two main clauses in a row, readers need a signal that one main clause is ending and another beginning. The usual signal is a comma with coordinating conjunction (*The ship was huge, and its mast stood eighty feet high*) or a semicolon (*The ship was huge; its mast stood eighty feet high*).

Two problems in punctuating main clauses deprive readers of this signal. One is the COMMA SPLICE, in which the clauses are joined (or spliced) *only* with a comma:

> **COMMA SPLICE**   The ship was huge, its mast stood eighty feet high.

The other is the FUSED SENTENCE (or RUN-ON SENTENCE), in which no punctuation or conjunction appears between the clauses.

> **FUSED SENTENCE**   The ship was huge its mast stood eighty feet high.

31a   **Separate main clauses not joined by *and, but,* or another coordinating conjunction.**

If your readers point out comma splices or fused sentences in your writing, you're not creating enough separation between main clauses in your sentences. The following guidelines can help you repair the problem.

cs / fs

31a

Revision of comma splices and fused sentences

❖ Underline the main clauses in your draft.
❖ When two main clauses fall in the same sentence, check the connection between them.
❖ If nothing falls between the clauses or only a comma does, revise in one of the following ways, depending on the relation you want to establish between the clauses. (See the text discussion for examples.)

Make the clauses into separate sentences.
Insert a comma followed by *and, but,* or another coordinating conjunction. Or, if the comma is already present, insert just the coordinating conjunction.
Insert a semicolon between clauses.
Subordinate one clause to the other.

┌─ KEY TERMS ─────────────────────────────────────

MAIN CLAUSE   A word group that contains a subject and a verb and does not begin with a subordinating word: *A dictionary is essential.*

COORDINATING CONJUNCTION   *And, but, or, nor, for, so, yet.* (See p. 95.)

Choose a method for revising comma splices or fused sentences depending on the meaning you intend:

❖ Make the clauses into separate sentences when the ideas expressed are only loosely related.

COMMA SPLICE   Chemistry has contributed much to our understanding of foods, many foods such as wheat and beans can be produced in the laboratory.

REVISED   Chemistry has contributed much to our understanding of foods⊙ Many foods such as wheat and beans can be produced in the laboratory.

ESL Making separate sentences may be the best option if you are used to writing very long sentences in your native language but often write comma splices in English.

❖ Insert a coordinating conjunction in a comma splice when the ideas in the main clauses are closely related and equally important.

COMMA SPLICE   Some laboratory-grown foods taste good, they are nutritious.

REVISED   Some laboratory-grown foods taste good, *and* they are nutritious.

In a fused sentence insert a comma and a coordinating conjunction.

FUSED   Chemists have made much progress they still have a way to go.

REVISED   Chemists have made much progress⊙ *but* they still have a way to go.

❖ Insert a semicolon between clauses if the relation between the ideas is very close and obvious without a conjunction.

COMMA SPLICE   Good taste is rare in laboratory-grown vegetables, they are usually bland.

REVISED   Good taste is rare in laboratory-grown vegetables⊙ they are usually bland.

❖ Subordinate one clause to the other when one idea is less important than the other.

COMMA SPLICE   The vitamins are adequate, the flavor is deficient.

REVISED   *Even though* the vitamins are adequate, the flavor is deficient.

cs / fs
31a

31b Separate main clauses related by *however, for example,* and so on.

Two groups of words that are not conjunctions describe how one main clause relates to another: CONJUNCTIVE ADVERBS and other TRANSITIONAL EXPRESSIONS.

Common conjunctive adverbs and transitional expressions

accordingly	for instance	in the meantime	otherwise
anyway	further	in the past	similarly
as a result	furthermore	likewise	so far
at last	hence	meanwhile	still
at length	however	moreover	that is
besides	incidentally	namely	then
certainly	in contrast	nevertheless	thereafter
consequently	indeed	nonetheless	therefore
even so	in fact	now	thus
finally	in other words	of course	to this end
for all that	in short	on the contrary	undoubtedly
for example	instead	on the whole	until now

(See p. 45 for a longer list of transitional expressions.)

When two clauses are related by a conjunctive adverb or another transitional expression, they must be separated by a period or by a semicolon. The adverb or expression is also generally set off by a comma or commas.

COMMA SPLICE	Most Americans refuse to give up unhealthful habits, consequently our medical costs are higher than those of many other countries.
REVISED	Most Americans refuse to give up unhealthful habits⊙ Consequently⊙ our medical costs are higher than those of many other countries.
REVISED	Most Americans refuse to give up unhealthful habits⊙ consequently⊙ our medical costs are higher than those of many other countries.

Conjunctive adverbs and transitional expressions are different from coordinating conjunctions (*and, but,* and so on) and subordinating conjunctions (*although, because,* and so on). Unlike conjunctions, conjunctive adverbs and transitional expressions do not join two clauses into a grammatical unit but merely describe the way two clauses relate in meaning. Thus, unlike conjunctions, conjunc-

cs / fs
31b

tive adverbs and transitional expressions can be moved from one place to another in a clause.

> Most Americans refuse to give up unhealthful habits; our medical costs, *consequently*, are higher than those of many other countries.

Note that commas set off the conjunctive adverb. (See p. 178.)

32 Mixed Sentences

A MIXED SENTENCE contains parts that do not fit together.

32a Match subjects and predicates in meaning.

In a sentence with mixed meaning, the subject is said to do or be something illogical. Such a mixture is sometimes called FAULTY PREDICATION because the predicate conflicts with the subject.

1. Illogical equation with *be*

When a form of *be* connects a subject and a word that describes the subject (a complement), the subject and complement must be logically related.

> MIXED   A *compromise* between the city and the country would
>
> be the ideal *place* to live.
>
> REVISED A *community* that offered the best qualities of both city
>
> and country would be the ideal *place* to live.

2. *Is when, is where*

Definitions require nouns on both sides of *be*. Clauses that define and begin with *when* or *where* are common in speech but should be avoided in writing.

┌─ KEY TERMS ───
SUBJECT   The part of a sentence that names who or what performs the action or makes the assertion of the verb: *Geese fly*. (See p. 96.)

PREDICATE   The part of a sentence containing the verb and asserting something about the subject: *Geese fly*. (See p. 96.)
└───

MIXED   An *examination* is *when you are tested* on what you know.

REVISED   An *examination* is a *test* of what you know.

3. *Reason is because*

The commonly heard construction *The reason is because . . .* is redundant since *because* means "for the reason that."

MIXED   The *reason* the temple requests donations *is because* the school needs expansion.

REVISED   The *reason* the temple requests donations *is that* the school needs expansion.

REVISED   The temple requests donations *because* the school needs expansion.

4. Other mixed meanings

Faulty predications are not confined to sentences with *be.*

MIXED   The *use* of emission controls *was created* to reduce air pollution.

REVISED   Emission *controls were created* to reduce air pollution.

mixed
32b

32b Untangle sentences that are mixed in grammar.

Many mixed sentences start with one grammatical plan or construction but end with a different one.

————modifier (prepositional phrase)———— verb
MIXED   By paying more attention to impressions than facts leads us to misjudge others.

This mixed sentence makes a prepositional phrase work as the subject of *leads,* but prepositional phrases function as modifiers, not as nouns, and thus not as sentence subjects.

————modifier (prepositional phrase)————
REVISED   By paying more attention to impressions than facts,
subject + verb
we *misjudge* others.

Mixed sentences are especially likely on a word processor when you connect parts of two sentences or rewrite half a sentence but not the other half. Mixed sentences may also occur when you don't focus your sentences on the subject and verb so that these elements carry the principal meaning. (See p. 80.) Here is another example:

subject ┌──────────modifier (subordinate clause)──────────
MIXED   The fact that someone may be considered guilty just for

associating with someone guilty.

subject verb
REVISED   The *fact is* that someone may be considered guilty just for associating with someone guilty.

32c   State parts of sentences, such as subjects, only once. ESL

In some languages other than English, certain parts of sentences may be repeated. These include the subject in any kind of clause or an object or adverb in an adjective clause. In English, however, these parts are stated only once in a clause.

1. Repetition of subject

You may be tempted to restate a subject as a pronoun before the verb. But the subject needs stating only once in its clause.

FAULTY   The *liquid it* reached a temperature of 180°F.
REVISED   The *liquid* reached a temperature of 180°F.

FAULTY   *Gases* in the liquid *they* escaped.
REVISED   *Gases* in the liquid escaped.

2. Repetition in an adjective clause

ADJECTIVE CLAUSES begin with *who, whom, whose, which, that, where,* and *when*. The beginning word replaces another word: the subject (*He is the person who called*), an object of a verb or preposition (*He is the person whom I mentioned*), or a preposition and pronoun (*He knows the office where [in which] the conference will occur*).

Do not state the word being replaced in an adjective clause by *who, whom,* and the like.

FAULTY   The technician *whom* the test depended on *her* was burned. [*Whom* should replace *her.*]
REVISED   The technician *whom* the test depended on was burned.

Adjective clauses beginning with *where* or *when* do not need an adverb such as *there* or *then*.

FAULTY   Gases escaped at a moment *when* the technician was un-
prepared *then*.

REVISED   Gases escaped at a moment *when* the technician was un-
prepared.

NOTE *Whom, which,* and similar words are sometimes omitted
but are still understood by the reader. Thus the word being replaced should not be stated.

FAULTY   Accidents rarely happen to technicians the lab has trained
them. [*Whom* is understood: . . . *technicians whom the lab
has trained.*]

REVISED   Accidents rarely happen to technicians the lab has
trained.

mixed
32c

Punctuation

IV

Punctuation

❖

End Punctuation

End a sentence with one of three punctuation marks: a period (.), a question mark (?), or an exclamation point (!).

33a Use a period after most sentences and in many abbreviations.

1. Statements, mild commands, and indirect questions

STATEMENT
The airline went bankrupt.   It no longer flies.

MILD COMMAND
Think of the possibilities.   Please consider others.

INDIRECT QUESTION
An INDIRECT QUESTION reports what someone asked but not in the exact form or words of the original question.

The judge asked why I had been driving with my lights off.
No one asked how we got home.

ESL Unlike a direct question, an indirect question uses the wording and subject-verb order of a statement: *The reporter asked why the negotiations failed* [not *why did the negotiations fail*].

2. Abbreviations

Use periods with most abbreviations involving small letters:

p.   Mrs.   e.g.   Minn.
Dr.   Mr.   i.e.   Feb.
Ph.D.   Ms.   a.m., p.m.   ft.

NOTE When an abbreviation falls at the end of a sentence, use only one period: *The school offers a Ph.D.*

Many abbreviations of two or more words using all-capital letters may be written with or without periods. Just be consistent.

BA or B.A.   US or U.S.   BC or B.C.   AM or A.M.

Omit periods from these abbreviations:

❖ The initials of a well-known person: *FDR, JFK.*
❖ The initials of an organization, corporation, or government agency: *IBM, USMC.*

❖ A postal abbreviation: *NY, AVE.*
❖ An ACRONYM, a pronounceable word formed from initials: *UNESCO, VISTA.*

33b Use a question mark after a direct question and sometimes to indicate doubt.

1. Direct questions

Who will follow her⟨?⟩
What is the difference between these two people⟨?⟩

After indirect questions, use a period: *We wondered who would follow her*⟨.⟩ (See the preceding page.)
Questions in a series are each followed by a question mark.

The officer asked how many times the suspect had been arrested. Three times⟨?⟩ Four times⟨?⟩ More than that⟨?⟩

2. Doubt

A question mark within parentheses can indicate doubt about a number or date.

The Greek philosopher Socrates was born in 470 (⟨?⟩) BC and died in 399 BC from drinking poison. [Socrates's birthdate is not known for sure.]

Use sentence structure and words, not a question mark, to express sarcasm or irony.

NOT   Stern's friendliness (?) bothered Crane.
BUT   Stern's *insincerity* bothered Crane.

.?!
33c

33c Use an exclamation point after an emphatic statement, interjection, or command.

No⟨!⟩ We must not lose this election⟨!⟩
Come here immediately⟨!⟩

┌─ KEY TERM ──────────────────────────────────────
│ INTERJECTION   A word that expresses feeling or commands atten-
│ tion, either alone or within a sentence: *Oh! Hey! Wow!* (See p. 96.)
└──

Follow mild interjections and commands with commas or periods, as appropriate: *Oh, call whenever you can.*

NOTE Use exclamation points sparingly, even in informal writing. Overused, they'll fail to impress readers, and they may make you sound overemphatic.

34 The Comma

The comma (,) is the most common punctuation mark inside sentences. Its main uses are shown in the box below.

Main uses of the comma

❖ To separate main clauses linked by a coordinating conjunction (next page):

The building is finished, *but* it has no tenants.

❖ To set off most introductory elements (next page):

Unfortunately, the only tenant pulled out.

❖ To set off nonrestrictive elements (p. 175):

The empty building symbolizes a weak local economy, *which affects everyone.*

The main cause, *the decline of local industry,* is not news.

❖ To separate items in series (p. 179):

The city needs *healthier businesses, new schools, and improved housing.*

❖ To separate two or more adjectives (p. 180):

A *tall, sleek* skyscraper is not needed.

❖ Other uses of the comma:

To set off other nonessential elements, such as absolute phrases, parenthetical expressions, and phrases expressing contrast (p. 178).
To separate parts of dates, addresses, long numbers (p. 181).
To separate quotations from words such as *she said* (p. 181).

See also p. 182 for when *not* to use the comma.

,
34

34a Use a comma before *and, but,* or another coordinating conjunction linking main clauses.

When a coordinating conjunction links words or phrases, do not use a comma: *Dugain plays⌒and sings Irish⌒and English folk songs.* However, *do* use a comma when a coordinating conjunction joins main clauses:

Caffeine can keep coffee drinkers alert⌄ *and* it may elevate their mood.

Caffeine was once thought to be safe⌄ *but* now researchers warn of harmful effects.

Coffee drinkers may suffer sleeplessness⌄ *for* the drug acts as a stimulant to the nervous system.

NOTE The comma goes *before,* not after, the coordinating conjunction: *Caffeine increases heart rate, and⌒it* [not *and, it*] *constricts blood vessels.*

EXCEPTION When main clauses are very short and closely related in meaning, you may omit the comma between them as long as the resulting sentence is clear: *Caffeine helps but it also hurts.* If you are in doubt about whether to use the comma in such a sentence, use it. It will always be correct.

34b Use a comma to set off most introductory elements.

An INTRODUCTORY ELEMENT begins a sentence and modifies a word or words in the main clause that follows. It is usually followed by a comma.

SUBORDINATE CLAUSE
Even when identical twins are raised apart⌄ they grow up very like each other.

34b

KEY TERMS

COORDINATING CONJUNCTIONS *And, but, or, nor,* and sometimes *for, so, yet.* (See p. 95.)

MAIN CLAUSE   A word group that contains a subject and a verb and does not begin with a subordinating word: *Water freezes at temperatures below 32°F.* (See p. 101.)

SUBORDINATE CLAUSE   A word group that contains a subject and a verb, begins with a subordinating word such as *because* or *who,* and is not a question: *When water freezes, crystals form.* (See p. 101.)

VERBAL OR VERBAL PHRASE

Explaining the similarity₍₂₎ some researchers claim that one's genes are one's destiny.

Concerned₍₂₎ other researchers deny the claim.

PREPOSITIONAL PHRASE

In a debate that has lasted centuries₍₂₎ scientists use identical twins to argue for or against genetic destiny.

TRANSITIONAL EXPRESSION

Of course₍₂₎ scientists can now look directly at the genes themselves to answer questions.

You may omit the comma after a short subordinate clause or prepositional phrase if its omission does not create confusion: *When snow falls⌒the city collapses. By the year 2000⌒the world population will top 6 billion.* But the comma is never wrong.

NOTE Take care to distinguish *-ing* words used as modifiers from *-ing* words used as subjects. The former almost always take a comma; the latter never do.

┌──────modifier──────┐   subject   verb
Studying identical twins₍₂₎ geneticists learn about inheritance.
┌────── subject ──────┐   verb
Studying identical twins⌒helps geneticists learn about inheritance.

34c Use a comma or commas to set off nonrestrictive elements.

Commas around part of a sentence often signal that the element is not essential to the meaning. This NONRESTRICTIVE ELEMENT may modify or rename the word it refers to, but it does not limit the word to a particular individual or group. The meaning of the word would still be clear if the element were deleted.

34c

KEY TERMS

VERBAL A verb form used as an adjective, adverb, or noun. A verbal plus any object or modifier is a VERBAL PHRASE: *frozen water, ready to freeze, rapid freezing.* (See p. 99.)

PREPOSITIONAL PHRASE A word group consisting of a preposition, such as *for* or *in,* followed by a noun or pronoun plus any modifiers: *in a jar, with a spoon.* (See p. 99.)

TRANSITIONAL EXPRESSION A word or phrase that shows the relationship between sentences: *for example, however, in fact, of course.* (See p. 44.)

A test for nonrestrictive and restrictive elements

1. Identify the element.

Hai Nguyen *who emigrated from Vietnam* lives in Denver.
Those *who emigrated with him* live elsewhere.

2. Remove the element. Does the fundamental meaning of the sentence change?

Hai Nguyen lives in Denver.   No.
Those live elsewhere.   YES. [Who are *Those?*]

3. If NO, the element is *nonrestrictive* and *should* be set off with punctuation.

Hai Nguyen⌒who emigrated from Vietnam⌒lives in Denver.

If YES, the element is *restrictive* and should *not* be set off with punctuation.

Those⌒who emigrated with him⌒live elsewhere.

NONRESTRICTIVE ELEMENT
The company⌒*which is located in Oklahoma*⌒has an excellent reputation.

In contrast, a RESTRICTIVE ELEMENT *does* limit the word it refers to: the element cannot be omitted without leaving the meaning too general. Because it is essential, a restrictive element is *not* set off with commas.

RESTRICTIVE ELEMENT
The company rewards employees⌒*who work hard.*

34c

Omitting the italicized words would distort the meaning: the company doesn't necessarily reward *all* employees, only the hardworking ones.

The same element in the same sentence may be restrictive or nonrestrictive depending on your intended meaning and the context in which the sentence appears.

RESTRICTIVE
Not all the bands were equally well received, however. The band⌒*playing old music*⌒held the audience's attention. The other groups created much less excitement. [*Playing old music* identifies a particular band.]

NONRESTRICTIVE
A new band called Fats made its debut on Saturday night. The band⌒*playing old music*⌒held the audience's attention. If this per-

formance is typical, the group has a bright future. [*Playing old music* adds information about a band already named.]

NOTE When a nonrestrictive element falls in the middle of a sentence, be sure to set it off with a pair of commas, one *before* and one *after* the element.

1. Nonrestrictive phrases and clauses

Most nonrestrictive phrases and subordinate clauses function as adjectives to modify nouns or pronouns. In every example below, the italicized words could be omitted with no loss of clarity:

> Elizabeth Blackwell was the first woman to graduate from an American medical school, *in 1849.* [Phrase.]
>
> She was a medical pioneer, *helping to found the first medical college for women.* [Phrase.]
>
> She taught at the school, *which was affiliated with the New York Infirmary.* [Clause.]
>
> Blackwell, *who published books and papers on medicine,* practiced pediatrics and gynecology. [Clause.]

NOTE Use *that* only in a restrictive clause, never in a nonrestrictive clause: . . . *school, which* [not *that*] *was affiliated.* . . . Many writers reserve *which* for nonrestrictive clauses.

2. Nonrestrictive appositives

Appositives may also be restrictive or nonrestrictive, depending on meaning and context. A nonrestrictive appositive merely adds information about the word it refers to:

> Toni Morrison's fifth novel, *Beloved,* won the Pulitzer Prize in 1988. [The word *fifth* identifies the novel, while the title adds a detail.]

In contrast, a restrictive appositive limits or defines the word it refers to.

34c

KEY TERMS

PHRASE   A word group lacking a subject or a verb or both: *in Duluth, carrying water.* (See p. 99.)

SUBORDINATE CLAUSE   A word group that contains a subject and a verb, begins with a subordinating word such as *who* or *although,* and is not a question: *Samson, who won a gold medal, coaches in Utah.* (See p. 101.)

APPOSITIVE   A noun that renames another noun immediately before it: *His wife, Kyra Sedgwick, is also an actor.* (See p. 101.)

Morrison's novel◯*The Bluest Eye*◯is about an African American girl who longs for blue eyes. [Morrison has written more than one novel, so the title is essential to identify the intended one.]

34d   Use a comma or commas to set off other nonessential elements.

Like nonrestrictive modifiers or appositives, many other elements contribute to texture, tone, or overall clarity but are not essential to the meaning. Unlike nonrestrictive elements, these other nonessential elements generally do not refer to any specific word in the sentence.

NOTE Use a pair of commas—one before, one after—when any of these elements falls in the middle of a sentence.

ABSOLUTE PHRASES

Domestic recycling having succeeded◯ the city now wants to extend the program to businesses.

Many businesses◯ *their profits already squeezed*◯ resist recycling.

PARENTHETICAL AND TRANSITIONAL EXPRESSIONS

Generally, set off parenthetical and transitional expressions with commas:

The world's most celebrated holiday is◯ *perhaps surprisingly*◯ New Year's Day. [Parenthetical expression.]

Interestingly◯ Americans have relatively few holidays. [Parenthetical expression.]

American workers◯ *for example*◯ receive fewer holidays than European workers do. [Transitional expression.]

(Dashes and parentheses may also set off parenthetical expressions. See pp. 196–97.)

When a transitional expression links main clauses, precede it with a semicolon and follow it with a comma. (See p. 185.)

34d

KEY TERMS

ABSOLUTE PHRASE   A phrase modifying a whole main clause and consisting of a participle and its subject: *Their homework completed, the children watched TV.* (See p. 100.)

PARENTHETICAL EXPRESSION   An explanatory or supplemental word or phrase, such as *all things considered, to be frank,* or a brief example or fact. (See p. 197.)

TRANSITIONAL EXPRESSION   A word or phrase that shows the relationship between sentences: *for example, however, in fact, of course.* (See p. 44.)

European workers often have long paid vacations⨀ *indeed*⨀ they may receive a full month.

NOTE The conjunctions *and* and *but*, sometimes used as transitional expressions, are not followed by commas (see p. 183). Nor are commas required after some transitional expressions that we read without pauses, such as *also, hence, next, now,* and *thus.* A few transitional expressions, notably *therefore* and *instead,* do not need commas when they fall inside or at the ends of clauses.

American workers⨀ *thus*⨀ put in more work days. But⨀ the days themselves may be shorter.

PHRASES OF CONTRAST

The substance⨀ *not the style*⨀ is important.
Substance⨀ *unlike style*⨀ cannot be faked.

TAG QUESTIONS

Jones should be allowed to vote⨀ *should he not?*
They don't stop to consider others⨀ *do they?*

YES AND NO

Yes⨀ the editorial did have a point.
No⨀ that can never be.

WORDS OF DIRECT ADDRESS

Cody⨀ please bring me the newspaper.
With all due respect⨀ *sir*⨀ I will not.

MILD INTERJECTIONS

Well⨀ you will never know who did it.
Oh⨀ they forgot all about the baby.

34e Use commas between items in a series.

34e

A SERIES consists of three or more items of equal importance. The items may be words, phrases, or clauses.

Anna Spingle *married at the age of seventeen*⨀ *had three children by twenty-one*⨀ *and divorced at twenty-two.*

She worked as *a cook*⨀ *a baby-sitter*⨀ *and a crossing guard.*

KEY TERMS

TAG QUESTION A question at the end of a statement, consisting of a pronoun, a helping verb, and sometimes *not: It isn't wet, is it?*

INTERJECTION A word that expresses feeling or commands attention: *Oh, must we?*

Some writers omit the comma before the coordinating conjunction in a series (*Breakfast consisted of coffee, eggs and kippers*). But the final comma is never wrong, and it always helps the reader see the last two items as separate.

34f Use commas between two or more adjectives that equally modify the same word.

Adjectives that equally modify the same word—COORDINATE ADJECTIVES—may be separated either by *and* or by a comma.

Spingle's *scratched and dented* car is an eyesore, but it gets her to work.

She has dreams of a *sleek, shiny* car.

Adjectives are not coordinate—and should not be separated by commas—when the one nearer the noun is more closely related to the noun in meaning.

Spingle's children work at *various odd* jobs.
They all expect to go to a *nearby community* college.

Tests for commas with adjectives

1. Identify the adjectives.

    She was a *faithful sincere* friend.
    They are *dedicated medical* students.

2. Can the adjectives be reversed without changing meaning?

    She was a *sincere faithful* friend.   YES.
    They are *medical dedicated* students.   NO.

3. Can the word *and* be inserted between the adjectives without changing meaning?

    She was a *faithful and sincere* friend.   YES.
    They are *dedicated and medical* students.   NO.

4. If YES to *both* questions, the adjectives *should* be separated by a comma.

    She was a *faithful, sincere* friend.

5. If NO to both questions, the adjectives should *not* be separated by a comma.

    They are *dedicated medical* students.

---

^
34f

34g Use commas in dates, addresses, place names, and long numbers.

When they appear within sentences, dates, addresses, and place names punctuated with commas are also ended with commas.

DATES

July 4, 1776, was the day the Declaration was signed.

The bombing of Pearl Harbor on Sunday, December 7, 1941, prompted American entry into World War II.

Do not use commas between the parts of a date in inverted order (*15 December 1992*) or in dates consisting of a month or season and a year (*December 1941*).

ADDRESSES AND PLACE NAMES

Use the address 220 Cornell Road, Woodside, California 94062, for all correspondence.

Columbus, Ohio, is the location of Ohio State University.

Do not use a comma between a state name and a zip code.

LONG NUMBERS

Use the comma to separate the figures in long numbers into groups of three, counting from the right. With numbers of four digits, the comma is optional.

The new assembly plant cost $7,525,000.
A kilometer is 3,281 feet (*or* 3281 feet).

ESL Usage in American English differs from that in some other languages, which use a period, not a comma, to separate the figures in long numbers.

34h Use commas with quotations according to standard practice.

The words *she said, he writes,* and so on identify the source of a quotation. These identifying words should be separated from the quotation by punctuation, usually a comma or commas.

Eleanor Roosevelt said, "You must do the thing you think you cannot do."

"Knowledge is power," wrote Francis Bacon.

"The shore has a dual nature," observes Rachel Carson, "changing with the swing of the tides." [The identifying words interrupt the quotation at a comma and thus end with a comma.]

EXCEPTIONS When explanatory words interrupt a quotation between main clauses, follow the explanatory words with a semicolon or a period. The choice depends on the punctuation of the original.

> NOT   "That part of my life was over," she wrote, "his words had sealed it shut."
>
> BUT   "That part of my life was over," she wrote⊙ "His words had sealed it shut." [*She wrote* interrupts the quotation at a period.]
>
> OR   "That part of my life was over," she wrote⊙ "his words had sealed it shut." [*She wrote* interrupts the quotation at a semicolon.]

Do not use a comma when identifying words follow a quotation ending in an exclamation point or a question mark.

> "Claude⊙" Mrs. Harrison called.
> "Why must I come home⊙" he asked.

Do not use a comma with a quotation that is integrated into your sentence structure, including one introduced by *that:*

> James Baldwin insists that⊙ "one must never, in one's life, accept . . . injustices as commonplace."
>
> Baldwin thought that the violence of a riot⊙ "had been devised as a corrective⊙" to his own violence.

Do not use a comma with a quoted title unless it is a nonrestrictive appositive.

> The Beatles recorded⊙ "She Loves Me⊙" in the early 1960s.

34i   Delete commas where they are not required.

Commas can make sentences choppy and even confusing if they are used more often than needed or in violation of rules 34a–34h. The most common spots for misused commas are discussed below.

1. Between subject and verb, verb and object, or preposition and object

> NOT   The returning *soldiers, received* a warm welcome. [Separated subject and verb.]

KEY TERM

NONRESTRICTIVE APPOSITIVE   A word or words that rename an immediately preceding noun but do not limit or define the noun: *The author's first story, "Biloxi," won a prize.* (See p. 177.)

---

no ⟨⟩
34i

BUT   The returning *soldiers received* a warm welcome.

NOT   They had *chosen, to fight* for their country *despite, the risks.*
[Separated verb *chosen* and its object; separated preposition *despite* and its object.]

BUT   They had *chosen to fight* for their country *despite the risks.*

2. In compound constructions

Compound constructions consisting of two elements almost never require a comma. The only exception is the sentence consisting of two main clauses linked by a coordinating conjunction: *The computer failed, but employees kept working* (see p. 174).

NOT   ⌐————————compound subject————————⌐
Banks, and other financial institutions have helped older
⌐———compound object of preposition———⌐
people with *money management, and investment.*

BUT   Banks and other financial institutions have helped older people with money management and investment.

NOT   ⌐—————————compound predicate—————————⌐
One bank *created* special accounts for older people, *and held*
⌐compound object of verb⌐
classes, and workshops.

BUT   One bank created special accounts for older people and held classes and workshops.

3. After a conjunction

NOT   Parents of adolescents notice increased conflict at puberty, *and,* they complain of bickering.

BUT   Parents of adolescents notice increased conflict at puberty, and they complain of bickering.

NOT   *Although,* other primates leave the family at adolescence, humans do not.

BUT   Although other primates leave the family at adolescence, humans do not.

no ⌃
34i

⌐ KEY TERMS ————

COMPOUND CONSTRUCTION   Two or more words, phrases, or clauses connected by a coordinating conjunction, usually *and, but, or, nor: man and woman, old or young, leaking oil and spewing steam.*

CONJUNCTION   A connecting word such as a COORDINATING CONJUNCTION (*and, but, or,* and so on) or a SUBORDINATING CONJUNCTION (*although, because, when,* and so on). (See p. 95.)

4. Around restrictive elements

NOT   Hawthorne's work, *The Scarlet Letter,* was the first major American novel. [The title is essential to distinguish the novel from the rest of Hawthorne's work.]

BUT   Hawthorne's work⌒ *The Scarlet Letter*⌒ was the first major American novel.

NOT   The symbols, *that Hawthorne used,* influenced other novelists. [The clause identifies which symbols were influential.]

BUT   The symbols⌒that Hawthorne used⌒influenced other novelists.

5. Around a series

Commas separate the items *within* a series (p. 179) but do not separate the series from the rest of the sentence.

NOT   The skills of, *hunting, herding, and agriculture,* sustained the Native Americans.

BUT   The skills of⌒hunting, herding, and agriculture⌒sustained the Native Americans.

6. Before an indirect quotation

NOT   The report *concluded, that* dieting could be more dangerous than overeating.

BUT   The report concluded⌒that dieting could be more dangerous than overeating.

35 The Semicolon

;
35

The semicolon (;) separates equal and balanced sentence elements—usually main clauses (opposite) and occasionally items in series (p. 186).

KEY TERMS

RESTRICTIVE ELEMENT   Limits (or restricts) the word it refers to and thus can't be omitted without leaving the meaning too general. (See p. 176.)

INDIRECT QUOTATION   Reports what someone said or wrote, but not in the exact words of the original.

MAIN CLAUSE   A word group that contains a subject and a verb and does not begin with a subordinating word: *Parks help cities breathe.*

35a Use a semicolon between main clauses not joined by *and*, *but*, or another coordinating conjunction.

When no coordinating conjunction links two main clauses, the clauses should be separated by a semicolon.

> A new ulcer drug arrived on the market with a mixed reputation; doctors find that the drug works but worry about its side effects.
>
> The side effects are not minor; some leave the patient quite uncomfortable or even ill.

NOTE This rule prevents the errors known as comma splice and fused sentence. (See pp. 161–63.)

35b Use a semicolon between main clauses related by *however, for example,* and so on.

When a conjunctive adverb or another transitional expression relates two main clauses in a single sentence, the clauses should be separated with a semicolon:

> An American immigrant, Levi Strauss, invented blue jeans in the 1860s; *eventually*, his product clothed working men throughout the West.

The position of the semicolon between main clauses never changes, but the conjunctive adverb or transitional expression may move around within the second clause. Wherever the adverb or expression falls, it is usually set off with a comma or commas. (See p. 178.)

> Blue jeans have become fashionable all over the world; the American originators, *however,* still wear more jeans than anyone else.
>
> Blue jeans have become fashionable all over the world; the American originators still wear more jeans than anyone else, *however.*

;
35b

KEY TERMS

COORDINATING CONJUNCTIONS   *And, but, or, nor,* and sometimes *for, so, yet.*

CONJUNCTIVE ADVERB   A modifier that describes the relation of the ideas in two clauses, such as *consequently, hence, however, indeed, instead, nonetheless, otherwise, still, then, therefore, thus.* (See p. 164.)

TRANSITIONAL EXPRESSION   A word or phrase that shows the relationship between sentences. Transitional expressions include conjunctive adverbs as well as *for example, in fact, of course,* and many other words and phrases. (See p. 44.)

NOTE This rule prevents the errors known as comma splice and fused sentence. (See pp. 164–65.)

> **35c** Use semicolons between main clauses or series items containing commas.

Normally, commas separate main clauses linked by coordinating conjunctions (*and, but, or, nor*) and items in a series. But when the clauses or series items contain commas, a semicolon between them makes the sentence easier to read.

> Lewis and Clark led the men of their party with consummate skill, inspiring and encouraging them, doctoring and caring for them⨀ *and* they kept voluminous journals.   —PAGE SMITH

> The custody case involved Amy Dalton, the child⨀ Ellen and Mark Dalton, the parents⨀and Ruth and Hal Blum, the grandparents.

> **35d** Delete or replace unneeded semicolons.

Too many semicolons can make writing choppy. And semicolons are often misused in certain constructions that call for other punctuation or no punctuation.

1. Between a main clause and subordinate clause or phrase

The semicolon does not separate unequal parts, such as main clauses and subordinate clauses or phrases.

> **NOT**   According to African authorities; only about 35,000 Pygmies exist today.
>
> **BUT**   According to African authorities⨀ only about 35,000 Pygmies exist today.
>
> **NOT**   They are in danger of extinction; because of encroaching development.
>
> **BUT**   They are in danger of extinction◯because of encroaching development.

2. Before a series or explanation

Colons and dashes, not semicolons, introduce series, explanations, and so forth. (See pp. 187 and 196.)

> **NOT**   Teachers have heard all sorts of reasons why students do poorly; psychological problems, family illness, too much work, too little time.

BUT   Teachers have heard all sorts of reasons why students do poorly: psychological problems, family illness, too much work, too little time.

36 The Colon

The colon (:) is mainly a mark of introduction: it signals that the words following will explain or amplify (below). The colon also has several conventional uses, such as in expressions of time (p. 188).

36a   **Use a colon to introduce a concluding explanation, series, appositive, or long or formal quotation.**

As an introducer, a colon is always preceded by a complete main clause. It may or may not be followed by a main clause. This is one way the colon differs from the semicolon, which generally separates main clauses only. (See pp. 184–85.)

EXPLANATION

Soul food has a deceptively simple definition: the ethnic cooking of African Americans.

Sometimes a concluding explanation is preceded by *the following* or *as follows* and a colon.

A more precise definition might be *the following*: soul food draws on ingredients, cooking methods, and dishes originating in Africa, brought to the New World by slaves, and modified or supplemented in the Caribbean and the American South.

NOTE A complete sentence *after* a colon may begin with a capital letter or a small letter (as in the example above). Just be consistent throughout an essay.

:
36a

┌ **KEY TERMS** ──────────────────────────────

MAIN CLAUSE   A word group that contains a subject and a verb and does not begin with a subordinating word: *Soul food is varied.* (See p. 101.)

APPOSITIVE   A noun or noun substitute that renames another noun immediately before it: *my brother, Jack.* (See p. 101.)

SERIES
At least three soul food dishes are familiar to most Americans(:) fried chicken, barbecued spareribs, and sweet potatoes.

APPOSITIVE
Soul food has one disadvantage(:) fat.

Namely, that is, and other expressions that introduce appositives *follow* the colon: *Soul food has one disadvantage(:) namely, fat.*

LONG OR FORMAL QUOTATION
One soul food chef has a solution(:) "Soul food doesn't have to be greasy to taste good. . . . Instead of using ham hocks to flavor beans, I use smoked turkey wings. The soulful, smoky taste remains, but without all the fat of pork."

36b **Use a colon after the salutation of a business letter, between a title and subtitle, between divisions of time, and in biblical citations.**

SALUTATION OF BUSINESS LETTER
Dear Ms. Burak(:)

TITLE AND SUBTITLE
Charles Dickens(:) An Introduction to His Novels

TIME		**BIBLICAL CITATION**
12(:)26	6(:)00	1 Corinthians 3(:)6–7

36c **Delete or replace unneeded colons.**

Use the colon only at the end of a main clause. Do not use it in these situations:

❖ Delete a colon after a verb:

NOT The best-known soul food dish is: fried chicken.
BUT The best-known soul food dish is◯fried chicken.

❖ Delete a colon after *such as* or *including:*

NOT Many Americans have not tasted delicacies such as: chitlins and black-eyed peas.
BUT Many Americans have not tasted delicacies such as◯chitlins and black-eyed peas.

❖ Delete a colon after a preposition:

NOT Soul food recipes can be found in: mainstream cookbooks as well as specialized references.

:
36c

BUT   Soul food recipes can be found in◯ mainstream cookbooks as well as specialized references.

37 The Apostrophe

The apostrophe (') appears as part of a word to indicate possession (below), the omission of one or more letters (p. 191), or (in a few cases) plural number (p. 192).

37a Use the apostrophe and sometimes -s to form possessive nouns and indefinite pronouns.

A noun or indefinite pronoun shows possession with an apostrophe and, usually, an *s: the dog◯'s hair, everyone◯'s hope.*

NOTE Apostrophes are easy to misuse. For safety's sake, check your drafts to be sure that all words ending in -s neither omit needed apostrophes nor add unneeded ones. Also, remember that the apostrophe or apostrophe-plus-s is an *addition.* Before this addition, always spell the name of the owner or owners without dropping or adding letters.

You can use your computer to search for words ending in -s so that you can check their form. However, your computer cannot tell you that you've misused an apostrophe. A spelling checker can say only whether a word matches an entry in its dictionary, not whether that word is appropriate for the context in which you've used it. (See p. 35 for more on spelling checkers.)

1. Singular words: Add -'s.

Bill *Boughton◯'s* skillful card tricks amaze children.
Anyone◯'s eyes would widen.
Most tricks will pique an *adult◯'s* curiosity, too.

The -'s ending for singular words pertains also to singular words ending in -s, as the next examples show.

37a

KEY TERMS

PREPOSITION   *In, on, outside,* or another word that takes a noun or pronoun as its object: *in the house.* (See p. 94.)

INDEFINITE PRONOUN   A pronoun that does not refer to a specific person or thing, such as *anyone, each, everybody, no one,* or *something.* (See p. 125.)

Uses and misuses of the apostrophe

USES	MISUSES
Possessives of nouns and indefinite pronouns (p. 189)	Singular, not plural, possessives (p. 190)

SINGULAR	PLURAL
Ms. Park's	the Parks'
everyone's	two weeks'

	NOT	BUT
	the Kim's car	the Kims' car
	boy's fathers	boys' fathers

Contractions (p. 191)

it's a girl	shouldn't
you're	won't

Plurals of nouns (p. 191)

NOT	BUT
book's are	books are
the Freed's	the Freeds

Optional: plurals of abbreviations and of letters, etc., named as words (p. 192)

C's or Cs	6's or 6s
if's or ifs	

Third-person singulars of verbs (p. 191)

NOT	BUT
swim's	swims

Possessives of personal pronouns (p. 191)

NOT	BUT
it's toes	its toes
your's	yours

Henry *James's* novels reward the patient reader.
The *business's* customers filed suit.

EXCEPTION An apostrophe alone may be added to a singular word ending in -*s* when another *s* would make the word difficult to say: *Moses' mother, Joan Rivers' jokes*. But the added -*s* is never wrong (*Moses's, Rivers's*).

37a

2. **Plural words ending in -*s*: Add -' only.**

    Workers' incomes have fallen slightly over the past year.
    Many students benefit from several *years'* work after high school.
    The *Jameses'* talents are extraordinary.

    Note the difference in the possessives of singular and plural words ending in -*s*. The singular form usually takes -'*s*: *James's*. The plural takes only the apostrophe: *Jameses'*.

3. **Plural words not ending in -*s*: Add -'*s*.**

    Children's educations are at stake.
    We need to attract the *media's* attention.

4. Compound words: Add -'s only to the last word.

The *brother-in-law's* business failed.
Taxes are always *somebody else's* fault.

5. Two or more owners: Add -'s depending on possession.

INDIVIDUAL POSSESSION

Youngman's and Mason's comedy techniques are similar. [Each comedian has his own technique.]

JOINT POSSESSION

The child recovered despite her *mother and father's* neglect. [The mother and father were jointly neglectful.]

37b Delete or replace any apostrophe in a plural noun, a singular verb, or a possessive personal pronoun.

1. Plural nouns

The plurals of nouns are generally formed by adding -*s* or -*es*: *boys, families, Joneses, Murphys.* Don't add an apostrophe to form the plural.

NOT   The *Jones'* controlled the *firm's* until 1996.
BUT   The *Joneses* controlled the *firms* until 1996.

2. Singular verbs

Verbs ending in -*s never* take an apostrophe.

NOT   The subway *break's* down less often now.
BUT   The subway *breaks* down less often now.

3. Possessives of personal pronouns

His, hers, its, ours, yours, theirs, and *whose* are possessive forms of *he, she, it, we, you, they,* and *who.* They do not take apostrophes.

NOT   The house is *her's. It's* roof leaks.
BUT   The house is *hers. Its* roof leaks.

Don't confuse possessive pronouns with contractions. See below.

37c Use the apostrophe to form contractions.

A CONTRACTION replaces one or more letters, numbers, or words with an apostrophe, as in the following examples.

37c

it is	it's	cannot	can't
they are	they're	does not	doesn't
you are	you're	were not	weren't
who is	who's	class of 1997	class of '97

NOTE Don't confuse contractions with personal pronouns.

CONTRACTIONS	**PERSONAL PRONOUNS**
It's a book.	*Its* cover is green.
They're coming.	*Their* car broke down.
You're right.	*Your* idea is good.
Who's coming?	*Whose* party is it?

37d **An apostrophe is often optional in the plurals of abbreviations and dates as well as letters, numbers, and words named as words.**

Use the apostrophe with most plural abbreviations that contain periods. With unpunctuated abbreviations and with dates, you can omit the apostrophe. (See p. 171 on using periods with abbreviations.)

Ph.D.'s	CD-ROMs	1990s
B.A.'s	BAs	

Add an *-s* to form the plural of a letter, number, or word that you are referring to as a word rather than using for its meaning. An apostrophe is optional. Just be consistent.

The sentence has too many <u>but</u>s [or <u>but</u>'s].
Two <u>3</u>s [or <u>3</u>'s] and two <u>&</u>s [or <u>&</u>'s] appeared at the end of each chapter.

NOTE Letters, numbers, and words named as words are underlined (italicized), but the added *-s* and any apostrophe are not. (See p. 226 on this use of underlining or italics.)

" "
38

---

38 Quotation Marks

Quotation marks—either double (" ") or single (' ')—mainly enclose direct quotations from speech and from writing.

NOTE Always use quotation marks in pairs, one at the beginning of a quotation and one at the end.

38a Use double quotation marks to enclose direct quotations.

A DIRECT QUOTATION reports what someone said or wrote, in the exact words of the original.

"Life," said the psychoanalyst Karen Horney, "remains a very efficient therapist."

Do not use quotation marks with an INDIRECT QUOTATION, which reports what someone said or wrote but not in the exact words.

The psychoanalyst Karen Horney said that life is a good therapist.

38b Use single quotation marks to enclose a quotation within a quotation.

"In formulating any philosophy," Woody Allen writes, "the first consideration must always be: What can we know? . . . Descartes hinted at the problem when he wrote, 'My mind can never know my body, although it has become quite friendly with my leg.'"

Notice that two different quotation marks appear at the end of the sentence—one single (to finish the interior quotation) and one double (to finish the main quotation).

38c Put quotation marks around the titles of works that are parts of other works.

Use quotation marks to enclose the titles of works that are released within larger works. Use underlining (italics) for all other titles, such as books and periodicals. (See p. 225.)

Titles to be enclosed in quotation marks
Other titles should be underlined (italicized). (See p. 225.)

SONG
"The Star-Spangled Banner"

SHORT STORY
"The Gift of the Magi"

SHORT POEM
"Mending Wall"

ARTICLE IN A PERIODICAL
"Does 'Scaring' Work?"

ESSAY
"Joey: A 'Mechanical Boy'"

EPISODE OF A TELEVISION OR RADIO PROGRAM
"The Mexican Connection"
   (on Sixty Minutes)

SUBDIVISION OF A BOOK
"The Mast Head" (Chapter 35 of Moby-Dick)

" "
38c

NOTE Use single quotation marks for a quotation within a quoted title, as in the article and essay titles in the box on the previous page. And enclose all punctuation in the title within the quotation marks, as in the article title.

38d Quotation marks may enclose words being used in a special sense.

On movie sets movable "wild walls" make a one-walled room seem four-walled on film.

NOTE Use underlining (italics) for defined words. (See p. 226.)

38e Delete quotation marks where they are not required.

TITLE OF YOUR PAPER
NOT "The Death Wish in One Poem by Robert Frost"
BUT The Death Wish in One Poem by Robert Frost
OR The Death Wish in "Stopping by Woods on a Snowy Evening"

COMMON NICKNAME
NOT As President, "Jimmy" Carter preferred to use his nickname.
BUT As President, Jimmy Carter preferred to use his nickname.

SLANG OR TRITE EXPRESSION
Quotation marks will not excuse slang or a trite expression that is inappropriate to your writing. If slang is appropriate, use it without quotation marks.

NOT We should support the President in his "hour of need" rather than "wimp out on him."
BUT We should give the President the support he needs rather than turn away like cowards.

38f Place other punctuation marks inside or outside quotation marks according to standard practice.

1. Commas and periods: Inside quotation marks

Swift uses irony in his essay "A Modest Proposal."

Many first-time readers are shocked to see infants described as "delicious."

"'A Modest Proposal,'" wrote one critic, "is so outrageous that it cannot be believed."

Exception When a parenthetical source citation immediately follows a quotation at the end of a sentence, the period follows the source citation: *One critic calls the essay "outrageous" (Olms 26).*

2. Colons and semicolons: Outside quotation marks

A few years ago the slogan in elementary education was "learning by playing"; now educators are concerned with teaching basic skills.

We all know the meaning of "basic skills": reading, writing, and arithmetic.

3. Dashes, question marks, and exclamation points: Inside quotation marks only if part of the quotation

When a dash, question mark, or exclamation point is part of the quotation, place it *inside* quotation marks. Don't use any other punctuation, such as a period or comma·

"But must you—" Marcia hesitated, afraid of the answer.
The stranger asked, "Where am I?"
"Go away!" I yelled.

When a dash, question mark, or exclamation point applies only to the larger sentence, not to the quotation, place it *outside* quotation marks—again, with no other punctuation:

One evocative line in English poetry—"After many a summer dies the swan"—was written by Alfred, Lord Tennyson.

Who said, "Now cracks a noble heart"?

The woman called me "stupid"!

When both the quotation and the larger sentence take a question mark or exclamation point, use only the one *inside* the quotation mark:

Did you say, "Who is she?"

39

39 Other Marks

The other marks of punctuation are the dash (next page), parentheses (p. 197), the ellipsis mark (p. 198), brackets (p. 199), and the slash (p. 200).

39a Use the dash or dashes to indicate shifts and to set off some sentence elements.

The dash (—) is mainly a mark of interruption: it signals a shift, insertion, or break. In your papers, form a dash with two hyphens (--). Do not add extra space before, after, or between the hyphens.

NOTE When an interrupting element starting with a dash falls in the middle of a sentence, be sure to add the closing dash to signal the end of the interruption. See the first example below.

1. Shifts in tone or thought

The novel—if one can call it that—appeared in 1994.
If the book had a plot—but a plot would be conventional.

2. Nonrestrictive elements

Dashes may be used instead of commas to set off and emphasize modifiers, parenthetical expressions, and other nonrestrictive elements, especially when these elements are internally punctuated.

The qualities Monet painted—sunlight, rich shadows, deep colors—abounded near the rivers and gardens he used as subjects.

Though they are close together—separated by only a few blocks—the two neighborhoods could be in different countries.

3. Introductory series and concluding series and explanations

Shortness of breath, skin discoloration or the sudden appearance of moles, persistent indigestion, the presence of small lumps—all these may signify cancer. [Introductory series.]

The patient undergoes a battery of tests—CAT scan, bronchoscopy, perhaps even biopsy. [Concluding series.]

Many patients are disturbed by the CAT scan—by the need to keep still for long periods in an exceedingly small space. [Concluding explanation.]

A colon could be used instead of a dash in the last two examples. The dash is more informal.

— 39a

⌐ KEY TERM ─────────────────────────────

NONRESTRICTIVE ELEMENT   Gives added information but does not limit (or restrict) the word it refers to. (See pp. 175–77.)

4. Overuse

Too many dashes can make writing jumpy or breathy.

Not   In all his life—eighty-seven years—my great-grandfather never allowed his picture to be taken—not even once. He claimed the "black box"—the camera—would steal his soul.

But   In all his eighty-seven years, my great-grandfather did not allow his picture to be taken even once. He claimed the "black box"—the camera—would steal his soul.

39b   Use parentheses to enclose nonessential elements.

Note Parentheses *always* come in pairs, one before and one after the punctuated material.

1. Parenthetical expressions

PARENTHETICAL EXPRESSIONS include explanations, facts, digressions, and examples that may be helpful or interesting but are not essential to meaning. Parentheses de-emphasize parenthetical expressions. (Commas emphasize them more and dashes still more.)

The population of Philadelphia (now about 1.6 million) has declined since 1950.

Note Don't put a comma before a parenthetical expression enclosed in parentheses. Punctuation after the parenthetical expression should be placed outside the closing parenthesis.

Not   Philadelphia's population compares with Houston's, (just over 1.6 million.)

But   Philadelphia's population compares with Houston's (just over 1.6 million).

**( )
39b**

When it falls between other complete sentences, a complete sentence enclosed in parentheses begins with a capital letter and ends with a period.

In general, coaches will tell you that scouts are just guys who can't coach. (But then, so are brain surgeons.)   —Roy Blount

2. Labels for lists

Outside the Middle East, the countries with the largest oil reserves are (1) Venezuela (63 billion barrels), (2) Russia (57 billion barrels), and (3) Mexico (51 billion barrels).

39c   Use the ellipsis mark to indicate omissions from quotations.

The ellipsis mark consists of three spaced periods (. . .). It generally indicates an omission from a quotation, as illustrated in the following excerpts from this quotation about the Philippines:

ORIGINAL QUOTATION

"It was the Cuba of the future. It was going the way of Iran. It was another Nicaragua, another Cambodia, another Vietnam. But all these places, awesome in their histories, are so different from each other that one couldn't help thinking: this kind of talk was a shorthand for a confusion. All that was being said was that something was happening in the Philippines. Or more plausibly, a lot of different things were happening in the Philippines. And a lot of people were feeling obliged to speak out about it."

—JAMES FENTON, "The Philippine Election"

1. OMISSION OF THE MIDDLE OF A SENTENCE

"But all these places . . . are so different from each other that one couldn't help thinking: this kind of talk was a shorthand for a confusion."

2. OMISSION OF THE END OF A SENTENCE (NO SOURCE CITATION)

"It was another Nicaragua . . . ." [The sentence period, closed up to the last word, precedes the ellipsis mark.]

3. OMISSION OF THE END OF A SENTENCE, WITH SOURCE CITATION

"It was another Nicaragua . . ." (Fenton 25). [When the quotation is followed by a parenthetical source citation, as here, the sentence period follows the citation.]

39c

4. OMISSION OF THE BEGINNING OF A SENTENCE

". . . [O]ne couldn't help thinking: this kind of talk was a shorthand for a confusion." [The brackets indicate a change in capitalization. See p. 222.]

5. OMISSION OF PARTS OF TWO SENTENCES

"All that was being said was that . . . a lot of different things were happening in the Philippines."

6. OMISSION OF ONE OR MORE SENTENCES

"It was the Cuba of the future. It was going the way of Iran. It was another Nicaragua, another Cambodia, another Vietnam . . . . All that was being said was that something was happening in the Philippines."

7. USE OF A PARTIAL SENTENCE

Fenton describes the "confusion" surrounding the Philippines. [No ellipsis mark needed.]

Note these features of the examples:

- ❖ Use an ellipsis mark when it is not otherwise clear that you have left out material from the source, as when the words you quote form a complete sentence that is different in the original (examples 1–5). You don't need an ellipsis mark at the beginning or end of a partial sentence because it will already be obvious that you omitted something (example 7).
- ❖ After a grammatically complete sentence, an ellipsis mark usually follows a sentence period and a space (examples 2 and 6). The exception occurs when a parenthetical source citation follows the quotation (example 3), in which case the sentence period falls after the citation.

If you omit one or more lines of poetry or paragraphs of prose from a quotation, use a separate line of ellipsis marks across the full width of the quotation to show the omission.

> In "Song: Love Armed" from 1676, Aphra Behn contrasts two
>
> lovers' experiences of a romance:
>
>> Love in fantastic triumph sate,
>>
>>> Whilst bleeding hearts around him flowed,
>>
>> . . . .
>>
>> But my poor heart alone is harmed,
>>
>>> Whilst thine the victor is, and free. (lines 1-2, 15-16)

(See p. 206 for the format of displayed quotations like this one.)

39d Use brackets to indicate changes in quotations.

Brackets have specialized uses in mathematical equations, but their main use for all kinds of writing is to indicate that you have altered a quotation to explain, clarify, or correct it.

"That Texaco station [just outside Chicago] is one of the busiest in the nation," said a company spokesperson.

The word *sic* (Latin for "in this manner") in brackets indicates that an error in the quotation appeared in the original and was not made by you. Do not underline or italicize *sic* in brackets.

According to the newspaper report, "The car slammed thru [*sic*] the railing and into oncoming traffic."

But don't use *sic* to make fun of a writer or to note errors in a passage that is clearly nonstandard.

39e   Use the slash between options and between lines of poetry.

Use the slash between options:

Some teachers oppose pass/fail courses.

The slash also separates lines of poetry that you run into your text. (Surround the slash with space.)

Many readers have sensed a reluctant turn away from death in Frost's lines "The woods are lovely, dark and deep, / But I have promises to keep" (13–14).

V

Conventions of Form and Appearance

❖

V

Conventions of Form and Appearance

❖

40 Document Format

Legible, consistent, and attractive documents are a service to your readers. This chapter describes and illustrates a basic format for academic papers (below) and some ways you can use a computer for designing documents (p. 207). (See Chapter 56 for the format of business documents.)

NOTE Trying to format a document while you draft it can interfere with the flow of your ideas. Except for choosing initial margins, line spacing, and typeface, leave formatting for the final, editing stage of revision.

40a Use an appropriate format for your academic papers.

The guidelines below are adapted from the *MLA Handbook for Writers of Research Papers*, the style book for English and some other disciplines. Most of these guidelines are standard, but instructors in various courses may expect you to follow different conventions. Check with your instructor for his or her preferences, or consult one of the style guides for specific disciplines, listed on pages 266–67. The style of the American Psychological Association is discussed on pages 318–20.

1. Paper and print

Use 8½″ × 11″ white bond paper of sixteen- or twenty-pound weight. Use the same type of paper throughout a project. If you use continuous paper folded like a fan at perforations, remove the strips of holes along the sides, and separate the pages at the folds.

Your typewriter's or printer's ribbon or cartridge should produce a dark impression. If you use a dot-matrix printer, make sure the characters are legible. (Show your instructor a sample of the type to be sure it is acceptable.)

2. Margins and spacing

Use one-inch margins on all sides of each page. (The top margin will contain the page numbers.) Use an even (or justified) right margin only if it does not leave wide spaces between words and thus interfere with readability.

Indent the first line of every paragraph one-half inch, and double-space throughout.

FIRST PAGE OF PAPER

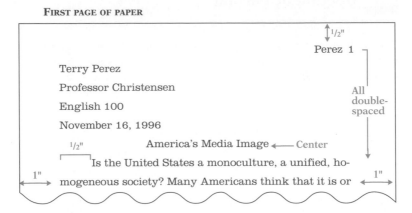

A LATER PAGE OF THE PAPER

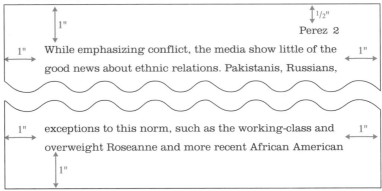

NOTE Don't try to achieve an assigned page count by increasing or decreasing margins or line spacing. If you're having trouble filling the specified pages, you may need to broaden your topic, explore it in more detail, or do more research. If you're having trouble fitting into the specified pages, you may need to narrow your topic or cut digressions.

3. Paging

Begin numbering your paper in the upper right of the first text page, and number consecutively through the end. Use Arabic numerals (1, 2, 3), and place your last name before the page number in case the pages become separated after you submit your paper.

ms
40a

Checklist for preparing an academic paper

❖ Have you used sturdy white paper measuring 8½″ × 11″?
❖ Have you used only one side of each page?
❖ Is the type dark?
❖ Is everything double-spaced?
❖ Do your name, the instructor's name, the course title, and the date appear on the first page?
❖ Is your paper titled and the title centered?
❖ Are the margins at least one inch on all sides?
❖ Are all the pages numbered consecutively in the upper right, starting with page 1 for the first text page? Does your last name appear before each page number?
❖ If you have used sources, have you cited them in your text and attached a list of works cited?
❖ Have you proofread the paper and corrected all errors?
❖ Are the pages of your paper clipped, stapled, folded, or bound, as requested by your instructor?

---

4. Title and identification

Provide your name and the date, plus any other information requested by your instructor, in the upper left of the first text page. Center the title, and capitalize words in it according to the guidelines on page 224. (See p. 24 for advice on creating titles.) Double-space all this opening material.

5. Text

Use a 10-point or 12-point typeface for the text (see p. 208), and space elements as illustrated in the sample opposite. Treat punctuation as follows:

❖ Leave one space between words.
❖ Leave one space after all punctuation, with these exceptions:

Dash (two hyphens)	book--its
Hyphen	one-half
Apostrophe within a word	book's
Between two or more adjacent marks	book.")

❖ Leave one space before the three dots of an ellipsis mark (see p. 198):

book . . . in
book. . . . The

ms
40a

❖ Don't start a line with a mark of punctuation other than a dash, an opening parenthesis, an opening quotation mark, an opening bracket, or an ellipsis mark.

❖ Don't end a line with an opening quotation mark, parenthesis, or bracket. Close these marks up to the word following.

❖ Don't break a two-hyphen dash or a three-dot ellipsis mark from one line to the next.

6. Quotations

Poetry

When you quote a single line from a poem, song, or verse play, run the line into your text and enclose it in quotation marks:

> Dylan Thomas remembered childhood as an idyllic time: "About the lilting house and happy as the grass was green" ("Fern Hill" line 2).

(The parenthetical information above and in the following examples provides source citations. See pp. 272–77 for an explanation.)

Poetry quotations of two or three lines may be placed in the text or displayed separately. In the text enclose the quotation in quotation marks and separate the lines with a slash surrounded by space:

> An example of Robert Frost's incisiveness is in two lines from "Death of the Hired Man": "Home is the place where, when you have to go there / They have to take you in" (119-20).

Quotations of more than three lines of poetry should always be separated from the text with space and an indention. *Do not add quotation marks.*

> Emily Dickinson stripped ideas to their essence, as in this description of "A narrow Fellow in the Grass," a snake:
>
> > I more than once at Noon
> > Have passed, I thought, a Whip lash
> > Unbraiding in the Sun
> > When stopping to secure it
> > It wrinkled, and was gone (12-16)

Double-space above, below, and throughout a displayed quotation. Indent the quotation one inch from the left margin.

Prose

Run a prose quotation of four or fewer typed lines into your text, and enclose it in quotation marks.

Separate quotations of five typed lines or more from the body of your paper. (Use such quotations sparingly. See p. 258.) *Do not add quotation marks.*

> In his 1967 study of the lives of unemployed black men, Elliot Liebow observes that "unskilled" construction work requires more experience and skill than is generally assumed.
>
> > A healthy, sturdy, active man of good intelligence requires from two to four weeks to break in on a construction job. . . . It frequently happens that his foreman or the craftsman he services is not willing to wait that long for him to get into condition or to learn at a glance the difference in size between a rough 2 x 8 and a finished 2 x 10. (62)

Double-space before, after, and throughout a displayed quotation. Indent the quotation one inch from the left.

Dialogue

When quoting conversations, begin a new paragraph for each speaker.

> "What shall I call you? Your name?" Andrews whispered rapidly, as with a high squeak the latch of the door rose.
> "Elizabeth," she said. "Elizabeth."
> > —GRAHAM GREENE, *The Man Within*

When you quote a single speaker for more than one paragraph, put quotation marks at the beginning of each paragraph but at the end of only the last paragraph.

40b   Designing documents

The preceding recommendations for document format will help you produce neat, legible papers, but sometimes your work may call for more. You may need headings to separate and label parts of the work, lists to highlight steps or conclusions, tables or graphs to organize data and show trends.

With computerized word processing, especially desktop publishing, it is possible to produce papers, reports, letters, and so on that look as if they have been professionally typeset and printed, like this book. But even if you work on a typewriter or a very basic word processor, many of the following guidelines can help you produce effective documents. The key elements are white space, type

ms
40b

styles and sizes, lists, headings, tables and illustrations, and sometimes color.

1. White space

The white space on a page eases crowding, highlights elements, and focuses readers' attention. On an otherwise full page, just the half-inch space of a paragraph indention gives readers a break and reassures them that you have divided ideas into manageable chunks. (See p. 39.)

White space appears mainly in margins and around headings and lists. Use minimum one-inch margins on all sides of the page. Make headings stand out: in double-spaced copy, double- or triple-space above and double-space below; in single-spaced copy, double-space above and below.

2. Type styles and sizes

Variations in the size of type and the style can affect the readability and the clarity of your work.

For your text, always choose a type size of 10 or 12 points. Here are some samples:

`12-point Courier`   12-point Times Roman

`10-point Courier`   10-point Times Roman

For text use a typeface with SERIFS—the small lines finishing the letters in the samples above. SANS SERIF typefaces (*sans* means "without") include this one commonly found on word processors:

12-point Helvetica
10-point Helvetica

Though fine for headings, sans serif typefaces can be more difficult than serif faces to read in extended text.

Within the text you can use underlining or *italic* or **boldface** or SMALL CAPITALS to emphasize key words or sentences. For academic writing, instructors often prefer underlining to italics, especially for titles in source citations. Italics are more common in business writing. No matter what your writing situation, however, use such emphasis selectively to complement your meaning, not to decorate your work. Many readers consider type embellishments to be distracting.

3. Lists

ms
40b

If your work contains a list of related items—for example, the steps in a process or the elements in a proposal—then consider indenting the items with numbers or bullets (centered dots, squares, diamonds, or other elements). Bulleted lists appear throughout this handbook, as below. A list is easier to read and remember than a paragraph and adds white space to the page. Many word processors can format a numbered or bulleted list automatically.

When formatting a list, follow these guidelines:

❖ Make the wording of the items consistent. In this list, for example, each item starts with a verb of command (*Make . . . , Limit . . . , Use . . .*). (See p. 61.)

❖ Limit the number of items in each list to six or seven. A longer list defeats the purpose of making the items memorable for readers.

❖ Use lists only for related and equivalent items: steps, reasons, elements, effects, features, guidelines, and so on.

4. Headings

In a research paper, business report, or similarly long and complex document, headings within the text can clarify organization and the relationships among parts.

Placement and wording

Overlapping, missing, or inconsistent headings can do your document more harm than good.

❖ Create an outline of your document in order to plan where headings should go. (See pp. 16 18.)

❖ Keep headings as short as possible while making them specific about the material that follows.

❖ Word headings consistently for instance, all questions (*What Is the Scientific Method?*), all phrases with *-ing* words (*Understanding the Scientific Method*), or all phrases with nouns (*The Scientific Method*).

Design

Even on a typewriter, you can design headings for visibility and clarity.

❖ Indicate the relative importance of headings with type size, positioning, and highlighting, such as capital letters and underlining.

FIRST-LEVEL HEADING

Second-Level Heading

Third-Level Heading

ms
40b

FIRST-LEVEL HEADING

Second-Level Heading

Third-Level Heading

❖ Keep the appearance simple: most reports or papers shouldn't need more than two type styles or two or three type sizes (including the body type). Except in promotional pieces, avoid extra-large letters and unusual styles of type (such as outline and shadow type).

❖ Don't break a page immediately after a heading. Push the heading to the next page.

NOTE Document format in psychology and some other social sciences requires a particular treatment of headings. See page 320.

5. Tables and illustrations

Tables and illustrations (graphs, charts, diagrams, photographs) can often make a point for you more efficiently and effectively than words can. Such visuals show data, make comparisons, explain processes, demonstrate changes, and represent what something looks like, among other uses.

NOTE Many organizations and academic disciplines have preferred styles for tables and figures. When in doubt about how to prepare and place visuals, ask your instructor or supervisor.

Content

Whether you're preparing a table or an illustration, consider the basics:

❖ Focus on a purpose for the table or illustration—a single point you want it to make. Otherwise, it may be too complex and may confuse readers.

❖ Provide a title for the table or illustration so that the reader knows immediately what its purpose and content are. Generally, a table's title falls above the table, whereas an illustration's title falls below.

❖ Make the table or illustration legible and attractive.

❖ Provide clear labels for all parts, such as columns and rows in a table, bars in a graph, and parts of a machine in a drawing. In the interest of clarity, avoid abbreviations unless you know your readers will understand them.

NOTE You may obtain your data or an entire visual from another source—for instance, from a book, journal article, CD-ROM database, or site on the World Wide Web. (You may be able to download a visual directly from an electronic source into your own document.) You must acknowledge any borrowed material in a source note (see p. 260). Each discipline has a slightly different style for such source notes. Those in the table below and the figures on page 212 reflect the style of the social sciences. See also pages 265–67.

Numbering and placement

Number and position tables and illustrations so that the reader knows what parts of the text they're relevant to and can find them easily.

* Number tables and figures separately (Table 1, Table 2, etc.; Figure 1, Figure 2, etc.).
* Refer to each table or figure (for instance, "See Figure 2") at the point(s) in the text where readers will benefit by consulting it.
* Unless your document includes many visuals, place each one on a page by itself immediately after the page that refers to it.

Tables

Tables usually summarize raw data, displaying the data concisely and clearly.

Table 1

Computers, Telephones, and Televisions per 1,000 People (1994)

Location	Computers	Telephones	Televisions
Worldwide	37	152	174
United States	365	965	900
Europe	93	508	419
Japan	105	645	625
Former Soviet republics	14	145	335

Note: From 8th Annual Computer Industry Almanac (p. 38), by K. P. Juliussen and E. Juliussen, 1995, Incline Village, NV: Computer Industry Almanac.

Illustrations

Illustrations often recast data into visual form. Pie charts, bar graphs, and line graphs are helpful for comparisons, such as changes and proportions.

ms
40b

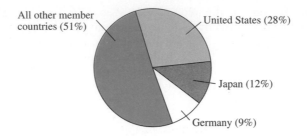

Figure 1. Member countries' assessments to United Nations budget of $1.1 billion in 1994. From "The U.N. at 50," by R. Mylan, 1995, October 18, *Newsweek,* p. 17.

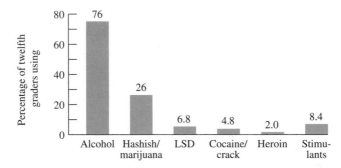

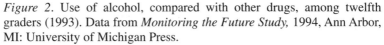

Figure 2. Use of alcohol, compared with other drugs, among twelfth graders (1993). Data from *Monitoring the Future Study,* 1994, Ann Arbor, MI: University of Michigan Press.

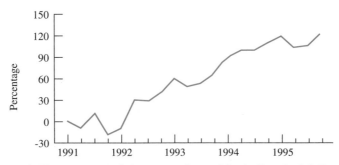

Figure 3. Five-year cumulative return for equities in Standard & Poor's 500 Index, 1991–1995.

ms
40b

6. Color

With a color printer and appropriate software you can produce documents that use color for bullets, headings, box borders, illustrations, and other elements. Academic papers and business documents consisting only of text and headings don't need color. (Ask your instructor or supervisor for his or her preferences.) If you do use color, follow these guidelines:

* Employ color to clarify and highlight your content. Too much color or too many colors on a page will distract rather than focus readers' attention.
* Typefaces in color can be hard to read. Use color only for boldfaced or large headings, and choose colors that make the type easily readable. Stick to the same color for all headings at the same level (for instance, red for primary headings, black for secondary headings).
* For bullets, box borders, lines, and other nontext elements, color can be used more decoratively to enliven the page. Still, stick to only one or two colors to keep the page clean.
* For illustrations, use color to distinguish the segments of charts, the lines of graphs, and the parts of diagrams. (See opposite for examples.) Use only as many colors as you need to make your illustration clear.

7. Samples of document design

Two partial samples of documents designed on computers appear on the next two pages. The first is from a business report intended to outline a problem and propose a solution. It illustrates a restrained use of typefaces, suitable for a formal business-writing situation. The report's problem-solution organization is clearly represented in its design with headings and other elements.

The second example, from a newsletter distributed to about fifty people, is designed to engage, motivate, and inform volunteers who teach reading to veterans of the armed services. Because of its purpose, this newsletter is livelier in appearance than the business report, using extra-large type for title and headings, lines, borders, and color to catch the eye of readers and focus their attention on distinct elements. The borders, rules, and column format of this newsletter are available on many word processors and all desktop publishers.

ms
40b

Canada Geese at ABC Institute: An Environmental Problem

Summary

The flock of Canada geese on and around ABC Institute's grounds has grown dramatically in recent years. What was once a source of pleasure for institute employees and others using the grounds has become a nuisance and an environmental problem. This report reviews the problem, considers the options for reducing the flock, and proposes as a solution the cooperation of ABC Institute, the municipalities around Taylor Lake, and the US Fish and Wildlife Service to reduce the flock by humane means.

The Problem

Canada geese began living at Taylor Lake, adjacent to ABC Institute, when they were relocated there in 1970 by the state game department. As a nonmigratory flock, the geese are present year-round, with the highest population each year occurring in fall, winter, and early spring, after the young have fledged.

In recent years the flock of geese at Taylor Lake has grown dramatically. The Audubon Society's annual Christmas bird census shows a thirty-fold increase from the 37 geese counted in 1972 to the 1125 counted in 1996. The following chart illustrates the increase between 1985 and 1996:

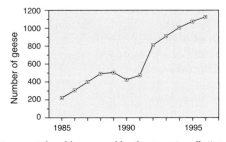

The principal environmental problem caused by the geese is pollution of grass and water by defecation. During high-population months, geese droppings cover the ABC Institute's grounds as well as the park's athletic fields and picnicking areas. The runoff from these droppings into Taylor Lake has substantially affected the quality of the lake's water, so that local authorities have twice (1995 and 1996) issued warnings against swimming.

The Solution

Several possible solutions to the goose overpopulation and resulting environmental problems are *not viable alternatives:*

- Harass the geese with dogs and audiovisual effects (light and noise) so that the geese choose to leave. This solution is inhumane to the geese and unpleasant for human neighbors.
- Feed the geese a chemical that will weaken the shells of their eggs and thus reduce growth of the flock. This solution is inhumane to the geese and also impractical, because geese are long-lived.
- Kill adult geese. This solution is, obviously, inhumane to the geese.

The most appropriate and humane solution is to thin the goose population by trapping and removing many geese (perhaps 600) to areas less populated by humans, such as wildlife preserves and wilderness areas. Though costly (see figures below), this solution would be efficient and harmless to the geese, provided that sizable netted enclosures are used for traps. [Discussion of solution continues, followed by "Recommendations."]

ms
40b

VA Literacy Volunteers

Springfield Veterans Administration Hospital   **SPRING 1997**

From the director

Can you help us? With more and more learners in the VA's literacy program, we need more and more tutors. You may know people who would be interested in participating in the program, if only they knew about it.

Those of you who have been tutoring VA patients in reading and writing know both the great need you fulfill and the great benefits you bring to your students. New tutors need no special skills (we'll provide the training), only patience and an interest in helping others.

We've scheduled an orientation meeting for Friday, June 6, at 6:30 PM. Please come and bring a friend who is willing to contribute a couple of hours a week to our work.

Thanks,
Nancy Thomas

IN THIS ISSUE

AWARDS FOR STUDENTS AND TUTORS AT ANNUAL DINNER

The annual SVAH literacy dinner on February 25 was a great success. George Bello obtained food and beverage contributions from area restaurants and suppliers, and the students decorated the dining room on the theme of books and reading. In all, eighty-six people attended.

The highlight of the night was the awards ceremony. Ten students, recommended by their tutors, received certificates recognizing their efforts and special accomplishments in learning to read and write:

Ramon Berva
Edward Byar
David Dunbar
Tony Garnier
Chris Giugni
Akili Haynes
Pat Laird
Jim Livingston
Paul Obeid
B. J. Resnansky

In addition, ten tutors received certificates commemorating five years of service at SVAH:

Anita Crumpton
Felix Cruz-Rivera
Bette Eigen
Kelly Bortoluzzi
Amitav Ghosh
Harriotte Henderson

Andy Obiso
Carla Puente
Robert Smith
Sara Villante

Congratulations to all!

New Guidelines on PTSD

Most of us are working with veterans who have been diagnosed with post-traumatic stress disorder. Because this disorder is often complicated by alcoholism, depression, anxiety, and other problems, the National Center for PTSD has issued some guidelines for helping PTSD patients in a way that reduces their stress:

▶ The hospital must know your tutoring schedule, and you need to sign in and out before and after each tutoring session.

▶ Cancellations are stressful for patients. Stick to your schedule.

▶ To protect patients' privacy, meet them only in designated visiting and tutoring areas, never in their rooms.

▶ Treat patients with dignity and respect, even when (as sometimes happens) they grow frustrated and angry. Seek help from a nurse or orderly if you need it.

ms
40b

41 Spelling

You can train yourself to spell better, and this chapter will tell you how. But you can also improve instantly by acquiring three habits:

- ❖ Carefully proofread your writing.
- ❖ Cultivate a healthy suspicion of your spellings.
- ❖ Compulsively check a dictionary whenever you doubt a spelling.

NOTE The spelling checkers for computerized word processors can help you find and track spelling errors in your papers. But their usefulness is limited, mainly because they can't spot the very common error of confusing words with similar spellings, such as *their/there/they're, to/too/two,* and any of the other groups in the list below. A spelling checker can supplement but can't substitute for your own care and attention.

41a Anticipate typical spelling problems.

Certain situations, such as misleading pronunciation, commonly lead to misspelling.

1. Pronunciation

In English, pronunciation of words is an unreliable guide to how they are spelled. Pronunciation is especially misleading with HOMONYMS, words pronounced the same but spelled differently. Some homonyms and near-homonyms appear below.

Words commonly confused	
accept (to receive)	bare (unclothed)
except (other than)	bear (to carry, or an animal)
affect (to have an influence on)	board (a plane of wood)
effect (result)	bored (uninterested)
all ready (prepared)	brake (stop)
already (by this time)	break (smash)
allusion (indirect reference)	buy (purchase)
illusion (erroneous belief or	by (next to)
perception)	cite (to quote an authority)
ascent (a movement up)	sight (the ability to see)
assent (agreement)	site (a place)

desert (to abandon)
dessert (after-dinner course)

discreet (reserved, respectful)
discrete (individual, distinct)

fair (average, or lovely)
fare (a fee for transportation)

forth (forward)
fourth (after *third*)

hear (to perceive by ear)
here (in this place)

heard (past tense of *hear*)
herd (a group of animals)

hole (an opening)
whole (complete)

its (possessive of *it*)
it's (contraction of *it is*)

know (to be certain)
no (the opposite of *yes*)

meat (flesh)
meet (encounter)

passed (past tense of *pass*)
past (after, or a time gone by)

patience (forbearance)
patients (persons under medical
    care)

peace (the absence of war)
piece (a portion of something)

plain (clear)
plane (a carpenter's tool, or an
    airborne vehicle)

presence (the state of being at
    hand)
presents (gifts)

principal (most important, or
    the head of a school)
principle (a basic truth or law)

rain (precipitation)
reign (to rule)
rein (a strap for controlling an
    animal)

right (correct)
rite (a religious ceremony)
write (to make letters)

road (a surface for driving)
rode (past tense of *ride*)

scene (where an action occurs)
seen (past participle of *see*)

stationary (unmoving)
stationery (writing paper)

their (possessive of *they*)
there (opposite of *here*)
they're (contraction of *they are*)

to (toward)
too (also)
two (following *one*)

waist (the middle of the body)
waste (discarded material)

weak (not strong)
week (Sunday through Saturday)

weather (climate)
whether (*if*, or introducing a
    choice)

which (one of a group)
witch (a sorcerer)

who's (contraction of *who is*)
whose (possessive of *who*)

your (possessive of *you*)
you're (contraction of *you are*)

2. Different forms of the same word

Often, the noun form and the verb form of the same word are spelled differently: for example, *advice* (noun) and *advise* (verb). Sometimes the noun and the adjective forms of the same word dif-

sp
41a

fer: *height* and *high*. Similar changes occur in the parts of some irregular verbs (*know, knew, known*) and the plurals of irregular nouns (*man, men*).

3. American vs. British spellings   ESL

If you learned English outside the United States, you may be accustomed to British rather than American spellings. Here are the chief differences:

AMERICAN	BRITISH
color, humor	colour, humour
theater, center	theatre, centre
canceled, traveled	cancelled, travelled
judgment	judgement
realize, civilize	realise, civilise
connection	connexion

41b   Follow spelling rules.

1. *Ie* vs. *ei*

To distinguish between *ie* and *ei,* use the familiar jingle:

I before *e,* except after *c,* or when pronounced "ay" as in *neighbor* and *weigh*.

i BEFORE *e*	believe	thief	hygiene
ei AFTER *c*	ceiling	conceive	perceive
ei SOUNDED AS "AY"	sleigh	eight	beige

EXCEPTIONS For some of the exceptions, remember this sentence:

The weird foreigner neither seizes leisure nor forfeits height.

2. Final *-e*

When adding an ending to a word ending in *-e,* drop the *-e* if the ending begins with a vowel.

advise + able = advisable   surprise + ing = surprising

Keep the *-e* if the ending begins with a consonant.

care + ful = careful   like + ly = likely

EXCEPTIONS Retain the *-e* after a soft *c* or *g,* to keep the sound of the consonant soft rather than hard: *courageous, changeable*. And drop the -*e* before a consonant when the -*e* is preceded by another vowel: *argue* + *ment* = *argument*, *true* + *ly* = *truly*.

3. Final -*y*

When adding an ending to a word ending in -*y*, change the *y* to *i* if it follows a consonant.

beauty, beauties   worry, worried   supply, supplies

But keep the *y* if it follows a vowel, if it ends a proper name, or if the ending is -*ing*.

day, days   Minsky, Minskys   cry, crying

4. Final consonants

When adding an ending to a word ending in a consonant, double the consonant if it is preceded by a single vowel or if the stress, once the ending is added, falls on the syllable finished by the consonant.

slap, slapping   submit, submitted   begin, beginning

Don't double the final consonant if it is preceded by two vowels or a vowel and another consonant or if the stress, once the ending is added, falls on some syllable other than the one finished by the consonant.

pair, paired   park, parking   refer, reference

5. Prefixes

When adding a prefix, do not drop a letter from or add a letter to the original word.

unnecessary   disappoint   misspell

6. Plurals

Most nouns form plurals by adding -*s* to the singular form. Add -*es* for the plural of nouns ending in -*s*, -*sh*, -*ch*, or -*x*.

boy, boys   kiss, kisses   church, churches

ESL Noncount nouns do not form plurals and so do not add -*s*. Examples include *equipment, intelligence,* and *wealth.* (See p. 149.)

Nouns ending in -*o* preceded by a vowel usually form the plural with -*s*. Those ending in -*o* preceded by a consonant usually form the plural with -*es*.

sp
41b

ratio, ratios   hero, heroes

Some very common nouns form irregular plurals.

child, children   man, men
mouse, mice   woman, women

Some English nouns that were originally Italian, Greek, Latin, or French form the plural according to their original language:

analysis, analyses   datum, data
basis, bases   medium, media
beau, beaux   phenomenon, phenomena
crisis, crises   piano, pianos
criterion, criteria   thesis, theses

A few such nouns may form irregular *or* regular plurals: for instance, *index, indices, indexes; curriculum, curricula, curriculums.* The regular plural is more contemporary.

With compound nouns, add *-s* to the main word of the compound. Sometimes this main word is not the last word.

city-states   fathers-in-law   passersby

---

42 The Hyphen

Always use a hyphen to divide a word between syllables from one line to the next. Also use it to form some COMPOUND WORDS expressing a combination of ideas, such as *cross-reference*. The following rules cover many but not all compounds. When you doubt the spelling of a compound word, consult a dictionary.

42a Use the hyphen in some compound adjectives.

When two or more words serve together as a single modifier before a noun, a hyphen forms the modifying words clearly into a unit.

She is a *well-known* actor.
No *English-speaking* people were in the room.

When such a compound adjective follows the noun, the hyphen is unnecessary.

hyph
42a

The actor is *well-known*.
Those people are *English-speaking*.

The hyphen is also unnecessary in a compound modifier containing an *-ly* adverb, even before the noun: *clearly-defined terms.*

When part of a compound adjective appears only once in two or more parallel compound adjectives, hyphens indicate which words the reader should mentally join with the missing part.

School-age children should have eight- or nine-o'clock bedtimes.

42b Use the hyphen in fractions and compound numbers.

Hyphens join the numerator and denominator of fractions: *one-half, three-fourths.* Hyphens also join the parts of the whole numbers *twenty-one* to *ninety-nine.*

42c Use the hyphen to attach some prefixes and suffixes.

Prefixes are usually attached to word stems without hyphens: *predetermine, unnatural, disengage.* However, a hyphen usually separates the two when the prefix precedes a capitalized word (*un-American*), when a capital letter combines with a word (*A-frame*), and when the combination links two of the same vowel or three of the same consonant (*de-emphasize, trill-like*). And some prefixes, such as *self-, all-,* and *ex-* (meaning "formerly"), usually require hyphens no matter what follows: *self-control, all-inclusive, ex-student.* The only suffix that regularly requires a hyphen is *-elect,* as in *president-elect.*

43 Capital Letters

The following conventions and a desk dictionary can help you decide whether to capitalize a particular word in most writing. The social, natural, and applied sciences require specialized capitalization for terminology, such as *Conditions A and B* or *Escherichia coli.* Consult one of the style guides listed on pages 266–67 for the requirements of the discipline you are writing in.

ESL Conventions of capitalization vary from language to language. English, for instance, is the only language to capitalize the first-person singular pronoun (*I*), and its practice of capitalizing

cap

43

proper nouns but not most common nouns also distinguishes it from some other languages.

43a   Capitalize the first word of every sentence.

Every writer should own a good dictionary.

When quoting other writers, you should reproduce the capital letters beginning their sentences or indicate that you have altered the source's capitalization. Whenever possible, integrate the quotation into your own sentence so that its capitalization coincides with yours:

"Psychotherapists often overlook the benefits of self-deception," the author argues.

The author argues that "the benefits of self-deception" are not always recognized by psychotherapists.

If you need to alter the capitalization in the source, indicate the change with brackets:

"[T]he benefits of self-deception" are not always recognized by psychotherapists, the author argues.

The author argues that "[p]sychotherapists often overlook the benefits of self-deception."

Note Capitalization of questions in a series is optional. Both of the following examples are correct.

Is the population a hundred? Two hundred? More?
Is the population a hundred? two hundred? more?

Also optional is capitalization of the first word in a complete sentence after a colon.

43b   Capitalize proper nouns, proper adjectives, and words used as essential parts of proper nouns.

1. Proper nouns and proper adjectives

Proper nouns name specific persons, places, and things: *Shakespeare, California, World War I*. **Proper adjectives** are formed from some proper nouns: *Shakespearean, Californian*. Capitalize all proper nouns and proper adjectives but not the articles (*a, an, the*) that precede them.

cap
43b

Proper nouns and adjectives to be capitalized

SPECIFIC PERSONS AND THINGS

Stephen King
Napoleon Bonaparte

Boulder Dam
the Empire State Building

SPECIFIC PLACES AND GEOGRAPHICAL REGIONS

New York City
China

the Mediterranean Sea
the Northeast, the South

But: northeast of the city, going south

DAYS OF THE WEEK, MONTHS, HOLIDAYS

Monday
May

Yom Kippur
Christmas

HISTORICAL EVENTS, DOCUMENTS, PERIODS, MOVEMENTS

the Vietnam War
the Constitution

the Renaissance
the Romantic Movement

GOVERNMENT OFFICES OR DEPARTMENTS AND INSTITUTIONS

House of Representatives
Department of Defense

Polk Municipal Court
Northeast High School

POLITICAL, SOCIAL, ATHLETIC, AND OTHER ORGANIZATIONS AND ASSOCIATIONS AND THEIR MEMBERS

Democratic Party, Democrats
Sierra Club
B'nai B'rith

League of Women Voters
Boston Celtics
Chicago Symphony Orchestra

RACES, NATIONALITIES, AND THEIR LANGUAGES

Native American
African American, Negro
Caucasian

Germans
Swahili
Italian

But: blacks, whites

RELIGIONS, THEIR FOLLOWERS, AND TERMS FOR THE SACRED

Christianity, Christians
Catholicism, Catholics
Judaism, Orthodox Jew
Islam, Moslems *or* Muslims

God
Allah
the Bible (*but* biblical)
the Koran

2. Common nouns used as essential parts of proper nouns

Capitalize the common nouns *street, avenue, park, river, ocean, lake, company, college, county,* and *memorial* when they are part of proper nouns naming specific places or institutions.

cap
43b

Main Street	Lake Superior
Central Park	Ford Motor Company
Mississippi River	Madison College
Pacific Ocean	George Washington Memorial

43c Capitalize most words in titles and subtitles of works.

Within your text, capitalize all the words in a title *except* the following: articles (*a, an, the*); *to* in infinitives; and connecting words (prepositions and conjunctions) of fewer than five letters. Capitalize even these short words when they are the first or last word in a title or when they fall after a colon or semicolon.

"Courtship Through the Ages"	*Management: A New Theory*
A Diamond Is Forever	"Once More to the Lake"
"Knowing Whom to Ask"	*An End to Live For*
Learning from Las Vegas	*File Under Architecture*

NOTE Some academic disciplines require a different treatment of titles within source citations, such as capitalizing only the first words of some or all titles. See pages 309–18 (APA style) and 335–38 (CBE style).

43d Capitalize titles preceding persons' names.

Before a person's name, capitalize his or her title. After or apart from the name, do not capitalize the title.

Professor Otto Osborne	Otto Osborne, a professor
Doctor Jane Covington	Jane Covington, a doctor
Governor Ella Moore	Ella Moore, the governor

NOTE   Many writers capitalize a title denoting very high rank even when it follows a name or is used alone: *Lyndon Johnson, past President of the United States.*

44 Underlining (Italics)

Underlining and *italic type* indicate the same thing: the word or words are being distinguished or emphasized. In business the almost universal use of computerized word processors makes both forms of highlighting possible, and italics may be preferred. In schools the use of italics is less common, and many disciplines continue to require underlining for works in source citations. Consult your instructor before you use italic type.

NOTE If you underline two or more words in a row, underline the space between the words, too: Criminal Statistics: Misuses of Numbers.

44a Underline the titles of works that appear independently.

Within your text, underline the titles of works, such as books and periodicals, that are published, released, or produced separately from other works. (See the box below.) Use quotation marks for all other titles, such as short stories, articles in periodicals, and episodes of television series. (See p. 193.)

Titles to be underlined (Italicized)
Other titles should be placed in quotation marks (see p. 193).

BOOKS
War and Peace
And the Band Played On

LONG POEMS
Beowulf
Paradise Lost

PLAYS
Hamlet
The Phantom of the Opera

PERIODICALS
Time
Philadelphia Inquirer

PAMPHLETS
The Truth About Alcoholism

PUBLISHED SPEECHES
Lincoln's Gettysburg Address

LONG MUSICAL WORKS
Tchaikovsky's Swan Lake
But: Symphony in C

MOVIES AND VIDEOTAPES
Schindler's List
How to Relax

TELEVISION AND RADIO PROGRAMS
The Shadow
Seinfeld

WORKS OF VISUAL ART
Michelangelo's David
the Mona Lisa

EXCEPTIONS Legal documents, the Bible, the Koran, and their parts are generally not underlined.

NOT   We studied the Book of Revelation in the Bible.
BUT   We studied the Book of Revelation in the Bible.

und
44a

44b **Underline the names of ships, aircraft, spacecraft, and trains.**

Challenger   Orient Express   Queen Elizabeth 2
Apollo XI   Montrealer   Spirit of St. Louis

44c **Underline foreign words that are not part of the English language.**

A foreign expression should be underlined when it has not been absorbed into our language. A dictionary will say whether a word is still considered foreign to English.

The scientific name for the brown trout is <u>Salmo trutta</u>. [The Latin scientific names for plants and animals are always underlined.]

The Latin <u>De gustibus non est disputandum</u> translates roughly as "There's no accounting for taste."

44d **Underline words being defined or words, letters, or numbers being named as words.**

The word <u>syzygy</u> refers to a straight line formed by three celestial bodies, as in the alignment of the earth, sun, and moon.

Some people say <u>th</u>, as in <u>thought</u>, with a faint <u>s</u> or <u>f</u> sound.

44e **Occasionally, underlining may be used for emphasis.**

Underlining can stress an important word or phrase, especially in reporting how someone said something. But use such emphasis very rarely, or your writing may sound immature or hysterical.

45 Abbreviations

The following guidelines on abbreviations pertain to the text of a nontechnical document. All academic disciplines use abbreviations in source citations, and much technical writing, such as in the sciences and engineering, uses many abbreviations in the document text. Consult one of the style guides listed on pages 266–67 for the in-text requirements of the discipline you are writing in.

NOTE Usage varies, but writers increasingly omit periods from abbreviations of two or more words written in all-capital letters: *US, BA, USMC.* See page 171 on punctuating abbreviations.

45a Use standard abbreviations for titles immediately before and after proper names.

BEFORE THE NAME	AFTER THE NAME
Dr. James Hsu	James Hsu, MD
Mr., Mrs., Ms., Hon.,	DDS, DVM, Ph.D.,
St., Rev., Msgr., Gen.	Ed.D., OSB, SJ, Sr., Jr.

Do not use abbreviations such as *Rev., Hon., Prof., Rep., Sen., Dr.,* and *St.* (for *Saint*) unless they appear before a proper name.

45b Familiar abbreviations and acronyms are acceptable in most writing.

An ACRONYM is an abbreviation that spells a pronounceable word, such as WHO, NATO, and AIDS. These and other abbreviations using initials are acceptable in most writing as long as they are familiar to readers.

INSTITUTIONS	LSU, UCLA, TCU
ORGANIZATIONS	CIA, FBI, YMCA, AFL-CIO
CORPORATIONS	IBM, CBS, ITT
PEOPLE	JFK, LBJ, FDR
COUNTRIES	USA

NOTE If a name or term (such as *operating room*) appears often in a piece of writing, then its abbreviation (*OR*) can cut down on extra words. Spell out the full term at its first appearance, indicate its abbreviation in parentheses, and then use the abbreviation.

45c Use *BC, AD, AM, PM, no.,* and *$* only with specific dates and numbers.

44 BC	11:26 AM (*or* a.m.)	no. 36 (*or* No. 36)
AD 1492	8:05 PM (*or* p.m.)	$7.41

The abbreviation BC ("before Christ") always follows a date, whereas AD (*anno Domini,* Latin for "in the year of the Lord") precedes a date.

NOTE BCE ("before the common era") and CE ("common era") are increasingly replacing BC and AD, respectively. Both follow the date.

ab
45c

45d **Generally, reserve Latin abbreviations for source citations and comments in parentheses.**

i.e.   *id est:* that is
cf.   *confer:* compare
e.g.   *exempli gratia:* for example
et al.   *et alii:* and others
etc.   *et cetera:* and so forth
NB   *nota bene:* note well

He said he would be gone a fortnight (i.e., two weeks)
Bloom et al., editors, *Anthology of Light Verse*
Trees, too, are susceptible to disease (e.g., Dutch elm disease).

(Note that these abbreviations are generally not italicized or underlined.)

Some writers avoid these abbreviations in formal writing, even within parentheses.

45e **Use *Inc., Bros., Co.,* or *&* (for *and*) only in official names of business firms.**

NOT   *The Santini bros.* operate a large moving firm in New York City *&* environs.

BUT   *The Santini brothers* operate a large moving firm in New York City *and* environs.

OR   *Santini Bros.* is a large moving firm in New York City *and* environs.

45f **Generally, spell out units of measurement and names of places, calendar designations, people, and courses.**

In most academic, general, and business writing, the types of words listed below should always be spelled out. (In source citations and technical writing, however, these words are more often abbreviated.)

UNITS OF MEASUREMENT
The dog is thirty *inches* [not *in.*] high.

GEOGRAPHICAL NAMES
The publisher is in *Massachusetts* [not *Mass.* or *MA*].

NAMES OF DAYS, MONTHS, AND HOLIDAYS
The truce was signed on *Tuesday* [not *Tues.*], *April* [not *Apr.*] 16.

NAMES OF PEOPLE
Robert [not *Robt.*] Frost writes accessible poems.

COURSES OF INSTRUCTION
I'm majoring in *political science* [not *poli. sci.*].

46 Numbers

This chapter addresses the use of numbers (numerals versus words) in the text of a document. All disciplines use many more numerals in source citations.

46a Use numerals according to standard practice in the field you are writing in.

Always use numerals for numbers that require more than two words to spell out:

The leap year has 366 days.
The population of Minot, North Dakota, is about *32,800*.

In nontechnical academic writing, spell out numbers of one or two words:

Twelve nations signed the treaty.

The ball game drew *forty-two thousand* people. [A hyphenated number may be considered one word.]

In much business writing, use numerals for all numbers over ten: *five reasons, 11 participants.* In technical academic and business writing, such as in science and engineering, use numerals for all numbers over ten, and use numerals for zero through nine when they refer to exact measurements: *2 liters, 1 hour.* (Technical usage does vary from discipline to discipline. Consult one of the style guides listed on pp. 266–67 for more details.)

NOTE Use a combination of numerals and words for round numbers over a million: *26 million, 2.45 billion.* And use either all numerals or all words when several numbers appear together in a passage, even if convention would require a mixture.

ESL In American English a comma separates the numerals in long numbers (*26,000*), and a period functions as a decimal point (*2.06*).

num
46a

46b Use numerals according to convention for dates, addresses, and other information.

DAYS AND YEARS

June 18, 1985   AD 12   456 BC   1999

PAGES, CHAPTERS, VOLUMES, ACTS, SCENES, LINES	**DECIMALS, PERCENTAGES, AND FRACTIONS**
Chapter 9, page 123	22.5 3½
Hamlet, act 5, scene 3	48% (*or* 48 percent)

ADDRESSES	**SCORES AND STATISTICS**
355 Clinton Avenue	21 to 7 a ratio of 8 to 1
Washington, DC 20036	

EXACT AMOUNTS OF MONEY	**THE TIME OF DAY**
$3.5 million $4.50	9:00 AM 3:45 PM

EXCEPTIONS Round dollar or cent amounts of only a few words may be expressed in words: *seventeen dollars; sixty cents.* When the word *o'clock* is used for the time of day, also express the number in words: *two o'clock* (not *2 o'clock*).

46c Spell out numbers that begin sentences.

For clarity, spell out any number that begins a sentence. If the number requires more than two words, reword the sentence so that the number falls later and can be expressed as a numeral.

NOT   *3.3 billion* people live in Asia.
BUT   The population of Asia is *3.3 billion*.

VI

Research and Documentation

VI

Research and Documentation

47 Research Strategy

Research writing gives you a chance to work like a detective solving a case. The mystery is the answer to a question you care about. The search for the answer leads you to consider what others think about your subject, to build on that information, and ultimately to become an expert in your own right.

Your investigation will be more productive and enjoyable if you anticipate the process (below), keep a research journal (below), plan your time (p. 234), choose an appropriate topic (p. 235), and refine the topic (p. 235). Chapters after this one discuss conducting a search (48), working with sources to write your paper (49), and documenting sources (50–53).

47a Viewing research writing as a process

Research writing is a *writing process:*

❖ You work within a particular situation of subject, purpose, and audience (see Chapter 1).
❖ You gather ideas and information about your subject (Chapter 2).
❖ You focus and arrange your ideas (Chapter 3).
❖ You draft to explore your meaning (Chapter 4).
❖ You revise and edit to develop, shape, and polish (Chapter 5).

Although the writing process seems neatly sequential in this list, you know from experience that the stages overlap—that, for instance, you may not realize your purpose until you're drafting. The same is true of the *research* writing process: you may begin drafting before you've gathered all the information you expect to find, and then while drafting you may discover a source that causes you to rethink your approach.

Anticipating the process of research writing can protect you from frustration as you pursue your subject into the occasional dead end or wonder sometimes whether your subject is mastering you, rather than the other way around. Anticipating the process can do more as well, giving you flexibility in your search and holding you open to discoveries.

47b Keeping a research journal

While working on a research project, carry index cards or a notebook with you at all times to use as a RESEARCH JOURNAL, a place to

233

47c

record your activities and ideas. (See pp. 7–8 on journal keeping.) In the journal's dated entries, you can write about the sources you consult, the leads you want to pursue, any difficulties you encounter, and, most important, your thoughts about sources, leads, difficulties, new directions, relationships, and anything else that strikes you. The very act of writing in the journal can expand and clarify your thinking.

The research journal is the place for tracking and developing your own ideas. Notes on what your sources actually say should be taken and organized separately, as discussed on pages 254–58.

47c Planning a research project

As soon as you receive an assignment for a research project, you can begin developing a strategy for completing it. The first step should be making a schedule that apportions the available time to the necessary work. A possible schedule appears below. (The page numbers refer to relevant discussions both earlier and later in this book.)

Complete
by:

_____	1. Finding and refining a topic (pp. 3–4, 235–36)
_____	2. Conducting a search for sources (pp. 236–51)

_____	3. Reading sources critically (pp. 251–54)
_____	4. Taking notes using summary, paraphrase, and direct quotation (pp. 254–58)

_____	5. Creating a focus and structure (pp. 13–19, 261–62)
_____	6. Drafting the paper (pp. 19–21, 262)

_____	7. Documenting sources (pp. 265–67)
_____	8. Revising and editing the paper (pp. 22–28, 267)
_____	9. Preparing and proofreading the final paper (pp. 28, 268)
_____	10. Final paper due

You can estimate that each segment marked off by a horizontal line will occupy *roughly* one-quarter of the total time—for example, a week in a four-week assignment or two weeks in an eight-week assignment. The most unpredictable segments are the first two, so it's wise to get started early enough to accommodate the unexpected.

47d Finding a topic

Before reading this section, you may want to review the suggestions given in Chapter 1 for finding and limiting a topic and for defining a purpose (pp. 3–5).

Seek a research subject that interests you and that you care about: a local public issue, a campus controversy, a medical problem, a business practice, a change in a sport, an intriguing public figure, a trend in the arts. Starting with your own views will motivate you, and you will be a participant in a dialogue when you begin examining sources. If no topic occurs to you, try freewriting, brainstorming, or clustering (pp. 8–11) to uncover your interests.

When you settle on a topic, ask the following questions about it. For each requirement, there are corresponding pitfalls.

❖ Are ample published sources of information available on the topic?

Avoid (*a*) very recent topics, such as the latest medical breakthrough, and (*b*) topics that are too removed geographically, such as a minor event in Australian history.

❖ Does the topic encourage research in the kinds and number of sources required by the assignment?

Avoid (*a*) topics that depend entirely on personal opinion and experience, such as the virtues of your hobby, and (*b*) topics that require research in only one source, such as a straight factual biography.

❖ Will the topic lead you to an objective assessment of sources and to defensible conclusions?

Avoid topics that rest entirely on belief or prejudice, such as when human life begins or why women (or men) are superior. Your readers are unlikely to be swayed from their own beliefs.

❖ Does the topic suit the length of paper assigned and the time given for research and writing?

Avoid broad topics that have too many sources to survey adequately, such as a major event in history.

47e Refining the topic

The more you refine your topic before you begin research, the more productive your research will be. Take some time to respond in your research journal to these questions:

❖ What led you to choose this topic? What can you say about it without any research? What opinions do you have about it, and why?
❖ What questions do you have about the topic? What kinds of information do you think you'll need in order to write about it?

Thinking about what you know and don't know can lead you to a RESEARCH QUESTION, a prompt that focuses and guides your work with sources. Try to narrow the question so that you can answer it in the time and space you have available. The question *What are the most effective weight-loss techniques?* is quite broad: whole books have been written on the subject. In contrast, the question *How well do liquid diets work?* or *How safe are the new weight-loss drugs?* is much narrower. Each question also requires more than a simple "Yes" or "No" answer, so that answering, even tentatively, demands thought about pros and cons, causes and effects.

As you read and write, your question will probably evolve to reflect your increasing knowledge of the subject, and eventually its answer will become your main idea, or thesis sentence (see p. 261).

48 Conducting a Search

Research writing is a process of creation: you find sources and coordinate them to develop and support your own ideas about your subject. This chapter discusses keeping track of sources (opposite), directing your search (p. 238), searching electronically (p. 239), and finding various kinds of sources (p. 242). Chapter 49 discusses the use of sources.

Two tips for researchers

❖ If you are unsure of how to locate or use your library's resources, ask a reference librarian. This person is very familiar with all the library's resources and with general and specialized research techniques, and it is his or her job to help you and others with research. Even very experienced researchers often consult reference librarians.
❖ If sources you need are not available from your library, you may be able to obtain them from another library, usually by mail, often by fax, sometimes electronically. Ask your librarian for help, and plan ahead: interlibrary loans can take a week or longer.

48a Keeping a working bibliography

Keep track of sources as you come across them with a WORKING BIBLIOGRAPHY, a record of all the information you need to locate the sources. Some instructors require that the working bibliography be submitted on note cards (one source to a card), and this system has the advantage of allowing the sources to be shuffled easily. But many researchers have abandoned note cards because computers can print out source information, sort sources, and even transfer data to the user's own disk. (See p. 241.)

Whatever system you use, you should have a bibliographic reference for each source you think may be useful, as detailed in the box below.

Information for a working bibliography

FOR A BOOK
Library call number
Name(s) of author(s), editor(s),
 translator(s), or others
 listed
Title and subtitle
Publication data:
 Place of publication
 Publisher's name
 Date of publication
Other important data, such as
 edition or volume number

FOR A PERIODICAL ARTICLE
Name(s) of author(s)
Title and subtitle of article
Title of periodical
Publication data:
 Volume number and issue
 number (if any) in which
 article appears
 Date of issue
 Page numbers on which arti-
 cle appears

FOR ELECTRONIC SOURCES
Name(s) of author(s)
Title and subtitle
Publication data if source is also
 published in print

Electronic publication data:
 Date of release or online posting
 Name and vendor (or pub-
 lisher) of a database or
 name of an online service
 or network (America On-
 line, Internet, etc.)
 Medium (CD-ROM or online)
 Format of online source
 (e-mail, Listserv, Web page,
 etc.)
Date you consulted the source
Electronic address

FOR OTHER SOURCES
Name(s) of author(s) or others
 listed, such as a government department or a
 recording artist
Title of the work
Format, such as unpublished
 letter, computer service, or
 live performance
Publication or production data:
 Publisher's or producer's
 name
 Date of publication, release,
 or production
 Identifying numbers (if any)

48b Setting goals for the search

When you start to look for sources, consider both what you need and what your library has to offer. For most topics, start with general sources, such as reference works or articles in popular periodicals, seeking the outlines of your subject, the range and depth of opinions on it. As you refine your views and your research question, move on to more specialized sources, such as scholarly books and periodicals or your own interviews or surveys.

A wide-ranging search, particularly on the Internet (p. 243), can turn up long lists of sources that are only partially relevant to your subject. For a paper of 1,500 to 2,500 words, try for ten to thirty promising titles in your working bibliography. For most subjects, try for a mix of sources, as described below. You can discover or infer most of this information from listings in directories, indexes, bibliographies, and catalogs.

Primary and secondary sources

As much as possible, you should rely on PRIMARY SOURCES, or firsthand accounts: historical documents (letters, speeches, and so on), eyewitness reports, works of literature, reports on experiments or surveys conducted by the writer, or your own interviews, experiments, observations, or correspondence.

In contrast, SECONDARY SOURCES report and analyze information drawn from other sources, often primary ones: a reporter's summary of a controversial issue, a historian's account of a battle, a critic's reading of a poem, a physicist's evaluation of several studies. Secondary sources may contain helpful summaries and interpretations that direct, support, and extend your own thinking. However, most research-writing assignments expect your own ideas to go beyond those in such sources.

Scholarly and popular sources

The scholarship of acknowledged experts is essential for depth, authority, and specificity. The general-interest views and information of popular sources can help you apply more scholarly approaches to daily life.

❖ Check the publisher. Is it a scholarly journal (such as *Education Forum*) or a publisher of scholarly books (such as Harvard University Press), or is it a popular magazine (such as *Time* or *Newsweek*) or a publisher of popular books (such as Little, Brown)?

* Check the author. Have you seen the name elsewhere, which might suggest that the author is an expert?
* Check the title. Is it technical, or does it use a general vocabulary?

Older and newer sources

Check the publication date. For most subjects a combination of older, established sources (such as books) and current sources (such as newspaper articles or interviews) will provide both background and up-to-date information. Only historical subjects or very current subjects require an emphasis on one extreme or another.

Impartial and biased sources

Seek a range of viewpoints. Sources that attempt to be impartial can offer an overview of your subject and trustworthy facts. Sources with clear biases can offer a diversity of opinion. Of course, to discover bias, you may have to read the source carefully (see p. 251); but even a bibliographical listing can be informative.

* Check the author. You may have heard of the author before as a respected researcher (thus more likely to be objective) or as a leading proponent of a certain view (less likely to be objective).
* Check the title. It may reveal something about point of view. (Consider these contrasting titles: "Drink Your Way to Weight Loss" versus "Nutritional Characteristics of Commercial Liquid Diet Products.")

Sources with helpful features

Does the source have a bibliography (which might direct you to other sources) or an index (which can help you find what you want) or illustrations (which could clarify important concepts)?

48c Searching electronically

During any research project, you will probably search one or more of the following computerized resources, either at the library or elsewhere, such as from your own computer:

* The library's catalog of holdings is a database allowing you to search for books and other sources. You type a subject, an author's name, or a title into a computer terminal, and the screen displays a list of all items matching your request. The catalog may include not only your library's holdings but also those of other schools nearby or in your state.

48c

❖ Databases on CD-ROM, or compact disk, include indexes, bibliographies, encyclopedias, and other references. You search such a database much as you search a catalog, by author, title, or subject. The CD-ROMs may be available at only certain computers in the library, but some schools distribute the databases over a network within the library or over the campus network.

❖ Online databases and text archives are stored on computers all over the world and are accessible over the Internet, either through your campus network, through a local Internet provider, or through a commercial service such as America Online. The online databases include many indexes, bibliographies, and other references. The text archives, containing the entire contents of sources, include the *New York Times* and other newspapers, *Time* and other magazines, academic journals, proceedings of professional conferences, reports of government agencies, and files of discussion groups. (See pp. 243–48 for more on searching online sources.)

1. Your access to sources

Finding answers to the following sets of questions will give you a head start on your electronic research and help smooth your way.

Computer access to library resources

Computers have changed research locations and times as well as research methods.

❖ Which, if any, library resources can be reached from computers elsewhere on campus or from home?
❖ What software or hardware do you need to reach the library?
❖ Whom do you ask for assistance in installing the software and connecting to the library?

Library resources and their formats

Knowing the library's holdings and their formats will help you plan and carry out your search.

❖ Which of the library's books are cataloged electronically? Some libraries have all their books listed electronically; others have only recent acquisitions—say, books less than ten years old.
❖ Which periodical indexes, bibliographies, and other reference works are available on CD-ROM or in other forms? (Whatever your library does not have may be available from another library nearby or over the Internet.)
❖ Do certain collections within the library have their own catalogs, either printed or electronic?

Ways to record information

A pencil and paper aren't necessarily your only tools for recording information.

48c

❖ Can you print search results in the library? Many libraries provide some printers so that users can print catalog items, periodical listings, and other references located on computer.
   Some libraries also restrict or charge for printing.
❖ Can you save search results on your own floppy disk? If so,
   you'll be able to rearrange and supplement source data easily
   for your working bibliography. But find out what hardware or
   software you need in order to "read" the search results on your
   own computer.

2. Keyword searches

Probably the most important element in an electronic search is
appropriate KEYWORDS, or DESCRIPTORS, to describe your subject.
Most electronic catalogs and databases, as well as many Internet
search engines, operate by keywords: you type words that define
your limited subject (see the box on the following page), and the
computer searches for sources using or indexed by those words. On
the broad subject of weight loss, keywords might include *liquid
diets, weight and nutrition,* and *weight-loss programs.*

To develop keywords, it helps to understand what they do
when you use them for a search. There is an important difference
between most databases and the search tools used on the Internet.

❖ Databases usually index sources by authors, titles, and publication years and also by keywords that describe the contents of
   sources. These keywords conform to the database's directory of
   terms. For the library's catalog, this directory is *Library of Congress Subject Headings (LCSH),* which is available in printed
   form in the library's reference room. Some other databases use
   LCSH as well, but many have their own directory. Using the
   database's directory will speed your search.
❖ The Internet itself has no directory like *LCSH* in which you can
   look up keywords to search with. Instead, there are so-called
   search engines that find all the Internet sources that use your
   keywords anywhere—author, title, summary, text—no matter
   how centrally or how often they are used. Keywords that are
   too broad can retrieve tens of thousands of listings.

You will probably have to use trial and error in developing your
keywords. Because different databases have different directories and
many search tools have no directory at all, you should count occa-

48d

Ways to refine keywords

You can refine your keywords in ways now standard, with some variations, among most databases and search engines. When in doubt about whether or how to use any of the following devices, consult the "Help" section of the resource you are using.

❖ Use the word *not* or the symbol – ("minus") to narrow your search by excluding irrelevant words: for instance, *(weight control) not exercise*.

❖ Use the word *and* or the symbol + to narrow your search by indicating that all the terms should appear in the source or its listing: for example, *(weight control) and (liquid diets)*.

❖ Use the word *or* to broaden your search: for example, *dieting or (weight loss) or (weight control)*.

❖ Use quotation marks or parentheses (as in the examples above) to indicate that you want to search for the entire phrase, not the separate words.

❖ To indicate that you will accept different versions of the same word, use a so-called wild card, such as *, in place of the optional letters: for example, *wom*n* includes both *woman* and *women*. (Some systems use ?, :, or + for a wild card instead of *.)

❖ Be sure to spell your keywords correctly. Some search tools will look for close matches or approximations, but correct spelling gives you the best chance of finding relevant sources.

sionally on running dry (turning up few or no sources) or hitting uncontrollable gushers (turning up hundreds or thousands of mostly irrelevant sources). But the process is not busywork—far from it. Besides leading you eventually to worthwhile sources, it can also teach you a great deal about your subject: how you can or should narrow it, how it is and is not described by others, what others consider interesting or debatable about it, what the major arguments are.

48d Finding sources

This section discusses the wide range of sources available to you, both electronically and in print:

❖ Reference works (opposite)
❖ The Internet, including the World Wide Web (p. 244) and other tools (p. 245), electronic mail (p. 247), Listservs (p. 247), Usenet newsgroups (p. 247), and synchronous communication (p. 248)
❖ Periodicals (p. 248)
❖ Pamphlets and government publications (p. 249)
❖ Books (p. 250)

❖ Your own sources, including interviews, surveys, and other primary sources you create (p. 250)

1. Reference works

REFERENCE WORKS (often available on CD-ROM or over the Internet) include encyclopedias, dictionaries, digests, bibliographies, indexes, atlases, almanacs, and handbooks. Your research *must* go beyond these sources, but they can help you decide whether your topic really interests you and whether it meets the requirements for a research paper (p. 235). Preliminary research in reference works can also help you develop keywords for computer searches (p. 241) and can direct you to more detailed sources on your topic.

Ask a librarian to give you a starting reference for your subject. The librarian can also tell you which works are available on CD-ROM, over the Internet, or in print.

2. The Internet

The Internet, linking millions of computers around the world, has a number of distinct advantages for researchers:

❖ Since Internet publication is faster than print or even CD-ROM publication, you may find more current information on the Internet than in your library.
❖ Many scholarly journals are published online. Some are published *only* online, not in print.
❖ You can supplement your library's holdings by searching other libraries' catalogs or obtaining documents over the Internet.
❖ You can get in touch with people who have an interest in your

---

Electronic addresses

Internet search programs let you find sources even if you don't know their addresses (called UNIFORM RESOURCE LOCATORS, or URLs). But you'll need the address to return directly to the source and to document the source if you want to use it in your final paper. Here is a translation of the address *http://www.nyu.edu/urban/leaders.html:*

❖ The initials *http* (for HyperText Transfer Protocol) specify the type of access at a particular location.
❖ The letters *www.nyu.edu* name the computer that houses the particular source: *nyu* stands for New York University; *edu* indicates that it is an educational institution.
❖ The rest of the address—*/urban/leaders.html*—specifies the location and name of the source.

48d

research topic by participating in a discussion group or conducting interviews online.

Gaining access to the Internet is easiest through the document retrieval system known as the World Wide Web.

The World Wide Web

Through the World Wide Web, you can travel from document to document and even from computer to computer by clicking on highlighted words or images that provide HYPERTEXT LINKS, instructions that tell the computer to find the new material specified. You can also experience sound, images, video, and animation.

To find sources on the Web, you use a SEARCH ENGINE that conducts keyword searches (see p. 241) or that outlines content in a series of directories. There are over thirty search engines available, all of them accessible via your Web browser by clicking on "Net Search." These are some of the most popular engines:

❖ Alta Vista allows you to conduct both simple and advanced searches using keywords. Alta Vista also allows you to specify the keywords that you think most important, so that sites containing those keywords will be listed first in the results. The following Alta Vista screen shot shows that around a hundred sources match the keywords *liquid diets*.

ALTA VISTA SEARCH RESULTS

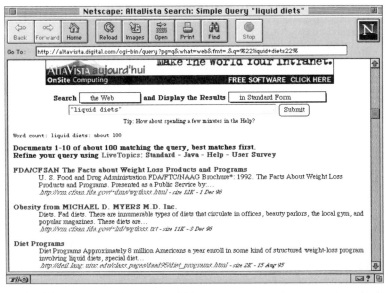

Internet tools in addition to the World Wide Web

The World Wide Web now encompasses many of the older tools for finding and using Internet sources. You may use any of these tools either through the Web or through a so-called shell account.

GOPHER

Until recently, Gopher was the preferred tool for locating and retrieving text documents over the Internet. It uses menus that are arranged in levels: they begin with general topics and become more specific as you proceed through a system. You can search for documents with the menus, or, using the search engine Veronica or Jughead, you can conduct a keyword search. Gopher remains popular and helpful, but many schools are now phasing it out in favor of the more interactive and flexible Web.

To visit a Gopher site from a shell account, type *Gopher* at the shell prompt followed by a space and then the address of the Gopher server you wish to reach. To visit a Gopher site from a Web browser, type *Gopher://* and the computer's address in the location window.

FILE TRANSFER PROTOCOL (FTP)

FTP allows you to transfer files to and from another computer over a network. The files may be software, documents (from government statistics to the texts of whole books), or graphics, sound, or video. Generally, you transfer files via "anonymous ftp," which lets you copy specified public files without having an account at the remote computer. A search engine named Archie can help you find FTP files by a keyword search of file titles.

With a shell account, type *ftp* followed by a space and the address of the FTP server. When asked to log in to the server, use the name "anonymous" and provide a password, usually your e-mail address. Then use commands to view the files listed at the site and to download them. If you are not working from a shell account, look for an application called Fetch to transfer files. To reach an FTP site with a Web browser, type *ftp://* and the computer's address in the location window. Web browsers have automated access to many FTP sites so that a simple click on a file name will transfer it to your computer or account.

TELNET

Telnet allows you to use a computer at another site on the Internet. You can, for instance, reach government computers or use your school's network from across the country. Often, you must have an account on the remote computer, or *host*, to be able to log in to it, but some hosts, such as libraries, do not require accounts.

To connect to a remote computer with a shell account, type *telnet* followed by a space and the host's address. With a Web browser, type *telnet://* and the address in the location window.

48d

* Excite allows you to search a directory compiled by a team of people reviewing Internet sites. It also allows simple keyword searches.
* Infoseek also allows you to search by directory or keyword. In addition, you can select the parts of the Internet that you want to search, such as newsgroups, corporate reports, or recent news.
* Lycos, which currently claims the largest catalog of Web sites, can be searched by directory or by keyword. Lycos also indexes sound, photographs, and other media, not just text documents.
* Magellan also allows you to search by directory or by keyword. You can search the entire Web, or you can limit your search to sites that have been reviewed and rated based on their content, organization, and use of technology.
* Yahoo allows you to search a subject directory or to request a keyword search that is forwarded to and conducted by other search engines. Yahoo is especially helpful with obscure topics because you're actually using seven or eight search engines at once.

Click on a search engine's "Help" button for information, such as how to format keyword searches and how to interpret the results of a search. Search engines generally list HITS, or sites that match your search criteria, in an order depending on the following: the number of times your search terms appear within a document; whether the terms appear at the beginning, middle, or end of a document; or whether the terms appear in the title or the address of the document.

When using a search engine, keep the following limitations and cautions in mind:

* Some Internet sites are designed and labeled as archives: they do not change except with additions. But other sites, such as those for newspapers and magazines, frequently replace old material with new. If you think you'll want to use something in such a site, you should consult it right away. If it seems useful, you should download it to your own computer or take notes from it (see pp. 254–55).
* Since anyone with the right hardware and software can place information on the Internet, you need to be especially careful about evaluating the individual sources you find (p. 251).
* Most works on the Internet are copyrighted just as print sources are, and you must acknowledge them when you use them (see p. 265). Keep records of the online sources that you find and use, such as their addresses and the dates you consulted them (see the list of elements to record on p. 237).

Electronic mail

With electronic mail (e-mail), you can send messages to and receive them from most people who use the Internet, as long as you know their addresses. As a research tool, e-mail allows you to communicate with others who may be interested in your topic. You may, for instance, carry on an e-mail conversation with a teacher at your school or with other students. Or you may interview an expert in another state to follow up on a scholarly article he or she published. (See p. 250 on conducting interviews, and see p. 368 for advice on e-mail format and etiquette.)

Listservs

A LISTSERV is a discussion group that operates by subscription, so that each subscriber automatically receives the contributions of all other subscribers via e-mail. Thousands of Listservs operate on the Internet, each with a particular purpose and audience.

To find lists that might be relevant to your research topic, use the keywords *list of listservs* (not *listserves*) to search the Web (p. 244). When you find a list that interests you, see if it has a compilation of frequently asked questions (FAQs), which will list the topics covered (and *not* covered) by the group and will answer common questions. Spend a week or two reading the list's messages before sending any questions or comments of your own. Reading but not participating (called LURKING) will verify whether the list is relevant to your topic (and vice versa) and whether a particular person might be able to answer your questions.

Although broad ranging and often very current, the information on Listservs is only as reliable as the subscriber who posts it. Listservs publish their subscriber lists, however, so you can find out who posted a message and communicate directly with that person. (See p. 252 for advice on evaluating online sources.)

Usenet newsgroups

Like Listservs, USENET NEWSGROUPS are forums in which people post messages on an enormous range of topics. However, newsgroups are not subscriber-based, and you do not receive postings automatically through your e-mail. Instead, you must visit the site. You can obtain a list of groups and other information by using the keywords *list of newsgroups*.

Newsgroups are roughly categorized by subject, indicated by the first letters of the address—for instance, *comp* for computers and computer science, *soc* for social issues, *biz* for business. This prefix will give you an idea of whether the group is relevant to your con-

48d

cerns. As with a Listserv, look for a newsgroup's frequently asked questions (FAQs) and lurk a while before jumping into the discussion.

Because newsgroups, unlike Listservs, are not subscriber-based, anyone can post messages on them, and you may not be able to find out who wrote a particular message. That makes it difficult to evaluate the reliability of a posting (see p. 252 on evaluating sources).

Synchronous communication

With SYNCHRONOUS (or simultaneous) COMMUNICATION, you and others can correspond in real time, as you might talk on the phone. Synchronous communication is often used for collaborative writing and editing (see p. 36). As a research tool, it can be helpful for conducting interviews (see p. 250), and you can also participate in academic conferences and debates.

Synchronous programs include IRC (Internet Relay Chat), which allows people anywhere in the world to talk with each other over "channels"; MUDs (multiuser domains or dungeons), which started as online versions of role-playing games but now feature scholarly discussions and other conversations; and MOOs (MUDs—object oriented), which allow more complex virtual environments in which to play games or hold discussions.

IRC requires special software, which may be installed on your school's computer. Some MUDs and MOOs can be reached via the Web, using the keywords *MUDs and MOOs*. Once you arrive at a site, you generally log on as a guest and receive directions for obtaining help.

3. Periodicals

PERIODICALS—journals, magazines, and newspapers—are invaluable sources of both current and specialized information. The difference between journals and magazines lies primarily in their content, readership, and frequency of issue.

❖ Magazines—such as *Psychology Today, Newsweek,* and *Esquire* —are nonspecialist publications intended for diverse readers. Most magazines appear weekly or monthly, and their pages are numbered anew with each issue.

❖ Journals often appear quarterly and contain specialized information intended for readers in a particular field. Examples include *American Anthropologist, Journal of Black Studies,* and *Journal of Chemical Education.* Many journals page each issue separately, but others number their pages consecutively through all the issues in a year (an annual volume). (The method of pagination determines how you cite a journal article in your list of works cited.)

Various indexes to periodicals—many available on CD-ROM or online—provide information on the articles in journals, magazines, and newspapers. The following are a few of the most widely used indexes:

- *InfoTrac:* more than fifteen hundred business, government, technical, and general-interest publications.
- *Humanities Index:* journals in language and literature, history, philosophy, and other humanities.
- *MLA International Bibliography of Books and Articles on the Modern Languages and Literatures:* books and periodicals on literature, linguistics, and languages.
- *New York Times Index:* articles in the most complete US newspaper.
- *Social Sciences Index:* journals in economics, psychology, political science, and other social sciences.
- *General Science Index:* journals in biology, chemistry, physics, and other sciences.
- *Readers' Guide to Periodical Literature:* over a hundred popular magazines.

Searching electronic periodical indexes is discussed under electronic searches on pages 239–42.

Every library lists its complete periodical holdings either in its main catalog (see p. 250) or in a separate catalog. Many periodicals are available on CD-ROM. If a periodical is not available electronically, recent issues are probably held in the library's periodical room. Back issues are usually stored elsewhere, either in bound volumes or on film that requires a special machine to read. A librarian will show you how to operate the machine.

4. Pamphlets and government publications

Organizations such as social-service groups, professional societies, and all branches of government publish pamphlets, compilations of data, and other sources that usually cannot be retrieved through the library's book catalog or periodicals listings.

Libraries store pamphlets and other loose materials in file drawers, called VERTICAL FILES. To find out what is available in pamphlet form, consult the *Vertical File Index: A Subject and Title Index to Selected Pamphlet Materials.*

Government publications provide a vast array of data, public records, and other historical and contemporary information. For US government publications, consult the *Monthly Catalog of US Government Publications,* available on computer. Many federal, state, and local government agencies post important publications—

48d

legislation, reports, press releases—on their own Web sites. You can find lists of sites for various federal agencies by using the keywords *United States federal government* with a search engine.

5. Books

Most academic libraries store their book catalogs on computer; however, older volumes—say, those acquired more than ten years ago—may still be cataloged in bound volumes or on film. (Few academic libraries use the once-familiar drawers of cards.)

You can search an electronic catalog for authors' names, titles, or keywords describing your subject. As much as possible, the keywords should match words in *Library of Congress Subject Headings* (*LCSH*), a multivolume work that lists the headings under which the Library of Congress catalogs books. See pages 241–42 for more on keyword searches.

6. Your own sources

Academic writing will often require you to conduct primary research for information of your own. For instance, you may need to analyze a poem, conduct an experiment, survey a group of people, or interview an expert.

An interview can be especially helpful for a research project because it allows you to ask questions precisely geared to your topic. You can conduct an interview in person, over the telephone, or online using electronic mail (see p. 247) or a form of synchronous communication such as Internet Relay Chat (see p. 248). A personal interview is preferable if you can arrange it, because you can see the person's expressions and gestures as well as hear his or her tone and words.

Here are a few guidelines for interviews:

❖ Call or write for an appointment. Tell the person exactly why you are calling, what you want to discuss, and how long you expect the interview to take. Be true to your word on all points.
❖ Prepare a list of open-ended questions to ask—perhaps ten or twelve for a one-hour interview. Plan on doing some research for these questions to discover background on the issues and your subject's published views on the issues.
❖ Give your subject time to consider your questions, and listen to your subject's answers so that you can ask appropriate follow-up questions.
❖ Take care in interpreting answers, especially if you are online and thus can't depend on facial expressions, gestures, and tone of voice to convey the subject's attitudes.

❖ For in-person and telephone interviews, keep careful notes or, if you have the equipment and your subject agrees, tape-record the interview. For online interviews, save the discussion in a file of its own.

❖ Before you quote your subject in your paper, check with him or her to ensure that the quotations are accurate.

❖ Send a thank-you note immediately after the interview. Promise your subject a copy of your finished paper, and send the paper promptly.

49 Working with Sources and Writing the Paper

This chapter shows you how to build on your research to make your topic your own and present your ideas to others. The chapter discusses reading your sources critically (below), taking notes while avoiding plagiarism (pp. 254 and 258), creating a thesis sentence and a structure for a draft (p. 261), integrating sources into your text (p. 262), documenting sources (p. 265), and revising, editing, and formatting the paper (p. 267).

ESL Making a topic your own requires thinking critically about sources and developing independent ideas. These goals may at first be uncomfortable for you if your native culture emphasizes understanding and respecting established authority over questioning and enlarging it. The information here will help you evaluate, manage, and write about sources so that you can become an expert in your own right and convincingly convey your expertise to others.

49a Reading sources critically

Research writing is much more than finding sources and reporting their contents. The challenge and interest come from *interacting* with sources, discovering their meanings, judging their quality, and creating relationships among them.

Such engagement requires CRITICAL READING, reading that looks beyond the surface of the words. To read critically, you analyze a text, identifying its main ideas, structure, evidence, or other relevant elements; you evaluate its usefulness or quality; and you relate it to other texts and to your own ideas.

49a

1. Evaluation

Not all the sources in your working bibliography will be useful to you. Some may prove irrelevant to your subject; others may prove unreliable. Before you settle in to take notes, scan your sources to evaluate the kind and extent of ideas and information they offer.

Relevance and reliability

Aim for the mix of sources discussed on pages 238–39: primary and secondary, scholarly and popular, older and newer, impartial and biased. For each source, try to answer the questions in the following box.

Questions for evaluating sources

❖ Is the work relevant?

Does the source devote some attention to your topic?
Where in the source are you likely to find relevant information or ideas?
Is the source appropriately specialized for your needs? Check the source's treatment of a topic you know something about, to ensure that it is neither too superficial nor too technical.
How important is the source likely to be for your writing?

❖ Is the work reliable?

How up to date is the source? Check the publication date.
Is the author an expert in the field? Look for an author biography, look up the author in a biographical reference, or trace the author over the Internet.
What is the author's bias? Check biographical information or the author's own preface or introduction. Consider what others have written about the author or the source.
Whatever his or her bias, does the author reason soundly, provide adequate evidence, and consider opposing views?

Evaluating electronic sources

Most books and periodical articles are reviewed before publication, so you can have some confidence in the information they contain. But many Internet sources are self-published by the author with no preliminary review by others, so you must be the sole judge of reliability. To a great extent, the same critical reading that serves you with books and periodical articles will help you evaluate Internet sources, too (see the box opposite). But you should do some digging as well:

❖ *Check electronic addresses.* Look for an abbreviation that tells you where the source originates: *edu* (educational institution, *gov* (government body), *org* (nonprofit organization), or *com* (commercial organization).

❖ *Check authorship.* Many sites list the author(s) or group(s) responsible for the site. You can research an author or group through a biographical dictionary or a keyword search of the World Wide Web (see p. 244). A site on the Web may provide links to information about or other work by an author or group. The author or group may also show up in your other sources.

❖ *Communicate directly with the author.* For a posting on a Listserv or a Usenet newsgroup, try to reach the author directly to ask about publications and background or to seek further information about your subject. Drop the source from your list if you can't trace the author or the author fails to respond to your requests for information.

❖ *Check for references or links to reliable sources.* The source may offer as support the titles of sources that you can trace and evaluate—articles in periodicals, other Internet sources, and so on. A Web site may include links to these other sources.

❖ *Evaluate the source as a whole.* For Web sites, especially, consider the purpose and value of links to other sites. Is the site trying to sell a particular product, service, or idea? Do some links raise questions about the intentions of the compiler—because the links are frivolous, say, or indecent?

❖ *Back up Internet sources.* Always consider Internet sources in the context of other sources so that you can distinguish singular, untested views from more mainstream views that have been subject to verification.

2. Synthesis

When you begin to locate the differences and similarities among sources, you move into the most significant part of research writing: forging relationships for your own purpose. This SYNTHESIS is an essential step in reading sources critically and continues through the drafting and revision of a research paper. As you infer connections—say, between one writer's opinions and another's or between two works by the same author—you create new knowledge.

49b

Your synthesis of sources will grow more detailed and sophisticated as you proceed through the research-writing process. Unless you are analyzing primary sources such as the works of a poet, at first read your sources quickly and selectively to obtain an overview of your topic and a sense of how the sources approach it. Don't get bogged down in taking detailed notes, but *do* record your ideas about sources in your research journal (p. 233):

❖ *Respond to sources.* Write down what your sources make you think. Do you agree or disagree with the author? Do you find his or her views narrow, or do they open up new approaches for you? Is there anything in the source that you need to research further before you can understand it? Does the source prompt questions that you should keep in mind while reading other sources?

❖ *Connect sources.* When you notice a link between sources, jot it down. Do two sources differ in their theories or their interpretations of facts? Does one source illuminate another—perhaps commenting or clarifying or supplying additional data? Do two or more sources report studies that support a theory you've read about or an idea of your own?

❖ *Heed your own insights.* Apart from ideas prompted by your sources, you are sure to come up with independent thoughts: a conviction, a point of confusion that suddenly becomes clear, a question you haven't seen anyone else ask. These insights may occur at unexpected times, so it's good practice to keep your research journal always close at hand.

49b **Taking notes using summary, paraphrase, and direct quotation**

You can accomplish a great deal of synthesis while taking notes from your sources. Note taking is not a mechanical process of copying from books. Rather, as you read and take notes you assess and organize the information in your sources.

Note A common trap in research writing is allowing your sources to control you, rather than vice versa. To avoid this trap, ask how each source illuminates the idea you are building. When you are taking notes, assign each note a heading from an outline (even a rough one) that you have devised to develop your idea.

You can take notes in any or all of four ways:

❖ Notes on file cards are easy to rearrange, but handwriting can be tedious.

❖ Notes on computer are also easy to rearrange and are easy to incorporate into your drafts, but they require a handy computer.

❖ Photocopies of sources save time and reduce the risk of misquoting sources; but the copies usually cost money, they are difficult to rearrange, and, most important, they do not require critical thinking about sources.

❖ Downloaded copies of sources—files transferred from the Internet to your own computer or floppy disk—share the advantages and disadvantages of photocopies. Downloading has the further advantage of enabling you to move quotations directly into your drafts.

Whatever system of note taking you use, make sure that each note has all the bibliographic information you'll need to cite the source in your paper if you decide to use the note. (See p. 237 for a list of information.) If you have a working bibliography, the note itself needs only a cross-reference to the full source information and then page numbers or other specifics about the note's location. Also give the note a topic heading that corresponds to a part of your subject, so you can see at a glance where the note fits. (See the samples on the following page.)

1. Summary

When you SUMMARIZE, you condense an extended idea or argument into a sentence or more in your own words. Summary is most useful when you want to record the gist of an author's idea without the background or supporting evidence. The sample note card at the top of the next page shows a summary of the following passage. The source is used in the sample paper on pages 299–304.

ORIGINAL

Most commercial [diet] programs are also beginning to pay more attention to counseling and exercise. Scientists say that developing new habits of eating and activity is the real key to long-term maintenance—and the only hope for breaking ties with a diet machine.

"They are trying to improve programs, but it's very variable," says Dr. Thomas A. Wadden, a weight-loss specialist at Syracuse University. "Some have lectures. But most people who are overweight need more than a lecture. Most people who are overweight know what they have to do—they know they should walk more and put their fork down in between bites— but have trouble doing it."

—ELISABETH ROSENTHAL, "Commercial Diets Lack Proof of Their Long-Term Success," *New York Times*, p. C11

49b

SUMMARY

Need for behavior modification
Rosenthal, p. C11

Commercial diets are now stressing the
essentials of long-term weight loss that
overweight people know but find difficult:
exercise more, and change eating habits
(quotes Dr. Thomas A. Wadden, Syracuse
U).

2. Paraphrase

When you PARAPHRASE, you follow much more closely the author's original presentation, but you still restate it in your own
words. Paraphrase is most useful when you want to present or examine an author's line of reasoning but don't feel the original words
merit direct quotation. Here is a paraphrase of the quotation from
Thomas Wadden in the *New York Times* passage on the previous
page:

PARAPHRASE

Need for behavior modification
Rosenthal, p. C11

Dr. Thomas A. Wadden (weight-loss expert,
Syracuse U) holds that although most
overweight people are aware that they need
to get more exercise and eat differently, they
find behavior change difficult.

Notice that the paraphrase follows the original but uses different words and different sentence structures. To achieve such a paraphrase, use the guidelines in the box below.

49b

Paraphrasing a source

❖ Read the relevant material several times to be sure you understand it.

❖ Restate the source's ideas in your own words and sentence structures. You need not put down in new words the whole passage or all the details. Select what is relevant to your topic, and restate only that. If complete sentences seem too detailed or cumbersome, use phrases, as in this example: *Exercising and changing eating habits—essential for weight loss but hard to do.*

❖ Be careful not to distort meaning. Don't change the source's emphasis or omit connecting words, qualifiers, and other material whose absence will confuse you later or cause you to misrepresent the source.

ESL If English is your second language, you may have difficulty paraphrasing the ideas in sources because synonyms don't occur to you or you don't see how to restructure sentences. Before attempting a paraphrase, read the original passage several times. Then, instead of "translating" line by line, try to state the gist of the passage without looking at it. Check your effort against the original to be sure you have captured the source author's meaning and emphasis without using his or her words and sentence structures. If you need a synonym for a word, look it up in a dictionary.

3. Direct quotation

In a paper analyzing primary sources such as literary works, you will use direct quotation extensively to illustrate and support your analysis. But you should quote from secondary sources only in the circumstances described in the box on the next page.

When taking a quotation from a source, copy the material *carefully*. Take down the author's exact wording, spelling, capitalization, and punctuation. Proofread every direct quotation *at least twice*, and be sure you have supplied big quotation marks so that later you won't confuse the direct quotation with a paraphrase or summary. If you want to make changes for clarity, use brackets (see p. 199). If you want to omit irrelevant words or sentences, use ellipsis marks, usually three spaced periods (see pp. 198–99).

49c

Tests for direct quotations

❖ The author's original satisfies one of these requirements:

The language is unusually vivid, bold, or inventive.
The quotation cannot be paraphrased without distortion or loss
    of meaning.
The words themselves are at issue in your interpretation.
The quotation represents and emphasizes a body of opinion or
    the view of an important expert.
The quotation emphatically reinforces your own idea.
The quotation is a graph, diagram, or table.

❖ The quotation is as short as possible.

It includes only material relevant to your point.
It is edited to eliminate examples and other unneeded material.

49c Avoiding plagiarism

PLAGIARISM (from a Latin word for "kidnapper") is the presentation of someone else's ideas or words as your own. Whether deliberate
or accidental, plagiarism is a serious and often punishable offense.

❖ *Deliberate* plagiarism:

Copying or downloading a phrase, a sentence, or a longer pas-
    sage from a source and passing it off as your own by omit-
    ting quotation marks and a source citation.
Summarizing or paraphrasing someone else's ideas without ac-
    knowledging your debt in a source citation.
Handing in as your own work a paper you have bought, had a
    friend write, or copied from another student.

❖ *Accidental* plagiarism:

Forgetting to place quotation marks around another writer's
    words.
Omitting a source citation from a paraphrase because of care-
    lessness.
Omitting a source citation for another's idea because you are
    unaware of the need to acknowledge the idea.

ESL More than in many other cultures, teachers in the United
States value students' original thinking and writing. In some other
cultures, for instance, students may be encouraged to copy the
words of scholars without acknowledgment, to demonstrate their

---

Checklist for avoiding plagiarism

❖ What type of source are you using: your own independent material, common knowledge, or someone else's independent material? You must acknowledge someone else's material.
❖ If you are quoting someone else's material, is the quotation exact? Have you inserted quotation marks around quotations run into the text? Have you shown omissions with ellipsis marks and additions with brackets?
❖ If you are paraphrasing or summarizing someone else's material, have you used your own words and sentence structures? Does your paraphrase or summary employ quotation marks when you resort to the author's exact language? Have you represented the author's meaning without distortion?
❖ If you are using someone else's material in your own online publication (such as a Web page), have you obtained permission?
❖ Is each use of someone else's material acknowledged in your text? Are all your source citations complete and accurate? (See p. 265.)
❖ Does your list of works cited include all the sources you have drawn from in writing your paper? (See p. 265.)

---

mastery of or respect for the scholars' work. But in the United States any use of another's words or ideas without a source citation is plagiarism and is unacceptable. When in doubt about the guidelines in this section, ask your instructor for advice.

1. What you need not acknowledge

Your independent material

Your own observations, thoughts, compilations of facts, or experimental results, expressed in your words and format, do not require acknowledgment. You should describe the basis for your conclusions so that readers can evaluate your thinking, but you need not cite sources for them.

Common knowledge

Common knowledge consists of the standard information on a subject as well as folk literature and commonsense observations.

❖ Standard information includes the major facts of history, such as the dates of Charlemagne's rule as emperor of Rome (800–14). It does not include interpretations of facts, such as a historian's opinion that Charlemagne was sometimes needlessly cruel in extending his power.

❖ Folk literature, such as the fairy tale "Snow White," is popularly known and cannot be traced to a particular writer. Literature traceable to a writer is not folk literature, even if it is very familiar.

❖ A commonsense observation is something most people know, such as that inflation is most troublesome for people with low and fixed incomes. An economist's argument about the effects of inflation on Chinese immigrants is not a commonsense observation.

If you do not know a subject well enough to determine whether a piece of information is common knowledge, make a record of the source as you would for any other quotation, paraphrase, or summary. As you read more about the subject, the information may come up repeatedly without acknowledgment, in which case it is probably common knowledge. But if you are still in doubt when you finish your research, always acknowledge the source.

2. What you must acknowledge

You must always acknowledge other people's independent material—that is, any facts or ideas that are not common knowledge or your own. The source may be anything, including a book, an article, a movie, an interview, a microfilmed document, a computer program, or a newsgroup posting. You must acknowledge not only ideas or facts themselves but also the language and format in which the ideas or facts appear, if you use them. That is, the wording, sentence structures, arrangement of ideas, and special graphics (such as a diagram) created by another writer belong to that writer just as his or her ideas do.

Copied language: Quotation marks and a source citation

The following example baldly plagiarizes the original quotation from Jessica Mitford's *Kind and Usual Punishment*, page 9. Without quotation marks or a source citation, the example matches Mitford's wording (underlined) and closely parallels her sentence structure:

ORIGINAL   The character and mentality of the keepers may be of more importance in understanding prisons than the character and mentality of the kept.

PLAGIARISM   But the character of prison officials (the keepers) is more important in understanding prisons than the character of prisoners (the kept).

To avoid plagiarism, the writer can paraphrase and cite the source (see the third example opposite) or use Mitford's actual words *in quotation marks* and *with a source citation* (here, in MLA style):

**REVISION
(QUOTATION)**   According to one critic of the penal system, "The character and mentality of the keepers may be of more importance in understanding prisons than the character and mentality of the kept" (Mitford 9).

49d

Paraphrase or summary: Original words and a source citation

The next example changes Mitford's sentence structure, but it still uses her words (underlined) without quotations marks and without a source citation:

PLAGIARISM   In understanding prisons, we should know more about the character and mentality of the keepers than of the kept.

To avoid plagiarism, the writer can use quotation marks and cite the source (see above) or *use his or her own words* and still *cite the source* (because the idea is Mitford's, not the writer's):

**REVISION
(PARAPHRASE)**   One critic of the penal system maintains that we may be able to learn more about prisons from the psychology of the prison officials than from that of the prisoners (Mitford 9).

49d Focusing, organizing, and drafting the paper

Before you begin using your source notes in a draft, give some thought to your main idea and your organization.

1. Thesis sentence

You began research with a question about your subject (see p. 236). Though that question may have evolved during research, you should be able to answer it once you've consulted most of your sources. Try to state that answer in a THESIS SENTENCE, an assertion that narrows your subject to a single assertion. The thesis sentence will give you a focus as you draft. (See pp. 13–15 for more on thesis sentences, including many examples.)

2. Organization

To create a structure for your paper, you'll need to synthesize, or forge relationships among ideas (see pp. 253–54). Here is one approach:

❖ Arrange your notes in groups of related ideas and information according to the subject headings you wrote on your notes. Each group should correspond to a main section of your paper:

a key idea of your own that supports the thesis and the evidence for that idea.

❖ Review your research journal for connections between sources and other thoughts that can help you organize your paper.

❖ Look objectively at your groups of notes. If some groups are skimpy, with few notes, consider whether you should drop the category or conduct more research to fill it out. If most of your notes fall into one or two groups, consider whether the categories are too broad and should be divided. (Does any of this rethinking affect your thesis sentence? If so, revise it accordingly.)

❖ Within each group, distinguish between the main idea of the group (which should be your own) and the supporting ideas and evidence (which should come from your sources).

See pages 15–19 for more on organizing a paper, including samples of both informal and formal outlines that can help you create a structure.

3. First draft

In drafting your paper, you do not have to proceed methodically from introduction to conclusion. Instead, draft in sections, beginning with the one you feel most confident about. Each section should center on a principal idea contributing to your thesis, a conclusion you have drawn from reading and responding to sources. Start the section by stating the idea; then support it with information, summaries, paraphrases, and quotations from your notes. Remember to insert source information from your notes as well.

If you have kept your notes on a computer, you can import them (and source information) directly into your draft and then rewrite and edit them so that they work for your ideas and fit into your sentences.

See pages 19–21 for more on drafting.

49e   Integrating sources into your text

The evidence of others' information and opinions should back up, not dominate, your own ideas. To synthesize evidence, you need to smooth the transitions between your ideas and words and those of your sources, and you need to give the reader a context for interpreting the borrowed material.

NOTE The examples in this section use the MLA style of source documentation, discussed in Chapter 50. The source citations not only acknowledge that material is borrowed but also help to indicate where the borrowed material begins or ends. (See p. 277.)

Conventions for handling quotations

❖ For guidelines on when to quote from sources, see p. 258.
❖ For the punctuation of identifying words such as *he insists,* see pp. 181–82.
❖ For guidelines on when to run quotations into your text and when to display them separately from your text, see pp. 206-07.
❖ For the use of brackets around words you add to quotations for clarity, see p. 199.
❖ For the use of the ellipsis mark (. . .) to indicate omissions from quotations, see pp. 198–99.

Introduction of borrowed material

Readers will be distracted from your point if borrowed material does not fit into your sentence. In the passage below, the writer has not meshed the structures of her own and her source's sentences:

> AWKWARD   One editor disagrees with this view and "a good reporter does not fail to separate opinions from facts" (Lyman 52).

In the following revision the writer adds words to integrate the quotation into her sentence:

> REVISED   One editor disagrees with this view, <u>maintaining that</u> "a good reporter does not fail to separate opinions from facts" (Lyman 52).

To mesh your own and your source's words, you may sometimes need to make a substitution or addition to the quotation, signaling your change with brackets:

> WORDS ADDED   "The tabloids [of England] are a journalistic case study in bad reporting," claims Lyman (52).
>
> VERB FORM CHANGED   A bad reporter, Lyman implies, is one who "[fails] to separate opinions from facts" (52). [The bracketed verb replaces *fail* in the original.]
>
> CAPITALIZATION CHANGED   "[T]o separate opinions from facts" is the work of a good reporter (Lyman 52). [See p. 222.]
>
> NOUN SUPPLIED FOR PRONOUN   The reliability of a news organization "depends on [reporters'] trustworthiness," says Lyman (52). [The bracketed noun replaces *their* in the original.]

Interpretation of borrowed material

Even when it does not conflict with your own sentence structure, borrowed material will be ineffective if you merely dump it in readers' laps without explaining how you intend it to be understood.

49e

DUMPED   Many news editors and reporters maintain that it is impossible to keep personal opinions from influencing the selection and presentation of facts. "True, news reporters, like everyone else, form impressions of what they see and hear. However, a good reporter does not fail to separate opinions from facts" (Lyman 52). [We must figure out for ourselves that the writer's sentence and the quotation state opposite points of view.]

REVISED   Many news editors and reporters maintain that it is impossible to keep personal opinions from influencing the selection and presentation of facts. Yet not all authorities agree with this view. One editor grants that "news reporters, like everyone else, form impressions of what they see and hear." But, he insists, "a good reporter does not fail to separate opinions from facts" (Lyman 52). [The writer's additions tell us what to expect in the quotation.]

The words *grants* and *insists* in the revised passage tell the reader what to expect in the quotations following. Below are some other verbs that indicate the source author's attitude or approach to what he or she is saying. (Note that these verbs are in the present tense, the appropriate tense for discussions of others' writings.)

AUTHOR IS NEUTRAL	AUTHOR INFERS OR SUGGESTS	AUTHOR ARGUES	AUTHOR IS UNEASY OR DISPARAGING
comments	analyzes	claims	belittles
describes	asks	contends	bemoans
explains	assesses	defends	complains
illustrates	concludes	disagrees	condemns
notes	considers	holds	deplores
observes	finds	insists	deprecates
points out	predicts	maintains	derides
records	proposes		laments
relates	reveals	AUTHOR AGREES	warns
reports	shows	admits	
says	speculates	agrees	
sees	suggests	concedes	
thinks	supposes	concurs	
writes		grants	

Your interpretive words may precede the borrowed material, as above, or they may interrupt or follow it:

ADDITION INTERRUPTS   "However," Lyman insists, "a good reporter does not fail to separate opinions from facts" (52).

ADDITION FOLLOWS   "[A] good reporter does not fail to separate opinions from facts," Lyman insists (52).

You can add information to a quotation to integrate it into your text and inform readers why you are using it. If your readers will recognize it, you can provide the author's name in the text:

49f

AUTHOR NAMED   Harold Lyman grants that "news reporters, like everyone else, form impressions of what they see and hear." But, Lyman insists, "a good reporter does not fail to separate opinions from facts" (52).

If the source title contributes information about the author or the context of the quotation, you can provide it in the text:

TITLE GIVEN   Harold Lyman, in his book *The Conscience of the Journalist*, grants that "news reporters, like everyone else, form impressions of what they see and hear." But, Lyman insists, "a good reporter does not fail to separate opinions from facts" (52).

Finally, if the quoted author's background and experience reinforce or clarify the quotation, you can provide these credentials in the text:

CREDENTIALS GIVEN   Harold Lyman, a newspaper editor for more than forty years, grants that "news reporters, like everyone else, form impressions of what they see and hear." But, Lyman insists, "a good reporter does not fail to separate opinions from facts" (52).

You need not name the author, source, or credentials in your text when you are simply establishing facts or weaving together facts and opinions from varied sources. In the following passage, the information is more important than the source, so the name of the source is confined to a parenthetical acknowledgment:

> To end the abuses of the British, many colonists were urging three actions: forming a united front, seceding from Britain, and taking control of their own international trade and diplomacy (Wills 325–36).

49f   Documenting sources

Every time you borrow the words, facts, or ideas of others, you must acknowledge the source to tell readers that you borrowed the material and where you borrowed it from.

Editors and teachers in most academic disciplines require special documentation formats (or styles) in their scholarly journals and in students' papers. All the styles use a citation in the text that serves two purposes: it signals that material is borrowed, and it refers readers to detailed information about the source so that they can locate both the source and the place in the source where the borrowed material appears. The detailed source information appears either in footnotes or at the end of the paper.

Aside from these essential similarities, the disciplines' documentation styles differ markedly in citation form, arrangement of source information, and other particulars. Each discipline's style reflects the needs of its practitioners for certain kinds of information presented in certain ways. For instance, the currency of a source is important in the social sciences, where studies build on and correct each other; thus in-text citations in the social sciences include a source's date of publication. In English, however, currency is less important, so in-text citations do not include date of publication.

The disciplines' documentation formats are described in style guides, including those in the following list. This book presents the styles of the guides that are marked *.

HUMANITIES

Chicago Manual of Style. 14th ed. 1993. (See pp. 329–34.)

*Gibaldi, Joseph. *MLA Handbook for Writers of Research Papers*. 4th ed. 1995. (See pp. 272–97.)

*Turabian, Kate L. *A Manual for Writers of Term Papers, Theses, and Dissertations*. 6th ed. Rev. John Grossman and Alice Bennett. 1996. (See pp. 329–34.)

SOCIAL SCIENCES

*American Psychological Association. *Publication Manual of the American Psychological Association*. 4th ed. 1994. (See pp. 307–18.)

American Sociological Association. "Editorial Guidelines." Inside front cover of each issue of *American Sociological Review*.

American Anthropological Association. "Style Guide and Information for Authors." *American Anthropologist* (1977): 774–79.

Linguistics Society of America. "LSA Style Sheet." Printed every December in *LSA Bulletin*.

SCIENCES AND MATHEMATICS

American Chemical Society. *ACS Style Guide: A Manual for Authors and Editors*. 2nd ed. 1997.

American Institute of Physics. *Style Manual for Guidance in the Preparation of Papers*. 4th ed. 1990.

American Mathematical Society. *A Manual for Authors of Mathematical Papers*. Rev. ed. 1990.

American Medical Association. *Manual of Style*. 8th ed. 1989.

Bates, Robert L., Rex Buchanan, and Marla Adkins-Heljeson, eds. *Geowriting: A Guide to Writing, Editing, and Printing in Earth Science*. 5th ed. 1992.

*Council of Biology Editors. *Scientific Style and Format: The CBE Manual for Authors, Editors, and Publishers.* 6th ed. 1994. (See pp. 335–38.)

Ask your instructor which style you should use. If your instructor does not require a particular documentation style, use the guide above that's most appropriate for the discipline you're writing in. Do follow one system for citing sources—and one system only—so that you provide all the necessary information in a consistent format.

NOTE Various computer programs can help you format your source citations in the style of your choice. Such a program will prompt you for needed information (author's name, book title, date of publication, and so on) and will arrange, capitalize, underline, and punctuate the information as required by the style. The program will remove some tedium from documenting sources, but it can't substitute for your own care and attention in giving your sources accurate and complete acknowledgment.

49g   Revising, editing, and formatting a research paper

Detailed advice on revising, editing, and proofreading—including checklists—appears in Chapter 5. In revising a research paper, take these additional steps:

❖ Ensure that your thesis sentence accurately describes your topic and your perspective as they emerged during drafting, so that the paper is unified and coherent.

❖ Be alert for structural problems. (Outlining your draft as suggested on p. 23 can help you see your structure at a glance.)

Illogical arrangements of ideas.
Inadequate emphasis of important points and overemphasis of minor points.
Imbalance between the views of others (support) and your own views (interpretation or analysis).

❖ Hunt out irrelevant ideas and facts that crept in just because you had notes on them.
❖ Look for places where supporting evidence is weak.
❖ Examine your explanations to be sure your readers will understand them. Define terms and clarify concepts that readers may be unfamiliar with.
❖ Integrate source material smoothly and clearly into your sentences.
❖ Cite your sources, following one of the styles in Chapters 50–53.

49g

The final draft of your paper should conform to the format recommended by your instructor or by the appropriate style guide. This book details two formats: that of the Modern Language Association (pp. 203–07), and that of the American Psychological Association (pp. 318–20). In any discipline you can use a computerized word processor to present your ideas effectively and attractively with readable typefaces, headings, illustrations, and other elements. See pages 207–15 for ideas.

Documenting Sources: MLA Style

❖

Documenting Sources: MLA Style

❖

Index to MLA works-cited models

MLA

50a

271

50 MLA Documentation

The style guide for English, foreign languages, and some other humanities is the *MLA Handbook for Writers of Research Papers*, published by the Modern Language Association. The documentation system of the *MLA Handbook* employs brief parenthetical citations within the text that direct readers to a list of works cited at the end of the text. This chapter describes this documentation system: writing citations (below), placing citations (p. 277), using supplementary notes (p. 278), and preparing the list of works cited (p. 279). A sample MLA paper concludes the chapter.

50a Writing MLA parenthetical text citations

1. Citation formats

The in-text citations of sources have two requirements:

* They must include just enough information for the reader to locate the appropriate source in your list of works cited.
* They must include just enough information for the reader to locate the place in the source where the borrowed material appears.

Usually, you can meet both these requirements by providing the author's last name and the page(s) in the source on which the material appears. The reader can find the source in your list of works cited and find the borrowed material in the source itself.

See the tabbed divider at page 270 for an index to the following models.

1. AUTHOR NOT NAMED IN YOUR TEXT

When you have not already named the author in your sentence, provide the author's last name and the page number(s), with no punctuation between them, in parentheses.

> One researcher concludes that "women impose a distinctive construction on moral problems, seeing moral dilemmas in terms of conflicting responsibilities" (Gilligan 105).

2. AUTHOR NAMED IN YOUR TEXT

If the author's name is already given in your text, you need not repeat it in the parenthetical citation. The citation gives just the page number(s).

One researcher, Carol Gilligan, concludes that "women impose a distinctive construction on moral problems, seeing moral dilemmas in terms of conflicting responsibilities" (105).

3. A WORK WITH TWO OR THREE AUTHORS

If the source has two or three authors, give all their last names in the text or in the citation. Separate two authors' names with "and":

As Frieden and Sagalyn observe, "The poor and the minorities were the leading victims of highway and renewal programs" (29).

According to one study, "The poor and the minorities were the leading victims of highway and renewal programs" (Frieden and Sagalyn 29).

With three authors, add commas and also "and" before the final name:

The text by Wilcox, Ault, and Agee discusses the "ethical dilemmas in public relations practice" (125).

One text discusses the "ethical dilemmas in public relations practice" (Wilcox, Ault, and Agee 125).

4. A WORK WITH MORE THAN THREE AUTHORS

If the source has more than three authors, you may list all their last names or use only the first author's name followed by "et al." (the abbreviation for the Latin "and others"). The choice depends on what you do in your list of works cited (see p. 280).

It took the combined forces of the Americans, Europeans, and Japanese to break the rebel siege of Beijing in 1900 (Lopez et al. 362).

It took the combined forces of the Americans, Europeans, and Japanese to break the rebel siege of Beijing in 1900 (Lopez, Blum, Cameron, and Barnes 362).

5. A WORK WITH NUMBERED PARAGRAPHS INSTEAD OF PAGES

Some electronic sources number each paragraph instead of each page. In citing passages in these sources, give the paragraph number(s) and distinguish them from page numbers: after the author's name, put a comma, a space, and the abbreviation "par." (one paragraph) or "pars." (more than one paragraph).

> Twins reared apart report similar feelings (Palfrey, pars. 6-7).

6. An entire work or a work with no page or paragraph numbers

When you cite an entire work rather than a part of it, the citation will not include any page or paragraph number. Try to work the author's name into your text, in which case you will not need a parenthetical citation. But remember that the source must appear in the list of works cited.

> Boyd deals with the need to acknowledge and come to terms with
>
> our fear of nuclear technology.

Use the same format when you cite a specific passage from a work that has no page or paragraph numbers, such as an online source. If the author's name does not appear in your text, put it in a parenthetical citation.

> Almost 20 percent of commercial banks have been audited for the
>
> practice (Friis).

7. A multivolume work

If you consulted only one volume of a multivolume work, your list of works cited will indicate as much (see p. 283), and you can treat the volume as any book. But if you consulted two or more volumes, your citation must indicate which one you are referring to. In the example the number 5 indicates the volume from which the quotation was taken; the number 438 indicates the page number in that volume.

> After issuing the Emancipation Proclamation, Lincoln said, "What
>
> I did, I did after very full deliberations, and under a very heavy
>
> and solemn sense of responsibility" (5: 438).

8. A work by an author of two or more works

If your list of works cited includes two or more works by the same author, give the appropriate title or a shortened version of it in the parenthetical citation. For this reference the full title is *The Arts and Human Development*.

> At about age seven, most children begin to use appropriate ges-
>
> tures to reinforce their stories (Gardner, Arts 144-45).

9. AN UNSIGNED WORK

Anonymous works are alphabetized by title in the list of works cited. In the text they are referred to by full or shortened title. This citation refers to an unsigned article titled "The Right to Die." (A page number is unnecessary because the article is no longer than a page.)

> One article notes that a death row inmate may demand his own execution to achieve a fleeting notoriety ("Right").

10. A GOVERNMENT PUBLICATION OR A WORK WITH A CORPORATE AUTHOR

If the author of the work is listed as a government body or a corporation, cite the work by that organization's name. If the name is long, work it into the text to avoid an intrusive citation.

> A 1996 report by the Hawaii Department of Education predicts an increase in enrollments (6).

11. AN INDIRECT SOURCE

When one of your sources quotes someone else and you want to use the quotation, try to find the original source and quote directly from it. If you can't find the original source, then your citation must indicate that your quotation of it is indirect. In the following citation "qtd. in" ("quoted in") says that Davino was quoted by Boyd:

> George Davino maintains that "even small children have vivid
>
> ideas about nuclear energy" (qtd. in Boyd 22).

The list of works cited then includes only Boyd (the work consulted), not Davino.

12. A LITERARY WORK

Novels, plays, and poems are often available in many editions, so your instructor may ask you to provide information that will help readers find the passage you cite no matter what edition they consult. For novels, the page number comes first, followed by a semicolon and then information on the appropriate part or chapter of the work.

> Toward the end of James's novel, Maggie suddenly feels "the thick
>
> breath of the definite--which was the intimate, the immediate, the
>
> familiar, as she hadn't had them for so long" (535; pt. 6, ch. 41).

For poems that are not divided into parts, you can omit the page number and supply the line number(s) for the quotation. To pre-

MLA

50a

vent confusion with page numbers, precede the number(s) with "line" or "lines" in the first citation; then just use the number(s).

> In Shakespeare's Sonnet 73 the speaker identifies with the trees of
> late autumn, "Bare ruined choirs, where late the sweet birds sang"
> (line 4). "In me," Shakespeare writes, "thou seest the glowing of
> such fire / That on the ashes of his youth doth lie" (9-10).

MLA

50a

For verse plays and poems that are divided into parts, omit a page number and cite the appropriate part—act (and scene, if any), canto, book, and so on—plus the line number(s). Use Arabic numerals for parts, including acts and scenes (3.4).

> Later in King Lear Shakespeare has the disguised Edgar say, "The
> prince of darkness is a gentleman" (3.4.147).

For prose plays, provide the page number followed by the act and scene, if any (see the reference to *Death of a Salesman* on p. 278).

13. THE BIBLE

When you cite passages of the Bible in parentheses, abbreviate the title of any book longer than four letters—for instance, "Gen." (Genesis), "1 Sam." (1 Samuel), "Ps." (Psalms), "Matt." (Matthew). Then give the chapter and verse(s) in Arabic numerals.

> According to the Bible, at Babel God "did . . . confound the lan-
> guage of all the earth" (Gen. 11.9).

14. AN ELECTRONIC SOURCE

Cite an electronic source as you would any other source: usually by author's name or, if there is no author, by title.

> Business forecasts for the fourth quarter tended to be optimistic
> (White 4).

This example cites a source with page numbers. For a source with paragraph numbers or no numbering, see models 5 and 6 (pp. 273–74).

15. MORE THAN ONE WORK

If you use a parenthetical citation to refer to more than a single work, separate the references with a semicolon.

> Two recent articles point out that a computer badly used can be
> less efficient than no computer at all (Gough and Hall 201;
> Richards 162).

Since long citations in the text can distract the reader, you may choose to cite several or more works in an endnote or footnote rather than in the text. See the next page.

2. Placement of parenthetical citations

Position text citations to accomplish two goals: (1) make it clear exactly where your borrowing begins and ends; (2) keep the citation as unobtrusive as possible. You can accomplish both goals by placing the parenthetical citation at the end of the sentence element containing the borrowed material. This sentence element may be a phrase or a clause, and it may begin, interrupt, or conclude the sentence. Usually, as in the examples below, the element ends with a punctuation mark.

MLA
50a

> The inflation rate might climb as high as 30 percent (Kim 164), an increase that could threaten the small nation's stability.

> The inflation rate, which might climb as high as 30 percent (Kim 164), could threaten the small nation's stability.

> The small nation's stability could be threatened by its inflation rate, which, one source predicts, might climb as high as 30 percent (Kim 164).

Notice that in the last example, the addition of "one source predicts" clarifies that Kim is responsible only for the inflation-rate prediction, not for the statement about stability.

For citations in your running text, generally place the parenthetical citation *before* any punctuation required by your sentence, as in the examples above. If the borrowed material is a quotation, place the citation *between* the closing quotation mark and the punctuation.

> Spelling argues that during the 1970s American automobile manufacturers met consumer needs "as well as could be expected" (26), but not everyone agrees with him.

The exception is a quotation ending in a question mark or exclamation point. Then use the appropriate punctuation inside the closing quotation mark, and follow the quotation with the text citation and a period.

> "Of what use is genius," Emerson asks, "if the organ . . . cannot find a focal distance within the actual horizon of human life?" ("Experience" 60). Mad genius is no genius.

When a citation appears after a quotation that ends in an ellipsis mark (. . .), place the citation between the closing quotation mark and the sentence period.

One observer maintains that "American manufacturers must bear

the blame for their poor sales . . ." (Rosenbaum 12).

When a citation appears at the end of a quotation set off from the text, place it one space *after* the punctuation ending the quotation. No additional punctuation is needed.

In Arthur Miller's Death of a Salesman, the most poignant defense

of Willie Loman comes from his wife, Linda:

> He's not the finest character that ever lived. But he's a
>
> human being, and a terrible thing is happening to him.
>
> So attention must be paid. He's not to be allowed to fall
>
> into his grave like an old dog. Attention, attention must
>
> finally be paid to such a person. (56; act 1)

(This citation of a play includes the act number as well as the page number. See p. 276.)

3. Footnotes or endnotes in special circumstances

Footnotes or endnotes may replace parenthetical citations when you cite several sources at once, when you comment on a source, or when you provide information that does not fit easily in the text. Signal a footnote or endnote in your text with a numeral raised above the appropriate line. Then write a note with the same numeral.

TEXT   At least five subsequent studies have confirmed these results.[1]

NOTE   [1] Abbott and Winger 266-68; Casner 27; Hoyenga

78-79; Marino 36; Tripp, Tripp, and Walk 179-83.

In a note the raised numeral is indented five spaces and followed by a space. If the note appears as a footnote, place it at the bottom of the page on which the citation appears, set it off from the text with quadruple spacing, and single-space the note itself. If the note appears as an endnote, place it in numerical order with the other endnotes on a page between the text and the list of works cited; double-space all the endnotes.

50b Preparing the MLA list of works cited

At the end of your paper, a list titled "Works Cited" includes all the sources you quoted, paraphrased, or summarized in your paper. (If your instructor asks you to include sources you examined but did not cite, title the list "Works Consulted.")

For the list of works cited, arrange your sources in alphabetical order by the last name of the author. If an author is not given in the source, alphabetize the source by the first main word of the title (excluding *A, An,* or *The*). Type the entire list double-spaced (both within and between entries). Indent the second and subsequent lines of each entry five spaces from the left. (See the sample on p. 304.)

NOTE An index to all the following models appears opposite the tabbed divider, on page 271. This index can be helpful when you need to combine formats. For example, to list a work by four authors appearing on a CD-ROM, you will have to draw on model 3 ("A book with more than three authors") and model 33 ("A source on CD-ROM").

1. Books

The basic format for a book includes the following elements:

Gilligan, Carol. *In a Different Voice: Psychological Theory and*

Women's Development. Cambridge: Harvard UP, 1983.

1. *Author.* Use the author's full name: the last name first, followed by a comma, and then the first name and any middle name or initial. End the name with a period and one space.
2. *Title.* Give the full title, including any subtitle. Underline the title, capitalize all important words (see p. 224), separate the main title and the subtitle with a colon and one space, and end the title with a period and one space.
3. *Publication information.* You can usually find this information on the book's title page or on the copyright page immediately following.

   a. The city of publication, followed by a colon and one space.
   b. The name of the publisher, followed by a comma. Shorten most publishers' names—in many cases to a single word. For instance, use "Little" for Little, Brown. For university presses, use the abbreviations "U" and "P," as in the example.
   c. The date of publication, ending with a period.

When other information is required for a reference, it is generally placed either between the author's name and the title or between the title and the publication information, as specified in the models below.

1. A BOOK WITH ONE AUTHOR

Gilligan, Carol. In a Different Voice: Psychological Theory and

Women's Development. Cambridge: Harvard UP, 1982.

2. A BOOK WITH TWO OR THREE AUTHORS

Frieden, Bernard J., and Lynne B. Sagalyn. Downtown, Inc.: How

America Rebuilds Cities. Cambridge: MIT P, 1989.

Wilcox, Dennis L., Phillip H. Ault, and Warren K. Agee. Public Re-

lations: Strategies and Tactics. 4th ed. New York: Harper,

1995.

Give the authors' names in the order provided on the title page. Reverse the first and last names of the first author *only*. Separate two authors' names with a comma and "and"; separate three authors' names with commas and with "and" before the third name.

3. A BOOK WITH MORE THAN THREE AUTHORS

Lopez, Robert S., et al. Civilizations: Western and World. Boston:

Little, 1975.

You may, but need not, give all authors' names if the work has more than three authors. If you choose not to give all names, provide the name of the first author only, and follow the name with a comma and the abbreviation "et al." (for the Latin *et alii,* meaning "and others").

4. TWO OR MORE WORKS BY THE SAME AUTHOR(S)

Gardner, Howard. The Arts and Human Development. New York:

Wiley, 1973.

---. The Quest for Mind: Piaget, Lévi-Strauss, and the Structuralist

Movement. New York: Knopf, 1973.

Give the author's name only in the first entry. For the second and any subsequent works by the same author, substitute three hyphens for the author's name. Within the set of entries for the author, list the sources alphabetically by the first main word of the title. Note that the three hyphens stand for *exactly* the same name or names. If the second source above were by Gardner and somebody else, both names would have to be given in full.

5. A BOOK WITH AN EDITOR

Ruitenbeek, Hendrick, ed. Freud as We Knew Him. Detroit: Wayne
State UP, 1973.

The abbreviation "ed.," separated from the name by a comma, identifies Ruitenbeek as the editor of the work.

6. A BOOK WITH AN AUTHOR AND AN EDITOR

Melville, Herman. The Confidence Man: His Masquerade. Ed. Hershel Parker. New York: Norton, 1971.

When citing the work of the author, give his or her name first, and give the editor's name after the title, preceded by "Ed." ("Edited by"). When citing the work of the editor, use the form above for a book with an editor, and give the author's name after the title preceded by "By": Parker, Hershel, ed. The Confidence Man: His Masquerade. By Herman Melville.

7. A TRANSLATION

Alighieri, Dante. The Inferno. Trans. John Ciardi. New York: NAL,
1971.

When citing the work of the author, give his or her name first, and give the translator's name after the title, preceded by "Trans." ("Translated by"). When citing the work of the translator, give his or her name first, followed by a comma and "trans."; then follow the title with "By" and the author's name: Ciardi, John, trans. The Inferno. By Dante Alighieri.

When a book you cite by author has a translator *and* an editor, give the translator's and editor's names in the order used on the book's title page. For a translated selection from an edited book, see model 19, page 284.

8. A BOOK WITH A CORPORATE AUTHOR

Lorenz, Inc. Research in Social Studies Teaching. Baltimore: Arrow, 1992.

List the name of the corporation, institution, or other body as author.

9. A GOVERNMENT PUBLICATION

Stiller, Ann. Historic Preservation and Tax Incentives. US Dept. of
Interior. Washington: GPO, 1996.

Hawaii. Dept. of Education. Kauai District Schools, Profile 1996-
97. Honolulu: Hawaii Dept. of Education, 1996.

United States. Cong. House. Committee on Ways and Means.

    Medicare Payment for Outpatient Occupational Therapy Ser-

    vices. 102nd Cong., 1st sess. Washington: GPO, 1991.

If an author is not listed for a government publication, give the appropriate agency as author. Provide information in the order illustrated, separating elements with a period and a space: the name of the government, the name of the agency (which may be abbreviated), and the title and publication information. For a congressional publication (last example), give the house and committee involved before the title, and give the number and session of Congress after the title. In the first and last examples, "GPO" stands for the US Government Printing Office.

10. AN ANONYMOUS BOOK

The Dorling Kindersley World Reference Atlas. London: Dorling,

    1994.

List an anonymous book by its full title. Alphabetize the book by the title's first main word (here "Dorling"), omitting *A, An,* or *The.*

11. THE BIBLE

The New English Bible. London: Oxford and Cambridge, 1970.

The Holy Bible. King James Version. Cleveland: World, n.d.

When citing the Bible, do not underline the title or the name of the version. The version may be included in the title (first example); if not, give it after the title (second example). The abbreviation "n.d." at the end of the second example indicates that the source lists no date of publication.

12. A LATER EDITION

Bollinger, Dwight L. Aspects of Language. 2nd ed. New York: Har-

    court, 1975.

For any edition after the first, place the edition number between the title and the publication information. Use the appropriate designation for editions that are named or dated rather than numbered—for instance, "Rev. ed." for "Revised edition."

13. A REPUBLISHED BOOK

James, Henry. The Golden Bowl. 1904. London: Penguin, 1966.

Place the original date of publication after the title, and then provide the full publication information for the source you are using.

14. A BOOK WITH A TITLE IN ITS TITLE

Eco, Umberto. Postscript to The Name of the Rose. Trans. William
    Weaver. New York: Harcourt, 1983.

When a book's title contains another book title (as here: The Name
of the Rose), do not underline the shorter title. When a book's title
contains a quotation or the title of a work normally placed in quotation marks, keep the quotation marks and underline both titles:
Critical Response to Henry James's "Beast in the Jungle." (Note
that the underlining extends under the closing quotation mark.)

MLA
50b

15. A WORK IN MORE THAN ONE VOLUME

Lincoln, Abraham. The Collected Works of Abraham Lincoln.
    Ed. Roy P. Basler. 8 vols. New Brunswick: Rutgers UP,
    1953.

Lincoln, Abraham. The Collected Works of Abraham Lincoln.
    Ed. Roy P. Basler. Vol. 5. New Brunswick: Rutgers UP,
    1953. 8 vols.

If you use two or more volumes of a multivolume work, give the
work's total number of volumes before the publication information
("8 vols." in the first example). Your text citation will indicate
which volume you are citing (see p. 274). If you use only one volume, give that volume number before the publication information
("Vol. 5" in the second example). You may add the total number of
volumes to the end of the entry ("8 vols." in the second example).

If you cite a multivolume work published over a period of
years, give the inclusive years as the publication date: for instance,
Cambridge: Harvard UP, 1978-90.

16. A WORK IN A SERIES

Bergman, Ingmar. The Seventh Seal. Mod. Film Scripts Ser. 12.
    New York: Simon, 1968.

Place the name of the series (not quoted or underlined) just before
the publication information. Abbreviate common words such as
modern and *series*. Add any series number after the series title.

17. PUBLISHED PROCEEDINGS OF A CONFERENCE

Watching Our Language: A Conference Sponsored by the Program
    in Architecture and Design Criticism. 6-8 May 1996. New
    York: Parsons School of Design, 1996.

Whether in or after the title of the conference, supply information about who sponsored the conference, when it was held, and who published the proceedings. If you are citing a particular presentation at the conference, treat it as a selection from an anthology (model 19).

18. AN ANTHOLOGY

Kennedy, X. J., and Dana Gioia, eds. Literature: An Introduction to

Fiction, Poetry, and Drama. 6th ed. New York: Harper, 1995.

When citing an entire anthology, give the name of the editor or editors (followed by "ed." or "eds.") and then the title of the anthology.

19. A SELECTION FROM AN ANTHOLOGY

Kafka, Franz. "The Metamorphosis." Trans. Willa and Edwin Muir.

Literature: An Introduction to Fiction, Poetry, and Drama.

6th ed. Ed. X. J. Kennedy and Dana Gioia. New York: Harper,

1995. 311-45.

The essentials of this listing are these: author of selection; title of selection (in quotation marks); title of anthology (underlined); editors' names preceded by "Ed." (meaning "Edited by"); publication information for the anthology; and inclusive page numbers for the selection (without the abbreviation "pp."). This source also requires a translator for the selection and an edition number for the anthology.

If the work you cite comes from a collection of works by one author and with no editor, use the following form:

Auden, W. H. "Family Ghosts." The Collected Poetry of W. H.

Auden. New York: Random, 1945. 132-33.

If the work you cite is a scholarly article that was previously printed elsewhere, provide the complete information for the earlier publication of the piece, followed by "Rpt. in" ("Reprinted in") and the information for the source in which you found the piece:

Gibian, George. "Traditional Symbolism in Crime and Punish-

ment." PMLA 70 (1955): 979-96. Rpt. in Crime and Punish-

ment. By Feodor Dostoevsky. Ed. George Gibian. Norton

Critical Editions. New York: Norton, 1964. 575-92.

20. TWO OR MORE SELECTIONS FROM THE SAME ANTHOLOGY

Chopin, Kate. "The Story of an Hour." Kennedy and Gioia 419-21.

Kennedy, X. J., and Dana Gioia, eds. <u>Literature: An Introduction to</u>

<u>Fiction, Poetry, and Drama</u>. 6th ed. New York: Harper, 1995.

Olsen, Tillie. "I Stand Here Ironing." Kennedy and Gioia 535-40.

When citing more than one selection from the same source, you may avoid repetition by giving the source in full (as in the Kennedy and Gioia entry) and then simply cross-referencing it in entries for the works you used. Thus, instead of full information for the Chopin and Olsen articles, give Kennedy's and Gioia's names and the appropriate pages in their book. Note that each entry appears in its proper alphabetical place among other works cited.

21. AN INTRODUCTION, PREFACE, FOREWORD, OR AFTERWORD

Donaldson, Norman. Introduction. <u>The Claverings</u>. By Anthony

Trollope. New York: Dover, 1977. vii-xv.

An introduction, foreword, or afterword is often written by someone other than the book's author. When citing such a work, give its name without quotation marks or underlining. Follow the title of the book with its author's name preceded by "By." Give the inclusive page numbers of the part you cite. (In the example above, the small Roman numerals indicate that the cited work is in the front matter of the book, before page 1.)

When the author of a preface or introduction is the same as the author of the book, give only the last name after the title:

Gould, Stephen Jay. Prologue. <u>The Flamingo's Smile: Reflections</u>

<u>in Natural History</u>. By Gould. New York: Norton, 1985. 13-

20.

22. AN ARTICLE IN A REFERENCE WORK

"Reckon." <u>Merriam-Webster's Collegiate Dictionary</u>. 10th ed.

1993.

Mark, Herman F. "Polymers." <u>The New Encyclopaedia Britannica:</u>

<u>Macropaedia</u>. 15th ed. 1991.

List an article in a reference work by its title (first example) unless the article is signed (second example). For works with entries arranged alphabetically, you need not include volume or page numbers. For well-known works like those listed above, you may also omit the editors' names and all publication information except any edition number and the year of publication. For works that are not well known, give full publication information.

2. Periodicals: Journals, magazines, and newspapers

The basic format for an article from a periodical includes the following information:

①_____ ②_____

Lever, Janet. "Sex Differences in the Games Children Play."

③_____

Social Problems 23 (1976): 478-87.
ⓐ   ⓑ   ⓒ   ⓓ

1. *Author.* Use the author's full name: the last name first, followed by a comma, and then the first name and any middle name or initial. End the name with a period and one space.
2. *Title of the article.* Give the full title, including any subtitle. Place the title in quotation marks, capitalize all important words in the title (see p. 224), and end the title with a period (inside the final quotation mark) and one space.
3. *Publication information.*
   a. The title of the periodical, underlined, followed by a space. Omit any *A, An,* or *The* from the beginning of the title.
   b. The volume and/or issue number (in Arabic numerals), followed by a space. See the note following.
   c. The date of publication, followed by a colon and a space. See the note following.
   d. The inclusive page numbers of the article (without the abbreviation "pp."). For the second number in inclusive page numbers over 100, provide only as many digits as needed for clarity (usually two): 100–01, 398–401, 1026–36.

NOTE The treatment of volume and issue numbers and publication dates varies depending on the kind of periodical being cited, as the models indicate. For the distinction between journals and magazines, see page 248.

23. A SIGNED ARTICLE IN A JOURNAL WITH CONTINUOUS PAGINATION THROUGHOUT THE ANNUAL VOLUME

Lever, Janet. "Sex Differences in the Games Children Play." Social

   Problems 23 (1976): 478-87.

Some journals number the pages of issues consecutively throughout a year, so that issue number 3 may begin on page 261. For this kind of journal, give the volume number after the title ("23" in the example above) and place the year of publication in parentheses.

24. A SIGNED ARTICLE IN A JOURNAL THAT PAGES ISSUES SEPARATELY OR THAT NUMBERS ONLY ISSUES, NOT VOLUMES

Dacey, June. "Management Participation in Corporate Buy-Outs."

   Management Perspectives 7.4 (1994): 20-31.

Some journals page each issue separately (starting each issue at page 1). For these journals, give the volume number, a period, and the issue number (as in "7.4" in the entry above). When citing an article in a journal that numbers only issues, not annual volumes, treat the issue number as if it were a volume number, as in model 23.

25. A SIGNED ARTICLE IN A MONTHLY OR BIMONTHLY MAGAZINE

Tilin, Andrew. "Selling the Dream." Worth Oct. 1996: 94-100.

Follow the magazine title with the month and the year of publication. (Abbreviate all months except May, June, and July.) Don't place the date in parentheses, and don't provide a volume or issue number.

26. A SIGNED ARTICLE IN A WEEKLY OR BIWEEKLY MAGAZINE

Stevens, Mark. "Low and Behold." New Republic 24 Dec. 1990: 27-
33.

Follow the magazine title with the day, the month (abbreviated), and the year of publication. (Abbreviate all months except May, June, and July.) Don't place the date in parentheses, and don't provide a volume or issue number.

27. A SIGNED ARTICLE IN A DAILY NEWSPAPER

Ramirez, Anthony. "Computer Groups Plan Standards." New York
Times 14 Dec. 1993, late ed.: D5.

Give the name of the newspaper as it appears on the first page (but without A, An, or The). Then follow model 26, with two differences: (1) If the newspaper lists an edition at the top of the first page, include that information after the date and a comma. (See "late ed." above.) (2) If the newspaper is divided into lettered or numbered sections, provide the section designation before the page number when the newspaper does the same (as in "D5" above); otherwise, provide the section designation before the colon (as in "sec. 1: 1+" below).

28. AN UNSIGNED ARTICLE

"The Right to Die." Time 11 Oct. 1976: 101.

"Protests Greet Pope in Holland." Boston Sunday Globe 12 May
1985, late ed., sec. 1: 1+.

Begin the entry for an unsigned article with the title of the article. (Alphabetize it by the first main word of the title.) The number "1+" indicates that the article does not run on consecutive pages but starts on page 1 and continues later in the issue.

29. An editorial or letter to the editor

"Bodily Intrusions." Editorial. New York Times 29 Aug. 1990, late
  ed.: A20.

Add the word "Editorial" or "Letter"—but without quotation marks
—after the title if there is one or after the author's name, as fol-lows:

Dowding, Michael. Letter. Economist 5-11 Jan. 1985: 4.

30. A review

Dunne, John Gregory. "The Secret of Danny Santiago." Rev. of Fa-
  mous All over Town, by Danny Santiago. New York Review
  of Books 16 Aug. 1984: 17-27.

"Rev." is an abbreviation for "Review." The name of the author of the
work being reviewed follows the title of the work, a comma, and "by."

31. An abstract of a dissertation or article

Steciw, Steven K. "Alterations to the Pessac Project of Le Corbusier."
  Diss. U of Cambridge, England, 1986. DAI 46 (1986): 565C.

For an abstract appearing in *Dissertation Abstracts* (*DA*) or *Dissertation Abstracts International* (*DAI*), give the author's name and the title, "Diss." (for "Dissertation"), the institution granting the author's
degree, the date of the dissertation, and the publication information.

For an abstract of an article, first provide the publication information for the article itself, followed by the information for the abstract:

Lever, Janet. "Sex Differences in the Games Children Play." Social
  Problems 23 (1976): 478-87. Psychological Abstracts 63
  (1976): item 1431.

3. Electronic sources

MLA formats for electronic sources vary according to the
medium and type of source (for instance, CD-ROM periodical, online database, online periodical). The models below follow the most
recent formats recommended by MLA, in its *MLA Style Manual and
Guide to Scholarly Publishing,* 2nd edition (1998). With online research constantly expanding and changing, these recent formats
are more extensive and up to date than those in the 1995 *MLA
Handbook*.

Note Online sources, such as those you reach through the
World Wide Web, require two special pieces of information:

❖ Because online sources are easy to change and thus do sometimes change, give the date when you consulted the source as
well as the date when the source was posted online. The posting date comes first, with other publication information. Your
access date falls near the end of the entry, just before the electronic address.

❖ To help your readers locate your online sources, give each
source's exact and complete electronic address. Enclose the address in angle brackets (< >), and place it at the end of the entry. If you must break an address from one line to the next, do
so *only* after a slash, and do not hyphenate.

MLA

50b

Try to locate all the information required in the following models, so that your readers can trace your sources with minimal difficulty. However, if you search for and still cannot find some
information, then give what you can find.

32. A SOURCE ON CD-ROM, DISKETTE, OR MAGNETIC TAPE

Treat sources on CD-ROM, diskette, or magnetic tape much as
you would sources in print, with two main additions: the medium
("CD-ROM," "Diskette," or "Magnetic tape," without quotation
marks) and the vendor (or distributor) of the electronic work, if one
is given as well as the publisher. Other additions depend on whether
the source is or is not a periodical and is or is not also published in
print.

A nonperiodical CD-ROM, diskette, or magnetic tape:

Shelley, Mary Wollstonecraft. Frankenstein. Classic Library.
CD-ROM. Alameda: Andromeda, 1993.

If you cite a single-issue CD-ROM, diskette, or tape, first provide its
author (1) and title (2). Underline titles of books or similarly long
works; use quotation marks for short works such as stories or parts
of books. Then give the underlined title of the entire disk or tape
(3), if there is a title; give the medium (4), without quotation marks
or underlining; and end with the disk's or tape's place of publication, publisher, and date of publication (5).

If the work you cite or the entire disk or tape has a version or
edition number, add it at the appropriate place, as shown in the
model below:

"Sugar." Concise Columbia Encyclopedia. 3rd ed. Microsoft Book-
shelf. CD-ROM. 1996-97 ed. Redmond: Microsoft, 1996.

This model also shows citation of a part of a work (in quotation
marks) with no author.

A periodical CD-ROM with information for a print version:

Ramirez, Anthony. "Computer Groups Plan Standards." New York

Times 14 Dec. 1993, late ed.: D5. New York Times Ondisc.

CD-ROM. UMI-Proquest. June 1994.

If you are citing a source on CD-ROM that's issued periodically (like a journal or magazine), look for information about a print version of the same source. (The information is usually at the beginning of the source.) If there is such information, provide it as in the model above (1), referring to pages 286-88 as needed. Then provide the following information on the CD-ROM version: the title of the CD-ROM (2), underlined; the medium, "CD-ROM" (3), without quotation marks or underlining; the name of the vendor (or distributor) of the CD-ROM (4); and the date of electronic publication (5).

A periodical CD-ROM without information for a print version:

"Vanguard Forecasts." Business Outlook. CD-ROM. Information

Access. Mar. 1997.

If a periodical source appears only on CD-ROM (not also in print), give only the CD-ROM title, the medium, the vendor, and the date.

33. ELECTRONIC MAIL OR AN ONLINE POSTING

Electronic mail:

Millon, Michele. "Re: Grief Therapy." E-mail to the author.

4 May 1997.

For e-mail, give the name of the writer (1); the title, if any, from the e-mail's subject heading (2), in quotation marks; a description of the transmission, including whom it was sent to (3); and the date of posting (4).

A discussion list:

Tourville, Michael. "European Currency Reform." 6 Jan. 1997.

Online posting. International Finance Discussion List.

22 Feb. 1997 <http://www.weg.isu.edu/finance-dl/>.

A discussion list or group, such as a Listserv, is subscribed to via e-mail (see p. 247). For a posting to a list, give the author's name (1); the title, if any, from the e-mail's subject heading (2), in quotation marks; the date of posting (3); the words "Online posting" (4), without quotation marks or underlining; the name of the list (5); the date you consulted the source (6); and the electronic address

(7). Whenever possible, cite an archived version of the posting. If the posting has an identifying number, insert it immediately after the list's name without intervening punctuation—for example, Art Finds Discussion List 22634.

A Usenet newsgroup:

Cramer, Sherry. "Recent Investment Practices in U.S. Business." 26 Mar. 1997. Online posting. 3 Apr. 1997 <news:biz.investment.current.2700>.

A Usenet newsgroup is not subscriber-based (see p. 247). For a posting to a newsgroup, give the author's name (1); the title from the subject heading (2), in quotation marks; the date of posting (3); "Online posting" (4), without quotation marks or underlining; the date you consulted the source (5); and, in angle brackets, the group's name preceded by "news:" (6), as in the example.

34. AN ONLINE SCHOLARLY PROJECT, REFERENCE DATABASE, OR PERSONAL OR PROFESSIONAL SITE

A scholarly project or database:

Scots Teaching and Research Network. Ed. John Corbett. 2 Feb. 1998. U of Glasgow. 5 Mar. 1998 <http://www.arts.gla.ac.uk/www/english/comet/starn/htm>.

When citing an entire project or database, provide the title (1), underlined; the name of any editor (2); the date of publication (3); the name of any organization or institution that sponsors the project or database (4); the date you consulted the source (5); and the electronic address (6). If the project or database has a version number, add it after the editor's name and before the date of publication—for instance, Vers. 3.2.

A short work within a scholarly project:

Barbour, John. "The Brus." Scots Teaching and Research Network. Ed. John Corbett. 2 Feb. 1998. U of Glasgow. 5 Mar. 1998 <http://www.arts.gla.ac.uk/www/english/comet/starn/poetry/ brus/contents/htm>.

For a poem, an article, or another short work published as part of a scholarly project, start with the author's name (1) and the title of the short work (2), in quotation marks. Then follow the model above for the complete project (3), but give the specific electronic address for the short work (4).

A personal or professional site:

Lederman, Leon. Topics in Modern Physics--Lederman. 12 Dec.

1997 <http://www-ed.fnal.gov/samplers/hsphys/people/

lederman.html>.

Cite a personal or professional site with the author's name (1); the title if any (2), underlined; the date you consulted the source (3); and the electronic address (4). If the source has no title, describe it with a label such as "Home page," without quotation marks or underlining. If it has a sponsoring organization or institution, add the name after the title.

35. AN ONLINE BOOK

A book published independently:

James, Henry. The Turn of the Screw. New York: Scribner's,

1908-09. 4 Mar. 1998 <http://www.americanliterature.com/

TS/TSINDX.HTML>.

For an online book published independently, not as part of a scholarly project or other larger site, provide the author's name (1); the underlined title of the book (2); any publication information for the original print version of the book (3); the date you consulted the source (4); and the electronic address (5). If the book was not published in print before, substitute the date of electronic publication for the print publication information. If the book has an editor or translator, include that information as in the following model.

A book within a scholarly project:

Austen, Jane. Emma. Ed. Ronald Blythe. Harmondsworth: Penguin,

1972. Oxford Text Archive. 1994. Oxford U. 15 Dec. 1997

<ftp://ota.ox.ac.uk/pub/ota/public/english/Austen/

emma.1519>.

For a book published as part of a scholarly project, first provide author and title (1), the name of any editor or translator (2), and any print publication information provided in the source (3). Add the title of the project (4), underlined; the date of electronic publication (5); the name of any sponsoring organization or institution (6); the date of your access (7); and the electronic address (8), which should direct readers to the book rather than to the project as a whole. If the project has an editor, add the name after the project's title (see the model on p. 291).

36. AN ARTICLE IN AN ONLINE PERIODICAL

An article in a scholarly journal:

Palfrey, Andrew. "Choice of Mates in Identical Twins." Modern

Psychology 4.1 (1996): 12 pars. 25 Feb. 1996 <http://

www.liasu.edu/modpsy/palfrey4(1).htm>.

Follow model 23 or 24 (p. 286) for a scholarly article (1), but add the date you consulted the source (2) and the electronic address (3). If the journal does not number pages in sequence, provide the total number of paragraphs (as in the example), pages, or other numbered sections. Omit such information if the source gives no numbering.

An article in a newspaper:

Still, Lucia. "On the Battlefields of Business, Millions of

Casualties." New York Times on the Web 3 Mar. 1996,

17 Aug. 1996 <http://www.nytimos.com/specials/downsize/

03down1.html>.

For an online newspaper article, provide the author's name (1); the title of the article (2), in quotation marks; the title of the online newspaper (3), underlined; the date of publication (4); the date you consulted the source (5); and the electronic address for the article (6). Provide section, page, or paragraph numbers if the newspaper does, as in model 27 (p. 287).

An article in a magazine:

Palevitz, Barry A., and Ricki Lewis. "Death Raises Safety

Issues for Primate Handlers." Scientist 2 Mar. 1998: 11.

27 Mar. 1998 <http://www.the-scientist.library.upenn.edu/

yr1998/mar/palevitz_pl_980302.html>.

Cite an article in an online magazine with the name(s) of the author(s) (1); the title of the article (2), in quotation marks; the title of the periodical (3), underlined; the date of publication (4); any page, paragraph, or other section numbers (5); the date you consulted the source (6); and the electronic address (7).

A review:

Detwiler, Donald S., and Chu Shao-Kang. Rev. of Important

Documents of the Republic of China, ed. Tan Quon Chin.

Journal of Military History 56.4 (1992): 669-84. 16 Sept.

1997 <http://www.jstor.org/fcgi-bin/jstor/viewitem.fcg/

08993718/96p0008x>.

Cite an online review following model 30 on page 288 and the appropriate model on the previous page for an online scholarly journal, newspaper, or magazine (1). Include the date you consulted the source (2) and the electronic address (3).

An editorial or letter to the editor:

Dobson, Ken. "Permanent Revolution--or Evolution?" Editorial. Physics Education 33.2 (1998): 75. 1 Apr. 1998 <http:// www.iop.org/EJ/S/1/NS0794600/?Mival=pe98033020001>.

For an online editorial or letter to the editor, follow model 29 on page 288 and the appropriate model on the previous page for an online scholarly journal, newspaper, or magazine (1). Include the date you consulted the source (2) and the electronic address (3).

37. A SYNCHRONOUS COMMUNICATION (MUD, MOO, ETC.)

Bruckman, Amy. MediaMOO Symposium: Virtual Worlds for Business? 20 Jan. 1998. MediaMOO. 26 Feb. 1998 <http:// www.cc.gatech.edu/fac/Amy.Bruckman/MediaMOO/ cscw-symposium-98.html>.

Cite a synchronous communication with the name of the speaker (1); a description of the event (2), without quotation marks or underlining; the date of the event (3); the forum (4); the date you consulted the source (5); and the electronic address (6). Whenever possible, cite an archived version of the communication.

38. COMPUTER SOFTWARE

Project Scheduler 8000. Vers. 3.1. Orlando: Scitor, 1997.

For software, provide the title (1), underlined; the version number (2); and the publication information (3), including place of publication, publisher, and date. If you consulted or obtained the software online, replace this publication information with the date of your access and the electronic address, as in previous examples.

4.   Other sources

39. A PAMPHLET

Medical Answers About AIDS. New York: Gay Men's Health Crisis, 1994.

Most pamphlets can be treated as books. In the example above, the pamphlet has no listed author, so the title comes first. If the pamphlet has an author, list his or her name first.

40. AN UNPUBLISHED DISSERTATION OR THESIS

Wilson, Stuart M. "John Stuart Mill as a Literary Critic." Diss. U of

Michigan, 1970.

The title is quoted rather than underlined. "Diss." stands for "Dissertation." "U of Michigan" is the institution that granted the author's degree.

41. A MUSICAL COMPOSITION OR WORK OF ART

Fauré, Gabriel. Sonata for Violin and Piano no. 1 in A major, op.

15.

Don't underline musical compositions identified only by form, number, and key. Do underline titled operas, ballets, and compositions (Carmen, Sleeping Beauty).

For a work of art, underline the title and include the name and location of the owner. For a work you see only in a photograph, provide the complete publication information, too, as in the following model. Omit such information only if you examined the actual work.

Sargent, John Singer. Venetian Doorway. Metropolitan Museum of

Art, New York. Sargent Watercolors. By Donelson F. Hoopes.

New York: Watson, 1976. 31.

42. A FILM OR VIDEO RECORDING

Schindler's List. Dir. Steven Spielberg. Perf. Liam Neeson and Ben

Kingsley. Universal, 1993.

Start with the title of the work you are citing, unless you are citing the contribution of a particular individual (see the next model). Give additional information (writer, lead performers, and so on) as seems appropriate. For a film, end with the film's distributor and date.

For a videocassette, filmstrip, or slide program, include the original release date (if any) and the medium (without underlining or quotation marks) before the distributor's name:

George Balanchine, chor. Serenade. Perf. San Francisco Ballet.

Dir. Hilary Bean. 1981. Videocassette. PBS Video, 1987.

43. A TELEVISION OR RADIO PROGRAM

Kenyon, Jane, and Donald Hall. "A Life Together." Bill Moyers'

Journal. PBS. WNET, New York. 17 Dec. 1993.

As in model 42, start with a title unless you are citing the work of a person or persons. The example above begins with the participants' names, then lists the episode title (in quotation marks) and the program title (underlined). Finish the entry with the name of the network, the local station and city, and the date.

44. A PERFORMANCE

The English Only Restaurant. By Silvio Martinez Palau. Dir.

> Susana Tubert. Puerto Rican Traveling Theater, New York.

> 27 July 1990.

Ozawa, Seiji, cond. Boston Symphony Orch. Concert. Symphony

> Hall, Boston. 25 Apr. 1997.

Place the title first unless you are citing the work of an individual (second example). Provide additional information about participants after the title, as well as the theater, city, and date. Note that the orchestra concert in the second example is neither quoted nor underlined.

45. A RECORDING

Siberry, Jane. "Caravan." Maria. Reprise, 1995.

Brahms, Johannes. Concerto no. 2 in B-flat, op. 83. Perf. Artur

> Rubinstein. Cond. Eugene Ormandy. Philadelphia Orch. LP.

> RCA, 1972.

Begin with the name of the individual whose work you are citing. If you're citing a song, give the title in quotation marks. Then provide the title of the recording. Underline the title (first example) unless it identifies a composition by form, number, and key (second example). After the title, provide the names of any artists not already listed, the medium if not compact disk ("LP" in the second example), the manufacturer of the recording, and the date of release.

46. A LETTER

Buttolph, Mrs. Laura E. Letter to Rev. and Mrs. C. C. Jones. 20

> June 1857. In The Children of Pride: A True Story of Georgia

> and the Civil War. Ed. Robert Manson Myers. New Haven:

> Yale UP, 1972. 334-35.

A published letter is listed under the writer's name. Specify that the source is a letter and to whom it was addressed, and give the date on which it was written. Treat the remaining information like that for a selection from an anthology (model 19, p. 284). (See also pp. 288

and 294 for the format of a letter to the editor of a periodical. And see pp. 290–91 for the format of e-mail or an online posting.)

For a letter you receive, give the name of the writer, note the fact that the letter was sent to you, and provide the date of the letter:

> Packer, Ann E. Letter to the author. 15 June 1994.

47. A LECTURE OR ADDRESS

> Carlone, Dennis. "Architecture for the City of 2000." Tenth Sympo-
> sium on Urban Issues. Cambridge City Hall, Cambridge. 22
> Oct. 1996.

Give the speaker's name, the title (in quotation marks), the title of the meeting, the name of the sponsoring organization, the location of the lecture, and the date.

48. AN INTERVIEW

> Graaf, Vera. Personal interview. 19 Dec. 1993.
>
> Christopher, Warren. Interview. Frontline. PBS. WGBH, Boston.
> 13 Feb. 1996.

Begin with the name of the person interviewed. For an interview you conducted, specify "Personal interview," "Telephone interview," "E-mail interview," or "IRC interview," as appropriate—without quotation marks or underlining—and then give the date. For an interview you read, heard, or saw, provide the title if any or "Interview" if not, along with other bibliographic information and the date.

49. A MAP OR OTHER ILLUSTRATION

> Women in the Armed Forces. Map. Women in the World: An Inter-
> national Atlas. By Joni Seager and Ann Olson. New York:
> Touchstone, 1992. 44-45.

List the illustration by its title (underlined). Provide a descriptive label ("Map," "Chart," "Table"), without underlining or quotation marks, and the publication information. If the creator of the illustration is credited in the source, put his or her name first in the entry, as with any author.

50c Examining a sample research paper in MLA style

The sample paper beginning on page 299 follows the guidelines of the *MLA Handbook* for overall format, as presented on pages 203–07, and for parenthetical citations and the list of works cited, as presented in this chapter. Marginal annotations highlight features of the paper.

A note on outlines

Some instructors ask students to submit a formal outline of the final paper. Advice on constructing such an outline appears on page 18, along with an example written in phrases (a topic outline). Below is an outline of the sample paper following, written in complete sentences. Note that the thesis sentence precedes either a topic or a sentence outline.

THESIS SENTENCE

Most liquid-diet programs fail to emphasize that successful weight loss demands a fundamental change in behavior, not a tasty low-calorie shake.

   I. Although once dangerous, liquid-diet programs are now safer.
     A. All programs have improved the calories and protein in liquid diets.
     B. Supervised programs monitor dieters' health.
   II. Unsupervised programs, such as Slim·Fast and Dynatrim, concern health-care professionals.
     A. They do not involve supervision.
     B. They encourage too-rapid weight loss.
     C. They do not encourage behavior modification.
  III. Most diet professionals consider behavior modification essential for long-term weight loss.
     A. Liquid-diet programs, which do not involve behavior modification, have poor results.
     B. Behavior modification involves a number of factors.
       1. Nutritionists suggest such practices as regular meals, small portions, and rewards.
       2. Weight Watchers and some other group programs emphasize eating real foods, understanding nutrition, and changing unhealthful habits.

If you attach an outline to your paper, use standard outline form (p. 18) and double-space all the lines. Place the outline before page 1 of the paper, and cover it with a title page containing the title, your name, and the course information; center this information on the page, and use double space or more between elements. If you use a title page, you do not need to repeat your name and the course information on page 1 of the paper, but do repeat the title.

Writer's name and page number.

Andrea Joseph

Ms. Diodati

English 101

April 18, 1997

Writer's name, course, instructor's name, date.

Drinking the Pounds Away

Title centered.

"Give us a week, we'll take off the weight" is a familiar jingle advertising the Slim Fast liquid diet. In our weight-conscious society, liquid-diet programs such as Slim Fast and Optifast promise quick weight loss with little effort on the dieter's part. But most of these programs fail to emphasize that successful weight loss demands a fundamental change in behavior, not a tasty low-calorie shake.

Double-space throughout.

Thesis sentence.

MLA

50c

When liquid diets were first introduced in the 1970s, they were so deficient nutritionally that they were actually dangerous. But according to Victor Frattali, a nutritionist at the US Food and Drug Administration, manufacturers have now raised calorie levels and use "high-quality protein" (qtd. in Sachs 48). In addition, liquid diets are now divided into two categories: those sold over the counter in drugstores and markets and those supervised by health-care professionals (Simko et al. 231).

Background information.

Citation form: indirect source (Frattali quoted by Sachs). Citation falls between quotation mark and sentence period.

Citation form: source with more than three authors.

Medically supervised programs, such as Optifast and Medifast, became popular when the talk-show host Oprah Winfrey broadcast that she lost sixty-seven pounds on the Optifast diet (Kirschner et al. 902). The twenty-six-week Optifast regimen consists of three stages: a fasting period when patients consume only liquid-protein shakes providing 420 to 800 calories a day; a "refeeding" stage when food is reintroduced into the diet; and a maintenance stage when patients practice eating sensibly (Beek 56).

Discussion of supervised programs.

Summary of source.

Citation form: author not named in the text.

Joseph 2

Medical supervision and psychological counseling are crucial parts of the Optifast program. Before admittance, patients must pass a physical examination to ensure that they do not have any conditions that might make the diet dangerous for them. During the diet, patients undergo frequent weight checks and blood and urine tests (Stocker-Ferguson 57). The Mayo Clinic Diet Manual concurs that patients should be closely monitored so that they do not suffer dehydration and loss of vital minerals (Pemberton et al. 190).

Oprah Winfrey's weight loss "provoked a new frenzy of public interest" in liquid diets (Kirschner et al. 902), but most people were medically ineligible for programs like Optifast. Over-the-counter liquid diets such as Slim·Fast and Dynatrim quickly appeared to meet consumer demand, and now celebrities speaking for these products almost guarantee weight loss. The drinks are easy to obtain and inexpensive (less than a dollar a serving), and their packaging makes losing weight seem effortless. According to the Slim·Fast instructions, the dieter can shed one or two pounds per week with a simple regimen: "Enjoy a Slim·Fast shake for breakfast, a mid-morning snack, another shake for lunch, a mid-afternoon snack . . . , then a satisfying, well-balanced dinner." Unlike with medically supervised programs, dieters are not required to attend meetings or consult health-care professionals. Medical supervision is not required because the addition of snacks and regular meals raises the calorie intake to at least 1200 compared to Optifast's maximum 800 (Kirschner et al. 902).

Although consumers overwhelmingly support the over-the-counter liquid diets, some health-care professionals are concerned about how the products are

---

MLA

50c

Discussion of risks of liquid diets.

Paragraph integrates information from two sources to describe risks.

Transition to unsupervised programs.

The writer uses Slim·Fast packaging as a primary source. Her analysis and conclusions are her own unless otherwise acknowledged.

Citation form: no parenthetical citation needed here because the author's name (Slim·Fast) is in the text and the product packaging has no pages.

Citation form: paraphrased source not named in the text.

Transition to professionals' concerns.

Joseph 3

marketed. For instance, Dr. Harriet Cane of the National Institute of Diabetes and Digestive and Kidney Diseases warns that "people with borderline diabetes or kidney disease can unknowingly 'diet' their way to serious illness." A can of Slim·Fast shake mix does post a warning in small type:

> Slim·Fast shakes should not be used as a sole source of nutrition; eat at least one well-balanced meal daily. . . . Anyone who is pregnant, nursing, has a health problem, is under the age of 18, or wants to lose more than 15 percent of their starting body weight should consult a physician before starting this or any weight loss program.

But the advertisements for Slim·Fast make the required meal sound like an optional treat, and they do not advise users to have a physical exam. Without supervision, dieters might eat the wrong proportions of nutrients or seriously undereat, losing weight faster than is safe for anyone, not just the categories of people listed in the warning (Beek 53).

The insert in a can of Slim·Fast mentions regular exercise and other forms of behavior modification, but the can label does not, nor, again, do the advertisements. And the insert actually encourages the use of the product as a crutch: "Behavior modification is a way of learning to change habits and Slim·Fast can help you. . . . Drink a satisfying Slim·Fast shake every day for breakfast or lunch." This advice shifts the responsibility for weight loss from the dieter to the product.

Most doctors and nutritionists agree that the will and effort of the dieter--especially in changing lifelong eating habits--are essential for long-term weight

---

Citation form: author named in the text and source not paginated.

MLA
50c

Quotation over four lines is indented one inch and double-spaced.

Writer's own analysis of the Slim·Fast packaging (through the next paragraph).

Ellipsis mark indicating omission from the quotation.

loss. Dr. Thomas A. Wadden, a leading expert in
weight loss, observes that although most overweight
people are aware they must get more exercise and eat
differently, they find behavior change difficult (qtd.
in Rosenthal C11). Still, as Newsweek's Melinda Beek
observes, people who have followed a liquid diet without behavior modification "haven't done anything to
improve their eating habits--unless they plan to drink
the powder for the rest of their lives" (55).

> Introduction to a paraphrase, giving source's name and credentials. (See the note card for this paraphrase on p. 256.)

MLA
50c

Indeed, long-term results with Slim-Fast and
other liquid diets are poor. One study of dieters on the
closely monitored Optifast program found that only
32 percent of the patients reached their goal weights,
and only 10 percent of these maintained their new
weight after eighteen months (Segal 13). (Oprah Winfrey's well-publicized battles with her weight provide
anecdotal evidence of the diet's weakness.) Dieters using over-the-counter products have even less success
at losing pounds and keeping them off (Kirschner
et al. 903; Segal 14).

> Paragraph integrates evidence from several sources.
>
> Summary of supporting data.
>
> Citation form: two sources.

What is the alternative? Two nutritionists offer
some simple modifications in behavior that can help
dieters learn to manage eating:

> Question emphasizing transition to behavior modification.

> Eat only at specified times and places; learn
> to eat more slowly; omit other activities,
> such as reading or watching television,
> while eating; use smaller plates and place
> portions directly on the plate rather than
> serve family style; and use a reward sys-
> tem. (Robinson and Lawler 481)

Weight Watchers and some other group programs
combine sensible eating of real foods (as opposed to
shakes and other substitutes) with counseling in
nutrition and behavior modification. During group

> Citation form: after displayed quotation, citation follows sentence period and one space.

Joseph 5

sessions conducted by nutritionists or therapists,
dieters try to identify and correct unhealthful eating
habits. One Weight Watchers participant, Ann Lorden,
explains that the counseling "helps you realize what
triggers your desire to eat, other than hunger, so that
you can keep yourself from having food you really
don't want or need."

    Liquid diets lure consumers with promises of
quick and easy weight loss, but the formulas are not
magic potions that absorb excess weight. A liquid diet
just lets a person avoid food. Only behavior modification helps a dieter learn to eat.

Primary
source:
personal
interview.

**MLA
50c**

Conclusion:
sharp contrast
between liquid
diets and
behavior
modification.

MLA

50c

Works Cited

Beek, Melinda. "The Losing Formula." Newsweek 17
    Apr. 1990: 53-58. InfoTrac: Magazine Index Plus.
    CD-ROM. Information Access. July 1994.

Cane, Harriet. "Beware Liquid Diets." Healthtouch
    Aug. 1996. 4 Mar. 1997 <http://
    www.healthtouch.com:80/cane/wcin/
    wcin002.html>.

Kirschner, M. A., et al. "Responsible Weight Loss in
    New Jersey." New Jersey Medicine 87 (1990):
    901-04. Medline. CD-ROM. CD Plus. Jan. 1991.

Lorden, Ann. Personal interview. 22 Mar. 1992.

Pemberton, Cecelia M., et al. Mayo Clinic Diet Manual:
    A Handbook of Dietary Practices. 7th ed.
    Philadelphia: Decker, 1996.

Robinson, Corrine H., and Marilyn R. Lawler. Normal
    and Therapeutic Nutrition. New York: Macmil-
    lan, 1982.

Rosenthal, Elisabeth. "Commercial Diets Lack Proof of
    Their Long-Term Success." New York Times 24
    Nov. 1992, late ed.: A1+. New York Times
    Ondisc. CD-ROM. UMI-Proquest. Jan. 1993.

Sachs, Andrea. "Drinking Yourself Skinny." Time 22
    Dec. 1988: 48-49. 21 Feb. 1997 <http://
    www.pathfinder.com/time/1988/dom/881222/
    health.drinking.html>.

Segal, Marian. "Modified Fast: A Sometime Solution to
    a Weighty Problem." FDA Consumer Apr. 1990:
    11-15. FDA FastSearch. CD-ROM. CDmatic. Sept.
    1990.

Simko, Margaret D., et al. Practical Nutrition: A
    Quick Reference for Health Care Practitioners.
    Rockville: Aspen, 1989.

Slim·Fast Foods. Label and insert with a can of Slim·
    Fast powdered mix. New York: Slim·Fast, 1997.

Stocker-Ferguson, Sharon. "Inside America's Hottest
    Diet Programs." Prevention Jan. 1990: 53-57.

New page for
works cited.

Heading
centered.

Sources are al-
phabetized by
authors' last
names.

Second and
subsequent
lines of each
source are in-
dented one-
half inch.

Double-space
throughout.

Documenting Sources: APA Style

APA

Documenting Sources:
APA Style

❖

---

51 Documenting Sources: APA Style

The documentation style of the American Psychological Association is used in psychology and some other social sciences and is very similar to the styles in sociology, economics, and other disciplines. The following adapts the APA style from the *Publication Manual of the American Psychological Association,* 4th ed. (1994).

51a Writing APA parenthetical text citations

In the APA style, parenthetical citations in the text refer to a list of sources at the end of the text. The basic parenthetical citation contains the author's last name, the date of publication, and often the page number from which material is borrowed.

1. AUTHOR NOT NAMED IN YOUR TEXT

One critic of Milgram's experiments said that the subjects "should have been fully informed of the possible effects on them" (Baumrind, 1968, p. 34).

When you do not name the author in your text, place in parentheses the author's name, the date of the source, and the page number(s) preceded by "p." or "pp." Separate the elements with commas. Position the reference so that it is clear what material is being documented *and* so that the reference fits as smoothly as possible into your sentence structure (see pp. 277–78).

2. AUTHOR NAMED IN YOUR TEXT

Baumrind (1968) said that the subjects in Milgram's study "should have been fully informed of the possible effects on them" (p. 34).

When you use the author's name in the text, do not repeat it in the reference. Place the date after the author's name and any page reference after the borrowed material. If you cite the same source again in the paragraph, you need not repeat the reference as long as it is clear that you are using the same source.

3. A WORK WITH TWO AUTHORS

Pepinsky and DeStefano (1987) demonstrate that a teacher's language often reveals hidden biases.

One study (Pepinsky & DeStefano, 1987) demonstrates hidden biases in teachers' language.

307

When given in the text, two authors' names are connected by "and." In a parenthetical citation, they are connected by an ampersand, "&."

4. A WORK WITH THREE TO FIVE AUTHORS

Pepinsky, Dunn, Rentl, and Corson (1983) further demonstrate

the biases evident in gestures.

In the first citation of a work with three to five authors, name all the authors, as in the example above. In the second and subsequent references to the work, give only the first author's name, followed by "et al." (Latin for "and others"):

In the work of Pepinsky et al. (1983), the loaded gestures include

head shakes and eye contact.

5. A WORK WITH SIX OR MORE AUTHORS

One study (Rutter et al., 1976) attempts to explain these geograph-

ical differences in adolescent experience.

For six or more authors, even in the first citation of the work, give only the first author's name, followed by "et al."

6. A WORK WITH A CORPORATE AUTHOR

An earlier prediction was even more somber (Lorenz, Inc., 1990).

For a work with a corporate or group author, treat the name of the corporation or group as if it were an individual's name.

7. AN ANONYMOUS WORK

One article ("Right to Die," 1976) noted that a death-row inmate

may crave notoriety.

For an anonymous or unsigned work, use the first two or three words of the title in place of an author's name, excluding an initial *The, A,* or *An.* Underline book and journal titles. Place quotation marks around article titles. (In the list of references, however, do not use quotation marks for article titles. See p. 310.) Capitalize the significant words in all titles cited in the text. (But in the reference list, treat only journal titles this way. See p. 310.)

8. ONE OF TWO OR MORE WORKS BY THE SAME AUTHOR(S)

At about age seven, most children begin to use appropriate ges-

tures to reinforce their stories (Gardner, 1973a, pp. 144-145).

APA
51a

If your reference list includes two or more works published by the same author(s) *in the same year,* the works should be lettered in the reference list (see p. 312). Then your parenthetical citation should include the appropriate letter, as in "1973a" in the example.

9. TWO OR MORE WORKS BY DIFFERENT AUTHORS

Two studies (Herskowitz, 1984; Marconi & Hamblen, 1990) found that periodic safety instruction can dramatically reduce employ-ees' accidents.

List the sources in alphabetical order by the first author's name. Insert a semicolon between sources.

10. AN INDIRECT SOURCE

Supporting data appear in a study by Wong (cited in Marconi & Hamblen, 1990).

The phrase "cited in" indicates that the reference to Wong's study was found in Marconi and Hamblen. You are obliged to acknowledge that you did not consult the original source (Wong) yourself. In the list of references, give only Marconi and Hamblen.

51b   Preparing the APA reference list

In APA style, the in-text parenthetical citations refer to the list of sources at the end of the text. This list, titled "References," includes full publication information on every source cited in the paper. Here is a sample of the first page:

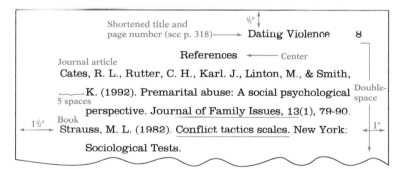

Prepare APA "References" as follows:

❖ Arrange sources alphabetically by the author's last name or, if there is no author, by the first main word of the title.
❖ Double-space all entries.
❖ Use an appropriate indention for each entry. For papers that will be published, the APA recommends indenting the first line of each entry five to seven spaces, like so:

> Rodriguez, R. (1982). A hunger of memory: The education of
>
> Richard Rodriguez. Boston: Godine.

When set into type for publication, the initial indentions are then converted into so-called hanging indentions, in which the first line is not indented while the others are. The hanging indention makes it easier for readers to spot authors' names, so the APA recognizes that students who are preparing final copy (not destined for publication) may wish to use the hanging indention for their references, like so:

APA
51b

> Rodriguez, R. (1982). A hunger of memory: The education of
>
>   Richard Rodriguez. Boston: Godine.

Because it is clearer for readers, the hanging indention is used in the sample on the previous page and throughout the following models for references, with a five-space indention for the second and subsequent lines of each entry. Ask your instructor which format he or she prefers.

❖ List all authors last-name first, separating names and parts of names with commas. Use initials for first and middle names. Use an ampersand (&) before the last author's name.
❖ In titles of books and articles, capitalize only the first word of the title, the first word of the subtitle, and proper names; all other words begin with small letters. In titles of journals, capitalize all significant words. Underline the titles of books and journals, along with any comma or period following. Do not underline or use quotation marks around the titles of articles.
❖ For sources that are not periodicals (such as books or government publications), give the city of publication. The following American cities do not require state names as well: Baltimore, Boston, Chicago, Los Angeles, New York, Philadelphia, and San Francisco. Follow their names with a colon. For all other cities, add a comma after the city name and give the two-letter postal abbreviation of the state. Then put a colon after the state.
❖ Also for nonperiodical sources, give the publisher's name after the place of publication and a colon. Use shortened names for many publishers (such as "Morrow" for William Morrow), and omit "Co.," "Inc.," and "Publishers." However, give full names

for associations, corporations, and university presses (such as "Harvard University Press"), and do not omit "Books" or "Press" from a publisher's name.

❖ Use the abbreviation "p." or "pp." before page numbers in books and in newspapers, but *not* in other periodicals. For inclusive page numbers, include all figures: "667-668."

❖ Separate the parts of the reference (author, date, title, and publication information) with a period and one space.

NOTE You may have to combine models to provide the necessary information on a source—for instance, combining "A book with two or more authors" (2) and "An online source" (19) for an online source with four authors.

1. A BOOK WITH ONE AUTHOR

Rodriguez, R. (1982). A hunger of memory: The education of

Richard Rodriguez. Boston: Godine.

The initial "R" appears instead of the author's first name, even though the author's full first name appears on the source. In the title, only the first words of title and subtitle and the proper name are capitalized.

2. A BOOK WITH TWO OR MORE AUTHORS

Nesselroade, J. R., & Baltes, P. B. (1979). Longitudinal research in

the study of behavioral development. New York: Academic

Press

An ampersand (&) separates the authors' names.

3. A BOOK WITH AN EDITOR

Dohrenwend, B. S., & Dohrenwend, B. P. (Eds.). (1974). Stressful

life events: Their nature and effects. New York: Wiley.

List the editors' names as if they were authors, but follow the last name with "(Eds.)."—or "(Ed.)." with only one editor. Note the periods inside and outside the final parenthesis.

4. A BOOK WITH A TRANSLATOR

Trajan, P. D. (1927). Psychology of animals (H. Simone, Trans.).

Washington, DC: Halperin.

The name of the translator appears in parentheses after the title, followed by a comma, "Trans.," a closing parenthesis, and a final period. Note also the absence of periods in "DC."

APA
51b

5. A BOOK WITH A CORPORATE AUTHOR

Lorenz, Inc. (1992). Research in social studies teaching. Baltimore: Arrow Books.

For a work with a corporate or group author, begin the entry with the corporate or group name. In the references list, alphabetize the work as if the first main word (excluding *The, A,* and *An*) were an author's last name.

6. AN ANONYMOUS BOOK

Merriam-Webster's collegiate dictionary (10th ed.). (1993). Springfield, MA: Merriam-Webster.

When no author is named, list the work under its title, and alphabetize it by the first main word (excluding *The, A, An*).

7. TWO OR MORE WORKS BY THE SAME AUTHOR(S)

Gardner, H. (1973a). The arts and human development. New York: Wiley.

Gardner, H. (1973b). The quest for mind: Piaget, Lévi-Strauss, and the structuralist movement. New York: Knopf.

When citing two or more works by exactly the same author(s), arrange the sources in order of their publication dates, earliest first. When citing two or more works by exactly the same author(s), published in the same year—as in the examples above—arrange them alphabetically by the first main word of the title and distinguish the sources by adding a letter to the date. Both the date *and* the letter are used in citing the source in the text (see pp. 308–09).

8. A LATER EDITION

Bollinger, D. L. (1975). Aspects of language (2nd ed.). New York: Harcourt Brace Jovanovich.

The edition number in parentheses follows the title and is followed by a period.

9. A WORK IN MORE THAN ONE VOLUME

Lincoln, A. (1953). The collected works of Abraham Lincoln (R. P. Basler, Ed.). (Vol. 5). New Brunswick, NJ: Rutgers University Press.

Lincoln, A. (1953). The collected works of Abraham Lincoln (R. P.
Basler, Ed.). (Vols. 1-8). New Brunswick, NJ: Rutgers University Press.

The first entry cites a single volume (5) in the eight-volume set. The
second cites all eight volumes. In the absence of an editor's name,
the description of volumes would follow the title directly: The collected works of Abraham Lincoln (Vol. 5).

10. AN ARTICLE OR CHAPTER IN AN EDITED BOOK

Paykel, E. S. (1974). Life stress and psychiatric disorder: Applica-
tions of the clinical approach. In B. S. Dohrenwend & B. P.
Dohrenwend (Eds.), Stressful life events: Their nature and effects (pp. 239-264). New York: Wiley.

Give the publication date of the collection (1974 above) as the publication date of the article or chapter. After the word "In," provide
the editors' names (in normal order), "(Eds.)," and a comma, the title of the collection, and the page numbers of the article in parentheses.

APA
51b

11. AN ARTICLE IN A JOURNAL WITH CONTINUOUS PAGINATION THROUGHOUT THE ANNUAL VOLUME

Emery, R. E. (1982). Marital turmoil: Interpersonal conflict and
the children of discord and divorce. Psychological Bulletin,
92, 310-330.

See page 248 for an explanation of journal pagination. Note that
you do not place the article title in quotation marks and that you
capitalize only the first words of the title and subtitle. In contrast,
you underline the journal title and capitalize all significant words.
Separate the volume number from the title with a comma and underline the number. Do not add "pp." before the page numbers.

12. AN ARTICLE IN A JOURNAL THAT PAGES ISSUES SEPARATELY

Dacey, J. (1994). Management participation in corporate buy-outs.
Management Perspectives, 7(4), 20-31.

Again, consult page 248 for an explanation of journal pagination. In
this case, place the issue number in parentheses after the volume
number without intervening space. Do *not* underline the issue number.

13. AN ARTICLE IN A MAGAZINE

Van Gelder, L. (1986, December). Countdown to motherhood:

　　When should you have a baby? Ms., 37-39, 74.

If a magazine has volume and issue numbers, give them as in models 11 and 12. Also give the full date of the issue: year, followed by a comma, month, and day (if any). Give all page numbers even when the article appears on discontinuous pages, without "pp."

14. AN ARTICLE IN A NEWSPAPER

Ramirez, A. (1993, December 14). Computer groups plan stan-

　　dards. The New York Times, p. D5.

Give month *and* date along with year of publication. Use The in the newspaper name if the paper itself does. For a newspaper (unlike a journal or magazine), precede the page number(s) with "p." or "pp."

APA
51b

15. AN UNSIGNED ARTICLE

The right to die. (1976, October 11). Time, 121, 101.

List and alphabetize the article under its title, as you would an anonymous book (model 6, p. 312).

16. A REVIEW

Dinnage, R. (1987, November 29). Against the master and his men

　　[Review of the book A mind of her own: The life of Karen

　　Horney]. The New York Times Book Review, 10-11.

If the review is not titled, use the bracketed information as the title, keeping the brackets.

17. COMPUTER SOFTWARE

Project scheduler 8000 [Computer software]. (1995). Orlando, FL:

　　Scitor.

Generally, give the title first, not underlined. Follow it with the type of source in brackets and then the date in parentheses. For publication information, give the location and name of the producer of the software.

18. A SOURCE ON CD-ROM

Ramirez, A. (1993, December 14). Computer groups plan standards.

　　The New York Times Ondisc [CD-ROM], p. D5. Available: UMI-

　　Proquest: New York Times Ondisc Item: 9340006210

Treat an article on CD-ROM as you would a print article from the same type of periodical—scholarly journal, newspaper, or magazine—but add the medium in brackets after the title, and supply the source and item or file number after "Available:" at the end of the entry.

The following model illustrates citation of an abstract on CD-ROM:

> Willard, B. L. (1992). Changes in occupational safety standards, 1970-1990 [CD-ROM]. Abstract from: Proquest File: Dissertation Abstracts Item: 7770763

19. AN ONLINE SOURCE

The online models given here are adapted from both the APA *Publication Manual* and *Electronic Style: A Guide to Citing Electronic Information*, by Xia Li and Nancy B. Crane (1993), which adapts APA style to a range of electronic sources and which the *Publication Manual* itself relies on.

NOTE For an online source that is not retrievable by others, the APA requires omitting the source from your list of references and citing it only in your text in parentheses: if the author is not already named, (G. M. Shay, personal communication, June 6, 1996); if the author is already named, (personal communication, June 6, 1996). Such nonretrievable sources generally include personal electronic mail and postings on electronic bulletin boards and discussion groups. However, some discussion groups archive their postings so that they are retrievable (see p. 247), and you may cite an archived posting in your reference list, as shown on page 316.

The following models illustrate several common online sources. In general, give author and title as you would for a printed source. Between these elements, provide the date of posting given by the source or, if no date is given, provide the date of your access to the source. For an online journal article, add the length (if given) after the article title (see the Palfrey entry below). After the title of the full source, provide the medium in brackets. At the end of the entry after "Available:" provide the electronic address and any other information (such as directory or file name) needed to retrieve the source. Do not add any period that is not part of an electronic address, even at the end of the entry.

An article in an online periodical:

> Palfrey, A. (1996, January). Choice of mates in identical twins [12 paragraphs]. Modern Psychology [Online serial], 4(1). Available: http://www.liasu.edu/modpsy/palfrey4(1).htm

Ramirez, A. (1993, December 14). Computer groups plan standards. The New York Times Online [Online], p. D5. Available: Nexis File: NYT

A source on the World Wide Web:

Leppik, P. (1996, January 21). The two rules of Internet security [Online]. Available: http://www.thinck.com/insec.html

An FTP (File Transfer Protocol) site:

Clarke. K. (1996, January). A "near" contract experience. E-Law-- Murdoch Electronic Journal of Law [Online serial], 3. Available: ftp://infolib.murdoch.edu.au/pub/subj/law/jnl/elaw/ comment/clarke.txt

A Gopher site:

Goetsch, S. (1995). And what about costume? Didaskalia: Ancient Theater Today [Online serial], 2(2). Available: gopher:// University of Warwick/Didaskalia/Didaskalia: Ancient Theater Today/03Features/Goetsch

A Telnet site:

Johnson, E. (1996, August 11). My house: Come on in. Houses of Cyberspace [Online]. Available: telnet://edwin.ohms.bookso .com 7777 @go #50827, press 10

An archived discussion group:

Campion, D. (1997, January 23). Cincinnati halfway houses. Corrections Alternatives Discussion List [Online]. Available e-mail: coralts@wau.edu

Cite e-mail, discussion-group messages, and other personal communications only in your text unless they are retrievable by others (see p. 315). The Listserv cited above is archived and so may be cited in the list of references.

A synchronous communication (IRC, MUD, MOO):

Chartreuse_Guest. (1996, February 13). Tuesday cafe session [Online]. Available: telnet://logos.daedalus.com:70/11/Alliance for Computers and Writing/NETORIC/Tuesday Cafe log 13Feb.

20. AN ABSTRACT OF AN ARTICLE OR DISSERTATION

Emery, R. E. (1982). Marital turmoil: Interpersonal conflict and

the children of discord and divorce. Psychological Bulletin,

92, 310-330. (From Psychological Abstracts, 69, Item 1320)

When you cite the abstract of an article, rather than the article itself, give full publication information for the article, followed, in parentheses, by the information for the collection of abstracts, including title, volume number, and either page number or other reference number ("Item 1320" above).

For an abstract of an unpublished doctoral dissertation, give the university and the year of the dissertation in parentheses after the title. Then give the source of the abstract, the volume number, and the page number.

Steciw, S. K. (1986). Alterations to the Pessac project of Le Cor-

busier (Doctoral dissertation, University of Cambridge, Cam

bridge, England, 1986). Dissertation Abstracts International,

46, 565C.

21. A REPORT

Gerald, K. (1958). Medico-moral problems in obstetric care (Report

No. NP-71). St. Louis, MO: Catholic Hospital Association.

Treat the report like a book, but provide any report number in parentheses immediately after the title, with no punctuation between them.

For a report from the Educational Resources Information Center (ERIC), provide the ERIC document number in parentheses at the end of the entry:

Jolson, M. K. (1981). Music education for preschoolers (Report No.

TC-622). New York: Teachers College, Columbia University.

(ERIC Document Reproduction Service No. ED 264 488)

22. A GOVERNMENT PUBLICATION

U.S. Commission on Civil Rights. (1983). Greater Baltimore com-

mitment. Washington, DC: Author.

If no individual is listed as author, list the publication under the name of the sponsoring agency. When the agency is both the author and the publisher, use "Author" in place of the publisher's name.

APA
51b

23. AN INTERVIEW

Brisick, W. C. (1988, July 1). [Interview with Ishmael Reed]. Publishers Weekly, 41-42.

List a published interview under the interviewer's name. Provide the publication information appropriate for the kind of source the interview appears in (here, a magazine). Immediately after the date, in brackets, specify that the piece is an interview and, if necessary, provide other identifying information. If the interview has its own title, insert it after the date, as with a review (model 16).

Note that interviews you conduct yourself are not included in the list of references. Instead, use an in-text parenthetical citation: if the subject is already named, (personal communication, July 7, 1996); if not, (L. Kogod, personal communication, July 7, 1996).

24. A VIDEOTAPE, RECORDING, OR OTHER AUDIOVISUAL SOURCE

Spielberg, S. (Director). (1993). Schindler's list [Videotape]. Los Angeles: Viacom.

Siberry, J. (1995). Caravan. On Maria [CD]. Burbank, CA: Reprise.

For audiovisual sources such as films, videotapes, television or radio programs, or recordings, begin with the name of the person whose work you are citing, followed by his or her function, if appropriate, in parentheses. Immediately after the title, give the medium in brackets. Then give the location and name of the distributor.

51c   Formatting a paper in APA style

The APA *Publication Manual* distinguishes between documents intended for publication (which will be set in type) and those submitted by students (which are final copy). The format illustrated on the facing page is appropriate for most undergraduate papers. Note these features:

- Use a 1½-inch margin on the left and 1-inch margins on the other sides. (The wider left margin allows for a binder.)
- Number pages consecutively, starting with the title page. Identify each page (including the title page) with a shortened version of the title as well as a page number, as illustrated opposite.
- Put the abstract (if there is one) on a page by itself immediately after the title page, with the centered heading "Abstract."
- Run into your text all quotations of fewer than forty words, and enclose them in quotation marks. For quotations of more than

TITLE PAGE

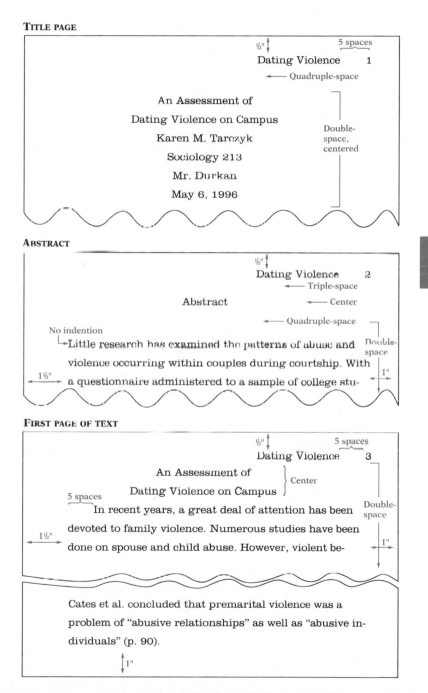

½" ↕   5 spaces

Dating Violence   1

← Quadruple-space

An Assessment of

Dating Violence on Campus

Karen M. Tarczyk

Sociology 213

Mr. Durkan

May 6, 1996

Double-space, centered

ABSTRACT

APA
51c

½" ↕

Dating Violence   2

← Triple-space

Abstract   ← Center

← Quadruple-space

No indention

↳Little research has examined the patterns of abuse and

violence occurring within couples during courtship. With

1½" →   a questionnaire administered to a sample of college stu-

Double-space

1"

FIRST PAGE OF TEXT

½" ↕   5 spaces

Dating Violence   3

An Assessment of

Dating Violence on Campus

Center

5 spaces

In recent years, a great deal of attention has been

1½" →   devoted to family violence. Numerous studies have been

done on spouse and child abuse. However, violent be-

Double-space

1"

Cates et al. concluded that premarital violence was a

problem of "abusive relationships" as well as "abusive in-

dividuals" (p. 90).

↕ 1"

forty words, set them off from your text by indenting all lines five spaces, double-spacing above and below. For student papers, the APA allows single-spacing of displayed quotations, like so:

Echoing the opinions of other Europeans at the time, Freud had a poor view of Americans:

> The Americans are really too bad. . . . Competition is much more pungent with them, not succeeding means civil death to every one, and they have no private resources apart from their profession, no hobby, games, love or other interests of a cultured person. And success means money. (1961, p. 86)

Do not use quotation marks around a quotation displayed in this way.

❖ Do not label the introduction with a heading. For other main sections of your paper, such as "Method" and "Results," type headings as follows:

First-Level Heading

Second-Level Heading

   Third-level heading. Run this heading into the text paragraph.

See page 322 for further examples of first-level and second-level headings.

❖ Present data in tables and figures (graphs or charts), as appropriate. (See the sample on p. 324 for a clear format to follow.) Begin each table or figure on a separate page. Number each kind of illustration consecutively and separately from the other (Table 1, Table 2, etc., and Figure 1, Figure 2, etc.). Refer to all tables and figures in your text—for instance, "(See Figure 3.)." Generally, place tables or figures immediately after the text references to them. (See pp. 210–12 for more on illustrations.)

❖ Type the reference list as illustrated on page 309 and again with the sample paper on page 325.

51d   Examining a sample research paper in APA style

The following excerpts from a sociology paper illustrate elements of a research paper using the APA style of documentation and format.

[New page.]

Dating Violence   1

Running head: shortened title and page number.

An Assessment of

Dating Violence on Campus

Karen M. Tarczyk

Sociology 213

Mr. Durkan

May 6, 1996

Title page.

[New page.]

Dating Violence   2

Abstract

Little research has examined the patterns of abuse and violence occurring within couples during courtship. A questionnaire administered to a sample of college students investigated the extent and nature of such abuse and violence. Results, interpretations, and implications for further research are discussed.

Abstract: summary of subject, research method, conclusions.

[New page.]

Dating Violence   3

An Assessment of

Dating Violence on Campus

In recent years, a great deal of attention has been devoted to family violence. Numerous studies have been done on spouse and child abuse. However, violent behavior occurs in dating relationships as well. The problem of dating violence has been relatively ignored by sociological research. It should be examined further since the premarital relationship is one context in which individuals learn and adopt behaviors that surface in marriage.

The sociologist James Makepeace (1979) con-

Double-space throughout.

Title repeated on first text page.

Introduction: presentation of the problem researched by the writer.

APA

51d

tends that courtship violence is a "potential mediating
link" between violence in one's family of orientation
and violence in one's later family of procreation (p.
103). His provocative study examining dating behaviors at Bemidji State University in Minnesota caused a
controversy. Makepeace reported that one-fifth of the
respondents had had at least one encounter with dating violence. He concluded by extending these percentages to students nationwide, suggesting the existence
of a major hidden social problem.

More recent research supports Makepeace's.
Cates, Rutter, Karl, Linton, and Smith (1992) found
that 22.3% of respondents at Oregon State University
had been either the victim or the perpetrator of premarital violence. In addition, in over half of the cases,
the abuse was reciprocal. Cates et al. concluded that
premarital violence was a problem of "abusive relationships" as well as "abusive individuals" (p. 90).
Another study (Cortes, 1996) found that so-called
date rape, while much more publicized and discussed,
was reported by many fewer woman respondents (2%)
than was other violence during courtship (21%) (pars.
6-8).

[The introduction continues.]

All these studies indicate a problem that is being
neglected. The present study's objective was to gather
information on the extent and nature of premarital violence and to discuss some possible interpretations.

Method

Sample

I conducted a survey of 200 students (134 females, 66 males) at a large state university in the
northeastern United States. The sample consisted of
students enrolled in an introductory sociology course.

APA
51d

[The explanation of method continues.]

The Questionnaire

A questionnaire exploring the personal dynamics of relationships was distributed during regularly scheduled class. Questions were answered anonymously in a 30-minute period. The survey consisted of three sections.

[The explanation of method continues.]

Section 3 required participants to provide information about their current dating relationships. Levels of stress and frustration, communication between partners, and patterns of decision making were examined. These variables were expected to influence the amount of violence in a relationship. The next part of the survey was adopted from Murray Strauss's Conflict Tactics Scales (1982). These scales contain 19 items designed to measure conflict and the means of conflict resolution, including reasoning, verbal aggression, and actual violence. The final page of the questionnaire contained general questions on the couple's use of alcohol, sexual activity, and overall satisfaction with the relationship.

APA
51d

Results

The incidence of verbal aggression and threatened and actual dating violence was examined. A high number of students, 50% (62 of 123 subjects), reported that they had been the victim of verbal abuse, either being insulted or sworn at. In addition, almost 14% (17 of 123) of respondents admitted being threatened with some type of violence, and more than 14% (18 of 123) reported being pushed, grabbed, or shoved. (See Table 1.)

"Results" section: summary and presentation of data.

[The explanation of results continues.]

Dating Violence   6

[Table on a page by itself.]

Table 1

Incidence of Courtship Violence

Table presents data in clear format.

Type of violence	Number of students reporting	Percentage of sample
Insulted or swore	62	50.4
Threatened to hit or throw something	17	13.8
Threw something	8	6.5
Pushed, grabbed, or shoved	18	14.6
Slapped	8	6.5
Kicked, bit, or hit with fist	7	5.7
Hit or tried to hit with something	2	1.6
Threatened with a knife or gun	1	0.8
Used a knife or gun	1	0.8

APA
51d

Discussion

"Discussion" section: interpretation of data and presentation of conclusions.

Violence within premarital relationships has been relatively ignored. The results of the present study indicate that abuse and force do occur in dating relationships. Although the percentages are small, so was the sample. Extending them to the entire campus population of 5,000 would mean significant numbers. For example, if the nearly 6% incidence of being kicked, bitten, or hit with a fist is typical, then 300 students might have experienced this type of violence. [The discussion continues.]

If the courtship period is characterized by abuse and violence, what accounts for it? The other sections of the survey examined some variables that appear to

Dating Violence   7

influence the relationship. Level of stress and frustration, both within the relationship and in the respon-
dent's life, was one such variable. The communication
level between partners, both the frequency of discussion and the frequency of agreement, was another.
[The discussion continues.]

The method of analyzing the data in this study,
utilizing frequency distributions, provided a clear
overview. However, more tests of significance and
correlation and a closer look at the social and individual variables affecting the relationship are war-
ranted. The courtship period may set the stage for
patterns of married life. It merits more attention.
[New page.]

APA
51d

Dating Violence   8

References

New page for
reference list.

Heading
centered.

Cates, R. L., Rutter, C. H., Karl, J., Linton, M., &
Smith, K. (1992). Premarital abuse: A social psychological perspective. Journal of Family Issues,
13(1), 79-90.

Sources are
alphabetized by
authors' last
names or first
words of titles.

Cortes, L. (1996). Beyond date rape: Violence during
courtship [20 paragraphs]. Electronic Journal of
Intimate Violence [Online serial], 5(2). Available:
www://acast.nova.edu/health/psy/file-disc/
file50.html

Double-space
throughout.

Second and
subsequent lines
of each source
are indented five
spaces (see p.
310).

Glaser, R., & Rutter, C. H. (Eds.). (1994). Familial violence [Special issue]. Family Relations, 43.

Makepeace, J. M. (1979). Courtship violence among
college students. Family Relations, 28, 97-103.

Socko performance on campus. (1981, June 7). Time,
126, 66-67. Magazine Database [Online]. Available: Dialog Item 81-24327

Strauss, M. L. (1982). Conflict tactics scales. New
York: Sociological Tests.

Documenting Sources: Chicago and CBE Styles

❖

Chicago
and CBE

Documenting Sources: Chicago and CBE Styles

❖

52 Chicago Documentation

History, art history, philosophy, and some other humanities use endnotes or footnotes to document sources, following one style recommended by the *Chicago Manual of Style*, 14th ed. (1993), and the student guide adapted from it, Kate L. Turabian's *A Manual for Writers of Term Papers, Theses, and Dissertations*, 6th ed., revised by John Grossman and Alice Bennett (1996). The Chicago note style is described below.

52a Distinguishing Chicago notes and works-cited entries

In the Chicago note style, raised numerals in the text refer to footnotes (bottoms of pages) or endnotes (end of paper) that contain complete source information. A separate list of works cited is optional: ask your instructor for his or her preference.

Single-space both footnotes and endnotes. Separate footnotes from the text with a short line:

In 1901, Madras, Bengal, and Punjab were a few of the huge Indian provinces governed by the British viceroy.[6] British rule, observes Stuart Cary Welch, "seemed as permanent as Mount Everest."[7]

——————— Line
5 spaces
    6. Martin Gilbert, Atlas of British History (New York: Dorset Press, 1968), 96.   ⎤ Single-space

                                                    — — Double-space
    7. Stuart Cary Welch, India: Art and Culture (New York: Metropolitan Museum of Art, 1985), 421.   ⎤ Single-space

↕ 1"

With endnotes, use the format on the following page for a list of works cited, substituting the heading "NOTES" and numbered entries as for footnotes.

For the list of sources at the end of the paper, use the format on the following page. Arrange the sources alphabetically by the authors' last names.

The following examples illustrate the essentials of a note and a works-cited entry.

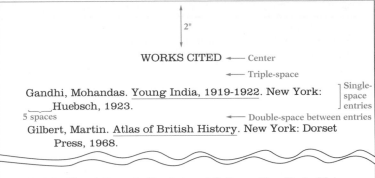

NOTE

   6. Martin Gilbert, <u>Atlas of British History</u> (New York: Dorset Press, 1968), 96.

WORKS CITED

Gilbert, Martin. <u>Atlas of British History</u>. New York: Dorset Press, 1968.

Notes and works-cited entries share certain features:

❖ Underline or italicize the titles of books and periodicals (ask your instructor for his or her preference).

❖ Enclose in quotation marks the titles of parts of books or articles in periodicals.

❖ Do not abbreviate publishers' names, but omit "Inc.," "Co.," and similar abbreviations.

❖ Do not use "p." or "pp." before page numbers.

Notes and works-cited entries also differ in important ways:

NOTE	**WORKS-CITED ENTRY**
Start with a number (typed on the line and followed by a period) that corresponds to the note number in the text.	Do not begin with a number.
Indent the first line five spaces.	Indent the second and subsequent lines five spaces.

NOTE	WORKS-CITED ENTRY
Give the author's name in normal order.	Begin with the author's last name.
Use commas between elements.	Use periods between elements.
Enclose publication information in parentheses, with no preceding punctuation.	Precede the publication information with a period, and don't use parentheses.
Include the specific page number(s) you borrowed from, omitting "p." or "pp."	Omit page numbers except for parts of books or articles in periodicals.

Many computerized word-processing programs will automatically position footnotes at the bottoms of appropriate pages. Some will automatically number notes and even renumber them if you add or delete one or more.

52b Models of Chicago notes and works-cited entries

In the following models for common sources, notes and works-cited entries appear together for easy reference. Be sure to use the numbered note form for notes and the unnumbered works-cited form for works-cited entries.

1. A BOOK WITH ONE, TWO, OR THREE AUTHORS

1. Carol Gilligan, In a Different Voice: Psychological Theory and Women's Development (Cambridge: Harvard University Press, 1982), 27.

Gilligan, Carol. In a Different Voice: Psychological Theory and Women's Development. Cambridge: Harvard University Press, 1982.

1. Bernard J. Frieden and Lynne B. Sagalyn, Downtown, Inc.: How America Rebuilds Cities (Cambridge: MIT Press, 1989), 16.

Frieden, Bernard J., and Lynne B. Sagalyn. Downtown, Inc.: How America Rebuilds Cities. Cambridge: MIT Press, 1989.

For a work with three authors, separate the authors' names with commas: Wilcox, Dennis L., Phillip H. Ault, and Warren K. Agee.

2. A BOOK WITH MORE THAN THREE AUTHORS

2. Joan Stryker and others, eds., Encyclopedia of American Life, 2d ed. (Boston: Winship, 1995), 126-28.

Stryker, Joan, William Hones, William Parker, and Sylvia Mannes, eds. Encyclopedia of American Life. 2d ed. Boston: Winship, 1995.

3. A BOOK WITH AN EDITOR

3. Hendrick Ruitenbeek, ed., Freud as We Knew Him (Detroit: Wayne State University Press, 1973), 64.

Ruitenbeek, Hendrick, ed. Freud as We Knew Him. Detroit: Wayne State University Press, 1973.

4. AN ANONYMOUS WORK

4. Merriam-Webster's Collegiate Dictionary, 10th ed. (Springfield, Mass.: Merriam-Webster, 1993).

Merriam-Webster's Collegiate Dictionary. 10th ed. Springfield, Mass.: Merriam-Webster, 1993.

5. A LATER EDITION

5. Dwight L. Bollinger, Aspects of Language, 2d ed. (New York: Harcourt Brace Jovanovich, 1975), 20.

Bollinger, Dwight L. Aspects of Language. 2d ed. New York: Harcourt Brace Jovanovich, 1975.

6. A WORK IN MORE THAN ONE VOLUME

6. Abraham Lincoln, The Collected Works of Abraham Lincoln, ed. Roy P. Basler (New Brunswick: Rutgers University Press, 1953), 5:426-28.

Lincoln, Abraham. The Collected Works of Abraham Lincoln. Ed. Roy P. Basler. Vol. 5. New Brunswick: Rutgers University Press, 1953.

7. A SELECTION FROM AN ANTHOLOGY

7. Rosetta Brooks, "Streetwise," in The New Urban Landscape, ed. Richard Martin (New York: Rizzoli, 1990), 38-39.

Brooks, Rosetta. "Streetwise." In The New Urban Landscape, ed. Richard Martin, 37-60. New York: Rizzoli, 1990.

8. AN ARTICLE IN A JOURNAL WITH CONTINUOUS PAGINATION THROUGHOUT THE ANNUAL VOLUME

8. Janet Lever, "Sex Differences in the Games Children Play," Social Problems 23 (1976): 482.

Lever, Janet. "Sex Differences in the Games Children Play." Social Problems 23 (1976): 478-87.

9. AN ARTICLE IN A JOURNAL THAT PAGES ISSUES SEPARATELY

9. June Dacey, "Management Participation in Corporate Buy-Outs," Management Perspectives 7, no. 4 (1994): 22.

Dacey, June. "Management Participation in Corporate Buy-Outs." Management Perspectives 7, no. 4 (1994): 20-31.

10. AN ARTICLE IN A POPULAR MAGAZINE

10. Mark Stevens, "Low and Behold," New Republic, 24 December 1990, 28.

Stevens, Mark. "Low and Behold." New Republic, 24 December 1990, 27-33.

11. AN ARTICLE IN A NEWSPAPER

11. Anthony Ramirez, "Computer Groups Plan Standards," New York Times, 14 December 1993, D5, late edition.

Ramirez, Anthony. "Computer Groups Plan Standards." New York Times, 14 December 1993, D5, late edition.

12. A GOVERNMENT PUBLICATION

12. House, Medicare Payment for Outpatient Physical and Occupational Therapy Services, 102d Cong., 1st sess., 1991, H. Doc. 409, 12-13.

U.S. House. Medicare Payment for Outpatient Physical and Occupational Therapy Services, 102d Cong., 1st sess., 1991. H. Doc. 409.

13. A WORK OF ART

13. John Singer Sargent, In Switzerland, watercolor, 1908, Metropolitan Museum of Art, New York.

Sargent, John Singer. In Switzerland, watercolor, 1908. Metropolitan Museum of Art, New York.

14. A SOURCE ON CD-ROM OR DISKETTE

14. Anthony Ramirez, "Computer Groups Plan Standards," New York Times, 14 December 1993, D5, late edition, New York Times Ondisc [CD-ROM], UMI-Proquest, June 1994.

Ramirez, Anthony. "Computer Groups Plan Standards." New York Times, 14 December 1993, D5, late edition. New York Times Ondisc [CD-ROM], UMI-Proquest, June 1994.

When a source is also published in print, as above, give the print information first, followed by the electronic information.

15. AN ONLINE SOURCE

15. Jane Austen, Emma [book online], ed. Ronald Blythe (Harmondsworth: Penguin, 1972), Oxford Text Archive, accessed 15 December 1995; available from ftp://ota.ox.ac.uk/pub/ota/public/english/Austen/emma.1519.

Austen, Jane. Emma [book online]. Ed. Ronald Blythe. Harmondsworth: Penguin, 1972. Oxford Text Archive. Accessed 15 December 1995. Available from ftp://ota.ox.ac.uk/pub/ota/public/english/Austen/emma.1519.

Give any print publication information first. End the entry with the date you consulted the source (after "accesssed") and the electronnic address for the source (after "available from").

15. Andrew Palfrey, "Choice of Mates in Identical Twins," Modern Psychology 4, no. 1 (1996): pars. 7-8 [journal online], accessed 25 February 1996; available from http://www.liasu.edu/modpsy/palfrey4(1).htm.

Palfrey, Andrew. "Choice of Mates in Identical Twins." Modern Psychology 4, no. 1 (1996) [journal online]. Accessed 25 February 1996. Available from http://www.liasu.edu/modpsy/palfrey4(1).htm.

16. TWO OR MORE CITATIONS OF THE SAME SOURCE

To minimize clutter and give a quick sense of how often you acknowledge a source, you may use a shortened form for subsequent citations of a source you have already cited fully.

You may use the Latin abbreviation "ibid." (meaning "in the same place") to refer to the same source cited in the preceding note:

8. Janet Lever, "Sex Differences in the Games Children Play," Social Problems 23 (1976): 482.

9. Ibid., 483.

For any source already cited in your notes, not just one cited immediately before, you may use the author's name and (if the author is responsible for more than one cited source) a shortened form of the title:

1. Carol Gilligan, In a Different Voice: Psychological Theory and Women's Development (Cambridge: Harvard University Press, 1982), 27.

2. Carol Gilligan, "Moral Development in the College Years," The Modern American College, ed. A. Chickering (San Francisco: Jossey-Bass, 1981), 286.

3. Gilligan, In a Different Voice, 47.

Omit the title if you are using only one source by the cited author.

53 CBE Documentation Style

A documentation style common in the health sciences, physics, mathematics, and other disciplines consists of in-text numbers that refer to a list of correspondingly numbered references. A version of this style, described here, appears in *Scientific Style and Format: The CBE Manual for Authors, Editors, and Publishers*, 6th ed. (1994). (CBE is the Council of Biology Editors.)

53a Using CBE numbered text citations

For CBE text citations, follow the examples and instructions below:

Two standard encyclopedias[1,2] use this term.

These forms of immunity have been extensively researched.[3]

According to one report,[4] research into some forms of viral immunity is almost nonexistent.

Hepburn and Tatin[2] do not discuss this project.

* Within the text, use a raised number or numbers to refer to numbered sources in the reference list that appears at the end of the text.
* The number for each source is based on the order in which you cite the source in the text: the first cited source is 1, the second is 2, and so on.
* When you cite a source you have already cited and numbered, use the original number again (see the last example above, which reuses the number 2 from the first example). This reuse is the key difference between the CBE numbered citations and numbered references to footnotes or endnotes (pp. 329–31). In the CBE style, each source has only one number, determined by the order in which the source is cited. With notes, in contrast, the numbering proceeds in sequence, so that sources have as many numbers as they have citations in the text.
* When you cite two or more sources at once, arrange their numbers in sequence and separate them with a comma and no space, as in the first example above.

NOTE Some versions of the numbered-citation style place citation numbers on the line of type (not raised) and between parentheses:

Two standard encyclopedias (1, 2) use this term.

CBE
53a

335

53b   Writing CBE numbered references

The list of references for the numbered-citation style begins on a new page at the end of the text. Here is part of the first page:

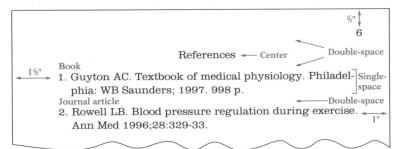

- ❖ Title the list of sources "References."
- ❖ Single-space each entry, and double-space between entries.
- ❖ Arrange the entries in numerical order—that is, in order of their citation in the text, *not* alphabetically.
- ❖ Begin each entry on a new line, and number it. Type the number on the line of type (not raised), and follow it with a period and a space. Indent subsequent lines of each entry directly under the first word of the first line.
- ❖ List authors' names with the last name first, followed by initials for first and middle names—for instance, Guyton AC in the first entry above. Do not use a comma after the last name or periods or space with initials.
- ❖ Separate authors' names with commas.
- ❖ Do not underline or use quotation marks for any titles.
- ❖ For journal titles of more than one word, use abbreviations for main words of six or more letters (without periods) and omit most prepositions, articles, and conjunctions. Capitalize each word. For example, *Annals of Medicine* becomes Ann Med (see the second entry above), and *Journal of Chemical and Biochemical Studies* becomes J Chem Biochem Stud.
- ❖ For book and article titles, capitalize only the first word and any proper nouns (see both entries above).
- ❖ For books, separate the name of the publisher from the date of publication with a semicolon and a space: WB Saunders; 1997. End the reference with the total number of pages in the book: 998 p.
- ❖ For a journal article, put the date of publication after the title of the journal, followed by the volume number and the inclusive page numbers for the article (with duplicated digits omitted):

Ann Med 1996;28:329-33. For a journal that pages each issue separately, add the month (and day, if relevant) after the year, and
add the issue number in unspaced parentheses after the volume
number: 1993 3 Mar;16(8):16–7. For all journals, use no punctuation between title and date of publication. Put an unspaced
semicolon between the date and volume number. Put an unspaced colon between the volume number (or parenthetical issue number) and the inclusive pages. (See models 6 and 7 below
for additional examples.)

1. A BOOK WITH ONE AUTHOR

1. Gould SJ. Time's arrow, time's cycle. Cambridge: Harvard Univ
   Pr; 1987. 222 p.

2. A BOOK WITH MORE THAN ONE AUTHOR

2. Hopburn PX, Tatin JM. Human physiology. 3rd ed. New York:
   Columbia Univ Pr; 1995. 1026 p.

3. A BOOK WITH AN EDITOR

3. Jonson P, editor. Anatomy yearbook. Los Angeles: Anatco;
   1997. 628 p.

4. A SELECTION FROM A BOOK

4. Krigel R, Laubenstein L, Muggia F. Kaposi's sarcoma. In: Ebbe-
   son P, Biggar RS, Melbye M, editors. AIDS: a basic guide for
   clinicians. 2nd ed. Philadelphia: WB Saunders; 1997. p 100-26.

CBE
53b

5. AN ANONYMOUS WORK

5. [Anonymous]. Health care for multiple sclerosis. New York: US
   Health Care; 1992. 86 p.

6. AN ARTICLE IN A JOURNAL WITH CONTINUOUS PAGINATION THROUGHOUT THE ANNUAL VOLUME

6. Ancino R, Carter KV, Elwin DJ. Factors contributing to viral
   immunity: a review of the research. Dev Biol 1993;40:156-9.

7. AN ARTICLE IN A JOURNAL THAT PAGES ISSUES SEPARATELY

7. Milbank Symposium. Medical decision making for the dying.
   Milbank Qtrly 1986 Feb;64(2):26-40.

8. AN ARTICLE IN A NEWSPAPER

8. Krauthammer C. Lifeboat ethics: the case of Baby Jesse. Washington Post 1986 June 13;Sect A:33 (col 1).

9. AN ARTICLE IN A MAGAZINE

9. Van Gelder L. Countdown to motherhood: when should you have a baby? Ms. 1986 Dec:37-39.

10. A GOVERNMENT PUBLICATION

10. House (US). Medicare payment for outpatient occupational therapy services. 102nd Cong., 1st Sess. House Doc nr 409; 1991.

11. AN ELECTRONIC SOURCE

11. Project scheduler 8000 [computer program]. Version 3.1. Orlando (FL): Scitor; 1995. 1 computer disk: 3½ in. Accompanied by: 1 manual. System requirements: IBM PC or fully compatible computer; DOS 5.0 or higher; 320K RAM; hard disk with a minimum of 2 MB of free space.

12. Grady GF. The here and now of hepatitis B immunization. Today's Medicine [serial online] 1993 May 2;Doc nr 2:[2620 words]. Available from: Public Access Computer Systems Forum PACS-L via the Internet. Accessed 1996 Jan 21.

13. Reich WT, ed. Encyclopedia of bioethics [CD-ROM]. New York: Free Pr; 1978.

CBE
53b

Special Types
of Writing

VII

Special Types of Writing

❖

VII Special Types of Writing

54 Writing an Argument

ARGUMENT is writing that attempts to articulate and support a position, often with the additional purpose of changing readers' minds or moving readers to action. A good argument is neither a cold exercise in logic nor an attempt to beat others into submission. It is a work of negotiation and problem solving in which both writer and reader search for the knowledge that will create common ground between them.

54a Using the elements of argument

In one simple scheme, an argument has three elements: assertions, evidence, and assumptions.

1. Assertions

ASSERTIONS are statements that require support. In an argument you state the central assertion outright as the THESIS SENTENCE, or main idea: it is what the argument is about. For instance:

The college needs a new chemistry laboratory to replace the existing outdated lab.

Assertions are usually statements of fact, opinion (a judgment based on facts), or belief. The thesis sentence of an argument should always assert an OPINION (such as the example above) because it is based on facts and is arguable on the basis of facts. (See also p. 13.) FACTS, in contrast, are not generally arguable because they are potentially verifiable—for example, *The cost of medical care is rising.* And BELIEFS, while seemingly arguable, are not based on facts and so cannot be contested on the basis of facts—for example, *The primary goal of government should be to provide equality of opportunity for all.* (Statements of fact and belief do not make thesis sentences, but they may serve as secondary assertions supporting the thesis.)

arg
54a

2. Evidence

EVIDENCE demonstrates the validity of your assertions. The evidence to support the assertion above about the need for a new chemistry lab might include the present lab's age, an inventory of facilities and equipment, and the testimony of chemistry professors.

There are several kinds of evidence:

- ❖ FACTS, statements whose truth can be verified: *Poland is slightly smaller than New Mexico.*
- ❖ STATISTICS, facts expressed as numbers: *Of those polled, 62 percent prefer a flat tax.*
- ❖ EXAMPLES, specific instances of the point being made: *Many groups, such as the elderly and the disabled, would benefit from this policy.*
- ❖ EXPERT OPINIONS, the judgments formed by authorities on the basis of their own examination of the facts: *Affirmative action is necessary to right past injustices, a point argued by Howard Glickstein, a past director of the US Commission on Civil Rights.*
- ❖ APPEALS to readers' beliefs or needs, statements that ask readers to accept an assertion in part because it states something they already accept as true without evidence: *The shabby, antiquated chemistry lab shames the school, making it seem a second-rate institution.*

Evidence must be reliable to be convincing. Ask these questions about your evidence:

- ❖ Is it accurate—trustworthy, exact, and undistorted?
- ❖ Is it relevant—authoritative, pertinent, and current?
- ❖ Is it representative—true to its context, neither under- nor overrepresenting any element of the sample it's drawn from?
- ❖ Is it adequate—plentiful and specific?

3. Assumptions

An ASSUMPTION is an opinion or belief that ties evidence to an assertion: the assumption explains why a particular piece of evidence is relevant to a particular assertion. For instance:

Assertion: The college needs a new chemistry laboratory.
Evidence (in part): The testimony of chemistry professors.
Assumption: Chemistry professors are the most capable of evaluating the present lab's quality.

Assumptions are not flaws in arguments but necessities. In writing an argument, however, you need to be aware of your own assumptions and how they influence your argument. If your readers do not share your assumptions or perceive that you are not forthright about your biases, they will be less receptive to your argument. (See the following discussion of reasonableness.)

arg
54a

54b Being reasonable

Reasonableness is essential if your argument is to establish common ground between you and your readers. Readers expect logical thinking, appropriate appeals, fairness toward the opposition, and, combining all of these, writing that is free of fallacies.

1. Logical thinking

The thesis of your argument is a conclusion you reach by reasoning about evidence. Two processes of reasoning, induction and deduction, are familiar to you even if you aren't familiar with their names.

Induction

When you're about to buy a used car, you consult friends, relatives, and consumer guides before deciding what kind of car to buy. Using INDUCTION, or INDUCTIVE REASONING, you make specific observations about cars (your evidence) and you induce, or infer, a GENERALIZATION about which car is most reliable. You might also use inductive reasoning in a term paper on print advertising:

Analyze advertisements in newspapers and magazines (evidence).
Read comments by advertisers, publishers, and critics (more evidence).
Form a conclusion about print advertising (generalization).

Reasoning inductively, you connect your evidence to your generalization (or assertion) by assuming that what is true in one set of circumstances (the ads you look at) is true in a similar set of circumstances (other ads). With induction you create new knowledge out of old.

The more evidence you accumulate, the more probable it is that your generalization is true. Note, however, that absolute certainty is not possible. At some point you must *assume* that your evidence justifies your generalization, for yourself and your readers. Most errors in inductive reasoning involve oversimplifying either the evidence or the generalization. See pages 345–47 on fallacies.

arg
54b

Deduction

You use DEDUCTION, or DEDUCTIVE REASONING, when you proceed from your generalization that Model X is the most reliable used car to your own specific circumstances (you want to buy a used car) to the conclusion that you should buy a Model X car. In deduction your assumption is the generalization you believe to be true. It links the evidence (new information) to the assertion (the conclusion you draw). With deduction you apply old information to new.

Say that you want the school administration to postpone new room fees for one dormitory. You can base your argument on a deductive SYLLOGISM:

> *Premise:* The administration should not raise fees on dorm rooms in bad condition. [A generalization or belief that you assume to be true.]
> *Premise:* The rooms in Polk Hall are in bad condition. [New information: a specific case of the first premise.]
> *Conclusion:* The administration should not raise fees on the rooms in Polk Hall.

As long as the premises of a syllogism are true, the conclusion derives logically and certainly from them. Errors in constructing syllogisms lie behind many of the fallacies discussed on pages 345–47.

2. Appropriate appeals

In most arguments you will combine RATIONAL APPEALS to readers' capacities for logical reasoning with EMOTIONAL APPEALS to readers' beliefs and feelings. The following example illustrates both: the second sentence makes a rational appeal (to the logic of financial gain), and the third sentence makes an emotional appeal (to the sense of fairness and open-mindedness).

> Advertising should show more physically challenged people. The millions of disabled Americans have considerable buying power, yet so far advertisers have made no attempt to tap that power. Further, by keeping the physically challenged out of the mainstream depicted in ads, advertisers encourage widespread prejudice against disability, prejudice that frightens and demeans those who hold it.

For an emotional appeal to be successful, it must be appropriate for the audience and the argument.

❖ It must not misjudge readers' actual feelings.
❖ It must not raise emotional issues that are irrelevant to the assertions and the evidence. (See p. 346 for a discussion of specific inappropriate appeals, such as bandwagon and ad hominem.)

A third kind of approach to readers, the ETHICAL APPEAL, is the sense you give of being a competent, fair person who is worth heeding. A rational appeal and an appropriate emotional appeal contribute to your ethical appeal, and so does your acknowledging

arg
54b

your opposition (see below). In addition, a sincere and even tone will assure readers that you are a balanced person who wants to reason with them.

A sincere and even tone need not exclude language with emotional appeal—words such as *frightens* and *demeans* at the end of the example about advertising. But avoid certain forms of expression that will mark you as unfair:

- ❖ Insulting words such as *idiotic* or *fascist*.
- ❖ Biased language such as *fags* or *broads* (see pp. 70–72).
- ❖ Sarcasm—for instance, using the sentence *What a brilliant idea* to indicate contempt for the idea and its originator.
- ❖ Exclamation points! They'll make you sound shrill!

3. Acknowledgment of the opposition

A good test of your fairness in argument is how you handle possible objections. Assuming your thesis is indeed arguable, then others can marshal their own evidence to support a different view or views. You need to find out what these other views are and what the support is for them. Then, in your argument, you need to take these views on, refute those you can, grant the validity of others, and demonstrate why, despite their validity, the opposing views are less compelling than your own. (See the sample essay on pp. 348–50 for examples.)

Before you draft your essay, list for yourself all the opposing views you can think of. You'll find them in your research, by talking to friends, and by critically thinking about your own ideas. Figure out which opposing views you can refute (do more research if necessary), and prepare to concede those views you can't refute. It's not a mark of weakness or failure to admit that the opposition has a point or two. Indeed, by showing yourself to be honest and fair, you strengthen your ethical appeal and thus your entire argument.

arg
54b

4. Fallacies

FALLACIES—errors in argument—either evade the issue of the argument or treat the argument as if it were much simpler than it is.

Evasions

An effective argument squarely faces the central issue or question it addresses. An ineffective argument may dodge the issue in one of the following ways:

- ❖ BEGGING THE QUESTION: treating an opinion that is open to question as if it were already proved or disproved.

The college library's expenses should be reduced by cutting subscriptions to useless periodicals. [Begged questions: Are some of the library's periodicals useless? Useless to whom?]

❖ NON SEQUITUR (Latin: "It does not follow"): linking two or more ideas that in fact have no logical connection.

If high school English were easier, fewer students would have trouble with the college English requirement. [Presumably, if high school English were easier, students would have *more* trouble.]

❖ APPEAL TO READERS' FEAR OR PITY: substituting emotions for reasoning.

She should not have to pay taxes because she is an aged widow with no friends or relatives. [Appeals to people's pity. Should age and loneliness, rather than income, determine a person's tax obligation?]

❖ BANDWAGON: inviting readers to accept an assertion because everyone else does.

As everyone knows, marijuana use leads to heroin addiction. [What is the evidence?]

❖ AD HOMINEM (Latin: "to the man"): attacking the qualities of the people holding an opposing view rather than the substance of the view itself.

One of the scientists has been treated for emotional problems, so his pessimism about nuclear waste merits no attention. [Do the scientist's previous emotional problems invalidate his current views?]

Oversimplifications

In a vain attempt to create something neatly convincing, an ineffective argument may conceal or ignore complexities in one of the following ways:

❖ HASTY GENERALIZATION: making an assertion on the basis of inadequate evidence.

People who care about the environment recycle their trash. [Many people who care about the environment may not have the option of recycling.]

❖ REDUCTIVE FALLACY: oversimplifying (reducing) the relation between causes and effects.

Poverty causes crime. [If so, then why do people who are not poor commit crimes? And why aren't all poor people criminals?]

❖ POST HOC FALLACY (from Latin, *post hoc, ergo propter hoc,* "after this, therefore because of this"): assuming that because *A* preceded *B,* then *A* must have caused *B.*

The town council erred in permitting the adult bookstore to open, for shortly afterward two women were assaulted. [It cannot be assumed without evidence that the women's assailants visited or were influenced by the bookstore.]

❖ EITHER/OR FALLACY: assuming that a complicated question has only two answers, one good and one bad, both good, or both bad.

Either we permit mandatory drug testing in the workplace or productivity will continue to decline. [Productivity is not necessarily dependent on drug testing.]

54c   Organizing an argument

One trusty scheme for organizing an argument appears below. (It is illustrated in the sample essay beginning on the next page.) You can modify this scheme to suit your subject, purpose, and audience.

❖ *Introduction:* Statement of the significance of the argument; background on the issue; statement of thesis. (See pp. 51–53 on introductions, pp. 13–15 on the thesis sentence.) The introduction may be one or more paragraphs, depending on the complexity of the issue, readers' knowledge of it, and the length of the whole paper.

❖ *Support for the thesis:* Assertions relating to the thesis, each developed in one or more paragraphs with the evidence for the assertion. If the argument consists of a string of supporting assertions, they are usually best arranged in order of increasing importance or persuasiveness. Sometimes the body of the argument will break into distinct sections, such as description of a problem, proposal for solving the problem, and advantages of the proposal. However arranged, the body is the meat of the argument and will run as long as needed.

❖ *Answering the opposition:* Refutation of opposing views, with evidence; concession to views more valid than your own; demonstration of your argument's greater strength. This material may come elsewhere in the argument, after the introduction or throughout the body. The choice depends mainly on whether you think readers need the opposition to be dealt with right away or can wait.

❖ *Conclusion:* Restatement of the thesis; summary of the argument; last appeal to readers. (See pp. 53–54 on conclusions.) The conclusion may be one or more paragraphs, depending on the complexity and the length of your argument.

arg
54c

54d Examining a sample argument

The following student essay illustrates the principles discussed in this chapter. As you read the essay, note especially the structure, the relation of assertions and supporting evidence, and signs of the writer's reasonableness.

Share the Ride

Every year we encounter more bad news about the environment, and a good portion of it is due to the private automobile. Respected scientists warn that carbon dioxide emissions, such as those from cars, may produce disastrous global warming. Soot, sulfur, and other automobile emissions are contributing to reduced air quality almost everywhere. The oil that powers cars comes from rapidly depleting reserves, leading to an unhappy choice between imports of foreign oil and exploration, such as off-shore drilling, that threatens the environment.

Introduction: identification of problem

In its own way Beverly Community College contributes to the problem. Campus parking lots are filled with about 1,800 cars every weekday, so that means 3,600 trips a day are made to and from campus. If just a third of the solo drivers shared rides with one another, the total trips to and from campus would be reduced by at least 600. It is time for the BCC community to make a difficult move toward an organized car-pooling system that would achieve this modest goal.

Thesis sentence: proposal for a solution

The first step in getting car-pools going is to form a task force of administrators, faculty, and students to devise a workable system. School records would be used to connect people who live near each other and would be willing to car-pool. With administration backing, the task force would initiate a school-wide campaign of meetings, rallies, posters, and other public-relations efforts to overcome resistance to car-pooling, answer questions, and win converts. The administration would assign staff to help with records and to keep the system current each term, since schedules and the student population change. As soon as administrators thought it was feasible, they could give a big boost to the system by creating monetary incentives to car-pool. Students who participate in car-pooling could receive a tuition rebate—say, $100 a term for full-time students. Faculty and staff could receive

Explanation of the proposal

equivalent bonuses. In addition, parking fees could be instituted to discourage driving to school.

The most obvious advantage of this proposal is that it would reduce car trips and thus air pollution and needless use of oil. Burning a single gallon of gasoline produces 20 pounds of carbon dioxide. If the average length of a trip to or from BCC is 10 miles (a conservative number) and the average car gets 30 miles to the gallon (a generous number), then it takes only 3 trips to burn a gallon of gasoline. Saving just 600 trips a day would keep 4,000 pounds of carbon dioxide out of the air. It would also keep 200 gallons of gasoline in the pumps.

That unused gasoline would also save money for participants. If a full-time student drove half as often as now, the gasoline savings would be about $30 a term, plus the savings in wear and tear on the car. If the school instituted a $100 tuition rebate, the cash savings would rise to $130 a term. If the school instituted a parking fee of, say, $1 a day, the cash savings would rise to more than $160 a term. (All figures assume that car-pools consist of two people who share driving and expenses equally.)

There are more abstract advantages, too. Individual freedom is a cherished right in our society, but it has no meaning outside the community. Like recycling and other environmental efforts, car-pooling would ask the individual to make a sacrifice on behalf of the community. Car-poolers would be actively participating in something larger than themselves, instead of just furthering their own self-interest.

Members of the BCC administration may point out that the proposed program asks for sacrifice from the school as well. They may object that rebates or bonuses and the costs of running the program are not feasible given the school's tight budget. True, $100 rebates or bonuses for an estimated 600 participants would cost $60,000 a term, and administrative time would also cost something. But considerable money could be raised by instituting a dollar parking fee, which could produce as much as $1,500 a day, nearly $100,000 a term, in revenue. Furthermore, sponsoring a car-pooling system is no more than many corporations do that encourage their employees to take public transportation by contributing to their monthly passes. Businesses, schools, and other institutions that require their people to assemble in one place should help reduce the environmental cost of commuting.

Support for the proposal: first advantage

Support for the proposal: second advantage

Support for the proposal: third advantage

Probable objection and response

arg

54d

Of course, it is the cost of commuters' convenience that will probably make or break the program. Students and faculty may have to arrive at school earlier than they want or leave later because of their car-pools. While considerable, this inconvenience could over time be turned to an advantage if car-poolers learned to use their extra on-campus time wisely to prepare for classes (work they would have to do at home anyway). In addition, this inconvenience might seem worthwhile in exchange for helping the environment and the concrete rewards of a rebate or bonus and savings on parking.

Probable objection and response

It is no small flaw in the proposal that not all commuters would be able to participate in the program, even if they wanted to. The fact is that many part-time faculty and students have schedules that are too complicated or erratic to permit car-pooling. Many teachers and students must make intermediate stops between their homes and BCC, such as for work. These commuters would not have access to the rebates or bonuses and still would be subject to the parking fee.

Probable objection

This unfairness is regrettable but, for now, unavoidable; we have to start somewhere. A change away from single-passenger cars to car-pools is like all other significant changes we must make on behalf of the environment. The shift in consciousness and responsibility will be halting and prolonged, and the costs and benefits will not always be distributed equally. One thing we can be sure of, however, is that the shift will not occur at all if we don't take the difficult first steps.

Response to probable objection and conclusion

—LEE MORRISON (student)

55 Reading and Writing About Literature

By Sylvan Barnet

Writers of literature—stories, novels, poems, and plays—are concerned with presenting human experience concretely, with *showing* rather than *telling*, with giving a sense of the feel of life. Reading and writing about literature thus require extremely close attention to the feel of the words. For instance, the word *woods* in Robert Frost's "Stopping by Woods on a Snowy Evening" has a rural, folksy quality that *forest* doesn't have, and many such small distinctions contribute to the poem's effect. When you read and write about literature, you interpret distinctions like these, forming an idea of a work that you support with evidence from it.

55a Reading literature

Reading literature critically involves interacting with a text, not in order to make negative judgments but in order to understand the work and evaluate its significance or quality. Such interaction is not passive, like scanning a newspaper or watching television. Instead, it is a process of engagement, of diving into the words themselves.

You will become more engaged if you write while you read. If you own the book you're reading, don't hesitate to underline or highlight passages that especially interest you for one reason or another. Don't hesitate to annotate the margins, indicating your pleasures, displeasures, and uncertainties with remarks such as *Nice detail* or *Do we need this long description?* or *Not believable.* If you don't own the book, make these notes on separate sheets or on your computer.

An effective way to interact with a text is to keep a READING JOURNAL. A journal is not a diary in which you record your doings but a place in which you develop and store your reflections on what you read, such as an answer to a question you may have posed in the margin of the text or a response to something said in class. You may, for instance, want to reflect on why your opinion is so different from that of another student. You may even make an entry in the form of a letter to the author or from one character to another. (See pp. 7–8 for more on journal keeping.)

55b Analyzing literature

1. Meaning in literature

In analyzing literature, you face right off the question of *meaning.* Readers disagree all the time over the meanings of works of literature, partly because (as noted earlier) literature *shows* rather than *tells:* it gives concrete images of imagined human experiences, but it usually does not say how we ought to understand the images. Further, readers bring different experiences to their reading and thus understand images differently. In writing about literature,

55b

KEY TERM

ANALYSIS   Separating something (such as a literary text) into its elements and interpreting the meaning, relationships, and significance of the elements.

then, we can offer only our *interpretation* of the meaning rather than *the* meaning. Still, most people agree that there are limits to interpretation: it must be supported by evidence that a reasonable person finds at least plausible if not totally convincing.

2. Analytical approaches

One reason interpretations of meaning differ is that readers approach literary works differently, focusing on certain elements and interpreting those elements distinctively. Some of the critical approaches you may encounter in studying literature are these:

❖ HISTORICAL CRITICISM focuses on the context in which a literary work was created and how that context affected the work. The critic may examine the author's social, political, and intellectual surroundings or may concentrate on the author's own biography: his or her life experiences or psychological makeup.

❖ FEMINIST CRITICISM focuses on the male domination of the literary canon—the body of work represented in the standard anthologies, discussed in the schools, and examined in the scholarly journals. Feminist critics are especially concerned with the writings of women and with the responses of women to the depiction of both sexes in literature.

❖ READER-RESPONSE CRITICISM focuses on the reactions of an audience to a work of literature, asking why readers respond as they do to a text. In this view the meaning of the text lies not just on the page but in the interaction between the work and its reader.

❖ DECONSTRUCTIVE CRITICISM regards a work of literature skeptically, resisting the obvious meanings and focusing on the ambiguities in the work, especially the internal contradictions. Perceiving that the relationship of words and their meanings is both arbitrary and forever changing—even within the same work—deconstructive critics emphasize multiple meanings and what a text does not say.

❖ FORMALIST CRITICISM (also called NEW CRITICISM) focuses primarily on a literary work as a constructed text, as an independent unity understood in itself rather than as an artifact of a particular context or reader response. Beginning with a personal response, the formalist critic tries to account for the response by examining the form of the work (hence *formalism*) and the relations among its elements.

55b

3. Questions for a literary analysis

A formalist approach to literature has certain advantages for inexperienced critics: it engages you immediately in the work of literature itself, without requiring extensive historical or cultural background, and it introduces the conventional elements of literature that all critical approaches discuss, even though they view the elements differently. The list below poses questions for each element that can help you think constructively and imaginatively about what you read.

* PLOT: the relationships and patterns of events. (Even a poem has a plot—for instance, a change in mood from grief to resignation.)

  What actions happen?
  What conflicts occur?
  How do the events connect to each other and to the whole?

* CHARACTERS: the people the author creates (including the narrator of a story or the speaker of a poem).

  Who are the principal people in the work?
  How do they interact?
  What do their actions, words, and thoughts reveal about their personalities and the personalities of others?
  Do the characters stay the same, or do they change? Why?

* POINT OF VIEW: the perspective or attitude of the speaker in a poem or the voice who tells a story. The point of view may be FIRST PERSON (a participant, using *I*) or THIRD PERSON (an outsider, using *he, she, it, they*). A first-person narrator may be a major or a minor character in the narrative, and may be RELIABLE or UNRELIABLE (unable to report events wholly or accurately). A third-person narrator may be OMNISCIENT (knows what goes on in all characters' minds), LIMITED (knows what goes on in the mind of only one or two characters), or OBJECTIVE (knows only what is external to the characters).

  Who is the narrator (or the speaker of a poem)?
  How does the narrator's point of view affect the narrative?

* TONE: the narrator's or speaker's attitude, perceived through the words (for instance, joyful, bitter, or confident).

  What tone (or tones) do you hear? If there is a change, how do you account for it?
  Is there an ironic contrast between the narrator's tone (for instance, confidence) and what you take to be the author's attitude (for instance, pity for human overconfidence)?

* IMAGERY: word pictures or visual details involving the senses (sight, sound, touch, smell, taste).

55b

What images does the writer use? What senses do they draw on?
What patterns are evident in the images (for instance, religious
  or commercial images)?
What is the significance of the imagery?

❖ SYMBOLISM: concrete things standing for larger and more abstract ideas (for instance, the American flag may symbolize
freedom, or a dead flower may symbolize mortality).

What symbols does the author use? What do they seem to signify?
How does the symbolism relate to the theme of the work?

❖ SETTING: the place where the action happens.

What does the locale contribute to the work?
Are scene shifts significant?

❖ FORM: the shape or structure of the work.

What *is* the form? (For example, a story might divide sharply in
  the middle, moving from happiness to sorrow.)
What parts of the work does the form emphasize, and why?

❖ THEME: the central idea, a conception of human experience
suggested by the work as a whole. Theme is neither plot (what
happens) nor subject (such as youth or mourning or marriage).
Rather it is what the author says with that plot about that subject.

Can you state the theme in a sentence? For instance, you might
  state the following about Kate Chopin's "The Story of an
  Hour" (p. 356): *Happiness depends partly on freedom.*
Do certain words, passages of dialogue or description, or situa-
  tions seem to represent the theme most clearly?
How do the work's elements combine to develop the theme?

❖ APPEAL: the degree to which the work pleases you.

What do you especially like or dislike about the work? Why?
Do you think your responses are unique, or would they be common to most readers? Why?

55c

55c Examining two literary works and sample papers

The following pages reprint two works of literature (a short
story and a poem), each followed by a student paper on the work.
In each student paper the author supports his or her ideas with

quotations, paraphrases, and summaries from the work being discussed, a primary source. In the second paper (p. 359), the author also draws sparingly on secondary sources (other critics' views), which further support his own views.

Note the following features of the students' papers:

* The writers do not merely summarize the literary works they write about. Occasionally, they briefly summarize to make their meaning clear, but their essays consist mostly of their own analysis.
* Each writer uses many quotations from the literary work to provide evidence for his or her ideas and to let readers hear the voice of the work.
* Both writers integrate quotations smoothly into their own sentences (see pp. 262–65).
* The writers use the present tense of verbs (*Chopin shows; Mrs. Mallard dies*) to describe both the literature author's work and the action in the work.

For the format of a literature paper, consult several other sections of this handbook.

* Use MLA document format for treatment of headings, margins, quotations, and other elements (pp. 203–07).
* Cite sources with MLA parenthetical text citations and a list of works cited (pp. 272–97).
* Use ellipsis marks (. . .) to indicate deletions from quotations (pp. 198–99). Use brackets to indicate additions to quotations (p. 199).

KEY TERMS

QUOTATION   An exact repetition of an author's words, placed in quotation marks. (See also pp. 193, 206–07.)

PARAPHRASE   A restatement of an author's words, closely following the author's line of thought but using different words and sentence structures. (See also pp. 256–57.)

SUMMARY   A condensation of an extended passage into a sentence or more. (See also pp. 255–56.)

PRIMARY SOURCE   A firsthand account: for instance, a historical document, a work of literature, or your own observations. (See also p. 238.)

SECONDARY SOURCE   A report on or analysis of other sources, often primary ones: for instance, a historian's account of a battle or a critic's view of a poem. (See also p. 238.)

55c

1. A short story and an essay about it

Short story

Kate Chopin

The Story of an Hour

Knowing that Mrs. Mallard was afflicted with a heart trouble, great care was taken to break to her as gently as possible the news of her husband's death.

It was her sister Josephine who told her, in broken sentences, veiled hints that revealed in half concealing. Her husband's friend Richards was there, too, near her. It was he who had been in the newspaper office when intelligence of the railroad disaster was received, with Brently Mallard's name leading the list of "killed." He had only taken the time to assure himself of its truth by a second telegram, and had hastened to forestall any less careful, less tender friend in bearing the sad message.

She did not hear the story as many women have heard the same, with a paralyzed inability to accept its significance. She wept at once with sudden, wild abandonment, in her sister's arms. When the storm of grief had spent itself she went away to her room alone. She would have no one follow her.

There stood, facing the open window, a comfortable, roomy armchair. Into this she sank, pressed down by a physical exhaustion that haunted her body and seemed to reach into her soul.

She could see in the open square before her house the tops of trees that were all aquiver with the new spring life. The delicious breath of rain was in the air. In the street below a peddler was crying his wares. The notes of a distant song which some one was singing reached her faintly, and countless sparrows were twittering in the eaves.

There were patches of blue sky showing here and there through the clouds that had met and piled one above the other in the west facing her window.

She sat with her head thrown back upon the cushion of the chair quite motionless, except when a sob came up into her throat and shook her, as a child who has cried itself to sleep continues to sob in its dreams.

She was young, with a fair, calm face, whose lines bespoke repression and even a certain strength. But now there was a dull stare in her eyes, whose gaze was fixed away off yonder on one of those patches of blue sky. It was not a glance of reflection, but rather indicated a suspension of intelligent thought.

There was something coming to her and she was waiting for it, fearfully. What was it? She did not know; it was too subtle and elusive to name. But she felt it creeping out of the sky, reaching toward her through the sounds, the scents, the color that filled the air.

Now her bosom rose and fell tumultuously. She was beginning to recognize this thing that was approaching to possess her,

55c

and she was striving to beat it back with her will—as powerless as her two white slender hands would have been.

When she abandoned herself a little whispered word escaped her slightly parted lips. She said it over and over under her breath: "Free, free, free!" The vacant stare and the look of terror that had followed it went from her eyes. They stayed keen and bright. Her pulses beat fast, and the coursing blood warmed and relaxed every inch of her body.

She did not stop to ask if it were not a monstrous joy that held her. A clear and exalted perception enabled her to dismiss the suggestion as trivial.

She knew that she would weep again when she saw the kind, tender hands folded in death; the face that had never looked save with love upon her, fixed and gray and dead. But she saw beyond that bitter moment a long procession of years to come that would belong to her absolutely. And she opened and spread her arms out to them in welcome.

There would be no one to live for her during those coming years; she would live for herself. There would be no powerful will bending her in the blind persistence with which men and women believe they have a right to impose a private will upon a fellow creature. A kind intention or a cruel intention made the act seem no less a crime as she looked upon it in that brief moment of illumination.

And yet she had loved him—sometimes. Often she had not. What did it matter! What could love, the unsolved mystery, count for in face of this possession of self-assertion which she suddenly recognized as the strongest impulse of her being.

"Free! Body and soul free!" she kept whispering.

Josephine was kneeling before the closed door with her lips to the keyhole, imploring for admission. "Louise, open the door! I beg; open the door—you will make yourself ill. What are you doing, Louise? For heaven's sake open the door."

"Go away. I am not making myself ill." No; she was drinking in the very elixir of life through that open window.

Her fancy was running riot along those days ahead of her. Spring days, and summer days, and all sorts of days that would be her own. She breathed a quick prayer that life might be long. It was only yesterday she had thought with a shudder that life might be long.

She arose at length and opened the door to her sister's importunities. There was a feverish triumph in her eyes, and she carried herself unwittingly like a goddess of Victory. She clasped her sister's waist and together they descended the stairs. Richards stood waiting for them at the bottom.

Some one was opening the front door with a latchkey. It was Brently Mallard who entered, a little travel-stained, composedly carrying his grip-sack and umbrella. He had been far from the scene of accident, and did not even know there had been one. He

55c

stood amazed at Josephine's piercing cry; at Richards' motion to screen him from the view of his wife.

But Richards was too late.

When the doctors came they said she had died of heart disease—of joy that kills.

An essay on fiction (no secondary sources)

Ironies of Life in Kate Chopin's "The Story of an Hour"

Kate Chopin's "The Story of an Hour"—which takes only a few minutes to read—has an ironic ending: Mrs. Mallard dies just when she is beginning to live. On first reading, the ending seems almost too ironic for belief. On rereading the story, however, one sees that the ending is believable partly because it is consistent with other ironies in the story.

After we know how the story turns out, if we reread it we find irony at the very start. Because Mrs. Mallard's friends and her sister assume, mistakenly, that she was deeply in love with her husband, Brently Mallard, they take great care to tell her gently of his death. They mean well, and in fact they do well, bringing her an hour of life, an hour of joyous freedom, but it is ironic that they think their news is sad. True, Mrs. Mallard at first expresses grief when she hears the news, but soon (unknown to her friends) she finds joy in it. So Richards's "sad message" (12), though sad in Richards's eyes, is in fact a happy message.

Among the small but significant ironic details is the statement near the end of the story that when Mallard entered the house, Richards tried to conceal him from Mrs. Mallard, but "Richards was too late" (13). This is ironic because almost at the start of the story, in the second paragraph, Richards "hastened" (12) to bring his sad message; if he had at the start been "too late" (13), Brently Mallard would have arrived at home first, and Mrs. Mallard's life would not have ended an hour later but would simply have gone on as it had been. Yet another irony at the end of the story is the diagnosis of the doctors. They say she died of "heart disease—of joy that kills" (13). In one sense they are right: Mrs. Mallard has for the last hour experienced a great joy. But of course the doctors totally misunderstand the joy that kills her. It is not joy at seeing her husband alive, but her realization that the great joy she experienced during the last hour is over.

All of these ironic details add richness to the story, but the central irony resides not in the well-intentioned but ironic actions of Richards, or in the unconsciously ironic words of the doctors, but in Mrs. Mallard's own life. She "sometimes" (13) loved her husband, but in a way she has been dead, a body subjected to her husband's will. Now, his apparent death brings her new life. Appropriately, this new life comes to her at the season of the year when "the tops of trees . . . were all aquiver with the new spring

55c

life" (12). But, ironically, her new life will last only an hour. She is "Free, free, free" (12-13), but only until her husband walks through the doorway. She looks forward to "summer days" (13), but she will not see even the end of this spring day. If her years of marriage were ironic, bringing her a sort of living death instead of joy, her new life is ironic too, not only because it grows out of her moment of grief for her supposedly dead husband, but also because her vision of "a long procession of years" (13) is cut short within an hour on a spring day.

Work Cited

Chopin, Kate. "The Story of an Hour." <u>Literature for Composition</u>. Ed. Sylvan Barnet et al. 4th ed. New York: Harper, 1996. 12-13.

— JANET VONG (student)

2. A poem and an essay about it

Poem

Gwendolyn Brooks

The Bean Eaters

They eat beans mostly, this old yellow pair.
Dinner is a casual affair.
Plain chipware on a plain and creaking wood,
Tin flatware.

Two who are Mostly Good.   5
Two who have lived their day,
But keep on putting on their clothes
And putting things away.

And remembering . . .
Remembering, with tinklings and twinges,   10
As they lean over the beans in their rented back room that is
    full of beads and receipts and dolls and cloths, tobacco
    crumbs, vases and fringes.

An essay on poetry (with secondary sources)

55c

Marking Time Versus Enduring in
Gwendolyn Brooks's "The Bean Eaters"

Gwendolyn Brooks's poem "The Bean Eaters" runs only eleven lines. It is written in plain language about very plain people. Yet its meaning is ambiguous. One critic, George E. Kent, says the old couple who eat beans "have had their day and exist now as time-markers" (141). However, another reader, D. H. Melhem, perceives not so much time marking as "endurance" in the old couple (123). Is this poem a despairing picture of old age or a more positive portrait?

"The Bean Eaters" describes an "old yellow pair" who "eat beans mostly" (line 1) off "Plain chipware" (3) with "Tin flatware"

(4) in "their rented back room" (11). Clearly, they are poor. Their existence is accompanied not by friends or relatives—children or grandchildren are not mentioned—but by memories and a few possessions (9-11). They are "Mostly Good" (5), words Brooks capitalizes at the end of a line, perhaps to stress the old people's adherence to traditional values as well as their lack of saintliness. They are unexceptional, whatever message they have for readers.

The isolated routine of the couple's life is something Brooks draws attention to with a separate stanza:

> Two who are Mostly Good.
> Two who have lived their day,
> But keep on putting on their clothes
> And putting things away. (5-8)

Brooks emphasizes how isolated the couple is by repeating "Two who." Then she emphasizes how routine their life is by repeating "putting."

A pessimistic reading of this poem seems justified. The critic Harry B. Shaw reads the lines just quoted as perhaps despairing: "they are putting things away as if winding down an operation and readying for withdrawal from activity" (80). However, Shaw observes, the word *But* also indicates the couple's "determination to go on living, a refusal to give up and let things go" (80). This dual meaning is at the heart of Brooks's poem: the old people live a meager existence, yes, but their will, their self-control, and their connection with another person—their essential humanity—are unharmed.

The truly positive nature of the poem is revealed in the last stanza. In Brooks's words, the old couple remember with some "twinges" perhaps, but also with "tinklings" (10), a cheerful image. As Melhem says, these people are "strong in mutual affection and shared memories" (123). And the final line, which is much longer than all the rest and which catalogs the evidence of the couple's long life together, is almost musically affirmative: "As they lean over the beans in their rented back room that is full of beads and receipts and dolls and cloths, tobacco crumbs, vases and fringes" (11).

What these people have is not much, but it is something.

Works Cited

Brooks, Gwendolyn. "The Bean Eaters." Literature: An Introduction to Fiction, Poetry, and Drama. Ed. X. J. Kennedy and Dana Gioia. 6th ed. New York: Harper, 1995. 655.

Kent, George E. A Life of Gwendolyn Brooks. Lexington: UP of Kentucky, 1990.

Melhem, D. H. Gwendolyn Brooks: Poetry and the Heroic Voice. Lexington: UP of Kentucky, 1987.

Shaw, Harry B. Gwendolyn Brooks. Twayne's United States Authors Ser. 395. Boston: Twayne, 1980.

—KENNETH SCHEFF (student)

55c

56 Writing for Business

When you write for business, you are addressing busy people who want to see quickly why you are writing and how they should respond to you. Follow these general guidelines:

- State your purpose right at the start.
- Be straightforward, clear, concise, objective, and courteous.
- Observe conventions of grammar and usage, which make your writing clear and impress your reader with your care.

ESL Business writing in your native culture may differ from American business writing. For instance, writers may be expected to begin with polite questions about the addressee or with compliments for the addressee's company. When writing to American business-people, get right to the point, even if at first your opening sounds abrupt or even impolite. See the examples on pages 362 and 367.

NOTE Pages 207–15 on document design offer additional pointers on typefaces, page layout, and other elements of a business document, along with examples.

56a Writing business letters and résumés

1. Business letter format

For any business letter, use either unlined white paper measuring $8\frac{1}{2}'' \times 11''$ or what is called letterhead stationery with your address printed at the top of the sheet. Type the letter single-spaced (with double space between elements) on only one side of a sheet.

A common form for business letters is illustrated on the next page.

- The RETURN-ADDRESS HEADING gives your address (but not your name) and the date. (If you are using stationery with a printed heading, you need only give the date.) Place your heading at least an inch from the top of the page. Align the heading at the left margin.
- The INSIDE ADDRESS shows the name, title, and complete address of the person you are writing to. Place the address at least two lines below the return-address heading.
- The SALUTATION greets the addressee. Position it at the left margin, two lines below the inside address and two lines above the body of the letter. Follow it with a colon. If you are not addressing someone whose name you know, use a job title (*Dear*

361

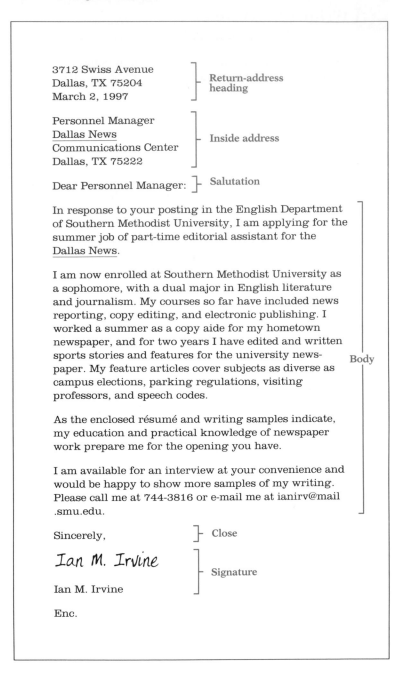

3712 Swiss Avenue
Dallas, TX 75204   Return-address heading
March 2, 1997

Personnel Manager
Dallas News   Inside address
Communications Center
Dallas, TX 75222

Dear Personnel Manager: Salutation

In response to your posting in the English Department of Southern Methodist University, I am applying for the summer job of part-time editorial assistant for the Dallas News.

I am now enrolled at Southern Methodist University as a sophomore, with a dual major in English literature and journalism. My courses so far have included news reporting, copy editing, and electronic publishing. I worked a summer as a copy aide for my hometown newspaper, and for two years I have edited and written sports stories and features for the university newspaper. My feature articles cover subjects as diverse as campus elections, parking regulations, visiting professors, and speech codes.   Body

As the enclosed résumé and writing samples indicate, my education and practical knowledge of newspaper work prepare me for the opening you have.

I am available for an interview at your convenience and would be happy to show more samples of my writing. Please call me at 744-3816 or e-mail me at ianirv@mail .smu.edu.

Sincerely,   Close

Ian M. Irvine   Signature

Ian M. Irvine

Enc.

56a

Personnel Manager) or use a general salutation (*Dear Smythe Shoes*). Use *Ms.* as the title for a woman when she has no other title, when you don't know how she prefers to be addressed, or when you know that she prefers *Ms.*

❖ The BODY of the letter, containing its substance, begins at the left margin. Instead of indenting the first line of each paragraph, insert an extra line of space between paragraphs.

❖ The letter's CLOSE begins two lines below the last line of the body and aligns at the left margin. The close should reflect the level of formality in the salutation: *Respectfully, Cordially, Yours truly,* and *Sincerely* are more formal closes; *Regards* and *Best wishes* are less formal. Capitalize only the first word, and follow the close with a comma.

❖ The SIGNATURE falls below the close and has two parts: your name typed four lines below the close, and your handwritten signature in the space between. Give your name as you sign checks and other documents.

❖ Below the signature at the left margin, you may want to include additional information such as *Enc.* (indicating an enclosure with the letter) or *cc: Margaret Zusky* (indicating that a copy is being sent to the person named).

Use an envelope that will accommodate the letter once it is folded horizontally in thirds. The envelope should show your name and address in the upper left corner and the addressee's name, title, and address in the center. For easy machine reading, the United States Postal Service recommends all capital letters and no punctuation (spaces separate the elements on a line), as in this address:

PERSONNEL MANAGER
DALLAS NEWS
COMMUNICATIONS CENTER
DALLAS TX 75222-0188

56a

2. Job-application letter

The sample on the facing page illustrates the key features of a job-application letter:

❖ The letter should be an interpretation of your résumé for a particular job, not a detailed account of the entire résumé. Instead of reciting your job history, highlight and reshape only the relevant parts.

❖ Announce at the outset what job you seek and how you heard about it.

❖ Include any special reason you have for applying, such as a specific career goal.

❖ Summarize your qualifications for this particular job, including relevant facts about education and employment history and emphasizing notable accomplishments. Mention that additional information appears in an accompanying résumé.

❖ At the end of the letter, mention that you are available for an interview at the convenience of the addressee, or specify when you will be available (for instance, when your current job or classes leave your free, or when you could travel to the employer's city).

3. Résumé

The résumé that you enclose with your letter of application can follow these guidelines:

❖ Provide the following, in table form: your name and address, career objective, education, employment history, any special skills or awards, and information about how to obtain your references. (See the sample on the facing page.)

❖ Use headings to mark the various sections of the résumé, spacing around them and within sections so that important information stands out.

❖ Limit your résumé to one page so that it can be quickly scanned. However, if your experience and education are extensive, a two-page résumé is preferable to a single cramped, unreadable page.

In preparing your résumé, you may wish to use some of the techniques of document design discussed on pages 207–15, such as variations in spacing and in type sizes and styles. One possibility for a résumé appears on page 366.

The sample résumé is only one possible type—for instance, you might want to organize your employment history by functions and skills (such as writing, editing, reporting). For more help and ideas, consult one of the many books devoted to application letters, résumés, and other elements of a job search. Two helpful guides are Richard N. Bolles, *What Color Is Your Parachute? A Practical Manual for Job-Hunters and Career Changers,* and Tom Jackson, *The Perfect Résumé.*

56b

56b Writing business memos

Business memorandums (memos, for short) address people within the same organization. A memo reports briefly and directly on a very specific topic: an answer to a question, a progress report, an evaluation.

Ian M. Irvine
3712 Swiss Avenue
Dallas, TX 75204
214-744-3816
E-mail: ianirv@mail.smu.edu

Position desired
Part-time editorial assistant.

Education
Southern Methodist University, 1995 to present.
Current standing: sophomore.
Major: English literature and journalism.
Journalism courses: news reporting, copy editing,
electronic publishing, communications arts, broadcast
journalism.

Abilene (Texas) Senior High School, 1991-1995.
Graduated with academic, college-preparatory degree.

Employment history
1995 to present. Reporter, Daily Campus, student newspaper of Southern Methodist University.
Write regular coverage of baseball, track, and soccer
teams. Write feature stories on campus policies and
events. Edit sports news, campus listings, features.

Summer 1996. Copy aide, Abilene Reporter-News.
Routed copy, ran errands, and assisted reporters with
research.

Summer 1995. Painter, Longhorn Painters, Abilene.
Prepared and painted exteriors and interiors of houses.

Special skills
Fluent in Spanish.
Proficient in Internet research and word processing.

References
Available on request:

Placement Office
Southern Methodist University
Dallas, TX 75275

56b

Ian M. Irvine   3712 Swiss Avenue
                                               Dallas, TX 75204
                                               214-744-3816
                                               ianirv@mail.smu.edu

---

**Position
desired**   Part-time editorial assistant.

Education   *Southern Methodist University,* 1995 to present.
                    Current standing: sophomore.
                    Major: English literature and journalism.
                    Journalism courses: news reporting, copy editing,
                    electronic publishing, communications arts, broad-
                    cast journalism.

                    Abilene (Texas) Senior High School, 1991-1995.
                    Graduated with academic, college-preparatory
                    degree.

**Employment   1995 to present. Reporter, *Daily Campus*, student
history**   newspaper of Southern Methodist University.
                    Write regular coverage of baseball, track, and soc-
                    cer teams. Write feature stories on campus policies
                    and events. Edit sports news, campus listings,
                    features.

                    Summer 1996. Copy aide, *Abilene Reporter-News*.
                    Routed copy, ran errands, and assisted reporters
                    with research.

                    Summer 1995. Painter, Longhorn Painters, Abilene.
                    Prepared and painted exteriors and interiors of
                    houses.

Special skills Fluent in Spanish.
                    Proficient in Internet research and word processing.

References   Available on request:

                    Placement Office
                    Southern Methodist University
                    Dallas, TX 75275

56b

Both the form and the structure of a memo are designed to get to the point and dispose of it quickly. State your reason for writing in the first sentence. Devote the first paragraph to a concise presentation of your answer, conclusion, or evaluation. In the rest of the memo explain your reasoning or evidence. Use headings or lists as appropriate to highlight key information. (See the sample below.)

Most companies have their own conventions for memo formats. The heading usually consists of the company name, the

---

Bigelow Wax Company

TO: Aileen Rosen, Director of Sales
FROM: Patricia Phillips, Territory 12 *PP*
DATE: March 17, 1997
SUBJECT: 1996 sales of Quick Wax in Territory 12

Since it was introduced in January of 1996, Quick Wax has been unsuccessful in Territory 12 and has not affected the sales of our Easy Shine. Discussions with customers and my own analysis of Quick Wax suggest three reasons for its failure to compete with our product.

1. Quick Wax has not received the promotion necessary for a new product. Advertising--primarily on radio-- has been sporadic and has not developed a clear, consistent image for the product. In addition, the Quick Wax sales representative in Territory 12 is new and inexperienced; he is not known to customers, and his sales pitch (which I once overheard) is weak. As far as I can tell, his efforts are not supported by phone calls or mailings from his home office.

2. When Quick Wax does make it to the store shelves, buyers do not choose it over our product. Though priced competitively with our product, Quick Wax is poorly packaged. The container seems smaller than ours, though in fact it holds the same eight ounces. The lettering on the Quick Wax package (red on blue) is difficult to read, in contrast to the white-on-green lettering on the Easy Shine package.

3. Our special purchase offers and my increased efforts to serve existing customers have had the intended effect of keeping customers satisfied with our product and reducing their inclination to stock something new.

Copies: L. Goldberger, Director of Marketing
            L. MacGregor, Customer Service Manager

56b

addressee's name, the writer's name (initialed in handwriting), the date, and a subject description or title. (See the sample.) The body of the memo is usually single-spaced, with double spacing between paragraphs and no paragraph indentions. An indication of who receives copies of the memo can be given two spaces below the last line of the body.

NOTE See page 214 for a sample of a business report, which is more formal in expression and format than a memo.

56c Writing faxes and electronic mail

Communicating via electronic devices, especially fax machines and computerized electronic mail (e-mail), speeds up correspondence but also creates new challenges. For both faxes and e-mail, the standards are the same as for other business correspondence: state your purpose at the outset and write straightforwardly, clearly, concisely, objectively, courteously, and correctly.

1. Faxes

For fax transmissions, follow the format of a letter (p. 361) or memo (p. 367), as appropriate. Provide a cover sheet containing the addressee's name, company, and fax number; the date, time, and subject; your own name and fax and telephone numbers (the telephone number is important in case something goes wrong with the transmission); and the total number of pages (including the cover sheet) in the fax.

Because fax transmissions can go astray, it's often wise to advise your addressee to expect a fax. Such advice is essential if the fax is confidential, because the machine is often shared. Transmission by fax can imply that the correspondence is urgent. If yours isn't, consider using the mail. (Swamping your correspondents with needless faxes can make you the boy who cried wolf when you really have an urgent message to transmit.)

56c

2. E-mail

Postings by electronic mail tend to be more offhand and informal than standard business letters on paper. E-mail can communicate very effectively with a little attention and structure:

❖ An e-mail posting announces itself in the reader's list of incoming mail, which may be extensive. Give your posting a title that accurately describes the contents, so that your reader knows what priority to assign it.

+ Compose e-mail offline. That will remove the pressure to write too quickly and give you the time to condense your message and edit it for grammar, punctuation, and spelling.
+ A posting will be more effective if it is tightly structured, with a clear forecast of its contents and a clear division into parts.
+ Because many e-mail users cannot display a posting while they are responding to it, your postings should center on one or two points. Then the reader has a better chance of responding to your whole message.
+ When you respond to someone else's posting, you can avoid re-stating it by excerpting relevant parts in your own message.
+ E-mail usually does not allow underlining, italics, or boldface, so you can't emphasize or highlight words conventionally. E-mail writers have devised some substitutes, including aster-isks before and after words to be emphasized (*I *will not* be able to attend*) or an underscore before and after a book title (*Measurements coincide with those in _Joule's Handbook_*) Don't use all-capital letters for emphasis: they yell too loudly.

Because it is sometimes anonymous as well as immediate, e-mail has been subject to abuses. Its users have developed some basic courtesies:

+ The headings in an e-mail message are usually dictated by the network, but for business correspondence you can still address your reader(s) by name and sign off with your own name.
+ Most e-mailers consider the medium more immediate than print mail and expect quick responses to their messages.
+ E-mail, like faxes, may be broadcast to many recipients at once with a few keystrokes. Avoid flooding your correspondents with irrelevant postings: target your messages only to those who can actually use them.
+ E-mail sometimes seems more free and impersonal than tele-phone conversations or print mail. But that's no justification for flaming, or attacking, correspondents. Address them re-spectfully and politely, as you would on paper.

56c

Glossary
of Usage

❖

Index

Glossary of Usage

❖

This glossary provides notes on words or phrases that often cause problems for writers. The recommendations for standard written English are based on current dictionaries and usage guides. Items labeled NONSTANDARD should be avoided in speech and especially in writing. Those labeled COLLOQUIAL and SLANG occur in speech and in some informal writing but are best avoided in the more formal writing usually expected in college and business. (Words and phrases labeled *colloquial* include those labeled by many dictionaries with the equivalent term *informal*.)

a, an Use *a* before words beginning with consonant sounds, including those spelled with an initial pronounced *h* and those spelled with vowels that are sounded as consonants: *a historian, a one-o'clock class, a university*. Use *an* before words that begin with vowel sounds, including those spelled with an initial silent *h*: *an orgy, an L, an honor*.

The article before an abbreviation depends on how the abbreviation is to be read: *She was once an AEC undersecretary* (*AEC* is to be read as three separate letters). *Many Americans opposed a SALT treaty* (*SALT* is to be read as one word, *salt*).

See also pp. 149–51 on the uses of *a/an* versus *the*.

accept, except *Accept* is a verb meaning "receive." *Except* is usually a preposition or conjunction meaning "but for" or "other than"; when it is used as a verb, it means "leave out." *I can accept all your suggestions except the last one. I'm sorry you excepted my last suggestion from your list.*

advice, advise *Advice* is a noun, and *advise* is a verb: *Take my advice; do as I advise you.*

affect, effect Usually *affect* is a verb, meaning "to influence," and *effect* is a noun, meaning "result": *The drug did not affect his driving; in fact, it seemed to have no effect at all.* But *effect* occasionally is used as a verb meaning "to bring about": *Her efforts effected a change.* And *affect* is used in psychology as a noun meaning "feeling or emotion": *One can infer much about affect from behavior.*

agree to, agree with *Agree to* means "consent to," and *agree with* means "be in accord with": *How can they agree to a treaty when they don't agree with each other about the terms?*

all ready, already   *All ready* means "completely prepared," and *already* means "by now" or "before now": *We were all ready to go to the movie, but it had already started.*

all right   *All right* is always two words. *Alright* is a common misspelling.

all together, altogether   *All together* means "in unison" or "gathered in one place." *Altogether* means "entirely." *It's not altogether true that our family never spends vacations all together.*

allusion, illusion   An *allusion* is an indirect reference, and an *illusion* is a deceptive appearance: *Paul's constant allusions to Shakespeare created the illusion that he was an intellectual.*

almost, most   *Almost* means "nearly"; *most* means "the greater number (or part) of." In formal writing, *most* should not be used as a substitute for *almost: We see each other almost* [not *most*] *every day.*

a lot   *A lot* is always two words, used informally to mean "many." *Alot* is a common misspelling.

among, between   In general, use *among* for relationships involving more than two people or for comparing one thing to a group to which it belongs. *The four of them agreed among themselves that the choice was between New York and Los Angeles.*

amount, number   Use *amount* with a singular noun that names something not countable (a noncount noun): *The amount of food varies.* Use *number* with a plural noun that names more than one of something countable (a plural count noun): *The number of calories must stay the same.*

and/or   *And/or* indicates three options: one or the other or both (*The decision is made by the mayor and/or the council*). If you mean all three options, *and/or* is appropriate. Otherwise, use *and* if you mean both, *or* if you mean either.

ante-, anti-   The prefix *ante-* means "before" (*antedate, antebellum*); *anti-* means "against" (*antiwar, antinuclear*). Before a capital letter or *i*, *anti-* takes a hyphen: *anti-Freudian, anti-isolationist.*

anxious, eager   *Anxious* means "nervous" or "worried" and is usually followed by *about*. *Eager* means "looking forward" and is usually followed by *to*. *I've been anxious about getting blisters. I'm eager* [not *anxious*] *to get new running shoes.*

anybody, any body; anyone, any one   *Anybody* and *anyone* are indefinite pronouns; *any body* is a noun modified by *any; any one* is a pronoun or adjective modified by *any. How can anybody communicate with any body of government? Can anyone help Amy? She has more work than any one person can handle.*

any more, anymore   *Any more* means "no more"; *anymore* means "now." Both are used in negative constructions. *He doesn't want any more. She doesn't live here anymore.*

anyplace   Colloquial for *anywhere.*

apt, liable, likely *Apt* and *likely* are interchangeable. Strictly speaking, though, *apt* means "having a tendency to": *Horace is apt to forget his lunch in the morning. Likely* means "probably going to": *Horace is leaving so early today that he's likely to catch the first bus.*

    Liable normally means "in danger of" and should be confined to situations with undesirable consequences: *Horace is liable to trip over that hose.* Strictly, *liable* means "responsible" or "exposed to": *The owner will be liable for Horace's injuries.*

are, is Use *are* with a plural subject (*books are*), *is* with a singular subject (*book is*).

as Substituting for *because, since,* or *while, as* may be vague or ambiguous: *As we were stopping to rest, we decided to eat lunch.* (Does *as* mean "while" or "because"?) *As* should never be used as a substitute for *whether* or *who. I'm not sure whether* [not *as*] *we can make it. That's the man who* [not *as*] *gave me directions.*

as, like In formal speech and writing, *like* should not introduce a full clause (with a subject and a verb) because it is a preposition. The preferred choice is *as* or *as if: The plan succeeded as* [not *like*] *we hoped. It seemed as if* [not *like*] *it might fail. Other plans like it have failed.*

as, than In comparisons, *as* and *than* precede a subjective-case pronoun when the pronoun is a subject: *I love you more than he* [*loves you*]. *As* and *than* precede an objective-case pronoun when the pronoun is an object: *I love you as much as* [*I love*] *him.* (See also p. 136.)

assure, ensure, insure *Assure* means "to promise": *He assured us that we would miss the traffic. Ensure* and *insure* often are used interchangeably to mean "make certain," but some reserve *insure* for matters of legal and financial protection and use *ensure* for more general meanings: *We left early to ensure that we would miss the traffic. It's expensive to insure yourself against floods.*

at The use of *at* after *where* is wordy and should be avoided: *Where are you meeting him?* is preferable to *Where are you meeting him at?*

awful, awfully Strictly speaking, *awful* means "awe-inspiring." As intensifiers meaning "very" or "extremely" (*He tried awfully hard*), *awful* and *awfully* should be avoided in formal speech or writing.

a while, awhile *Awhile* is an adverb; *a while* is an article and a noun. *I will be gone awhile* [not *a while*]. *I will be gone for a while* [not *awhile*].

bad, badly In formal speech and writing, *bad* should be used only as an adjective; the adverb is *badly. He felt bad because his tooth ached badly.* In *He felt bad,* the verb *felt* is a linking verb and the adjective *bad* describes the subject. See also p. 145.

being as, being that Colloquial for *because,* the preferable word in formal speech or writing: *Because* [not *Being as*] *the world is round, Columbus never did fall off the edge.*

beside, besides *Beside* is a preposition meaning "next to." *Besides* is a preposition meaning "except" or "in addition to" as well as an adverb meaning "in addition." *Besides, several other people besides you want to sit beside Dr. Christensen.*

better, had better   *Had better* (meaning "ought to") is a verb modified by an adverb. The verb is necessary and should not be omitted: *You had better* [not *better*] *go.*

between, among   See *among, between.*

bring, take   Use *bring* only for movement from a farther place to a nearer one and *take* for any other movement. *First take these books to the library for renewal; then take them to Mr. Daniels. Bring them back to me when he's finished.*

but, hardly, scarcely   These words are negative in their own right; using *not* with any of them produces a double negative (see p. 147). *We have but* [not *haven't got but*] *an hour before our plane leaves. I could hardly* [not *couldn't hardly*] *make out her face.*

but, however, yet   Each of these words is adequate to express contrast. Don't combine them. *He said he had finished, yet* [not *but yet*] *he continued.*

can, may   Strictly, *can* indicates capacity or ability, and *may* indicates permission: *If I may talk with you a moment, I believe I can solve your problem.*

censor, censure   To *censor* is to edit or remove from public view on moral or some other grounds; to *censure* is to give a formal scolding. *The lieutenant was censured by Major Taylor for censoring the letters her soldiers wrote home from boot camp.*

center around   *Center on* is more logical than, and preferable to, *center around.*

cite, sight, site   *Cite* is a verb usually meaning "quote," "commend," or "acknowledge": *You must cite your sources. Sight* is both a noun meaning "the ability to see" or "a view" and a verb meaning "perceive" or "observe": *What a sight you see when you sight Venus through a strong telescope. Site* is a noun meaning "place" or "location" or a verb meaning "situate": *The builder sited the house on an unlikely site.*

climatic, climactic   *Climatic* comes from *climate* and refers to the weather: *Last winter's temperatures may indicate a climatic change. Climactic* comes from *climax* and refers to a dramatic high point: *During the climactic duel between Hamlet and Laertes, Gertrude drinks poisoned wine.*

complement, compliment   To *complement* something is to add to, complete, or reinforce it: *Her yellow blouse complemented her black hair.* To *compliment* something is to make a flattering remark about it: *He complimented her on her hair. Complimentary* can also mean "free": *complimentary tickets.*

conscience, conscious   *Conscience* is a noun meaning "a sense of right and wrong"; *conscious* is an adjective meaning "aware" or "awake." *Though I was barely conscious, my conscience nagged me.*

contact Often used imprecisely as a verb instead of a more exact word such as *consult, talk with, telephone,* or *write to.*

continual, continuous *Continual* means "constantly recurring": *Most movies on television are continually interrupted by commercials. Continuous* means "unceasing": *Some cable channels present movies continuously without commercials.*

could of See *have, of.*

credible, creditable, credulous *Credible* means "believable": *It's a strange story, but it seems credible to me. Creditable* means "deserving of credit" or "worthy": *Steve gave a creditable performance. Credulous* means "gullible": *The credulous Claire believed Tim's lies.* See also *incredible, incredulous.*

criteria The plural of *criterion* (meaning "standard for judgment"): *Our criteria are strict. The most important criterion is a sense of humor.*

data The plural of *datum* (meaning "fact"). Though *data* is often used as a singular noun, most careful writers still treat it as plural: *The data fail* [not *fails*] *to support the hypothesis.*

device, devise *Device* is the noun, and *devise* is the verb: *Can you devise some device for getting his attention?*

different from, different than *Different from* is preferred: *His purpose is different from mine.* But *different than* is widely accepted when a construction using *from* would be wordy: *I'm a different person now than I used to be* is preferable to *I'm a different person now from the person I used to be.*

differ from, differ with To *differ from* is to be unlike: *The twins differ from each other only in their hairstyles.* To *differ with* is to disagree with: *I have to differ with you on that point.*

discreet, discrete *Discreet* (noun form *discretion*) means "tactful": *What's a discreet way of telling Maud to be quiet? Discrete* (noun form *discreteness*) means "separate and distinct": *Within a computer's memory are millions of discrete bits of information.*

disinterested, uninterested *Disinterested* means "impartial": *We chose Pete, as a disinterested third party, to decide who was right. Uninterested* means "bored" or "lacking interest": *Unfortunately, Pete was completely uninterested in the question.*

don't *Don't* is the contraction for *do not,* not for *does not: I don't care, you don't care,* and *he doesn't* [not *don't*] *care.*

due to the fact that Wordy for *because.*

eager, anxious See *anxious, eager.*

effect See *affect, effect.*

elicit, illicit *Elicit* is a verb meaning "bring out" or "call forth." *Illicit* is an adjective meaning "unlawful." *The crime elicited an outcry against illicit drugs.*

emigrate, immigrate   *Emigrate* means "to leave one place and move to another": *The Chus emigrated from Korea. Immigrate* means "to move into a place where one was not born": *They immigrated to the United States.*

ensure   See *assure, ensure, insure.*

enthused   Used colloquially as an adjective meaning "showing enthusiasm." The preferred adjective is *enthusiastic: The coach was enthusiastic* [not *enthused*] *about the team's victory.*

et al., etc.   Use *et al.,* the Latin abbreviation for "and other people," only in source citations for works with multiple authors: *Jones et al. Etc.,* the Latin abbreviation for "and other things," should be avoided in formal writing and should not be used to refer to people. When used, it should not substitute for precision, as in *The government provides health care, etc.*

everybody, every body; everyone, every one   *Everybody* and *everyone* are indefinite pronouns: *Everybody* [*everyone*] *knows Tom steals. Every one* is a pronoun modified by *every,* and *every body* a noun modified by *every.* Both refer to each thing or person of a specific group and are typically followed by *of: The game commissioner has stocked every body of fresh water in the state with fish, and now every one of our rivers is a potential trout stream.*

everyday, every day   *Everyday* is an adjective meaning "used daily" or "common"; *every day* is a noun modified by *every: Everyday problems tend to arise every day.*

everywheres   Nonstandard for *everywhere.*

except   See *accept, except.*

except for the fact that   Wordy for *except that.*

explicit, implicit   *Explicit* means "stated outright": *I left explicit instructions. Implicit* means "implied, unstated": *We had an implicit understanding.*

farther, further   *Farther* refers to additional distance (*How much farther is it to the beach?*), and *further* refers to additional time, amount, or other abstract matters (*I don't want to discuss this any further*).

fewer, less   *Fewer* refers to individual countable items (a plural count noun), *less* to general amounts (a noncount noun, always singular). *Skim milk has fewer calories than whole milk. We have less milk left than I thought.*

flaunt, flout   *Flaunt* means "show off": *If you have style, flaunt it. Flout* means "scorn" or "defy": *Hester Prynne flouted convention and paid the price.*

flunk   A colloquial substitute for *fail.*

fun   As an adjective, *fun* is colloquial and should be avoided in most writing: *It was a pleasurable* [not *fun*] *evening.*

further   See *farther, further.*

get This common verb is used in many slang and colloquial expressions: *get lost, that really gets me, getting on. Get* is easy to overuse: watch out for it in expressions such as *it's getting better* (substitute *improving*) and *we got done* (substitute *finished*).

good, well *Good* is an adjective, and *well* is nearly always an adverb: *Larry's a good dancer. He and Linda dance well together. Well* is properly used as an adjective only to refer to health: *You look well.* (*You look good,* in contrast, means "Your appearance is pleasing.")

good and Colloquial for "very": *I was very* [not *good and*] *tired.*

had better See *better, had better.*

had ought The *had* is unnecessary and should be omitted: *He ought* [not *had ought*] *to listen to his mother.*

hanged, hung Though both are past-tense forms of *hang, hanged* is used to refer to executions and *hung* is used for all other meanings: *Tom Dooley was hanged* [not *hung*] *from a white oak tree. I hung* [not *hanged*] *the picture you gave me.*

hardly See *but, hardly, scarcely.*

have, of Use *have,* not *of,* after helping verbs such as *could, should, would, may,* and *might: You should have* [not *should of*] *told me.*

he, she; he/she Convention has allowed the use of *he* to mean "he or she": *After the infant learns to creep, he progresses to crawling.* However, many writers today consider this usage inaccurate and unfair because it excludes females. The construction *he/she,* one substitute for *he,* is awkward and objectionable to most readers. The better choice is to use *he or she,* to make the pronoun plural, or to rephrase. For instance: *After the infant learns to creep, he or she progresses to crawling. After infants learn to creep, they progress to crawling. After learning to creep, the infant progresses to crawling.* See also pp. 72 and 139–40.

herself, himself See *myself, herself, himself, yourself.*

hisself Nonstandard for *himself.*

hopefully *Hopefully* means "with hope": *Freddy waited hopefully for a glimpse of Eliza.* The use of *hopefully* to mean "it is to be hoped," "I hope," or "let's hope" is now very common; but since many readers continue to object strongly to the usage, try to avoid it. *I hope* [not *Hopefully*] *the law will pass.*

idea, ideal An *idea* is a thought or conception. An *ideal* (noun) is a model of perfection or a goal. *Ideal* should not be used in place of *idea: The idea* [not *ideal*] *of the play is that our ideals often sustain us.*

if, whether For clarity, use *whether* rather than *if* when you are expressing an alternative: *If I laugh hard, people can't tell whether I'm crying.*

illicit See *elicit, illicit.*

illusion See *allusion, illusion.*

immigrate, emigrate See *emigrate, immigrate.*

implicit   See *explicit, implicit*.

imply, infer   Writers or speakers *imply*, meaning "suggest": *Jim's letter implies he's having a good time.* Readers or listeners *infer*, meaning "conclude": *From Jim's letter I infer he's having a good time.*

incredible, incredulous   *Incredible* means "unbelievable"; *incredulous* means "unbelieving": *When Nancy heard Dennis's incredible story, she was frankly incredulous.* See also *credible, creditable, credulous*.

individual, person, party   *Individual* should refer to a single human being in contrast to a group or should stress uniqueness: *The US Constitution places strong emphasis on the rights of the individual.* For other meanings *person* is preferable: *What person* [not *individual*] *wouldn't want the security promised in that advertisement? Party* means "group" (*Can you seat a party of four for dinner?*) and should not be used to refer to an individual except in legal documents. See also *people, persons*.

infer   See *imply, infer*.

in regards to   Nonstandard for *in regard to, as regards,* or *regarding*.

inside of, outside of   The *of* is unnecessary when *inside* and *outside* are used as prepositions: *Stay inside* [not *inside of*] *the house. The decision is outside* [not *outside of*] *my authority. Inside of* may refer colloquially to time, though in formal English *within* is preferred: *The law was passed within* [not *inside of*] *a year.*

insure   See *assure, ensure, insure*.

irregardless   Nonstandard for *regardless*.

is, are   See *are, is*.

is because   See *reason is because*.

is when, is where   These are faulty constructions in sentences that define: *Adolescence is a stage* [not *is when a person is*] *between childhood and adulthood. Socialism is a system in which* [not *is where*] *government owns the means of production.* See also pp. 165–66.

its, it's   *Its* is the pronoun *it* in the possessive case: *That plant is losing its leaves. It's* is a contraction for *it is: It's likely to die if you don't water it.* Many people confuse *it's* and *its* because possessives are most often formed with *-'s;* but the possessive *its*, like *his* and *hers*, never takes an apostrophe.

-ize, -wise   The suffix *-ize* changes a noun or adjective into a verb: *revolutionize, immunize.* The suffix *-wise* changes a noun or adjective into an adverb: *clockwise, otherwise, likewise.* Avoid the two suffixes except in established words: *I'm highly sensitive* [not *sensitized*] *to that kind of criticism. Financially* [not *Moneywise*], *it's a good time to buy real estate.*

kind of, sort of, type of   In formal speech and writing, avoid using *kind of* or *sort of* to mean "somewhat": *He was rather* [not *kind of*] *tall.*

　　　Kind, sort, and *type* are singular and take singular modifiers and verbs: *This kind of dog is easily trained.* Agreement errors often occur when these singular nouns are combined with the plural adjectives *these* and *those*: *These kinds* [not *kind*] *of dogs are easily trained. Kind, sort,* and *type* should be followed by *of* but not by *a*: *I don't know what type of* [not *type* or *type of a*] *dog that is.*

    Use *kind of, sort of,* or *type of* only when the word *kind, sort,* or *type* is important: *That was a strange* [not *strange sort of*] *statement.*

lay, lie   *Lay* means "put" or "place" and takes a direct object: *We could lay the tablecloth in the sun.* Its main forms are *lay, laid, laid. Lie* means "recline" or "be situated" and does not take an object: *I lie awake at night. The town lies east of the river.* Its main forms are *lie, lay, lain.* (See also pp. 106–07.)

leave, let   *Leave* and *let* are interchangeable only when followed by *alone: leave me alone* is the same as *let me alone.* Otherwise, *leave* means "depart" and *let* means "allow": *Jill would not let Sue leave.*

less   See *fewer, less.*

liable   See *apt, liable, likely.*

lie, lay   See *lay, lie.*

like, as   See *as, like.*

like, such as   Strictly, *such as* precedes an example that represents a larger subject, whereas *like* indicates that two subjects are comparable. *Steve has recordings of many great saxophonists such as Ben Webster and Lee Konitz. Steve wants to be a great jazz saxophonist like Ben Webster and Lee Konitz.*

likely   See *apt, liable, likely.*

literally   This word means "actually" or "just as the words say," and it should not be used to qualify or intensify expressions whose words are not to be taken at face value. The sentence *He was literally climbing the walls* describes a person behaving like an insect, not a person who is restless or anxious. For the latter meaning, *literally* should be omitted.

lose, loose   *Lose* means "mislay": *Did you lose a brown glove? Loose* means "unrestrained" or "not tight": *Ann's canary got loose. Loose* also can function as a verb meaning "let loose": *They loose the dogs as soon as they spot the bear.*

lots, lots of   Colloquial substitutes for *very many, a great many,* or *much.* Avoid *lots* and *lots of* in college or business writing.

may, can   See *can, may.*

may be, maybe   *May be* is a verb, and *maybe* is an adverb meaning "perhaps": *Tuesday may be a legal holiday. Maybe we won't have classes.*

may of   See *have, of.*

media   *Media* is the plural of *medium* and takes a plural verb: *All the news media are increasingly visual.* The singular verb is common, even in the media, but most careful writers still use the plural verb.

might of   See *have, of.*

Usage

moral, morale As a noun, *moral* means "ethical conclusion" or "lesson": *The moral of the story escapes me. Morale* means "spirit" or "state of mind": *Victory improved the team's morale.*

most, almost See *almost, most.*

must of See *have, of.*

myself, herself, himself, yourself The *-self* pronouns refer to or intensify another word or words: *Paul helped himself; Jill herself said so.* The *-self* pronouns are often used colloquially in place of personal pronouns, but that use should be avoided in formal speech and writing: *No one except me* [not *myself*] *saw the accident. Our delegates will be Susan and you* [not *yourself*].

nowheres Nonstandard for *nowhere.*

number See *amount, number.*

of, have See *have, of.*

off of *Of* is unnecessary. Use *off* or *from* rather than *off of: He jumped off* [or *from,* not *off of*] *the roof.*

OK, O.K., okay All three spellings are acceptable, but avoid this colloquial term in formal speech and writing.

on account of Wordy for *because of.*

on the other hand This transitional expression of contrast should be preceded by its mate, *on the one hand: On the one hand, we hoped for snow. On the other hand, we feared that it would harm the animals.* However, the two combined can be unwieldy, and a simple *but, however, yet,* or *in contrast* often suffices: *We hoped for snow. Yet we feared that it would harm the animals.*

outside of See *inside of, outside of.*

owing to the fact that Wordy for *because.*

party See *individual, person, party.*

people, persons In formal usage, *people* refers to a general group: *We the people of the United States. . . . Persons* refers to a collection of individuals: *Will the person or persons who saw the accident please notify. . . .* Except when emphasizing individuals, prefer *people* to *persons.* See also *individual, person, party.*

per Except in technical writing, an English equivalent is usually preferable to the Latin *per: $10 an* [not *per*] *hour; sent by* [not *per*] *parcel post; requested in* [not *per* or *as per*] *your letter.*

percent (per cent), percentage Both these terms refer to fractions of one hundred. *Percent* always follows a numeral (*40 percent of the voters*), and the word should be used instead of the symbol (%) in general writing. *Percentage* usually follows an adjective (*a high percentage*).

person See *individual, person, party.*

persons See *people, persons.*

Usage

phenomena The plural of *phenomenon* (meaning "perceivable fact" or "unusual occurrence"): *Many phenomena are not recorded. One phenomenon is attracting attention.*

plenty A colloquial substitute for *very: The reaction occurred very* [not *plenty*] *fast.*

plus *Plus* is standard as a preposition meaning "in addition to": *His income plus mine is sufficient.* But *plus* is colloquial as a conjunctive adverb: *Our organization is larger than theirs; moreover* [not *plus*], *we have more money.*

precede, proceed The verb *precede* means "come before": *My name precedes yours in the alphabet.* The verb *proceed* means "move on": *We were told to proceed to the waiting room.*

prejudice, prejudiced *Prejudice* is a noun; *prejudiced* is an adjective. Do not drop the *-d* from *prejudiced: I was fortunate that my parents were not prejudiced* [not *prejudice*].

pretty Overworked as an adverb meaning "rather" or "somewhat": *He was somewhat* [not *pretty*] *irked at the suggestion.*

previous to, prior to Wordy for *before.*

principal, principle *Principal* is an adjective meaning "foremost" or "major," a noun meaning "chief official," or, in finance, a noun meaning "capital sum." *Principle* is a noun only, meaning "rule" or "axiom." *Her principal reasons for confessing were her principles of right and wrong.*

proceed, precede See *precede, proceed.*

question of whether, question as to whether Wordy substitutes for *whether.*

raise, rise *Raise* means "lift" or "bring up" and takes a direct object: *The Kirks raise cattle.* Its main forms are *raise, raised, raised. Rise* means "get up" and does not take an object: *They must rise at dawn.* Its main forms are *rise, rose, risen.* (See also pp. 106–07.)

real, really In formal speech and writing, *real* should not be used as an adverb; *really* is the adverb and *real* an adjective. *Popular reaction to the announcement was really* [not *real*] *enthusiastic.*

reason is because Although colloquially common, this expression should be avoided in formal speech and writing. Use a *that* clause after *reason is: The reason he is absent is that* [not *is because*] *he is sick.* Or: *He is absent because he is sick.*

respectful, respective *Respectful* means "full of (or showing) respect": *Be respectful of other people. Respective* means "separate": *The French and the Germans occupied their respective trenches.*

rise, raise See *raise, rise.*

scarcely See *but, hardly, scarcely.*

sensual, sensuous   *Sensual* suggests sexuality; *sensuous* means "pleasing to the senses." *Stirred by the sensuous scent of meadow grass and flowers, Cheryl and Paul found their thoughts growing increasingly sensual.*

set, sit   *Set* means "put" or "place" and takes a direct object: *He sets the pitcher down.* Its main forms are *set, set, set. Sit* means "be seated" and does not take an object: *She sits on the sofa.* Its main forms are *sit, sat, sat.* (See also pp. 106–07.)

shall, will   *Will* is the future-tense helping verb for all persons: *I will go, you will go, they will go.* The main use of *shall* is for first-person questions requesting an opinion or consent: *Shall I order a pizza? Shall we dance? Shall* can also be used for the first person when a formal effect is desired (*I shall expect you around three*), and it is occasionally used with the second or third person to express the speaker's determination (*You shall do as I say*).

should of   See *have, of.*

sight, site, cite   See *cite, sight, site.*

since   *Since* mainly relates to time: *I've been waiting since noon.* But *since* is also often used to mean "because": *Since you ask, I'll tell you.* Revise sentences in which the word could have either meaning, such as *Since you left, my life is empty.*

sit, set   See *set, sit.*

site, cite, sight   See *cite, sight, site.*

so   Avoid using *so* alone or as a vague intensifier: *He was so late. So* needs to be followed by *that* and a clause that states a result: *He was so late that I left without him.*

somebody, some body; someone, some one   *Somebody* and *someone* are indefinite pronouns; *some body* is a noun modified by *some;* and *some one* is a pronoun or an adjective modified by *some. Somebody ought to invent a shampoo that will give hair some body. Someone told Janine she should choose some one plan and stick with it.*

someplace   Informal for *somewhere.*

sometime, sometimes, some time   *Sometime* means "at an indefinite time in the future": *Why don't you come up and see me sometime? Sometimes* means "now and then": *I still see my old friend Joe sometimes. Some time* means "a span of time": *I need some time to make the payments.*

somewheres   Nonstandard for *somewhere.*

sort of, sort of a   See *kind of, sort of, type of.*

such   Avoid using *such* as a vague intensifier: *It was such a cold winter. Such* should be followed by *that* and a clause that states a result: *It was such a cold winter that Napoleon's troops had to turn back.*

such as   See *like, such as.*

supposed to, used to   In both these expressions, the *-d* is essential: *I used to* [not *use to*] *think so. He's supposed to* [not *suppose to*] *meet us.*

sure   Colloquial when used as an adverb meaning *surely: James Madison sure was right about the need for the Bill of Rights.* If you merely want to be emphatic, use *certainly: Madison certainly was right.* If your goal is to convince a possibly reluctant reader, use *surely: Madison surely was right.*

sure and, sure to; try and, try to   *Sure to* and *try to* are the correct forms: *Be sure to* [not *sure and*] *buy milk. Try to* [not *Try and*] *find some decent tomatoes.*

take, bring   See *bring, take.*

than, as   See *as, than.*

than, then   *Than* is a conjunction used in comparisons, *then* an adverb indicating time: *Holmes knew then that Moriarty was wilier than he had thought.*

that, which   *That* always introduces restrictive clauses: *We should use the lettuce that Susan bought* (*that Susan bought* limits the lettuce to a particular lettuce). *Which* can introduce both restrictive and nonrestrictive clauses, but many writers reserve *which* only for nonrestrictive clauses: *The leftover lettuce, which is in the refrigerator, would make a good salad* (*which is in the refrigerator* simply provides more information about the lettuce we already know of). Restrictive clauses (with *that* or *which*) are not set off by commas; nonrestrictive clauses (with *which*) are. See also pp. 175–77.

that, which, who   Use *that* for animals, things, and sometimes collective or anonymous people: *The rocket that failed cost millions. Infants that walk need constant tending.* Use *which* only for animals and things: *The river, which flows south, divides two countries.* Use *who* only for people and for animals with names: *Dorothy is the girl who visits Oz. Her dog, Toto, who accompanies her, gives her courage.*

their, there, they're   *Their* is the possessive form of *they: Give them their money. There* indicates place (*I saw her standing there*) or functions as an expletive (*There is a hole behind you*). *They're* is a contraction for *they are: They're going fast.*

theirselves   Nonstandard for *themselves.*

then, than   See *than, then.*

these kind, these sort, these type, those kind   See *kind of, sort of, type of.*

thru   A colloquial spelling of *through* that should be avoided in all academic and business writing.

to, too, two   *To* is a preposition; *too* is an adverb meaning "also" or "excessively"; and *two* is a number. *I too have been to Europe two times.*

too   Avoid using *too* as an intensifier meaning "very": *Monkeys are too mean.* If you do use *too*, explain the consequences of the excessive quality: *Monkeys are too mean to make good pets.*

toward, towards   Both are acceptable, though *toward* is preferred. Use one or the other consistently.

try and, try to   See *sure and, sure to; try and, try to.*

type of   See *kind of, sort of, type of.* Don't use *type* without *of: It was a family type of* [not *type*] *restaurant.* Or better: *It was a family restaurant.*

uninterested   See *disinterested, uninterested.*

unique   *Unique* means "the only one of its kind" and so cannot sensibly be modified with words such as *very* or *most: That was a unique* [not *a very unique* or *the most unique*] *movie.*

usage, use   *Usage* refers to conventions, most often those of a language: *Is "hadn't ought" proper usage? Usage* is often misused in place of the noun *use: Wise use* [not *usage*] *of insulation can save fuel.*

use, utilize   Utilize can be used to mean "make good use of": *Many teachers utilize computers for instruction.* But for all other senses of "place in service" or "employ," prefer *use.*

used to   See *supposed to, used to.*

wait for, wait on   In formal speech and writing, *wait for* means "await" (*I'm waiting for Paul*) and *wait on* means "serve" (*The owner of the store herself waited on us*).

ways   Colloquial as a substitute for *way: We have only a little way* [not *ways*] *to go.*

well   See *good, well.*

whether, if   See *if, whether.*

which   See *that, which.*

which, who, that   See *that, which, who.*

who's, whose   *Who's* is the contraction of *who is: Who's at the door? Whose* is the possessive form of *who: Whose book is that?*

will, shall   See *shall, will.*

-wise   See *-ize, -wise.*

would have   Avoid this construction in place of *had* in clauses that begin *if* and state a condition contrary to fact: *If the tree had* [not *would have*] *withstood the fire, it would have been the oldest in town.* See also p. 120.

would of   See *have, of.*

you   In all but very formal writing, *you* is generally appropriate as long as it means "you, the reader." In all writing, avoid indefinite uses of *you,* such as *In one ancient tribe your first loyalty was to your parents.* See also p. 143.

your, you're   *Your* is the possessive form of *you: Your dinner is ready. You're* is the contraction of *you are: You're bound to be late.*

yourself   See *myself, herself, himself, yourself.*

Usage

Index

❖

Page numbers in **boldface** refer to main definitions in the text.

Index

387

choosing between, 373
rules for use of (ESL), 148–51
Analysis (division)
in critical reading of literature, 352–54
in critical reading of research sources, 252–53
in essay development, 12
in paragraph development, 48–49
and
ampersand (&) for, 228
antecedents of pronouns joined by, 138
comma with, 174, 179, 183
as coordinating conjunction, 95
main clauses not joined by, 162–63
parallelism with, 59–60
semicolon with, 185
subjects joined by, 124, 183
and/or, 374
angry with, 77
Anonymous or unsigned works
APA style: in parenthetical citation, 308; in reference list, 312, 314
CBE reference-list form for, 337
Chicago note and works-cited forms for, 332
MLA style: in list of works cited, 282, 287; in parenthetical citation, 275
ante-, anti-, 374
Antecedents
agreement of pronouns and, 137–40
collective nouns as, 140
defined, **126, 137**
indefinite pronouns as, 138–40
reference of pronouns to, 140–43
Anthology
APA reference-list form for, 313
Chicago note and works-cited forms for, 332
MLA works-cited form for, 284–85
anti-, ante-, 374
anxious, eager, 374
any
agreement of pronoun with, 138–40
agreement of verb with, 125

any, any other, 147
anybody
agreement of pronoun with, 138–40
agreement of verb with, 125
vs. *any body*, 374
any more, anymore, 374
anyone
agreement of pronoun with, 138–40
agreement of verb with, 125
vs. *any one*, 374
anyplace, 374
anything
agreement of pronoun with, 138–40
agreement of verb with, 125
anyway, semicolon and comma with, 164
APA style
for document format, 318–20
for parenthetical citations: index to, 306; models of, 307–09
for reference list: guidelines for, 309–11; index to, 306; models of, 311–18
sample research paper using, 320–25
Apostrophe, 189–92
to form contractions, 191–92
to form plurals of letters, etc., used as words, 192
to form possessives, 91, 189–91
misuses of, with plural noun, singular verb, or possessive personal pronoun, 191, 192
space with, 205
Appeal, of literary work, **354**
Appeals, in argument
appropriate, 344–45
as evidence, 342
inappropriate, 345
Appositive
case of pronoun in, 136
colon to introduce, 187–88
comma with nonrestrictive, 177–78
defined, **101**
apt, liable, likely, 375
are, is, 375
Argument(s), **341–50**
elements of, 341–42
fallacies in, 345–47

Quotation(s), direct. *See also* Indirect quotations
accuracy of, 257–58
acknowledging source of, 260
avoiding plagiarism with, 258–61
brackets for changes in, 199–200, 222
capitalization in, 222
changes in, 198–99, 222, 257–58
colon before, 188
comma with, 181–82
criteria for using, 257–58
defined, **193**
of dialogue, 207
displayed separately from text, 206–07
documenting, 265–67
ellipsis mark for omissions from, 198–99
introducing, in a paper, 263–65
and note taking, 257–58
omissions from, 198–99
vs. paraphrase and summary, 256–57
of poetry, 206
of prose, 206–07
quotation marks with, 193, 194–95
within quotations, 193
she said and other identifying words with, 181–82
sic in, 199–200
slash with, 200
Quotation marks, 192–95
avoiding unnecessary, 194
for dialogue, 207
for direct quotations, 192–93, 260–61
double, 193
with other punctuation, 194–95
with poetry, 206
with prose, 206–07
for quotation within quotation, 193
single, 193
space with, 205
for titles of works, 193–94
for words used in special sense, 194

R

Races of people, capitalization of, 223

Radio programs. *See* Television and radio programs
rain, reign, rein, 217
raise, rise, 106–07, 383
Rational appeals, **344**
Reader-response criticism, 352
Readers. *See* Audience
Readers' Guide to Periodical Literature, 249
Reading
critical, 12–13, 251–54, 262
for essay development, 12–13
literature, 350–55
research sources, 251–54, 262
for revision, 22–23
Reading journal, **351**
real, really, 383
Reasonableness, in arguments, 343–47
acknowledgment of opposition, 345, 347
appropriate appeals, 344–45
fallacies, 346–47
logical thinking, 343–44
reason is because, 166, 383
Recordings
MLA works-cited form for, 296
titles of: quotation marks for songs, 193; underlining (italics) for longer works, 225
Reductive fallacy, **346**
Reference librarian, 236
Reference list. *See* APA style; CBE style; Chicago style; MLA style
Reference of pronouns, 140–43
to clear antecedent, 141
to close antecedent, 141
to implied nouns, 142
to indefinite *it, they, you,* 142–43
to specific antecedent, 142
to vague *this, that, which, it,* 141–42
References, parenthetical. *See* Parenthetical text citations
Reference works
electronic, 240, 243
MLA works-cited form for, 285, 291
as research paper sources, 243
style guides, 266–67
Reflexive pronouns, **91**
Regular verbs
defined, **104**
vs. irregular verbs, 104–06
reign, rein, rain, 217

Index

ESL GUIDE

Throughout the handbook the symbol ESL signals topics of special interest to students using English as a second language. The index below arranges these topics for easy reference. Because ESL material is thoroughly integrated with the rest of the handbook, you can follow any of the page numbers given to reach a broader discussion of the topic as well.

CONTENTS

ESL Guide on reverse

EDITING SYMBOLS

Boldface numbers and letters refer to chapters and sections of the handbook.

ab	Faulty abbreviation, **45**		;	Semicolon, **35**
ad	Misuse of adjective or adverb, **28**		:	Colon, **36**
agr	Error in agreement, **23, 26**		⸕	Apostrophe, **37**
ap	Apostrophe needed or misused, **37**		" "	Quotation marks, **38**
appr	Inappropriate word, **12a**		— ( ) . . . [ ] /	Dash, parentheses, ellipsis mark, brackets, slash, **39**
arg	Faulty argument, **51**		par, ¶	Start new paragraph, **7**
awk	Awkward construction		¶ coh	Paragraph not coherent, **7b**
cap	Use capital letter, **43**		¶ dev	Paragraph not developed, **7c**
case	Error in case form, **25**		¶ un	Paragraph not unified, **7a**
cit	Missing source citation or error in form of citation, **50–53**		pass	Ineffective passive voice, **22a**
			pn agr	Error in pronoun-antecedent agreement, **26**
coh	Coherence lacking, **3b-3, 7b**		ref	Error in pronoun reference, **27**
con	Be more concise, **14**			
coord	Coordination needed, **8**		rep	Unnecessary repetition, **14b**
cs	Comma splice, **31**		rev	Revise or proofread, **5**
d	Ineffective diction (word choice), **12**		run-on	Run-on (fused) sentence, **31**
			shift	Inconsistency, **20c, 21b, 22b, 27d**
det	Error in use of determiner, **28f**		sp	Misspelled word, **41**
dm	Dangling modifier, **29b**		spec	Be more specific, **7c, 12b-2**
emph	Emphasis lacking or faulty, **10**		sub	Subordination needed or faulty, **10**
exact	Inexact word, **12b**			
frag	Sentence fragment, **30**		t	Error in verb tense, **20**
fs	Fused sentence, **31**		t seq	Error in tense sequence, **20d**
gr	Error in grammar, **15–18**		trans	Transition needed, **7b-6**
hyph	Error in use of hyphen, **42**		und	Underline (italicize), **44**
inc	Incomplete construction, **13**		usage	See Glossary of Usage, p. 373
ital	Italicize (underline), **44**		var	Vary sentence structure, **11**
k	Awkward construction		vb	Error in verb form, **19**
lc	Use lowercase letter, **43**		vb agr	Error in subject-verb agreement, **23**
mixed	Mixed construction, **32**			
mm	Misplaced modifier, **29a**		w	Wordy, **14**
mng	Meaning unclear		ww	Wrong word, **12b-1**
ms	Error in manuscript form, **40**		//	Faulty parallelism, **9**
no cap	Unnecessary capital letter, **43**		#	Separate with a space
no ⸕	Comma not needed, **34i**		◡	Close up the space
no ¶	No new paragraph needed, **7**		⸝	Delete
num	Error in use of numbers, **46**		t⟨eh⟩	Transpose letters or words
p	Error in punctuation, **33–39**		x	Obvious error
. ? !	Period, question mark, exclamation point, **33**		∧	Something missing, **13**
⸕	Comma, **34**		??	Manuscript illegible or meaning unclear